Industrial Relations in the San Francisco
Bay Area, 1900-1918

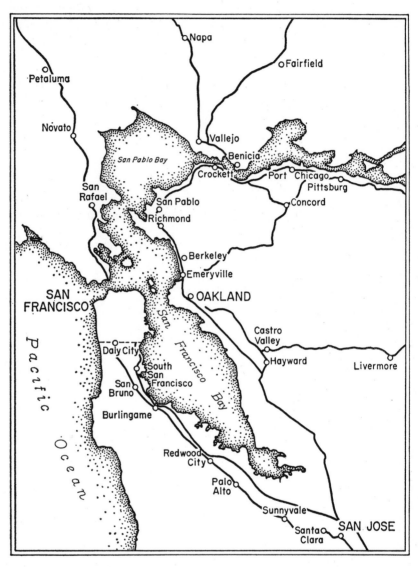

THE SAN FRANCISCO BAY AREA (Base Map Copyright by Rand McNally & Company, R. L. 59-S.F.-21)

Publications of the
Institute of Industrial Relations
University of California

Industrial Relations

in the San Francisco Bay

Area, 1900-1918

ROBERT EDWARD LEE KNIGHT

Berkeley and Los Angeles · 1960

UNIVERSITY OF CALIFORNIA PRESS

UNIVERSITY OF CALIFORNIA PRESS
BERKELEY AND LOS ANGELES

CAMBRIDGE UNIVERSITY PRESS
LONDON, ENGLAND

© 1960, BY
THE REGENTS OF THE UNIVERSITY OF CALIFORNIA
LIBRARY OF CONGRESS CATALOG CARD NO. 59-15332
PRINTED IN THE UNITED STATES OF AMERICA

To Mary

Foreword

ALTHOUGH THE ORIGINS of union organization in the San Francisco area can be traced back to the Gold Rush era, it was not until the first two decades of the present century that San Francisco acquired its reputation as a stronghold of unionism. This was the period when P. H. McCarthy acquired and maintained control of the building trades, when unionism spread to industries and occupations that were scarcely organized at all in other communities, when the Union Labor Party and "Boss" Ruef captured control of the city government for a six-year period, and when multi-employer bargaining became an accepted feature of the San Francisco scene. It was also the period during which the famed Mooney-Billings episode took place.

Thus the history of labor relations in northern California from 1900 through World War I is of unusual interest. What accounted for the phenomenal growth of unionism in San Francisco around the turn of the century and for its success among groups of relatively unskilled workers who were then considered largely unorganizable in other parts of the country? How did employers respond to the challenge presented by the growth of unionism, and what factors explain the failure of the various efforts to restore the area to open-shop conditions? Why was it that multi-employer bargaining became customary in a number of industries, while attempts to form strong employers' organizations which cut across industry boundaries and embraced the entire management community proved abortive?

These are the questions that provide the focus for Dr. Knight's careful and scholarly study. The author was a member of the research staff of the Institute of Industrial Relations throughout the three-year period during which the volume was in preparation. He was fortunate in being able to interview many "old-timers" who played a personal part in the events he describes, as well as to consult all the available documentary material relating to the period. And, following in the tradition of Ira B. Cross, whose *History of the Labor Movement in California* (1935) deals chiefly with developments in the latter part of the nineteenth century, Dr. Knight displays skill in portraying the economic background which played a decisive role in shaping developments in industrial relations throughout the period.

Arthur M. Ross, *Director*
Institute of Industrial Relations
University of California, Berkeley

Acknowledgments

SINCE early 1955, when I first began work on this book as a staff member of the Institute of Industrial Relations, University of California, Berkeley, I have incurred debts of gratitude to many people. To Arthur Ross, Director of the Institute, I am particularly grateful for the support and encouragement he gave me throughout this project. Margaret Gordon, the Institute's Associate Director, read the manuscript at its successive stages and was an unfailing source of welcome advice in numerous consultations. Professor Ira B. Cross conferred with me at an early point in the work, and drew generously upon his own experience in writing *A History of the Labor Movement in California.* From Irving Bernstein, of the Institute of Industrial Relations, University of California, Los Angeles, I received valuable counsel concerning the planning of my research. Charles A. Gulick read the first draft of the completed manuscript with a careful and critical eye, and offered many cogent suggestions for improvements in organization and style.

There are others to whom I am especially indebted: Sam Kagel, for his initial encouragement of this undertaking and his advice concerning people to interview; Corinne Gilb, for the valuable interview material gathered in her Oral History Project; Archie Green, for the use of his unique private library of Bay Area labor documents and for his lively interest in the progress of this book; Grace H. Stimson, of the University of California Press, for her editing of the final manuscript. I wish to extend thanks, also, to Gwendolyn Lloyd, Margaret Mould, and the other members of the library and clerical staff of the Berkeley Institute.

To the former students of the University of California who, over the past sixty years, have written M.A. and Ph.D. theses on various aspects of the Bay Area and California labor movements, my obligation is very great indeed. Their work has contributed in large measure to the material for this history. Likewise, I received invaluable aid from the men who, in personal interviews, helped to re-create for me the Bay Area labor scene in the first two decades of this century: George Bahrs, Warren K. Billings, Colbert Coldwell, John Forbes, Andrew J. Gallagher, James Galliano, Henry F. Grady, Luis Ireland, Frederick Koster, Atholl McBean, Edwin McKenzie, Ernie P. Marsh, James Rickets, Tom Roberts, Paul Scharrenberg, G. A. Silverthorn, Judge Marcus C. Sloss, and Al Wynn.

Finally, I want to express my deep gratitude to my wife for her frequent advice on matters of style and presentation, and for the many hours she devoted to typing and proofreading, in the long task of bringing this manuscript to completion.

R. E. L. K.

Contents

Chapter I | *The Background*
Years

In the San Francisco Bay Area, at the beginning of the year 1900, there existed few established collective bargaining relationships in the modern sense of the term. A relatively small minority of wage earners held membership in unions, and formal agreements between employers and unions were rare. The terms of employment for most workers were set unilaterally by their employers under the prevailing conditions of supply and demand in the local labor market, and were subject to change upon little or no notice. The situation was similar when the terms were set by employer acceptance of union demands, for these terms were seldom guaranteed by contract for any fixed period. A change in the economic environment, or a real or assumed shift in the relative strength of union and employer, might bring on an attempt by either party to alter wages, hours, or other conditions of employment. The relationships between employers and workers were thus quite fluid, as yet unstructured by organization on both sides and by collective bargaining agreements.

The major areas of labor strength in early 1900 were the building trades, the printing trades, and the brewery industry. Here unions had maintained a continuous existence for some years, had managed to organize the bulk of the workers in their respective jurisdictions, and had demonstrated their power to win favorable conditions. Unions also possessed significant strength among certain other groups of Bay Area workers. In the San Francisco shipbuilding industry, the highly skilled calkers were thoroughly organized into one of the oldest unions in California. Along the water front, the several unions of longshoremen were growing in membership and power, especially the Longshore Lumbermen's Association, composed of the skilled cargo handlers in the flourishing coastwise lumber trade. Offshore, the Sailors' Union of the Pacific and the Marine Firemen's Union were rapidly regaining their strength of earlier years. In the metal trades, a substantial minority of the skilled craftsmen were members of unions which had maintained continuous existence for a decade or more. Preëminent among these was the veteran Molders' Union, active in local foundries since the 1860's. By early 1900 it had again thoroughly organized its Bay Area jurisdiction, although it had achieved recognition from but few employers.

Minor pockets of union strength existed in other trades, but most groups of workers in the local labor force either had not recently been touched by unionization or contained only nuclei of small unions, most of them newly formed. These nuclei were especially few and weak among relatively unskilled workers, women workers, and those not members of recognized crafts.

The two principal terms of employment, wages and hours, varied widely among the different categories of workers. A workweek of six full days was standard for virtually all manual occupations. The eight-hour day and forty-eight-hour week were almost universal in the San Francisco building trades, at union scales of $3 and $4 per day for most crafts, and as high as $5 for bricklayers. Printing tradesmen had achieved the eight-hour day on newspapers in 1899, but as of 1900 were still working a nine-hour day in book and job printing firms, with journeymen printers receiving a union scale of $3.50 per day. In the metal trades, a ten-hour day was standard for skilled and unskilled workers; machinists, molders, and boilermakers received daily wages of $3.25 to $3.50. The large majority of the other Bay Area manufacturing industries operated on either a nine- or ten-hour day, with daily wage rates for most skilled craftsmen falling in a range of $2.75 to $3.50. By contrast, wages of helpers and apprentices in the skilled crafts were sharply below this level, frequently only one-third to one-half of the rate for journeymen. For common, unskilled heavy labor, in manufacturing and other industries, the prevailing rate was $1.75 to $2 per day.[1]

Certain groups of Bay Area workers, in early 1900, were subject to working schedules which, if not leaving them in a state of exhaustion at the close of the workday, left them thin margins of waking time for leisure and family life. Clerks in retail stores were on duty throughout the store shopping hours, which in many lines of retailing ran to 7 P.M. or later on weeknights, and to very late on Saturday nights. Many stores, moreover, remained open on Sundays. Butchers and bakers in retail meat markets and bakeries kept similar weekly working hours. Cooks and waiters worked seven days a week in hotels and restaurants, usually on a thirteen-hour schedule. Conductors and motormen on local street railways, engaged in work both physically and nervously exhausting, were on a daily schedule of eleven to twelve hours within a fourteen-hour period. Drivers in many of the teaming trades worked twelve or more hours a day, and frequently seven days a week. Milk wagon drivers, making deliveries as early as 3 A.M., worked especially long and irregular hours. Drivers of hacks, the 1900 equivalent of taxis, typically kept a twelve-hour schedule. The general teamsters employed by the members of the San Francisco Draymen's Association earned an average weekly wage of $14, for a seven-day week and hours that often ran well beyond twelve per day. Steam laundry workers, mainly women, labored under hot and noisy conditions from seven in the morning until frequently eight or later at night, six days a week. The average weekly earnings of experienced women laundry workers were at most $10 to $11. Bakers, milkers, stable employees, fruit packers, and cannery workers also worked long hours for low wages. Their earnings averaged $1.25 to $2 a day.[2]

This sampling of hours and wages in local industry at the turn of the century describes the base from which these terms of employment were to move in the years ahead. For by early 1900 the economy of the Bay Area, as of the nation, was in a period of accelerated growth, under boom conditions, and opportunities for gains by organized workers were expanding rapidly. The San Francisco labor movement, accordingly, was experiencing a vigorous revival, which was to carry it to a height of power it had never before attained during almost fifty years of existence.

The Background of Fifty Years

The swiftly growing unionism of early 1900 was a phase in a history of ebbs and flows in the strength of San Francisco labor reaching as far back as the 1850's. Under the stimulus of the California gold rush, beginning in the winter of 1848–49, a city was created with feverish speed on the shores of San Francisco Bay. With its creation appeared the first banding together of workers for organized action in the Bay Area.

At the time of the first discovery of gold, in January, 1848, San Francisco was a minor trading settlement with a population well under 1,000. By 1850 it was a city of more than 30,000, a rapidly built boom town that would remain and grow long after the initial flush of the boom had subsided. Its strategic position had transformed the quiet port settlement into the chief supply base for the thousands of gold seekers swarming into northern California, and had made it a busy hive humming with the activities of shipping, trade, and construction.

By the fall of 1848 an acute labor shortage existed in San Francisco. The lure of sudden riches had drawn much of the local citizenry to the gold country, while simultaneously an urgent demand had arisen for the labor needed to handle the increasing stream of goods flowing into the port, and to erect warehouses, hotels, saloons, and other buildings. Wage rates leaped sharply upward in 1848–49, as employers bid against one another—and against the glittering temptations of the search for gold—to recruit workers.[3] The expanding economy of the newly created city demanded labor services in a rapidly growing number of trades and occupations. This new labor force was supplied by workers drawn to California by reports of plentiful employment at high wages, and by participants in the gold rush, thousands of whom poured back into San Francisco as their luck and supplies gave out.

The Embryo of a Labor Movement

In the words of the California labor historian, Lucile Eaves, "There are evidences of such early trade-union activity in San Francisco that one is tempted to believe that the craftsmen met each other on the way to California and agreed to unite." [4] No formal organization actually appeared before 1850, when printers formed the San Francisco Typographical Society, the first trade union on the Pacific Coast. But in November, 1849, a group of carpenters joined together to demand an increase in the prevailing wage from $12 to $16 per day. When this was refused, they staged a brief strike before settling for a compromise rate of $14.[5] This was the first recorded instance of concerted action by workers in San Francisco. It was typical of a number of such incidents occurring sporadically in the next few years. Men employed in a trade would come together to form an *ad hoc* organization, for offensive or defensive action. The immediate stimulus was usually a determination to enforce a higher wage rate, but occasionally it was the intent to resist a cut in wages.

A frontier society existed in San Francisco in the early 1850's, a highly democratic one. The men from among whom the San Francisco labor force of this period was drawn possessed characteristics predisposing them toward aggressive action in their own behalf. They were energetic, adventuresome men who had come to California for material gain. When they sought work, they were insistent upon satisfactory wages, and quick to act to gain them. Under the semilawless frontier conditions, they could be violent in enforcing their demands. The winter of 1849–50 offered an illustration of this. Thousands of miners wintered in San Francisco, temporarily flooding the labor market. One of them, writing shortly afterward, vividly described mass meetings of hundreds of unemployed men, "armed with bowie-knives and fire-arms, and often intoxicated." At these meetings, speakers engaged in "furious tirades forbidding foreigners to seek employment . . . and holding out a deadly threat to all who dared labor under the fixed rate of payment, ten dollars per day." These were not idle threats, he reported, for from a high cliff overlooking the sea "three poor fellows had been hurled who had worked under wages or were suspected of having done so." [6]

San Francisco's traditional position as an area of high wages thus stemmed from its earliest years. The combination of an aggressive work force and recurrent labor shortages in the expanding local economy was largely influential in establishing this position. An important contributing factor was the high level of prices which resulted from the abundance of gold—the medium of exchange—and the heavy shipping costs incurred by goods sent from Eastern suppliers. These factors, in varying degrees, remained influential over the decades ahead in maintaining relatively high wages for San Francisco workers.

Wages did not remain, however, at the inflated levels of 1848–49. They moved downward under the pressure of a great influx of newcomers in 1850–1852 and under the impact of several shocks administered to the local economy by drops in gold output, financial failures of speculative merchants and bankers, and fires that laid waste much of the newly built town. By the summer of 1853 the carpenters were again banding together to establish a standard wage of $8 per day—only one-half the rate for which they had struck in late 1849.[7] Although still highly paid by comparison with wage earners in the East, San Francisco labor no longer commanded its former extraordinary premium price.

In 1853 the flow of gold seekers lessened greatly, and for the remainder of the decade the San Francisco population grew comparatively slowly. Meanwhile, conditions of law and order became more settled. In 1851 some hundreds of citizens had organized the Committee of Vigilance, which functioned for several months combating the prevalent crime and violence. In early 1856 a renewed wave of criminality stimulated the formation of the second Committee of Vigilance. Composed of 5,000 or more men, this extralegal organization demonstrated its power through the summer of 1856, conducting public investigations, trials, deportations, and executions of undesirable citizens.[8] It established not only law and order in San Francisco, but a tradition. At times of threatened disorder in years to come, Californians would be quick to invoke the spirit of the reformers of the 1850's and call for vigilante action.

In the period of slower growth after 1852, labor organizations were formed among building tradesmen, printers, longshoremen, teamsters, and other groups of workers. Organizing was especially active in 1853, under the favorable conditions of a temporary building boom and a renewed labor shortage. The middle years of the decade, however, brought substantial unemployment and lower levels of wages and prices. The output of the gold mines, upon which San Francisco prosperity was largely dependent, fell off greatly in 1854–55. Not until 1858 did a strong revival begin in the local economy. The silver-mining boom which developed in 1859 in western Nevada gave added impetus to this revival. San Francisco thus ended the decade of the 1850's in an atmosphere of renewed expansion.[9]

Unionism in the 1860's

In 1860–1861 labor organizations existed in San Francisco among printers, building tradesmen, longshoremen, shipwrights, teamsters, cigar makers, and a handful of other groups.[10] Although this was much the same set of trades caught up in the first wave of unionization in the early 1850's, it is doubtful that more than one or two of these organizations had maintained continuous existence since then. In the mobile new California society, men moved comparatively easily from one trade to another, and from working for wages to self-employment. A settled body of wage earners, conscious of themselves as such, was slow to develop. Most of the unions formed in the 1850's dissolved within a few months or years. Many of their members moved into other occupations; others lost interest after the immediate circumstances which originally stimulated unionization had changed. These early labor organizations almost totally lacked attributes that gave strength and permanence to later unions: experienced leadership; trade-union traditions; treasuries; systematic financing; affiliation with national labor organizations; and machinery for developing mutual assistance to and coöperation with other unions.

The population of San Francisco more than doubled in the 1860's, rising from approximately 60,000 to almost 150,000. In this period of expansion and prosperity, unions established themselves on a broader, firmer basis. A rising cost of living and renewed tightness in the labor market stimulated organization. The Civil War gave an inflationary push to prices and, by restricting the flow of goods from Eastern suppliers, speeded the growth of local manufacturing to supply the Western market. During the decade the industrial base of the San Francisco economy expanded greatly, with a consequent increase in the demand for labor. These favorable conditions fostered union activity. By the end of 1863 a number of vigorous new unions had appeared, notably among metal trades craftsmen, bakers, shoeworkers, tailors, and culinary workers. Organization even reached out beyond the area of strictly manual work. Retail clerks formed an association in 1863 and began their perennial struggle for earlier closing hours.[11]

With this renewed union activity came an increased ability on the part of workers to maintain their organizations, coöperate with other groups of wage earners, and engage successfully in contests with employers. A number of unions struck to enforce demands in 1863, usually with favorable outcomes. From one of these strikes, a prolonged struggle by the new union of tailors, there emerged the first city central labor council to be formed in California. Recognizing the urgent need for mutual assistance among unions, the tailors took the initiative in 1863 in organizing the San Francisco Trades' Union. This central council, by early 1864, embraced fifteen unions with a total membership perhaps as high as 3,000.[12]

In the 1860's employers also began to organize. The development of employers' associations, which was to be one of the outstanding features of San Francisco industrial relations, can be dated from 1861, when the restaurant owners joined together in the first employers' protective association on the Pacific Coast. In 1863 the organized restaurant proprietors apparently defeated a strike by their waiters.[13]

The following year brought the first prolonged battle between workers and an employers' association in any San Francisco industry. In the spring of 1864 the unions of molders and boilermakers struck a number of metal trades firms, demanding wages of $5 for the prevailing ten-hour day. The struck firms promptly formed an employers' association and made a determined effort to overcome one of the major sources of strength to San Francisco unions—the expense and slowness of importing strikebreakers from the East. Molders and boilermakers were recruited in Atlantic seaboard cities and sent to San Francisco by ship and the overland route across Panama. These skilled craftsmen, however, were contacted in Panama by union representatives and persuaded to join the strikers upon their arrival. Checkmated, the employers acceded to the wage demands. The first major dispute in the local metal trades industry thus ended in union victory.[14]

Another development of interest in the 1860's was the appearance, for the first time, of explicit union demands for closed-shop conditions. These demands seem to have been confined almost entirely to the building trades, where a number of unions insisted that their members would not work on any job employing non-union men within their respective crafts. Late in the decade the carpenters' union introduced the systematic inspection of construction sites to assure that none other than its members were at work. It thereby became the first San Francisco union to utilize a "walking delegate." [15]

After 1863 the pace of unionization slackened. Some new unions were formed, however, and most organizations maintained an active existence through the favorable years of the decade. From late 1865 the main efforts of labor were channeled into a drive for shorter hours. Since the 1850's the ten-hour day had been standard for almost all skilled craftsmen, and apparently for the majority of unskilled workers. In the 1860's came intensified efforts by organized workers throughout the nation to win the eight-hour day, the treasured goal and symbol of achievement toward which labor was to strive for years to come.

San Francisco unions, though still in the most limited of contact with organized labor in the East, participated vigorously in this eight-hour movement. The Trades' Union directed a coördinated labor campaign to win passage of an eight-hour law by the 1866 session of the state legislature. The proposed law was defeated by only a slim majority. Relying upon economic power rather than political action, a number of San Francisco building trades unions unilaterally instituted the eight-hour day. Outside the building trades, the one major area of success was among the shipwrights, calkers, and several other categories of skilled craftsmen in the shipbuilding and ship repair industry. Some struggles over this issue came in 1867. Although the carpenters, the largest body of craftsmen in the building trades, easily established the eight-hour day on construction jobs in San Francisco and Oakland, they met stiff opposition from Bay Area planing mills. In mid-1867, consequently, the carpenters resorted to a tactic later used by various local unions: they organized a union-owned coöperative planing mill to provide "eight-hour lumber" to building contractors. After a prolonged contest, most of the millowners accepted the shorter day. A less one-sided battle developed in the summer of 1867, when several steamship companies decided to end their passive acquiescence in the eight-hour day established the previous year by unions in the ship repair crafts. The companies locked out these craftsmen, advertised in the East for replacements willing to work nine hours a day, and managed to import almost fifty skilled men into San Francisco. The lockout was evidently ended by negotiations in the fall of 1867. The eight-hour day remained in effect, but only at the cost of wage cuts imposed by the employers upon the workers.[16]

Another effort to combat the shorter workday was undertaken in mid-1867 by a group of employers who formed the Ten-Hour Association. The association pleaded for the use of "all just and honorable measures to prevent the eight-hour labor system being adopted in this city . . . knowing as we do that it is incompatible with the best interests and growth of the city." [17] Unable to elicit widespread employer support, however, the association had but a brief and ineffective existence.

The spread of the eight-hour day beyond the building trades remained negligible, but unions continued their efforts to win legislation that would shorten the workday throughout all industry. Labor historian Lucile Eaves has advanced the hypothesis that San Francisco workers in the late 1860's turned to political action primarily because many unions had become reluctant to engage in direct economic struggles with employers.[18] Certainly employers in several industries had demonstrated their ability to resist demands, organize for unified action, and secure strike-breakers. Unionists had watched a few strikes suffer thorough defeat: for example, a marine firemen's strike in 1866 and a shoe-workers' strike in 1867.[19] Having observed such setbacks as these, labor may well have developed a heightened sense of caution.

Unions displayed great interest in political activity in 1867, when for the first time organized labor made significant efforts to influence local and state elections in California. A state-wide Workingmen's Convention, held in San Francisco, endorsed candidates favorable to an eight-hour law, prohibition of Chinese immigration, and other legislation of benefit to workers. Like many later ventures of labor into California politics, the Workingmen's Convention found its effectiveness in unifying the worker vote marred by wranglings over endorsements and widespread suspicion of the political ambitions of some of its leaders. It did awaken political candidates, however, to the existence of a potent labor vote. Many of them, including the large majority of those who won election to the state legislature from San Francisco in 1867, pledged themselves to support the measures desired by labor.[20]

Late in 1867 San Francisco unions formed a new central body, the Mechanics' State Council. Their original central council, the Trades' Union, had dissolved the previous year as a result of internal dissension. Although the new organization was state-wide in scope, its leadership and most of its membership were provided by San Francisco unionists. By mid-1868 the council had twenty-one affiliated unions, with an estimated 6,000 members.[21] It was active for several years in support of the eight-hour movement. Despite its numerical strength, the council exercised only a minor influence upon labor relations in San Francisco.

The Chinese Issue

A major long-term influence on the local labor scene—the anti-Chinese movement—developed stronger force in the late 1860's. The intense antagonism toward the Chinese had developed early; it had been aroused during the years of the gold rush, which brought approximately 50,000 Orientals into California by 1855. The Chinese forty-niners, along with Mexicans and South Americans, were frequent victims of organized intimidation and violence on the part of miners of native American and north European origin, who were determined to drive all "foreigners" from the gold fields. Less crude harassment soon appeared in the form of a series of laws, passed by the state legislature during the 1850's and later, which aimed at cutting off further immigration from China or confining the Chinese to certain occupations. These discriminatory laws were rendered virtually ineffective, however, by court decisions which declared most of them unconstitutional.[22]

As the flow of Oriental immigrants continued through the late 1850's and the 1860's, though at a reduced volume, San Francisco wage earners became increasingly aware that it created an economic problem. Probably a majority of local employers also opposed the continued immigration. Nevertheless, the growing number of Chinese in San Francisco offered employers a tempting body of low-wage labor. Although some white employers were eventually threatened with extinction by the competition of Chinese firms, San Francisco workers were convinced that the Oriental was primarily a menace to the wages and conditions of white labor. During the 1860's Chinese came to make up a large portion of the work force in a widening circle of industries. Particularly affected were the laundry, culinary, and other service trades, and such light manufacturing industries as those producing cigars, shoes, clothing, paper boxes and bags, woolen textiles, and soap.[23]

In February, 1867, a strike of white shoeworkers led to violence against Orientals employed in that industry. In the same month a riot was precipitated by the discharge of a group of white construction laborers and their replacement by lower-paid Chinese. These outbursts were followed by meetings and the formation in San Francisco of the Pacific Coast Anti-Coolie Association.[24] This was the first in a series of short-lived, similar organizations created in the next few years. White workers in San Francisco thus ended their period of prosperity in the 1860's on a note of increased antagonism toward the Chinese, an antagonism that would become more explosive in the decade ahead.

Rollback of Labor's Gains in 1869

The year 1869 ushered in a period of defeat and inactivity for San Francisco labor. An unusually large number of migrants arrived from the East in 1868–69. Many of these were attracted by the California Labor and Employment Exchange, an agency created by San Francisco employers to advertise the high wages and ready employment that awaited workers in the West.[25] This exchange was the forerunner of later organizations established by employers at various times to stimulate migration to California. Unions perennially opposed such organizations, protesting that their purpose was to flood the local labor market in order to break down wages and working conditions.

The 1868–69 inpouring of new arrivals proved, in fact, too great for the San Francisco economy to absorb. Unemployment became increasingly heavy throughout 1869. A serious business depression began during that year. Lowered output from California's major industries of agriculture and gold mining reduced the flow of commerce through San Francisco, while completion of the transcontinental railroad exposed merchants and manufacturers to painfully intensified competition from Eastern firms. The joining of the Central Pacific and Union Pacific railroads in May, 1869, at Promontory Point, Utah, was a milestone in the history of California; it established an essential facility for the long-run expansion of the state's population and economy. The immediate consequence, however, was to aggravate the local depression by enabling Eastern manufacturers and wholesalers to cut deeply into markets previously supplied largely by goods manufactured in San Francisco or shipped there for distribution throughout the West.[26]

The completion of the transcontinental railroad in 1869 also helped to undermine the economic position of San Francisco workers. Thousands of Chinese, Irish, and other laborers who had been employed in railroad construction poured back into San Francisco to seek work, further demoralizing the labor market. These relatively unskilled laborers offered only a minor threat to the wages and conditions of skilled workers. But the bargaining power of skilled craftsmen was seriously menaced by the new rail connection with the East, which made it easy for employers to tap the supply of labor in Chicago and other industrial centers. From 1869 on, local unions of skilled workers could no longer undertake strikes with the comfortable assurance that weeks must elapse before strikebreakers could reach the city. The protective geographical barrier behind which the San Francisco labor movement had flourished in the 1860's was permanently breached.

Along with depression, unemployment, and falling prices came efforts by employers to cut wages and eliminate the eight-hour day so recently won by building tradesmen and workers in several other crafts. For the most part, these efforts appear to have met little organized resistance. A few San Francisco unions launched determined strikes in 1869–1870, but without success. The most notable conflict was a stubborn strike by the Molders' Union against a wage cut imposed by the Union Iron Works and the Risdon Iron Works, two of the largest firms in the city. The futile struggle, prolonged for months, virtually disintegrated the union.[27]

By early 1870 acute depression prevailed in San Francisco,

with the number of unemployed at a level never before seen. The situation provoked increasing agitation against the Chinese. Efforts, almost entirely ineffective, were made to force employers to get rid of Chinese workers; boycotts were proclaimed against some firms that refused to comply. The Mechanics' State Council took a leading part in this agitation. This was the council's last significant action, for late in 1870 it fell apart over internal quarrels brought on by the political ambitions of some of its leaders. The consequent lack of effective central direction handicapped the local labor movement in weathering the rough years of the 1870's. The building trades unions, well organized in the 1860's, also lost strength after 1869. Several of the crafts apparently retained the eight-hour day for a few years, but none held it throughout the 1870's. No union in the building trades, in fact, survived continuously and actively through the entire decade.[28]

Business had revived considerably by 1872, but setbacks in the middle years of the decade prevented the attainment of a sustained high level of activity. The flow of migrants, moreover, swelled the labor force more rapidly than the local economy could provide jobs. Although the population growth of San Francisco in the 1870's was at a percentage rate far below that of the 1860's, it was almost as large absolutely. By 1880 the city had more than 230,000 residents. With unemployment continuing to harass labor, few unions appear to have maintained an active existence throughout the 1870's. The local labor scene in the middle years of the decade was typically one of apathy among workers, dotted by brief spurts of organization in individual trades, occasional short strikes, and several attempts to form new central labor councils.

Although unions largely eschewed direct efforts to win gains from employers in the 1870's, they continued to direct much energy against the Chinese, an opponent less able to strike back. As immigration from the Orient continued, it provided white workers a ready explanation for unemployment and low wages. Accordingly, a vigorous anti-Chinese campaign was maintained through the mid-1870's by a series of briefly flourishing organizations which held mass meetings, distributed propaganda, and appealed to the federal government for a ban on further immigration. Out of this continued agitation developed a weapon that was employed far beyond the spatial and temporal limits of the California anti-Chinese movement. The San Francisco Cigarmakers' Union, striving desperately to survive against Chinese competition, began in 1874 to place a white label on boxes of cigars produced by their members. This was the first recorded use in American labor history of the tactic of labeling a consumer good in order to facilitate a consumption boycott against "unfair" products not bearing the label.[29] From its initial use in San Francisco, the union label evolved into one of labor's most widespread, effective devices for applying economic pressure to manufacturers of consumer goods.

Chinese immigration was particularly heavy in 1876, augmenting the labor force just as San Francisco was approaching a period of depression and serious unemployment. By early 1877 a severe decline in business activity was under way. Through the spring and summer the unemployed swelled in number, growing increasingly bitter and restless.

To San Francisco wage earners the depression of 1877 came as a culminating blow after years of low wages, recurrent unemployment, and growing Chinese competition for jobs. Their resentment, when it broke forth, was channeled into mob demonstrations. The immediate occasion touching off the outburst arose from developments in the East, where labor was also restive in the depression year of 1877. In the summer a wave of strikes swept over most of the major Eastern railroads. These strikes were by far the most widespread and violent the nation had ever seen. Not only state militia but, for the first time in an American labor conflict, federal troops were ordered out to control the strikers. In Pittsburgh, on July 21, state militia opened fire on a mob of strikers and strike sympathizers, killing and wounding almost fifty people. Immediate reaction came in the form of serious rioting in Pittsburgh and angry protest by workers' organizations elsewhere. At San Francisco, on the night of July 23, an estimated 8,000 people gathered in an open-air mass meeting called in support of the Eastern railroad strikers. The meeting was orderly, but anti-Chinese agitators seized advantage of the prevailing atmosphere of anger and tension. Excited by an outbreak of petty assault upon Chinese bystanders, part of the crowd was soon drawn off into a mushrooming mob that swarmed through the city, venting at last its hatred of the Chinese. During the night it wrecked a score of Chinese laundries and other establishments, doing thousands of dollars worth of property damage.[30]

Once aroused, the mob spirit continued to animate a dangerously large number of San Franciscans. In addition to rowdies and hoodlums, many jobless men joined mobs that agitated the city for almost a week. As the mob anger spread to include white employers of Chinese, San Francisco businessmen and property owners feared a general uprising, motivated by class hatred against the well-to-do. They reacted characteristically by forming a committee of safety, designed as a reincarnation of the Vigilance Committee of 1856. The several thousand members of the committee, along with militia and police, restored order within a few days, but only after several men had been killed.[31]

Despite the return of surface calm, thousands of workers remained resentful and ready to respond to class-conscious leadership. An Irish-born drayage firm proprietor, Dennis Kearney, was quick to cast himself in the role of their Messiah. In the early fall of 1877, amid continuing depression and unemployment, Kearney began holding open-air meetings in San Francisco. In addition, he organized the Workingmen's Party of California, with a platform that combined threats of violence against the Chinese with heated denunciations of wealthy capitalists.[32] The combination proved popular; the membership of the new party grew rapidly and spread to other parts of the state. Kearney drew increasing numbers to his open-air meetings, at which he displayed a talent for bombast worthy of a Falstaff. He directed his oratory mainly against the Chinese and their employers, but also fulminated against the capitalist exploiters of the working class. Although his assaults on the established order seem to have been almost exclusively verbal, the months of rabble-rousing kept prosperous citizens tense and alarmed. They scarcely found it reassuring to hear Kearney regaling large crowds with such bloodthirsty promises as, "When the Chinese question is settled, we can discuss whether it would be better to hang, shoot, or cut the capitalists to pieces." [33] Property owners formed another vigilance committee, and police and militia were kept alerted against a renewed outbreak of rioting.

Early in 1878 Kearney turned to the calmer pursuits of politics, and the mob demonstrations dwindled away. But the winter's unrest had brought a significant development. For the first time, state legislation and San Francisco city ordinances were passed placing limitations upon the rights of free speech and assembly. The public advocacy of violence against property was made a felony.[34] Although little effort was made to enforce these curbs, they indicated a hardening of class lines in California's heretofore loose and easy democratic society.

In 1878 San Francisco workers, still beset by unemployment and filled with a sense of grievance, turned their interests to political action under the leadership of Kearney's Workingmen's Party. Denouncing alleged abuses by privileged corporations and promising to redeem government from the control of business interests, the new party quickly developed strength throughout the state. It made an impressive showing in 1878, electing a mayor of Oakland, a number of other candidates for state and local office, and approximately one-third of the delegates to a convention called to revise the state constitution. The new constitution, adopted in 1879, reflected the depression, discontent, and protest of the late 1870's. Over the strong opposition of business interests, curbs were placed on stock exchange practices and on railroads, banks, and other corporations. The constitution also included an article prohibiting the hiring of Chinese by any corporations formed under state law, but this provision proved legally unenforceable.[35]

On the economic front, San Francisco workers remained relatively inactive during 1878–1880, years of poor business conditions and slack demand for labor. Nevertheless, unions retained a significant membership. Early in 1878 the interest aroused by the Workingmen's Party helped stimulate the formation of another central labor body, the San Francisco Trades Assembly, which soon expanded to include fourteen unions with a claimed membership of 4,000.[36] The assembly had only a negligible influence on labor relations in the closing years of the decade, but it continued in active existence.

The Workingmen's Party survived as an effective political force only through 1879, when it elected numerous members of the state legislature and a mayor of San Francisco. Factional squabbles disrupted it in 1880.[37] Its temporary successes, beyond mildly frightening business interests, had no impact upon labor relations. The support won by the party showed the disposition of Bay Area workers to rebel against adverse economic conditions. Their energy, however, had been diverted into a loosely framed, ephemeral movement of political protest, rather than into a systematic effort to build up the economic power of organized labor.

The 1880's: A New Era in Labor Relations

In 1881 came business revival, bringing with it a new wave of union growth. San Francisco workers entered upon a period of development and of unprecedented organizational activity. During the 1880's labor relations moved into their modern phase in San Francisco, with union-employer struggles concerning not only wages and hours, but most issues that are still the subject of dispute, such as the union shop, exclusive hiring through union offices, apprenticeship rules, unionization of foremen, and adjustment of work loads. These contests evoked organizational and combative techniques that had a modern flavor, as unions resorted increasingly to boycotts, picketing, sympathy strikes, secondary boycotts, and the systematic collection of funds to support strikes. Employers wielded with growing skill such counterweapons as lockouts, importation of strikebreakers, and the black-listing of militant unionists.

In the 1880's both workers and employers made the leap to a new level of organization. This was the first period in which a significant proportion of the new unions formed remained in existence for more than a few years. A number of the unions born then in San Francisco are thriving at the present day, having by now led active lives for three-quarters of a century. The 1880's brought the first widespread affiliation of local unions with national trade unions, which had been growing in number since the 1860's. San Francisco labor finally formed a lasting central council. And there now appeared on the scene men who embarked on lifetime careers of union leadership, some of which stretched well into the present century.

Organization also blossomed extensively, for the first time, among employers in many industries. Unlike their forerunners in San Francisco, several of these employer associations of the 1880's remained active for some years beyond the immediate crises that brought them into existence. Employers' associations, however, still lagged behind unions in developing the capacity for continuous survival. Arising in response to union pressure, they tended to lapse into inertia or dissolution during periods of labor quiescence.

In contrast to the preceding period, the 1880's were for the most part years of healthy business activity and high employment. Moreover, the economic position of San Francisco wage earners was enhanced by the enactment in 1882 of federal legislation which suspended for a ten-year period all immigration of Chinese laborers.[38] Unions continued sporadic anti-Chinese agitation for some years, but the Chinese threat was thereafter a diminishing one. In the 1880's the population of San Francisco increased from slightly more than 230,000 to almost 300,000. Across the Bay, Oakland—a city of growing economic importance as the Pacific Coast terminus of the transcontinental railroad—reached a population of almost 50,000.

The business revival of 1881 coincided with a change of leadership in the San Francisco Trades Assembly. In that year Frank Roney, a member of the Molders' Union and a former Irish revolutionary, became president of the central body. The American labor movement was by then striving for effective nationwide coördination, and Roney was active in inducing the assembly to send a delegate in 1881 to a union convention in Pittsburgh. The assembly and a few individual San Francisco unions affiliated with the new national organization which emerged from this convention—a loosely organized, as yet weak, body of unions that in 1886 became the American Federation of Labor.[39]

Frank Roney's leadership revitalized the Trades Assembly, which had declined by 1881 to a handful of unions with a total membership of about 1,200. During 1882–1883 the assembly took part in a burst of organizing activity which created about twenty-five new unions. By the end of 1883 there were more than fifty unions in San Francisco. Organization was strong in almost every craft of the building trades, and unions of widely varying strength were active among metal tradesmen, shipbuilding craftsmen, printing tradesmen, teamsters, longshoremen, culinary workers, butchers, bakers, tailors, and several other groups. A minor wave of unionization in Oakland was confined almost exclusively to a few building trades crafts.[40] Not all these Bay Area unions survived the decade, and many displayed little energy or effectiveness. Organization was, however, far more widely and solidly rooted than ever before.

During the prosperous year of 1882, building trades unions met general success in establishing shorter hours and higher wage rates. By early 1883 their standard workday had been cut from ten to nine hours; two or three crafts had even regained the eight-hour day. The drive for improved wages and conditions spread to unions in other industries during 1883, and in the summer there were brief strikes by printers, shoeworkers, longshoremen, coopers, telegraph operators, and a few other crafts. About one-half of the strikes were successful. The marked increase in union aggressiveness stimulated employers to form the Merchants' and Manufacturers' Association in October, 1883. This was the first significant San Francisco organization to combine employers from different industries in a central body for mutual defense against organized labor. It seems, however, to have displayed little forceful activity during its few years of existence.[41]

A decline in business, beginning in 1883, brought increased unemployment in 1884 and some employer attempts to cut wages. Several unions, mainly in the metal trades, called brief strikes over such issues as apprenticeship regulations and employment of non-union craftsmen, but the chief strikes of the year were against pay reductions. A small union of ironworkers failed in a prolonged strike against a wage-cutting Oakland plant. Painters in San Francisco and Oakland struck successfully against a number of painting contractors attempting to return to the ten-hour day at a low daily wage. The strike involved a recently organized association of master painters, one of several such specialty building trades employers' associations formed in 1884.[42]

The Merchants' and Manufacturers' Association, however, found little opportunity for action in 1884–1885. The Trades Assembly likewise played an insignificant role. Despite the expansion of unionism in the early 1880's, the assembly only briefly retained the affiliation of most unions. Frank Roney left the presidency after one term, and other active leaders diverted their interests to a colorful organization headed by militant Bay Area Socialists and bearing the pretentious title, International Workingmen's Association. By early 1884 the Trades Assembly was moribund, and its dissolution came soon afterward.[43]

Business continued depressed, with severe unemployment in San Francisco in 1885. But this depression, unlike those of the past, found many unions too firmly rooted to be swept away. Two attempts in 1885 to reduce wages boomeranged on employers, in fact, by stimulating the creation of important new unions. Early in the year several leading metal trades firms cut wages by 15 per cent. In reaction came the almost overnight formation of unions of machinists, boilermakers, and patternmakers. These joined with the blacksmiths and the molders in a strike that affected more than 1,000 men and within a few weeks won restoration of the former wage scales. Soon after the strike the metal tradesmen established a central council for joint consultation and support, the first such body formed in any American city. Among the founders were Frank Roney and Joseph F. Valentine, a young member of the Molders' Union whose subsequent career led to nationwide prominence as a labor leader. The second attempt to cut wages, made by shipowners in the coastal shipping trade, stimulated formation of the Coast Seamen's Union, which within a few months became the largest individual union on the Pacific Coast. The new union met fair success in a prolonged battle against the lowered wage scale.[44]

Ferment in 1886

Aside from the metal trades and shipping disputes, local labor relations remained generally quiet in 1885. With the upturn of business in 1886, however, union activity and industrial conflict jumped to a new high level in San Francisco. The year 1886, marked by such events as the Haymarket Riot and the founding of the AFL, was one of the most memorable in American labor history. In San Francisco the year opened with the formation in January of a new central body, the Federated Trades Council. With Frank Roney as its first president, the council rapidly grew to a membership of more than fifty affiliated unions, including several from Oakland and other northern California cities. In a surge of organizing activity, more than twenty new unions were established in San Francisco in early 1886, and on May 11 an estimated 10,000 union members marched in the largest workers' parade the city had ever witnessed. A forerunner of Labor Day celebrations to come, the event was symbolic of labor's growing strength.[45]

The major labor disputes of 1886 revealed a tendency for the scope of conflict to broaden beyond the simple pattern of a contest between an individual union and an individual employer over issues of wages and hours. In the spring the Typographical Union struck two daily newspapers to enforce its demand for a strict union shop. The local labor movement backed the strike with a vigorous boycott campaign which included pressure on newspaper advertisers, and the struggle ended in union victory. In July several streetcar companies discharged workers identified as members of a large new carmen's union. The resulting strike established a pattern of violence characteristic of future Bay Area street railway disputes. Attempts to maintain operations brought forth mobs of strike sympathizers, who hurled rocks at the moving cars and overturned several. After a few days of disorder, peace was restored by employer promises to cease discharging union members.[46]

The 1886 streetcar conflict coincided with prolonged strikes of the unions of seamen and metal tradesmen. The boilermakers had struck the large Union Iron Works in May, demanding the discharge of certain nonunion men. The metal tradesmen's new federation, the Iron Trades Council, called out other union members at the plant in support of the boilermakers. Meanwhile, marine firemen struck one of the ships of the Oceanic Steamship Company, demanding lighter work loads. The Federated Trades Council then intervened with the most sweeping action yet taken by a San Francisco central labor body in support of a strike. Unable to persuade the company to arbitrate the issue, the council ordered a strike of every union seaman employed on Oceanic vessels. In addition, the council commanded the boilermakers' union to strike the Risdon Iron Works when that firm continued doing repair work on Oceanic ships.[47]

These strikes broke down in the face of strong employer opposition. The Union Iron Works imported strikebreakers from the East and joined with other metal trades firms to form the Engineers' and Iron Founders' Association, a solidly organized body of employers. The Iron Trades Council, by contrast, failed to maintain unity among its members. The strikers returned to work at Risdon within a few weeks, and by early September the metal trades unions had, one by one, called off the Union Iron Works strike.[48]

The Oceanic Steamship Company strike dragged on longer, but was no more successful. In June, 1886, a group of employers formed the Ship Owners' Protective Association, which not only supported Oceanic but initiated broad antiunion countermeasures. It set up a central shipping office through which the association's members required all seamen to be cleared for employment and hired—a new hiring procedure well adapted to the elimination of active unionists from the industry. In August, protesting the hiring system, the Coast Seamen's Union proclaimed a strike against every firm in the Ship Owners' Association. But the strike eventually went down to defeat, leaving the union reduced in membership and too weak to ward off ensuing wage reductions.[49]

The year 1886 closed with another violent street railway strike. In December carmen struck two San Francisco streetcar companies in an attempt to win improved wages and hours. The strike, which lasted into the early spring of 1887, was featured by assaults on strikebreakers, repeated attempts to dynamite moving cars, and damage to the cars from rock-throwing mobs. Although this struggle failed, it demonstrated increased awareness among unionists of the importance of organized financial support to strikers. Local unions donated more than $10,000 to keep the strike going for so long a period.[50]

Despite the failure of most of the major strikes of 1886, San Francisco labor remained substantially organized in a wider range of industries than ever before. Among employers, also, there was increasing recognition of the need for organization. In a reaction to expanding unionism, employers' associations were active during 1887 not only in shipping and the metal trades, but in the brewing, baking, restaurant, construction, furniture manufacturing, and several other industries. Frank Roney optimistically concluded that this development offered an opportunity for the establishment of more peaceful labor relations. As president of the Federated Trades Council he proposed to a group of employers that they join with the council in creating a permanent board of arbitration to settle local labor disputes. The proposal was rejected because, Roney believed, employers were unwilling to accord formal recognition to unions.[51]

During 1887, a year of continued prosperity, some organized workers scored significant gains. By the end of the year the bakers had persuaded a majority of San Francisco and Oakland bakeries to reduce their grueling schedule of a fourteen-hour day and a seven-day week to a six-day, sixty-four-hour week, with hiring exclusively through union offices. In May the brewery workers, who also worked intolerably long hours, demanded higher wages, a sixty-three-hour week, and a strict union shop. When employers rejected the union shop, a strike and boycott resulted; after two months the breweries signed a detailed, formal contract embodying the union demands. This victory gave evidence of the added strength San Francisco labor was acquiring by increasing its ties with the national labor movement. The national union of brewery workers greatly aided the strikers through payment of generous benefits.[52]

In the following year, however, organized employers launched counterattacks against the brewery and bakery unions. Early in 1888, after careful preparation, a bakery employers' association provoked the industry's workers into a strike to preserve the gains they had just won. In an ill-considered attempt to aid the bakers, leaders of the large union of cooks and waiters ordered a sympathy strike of its entire membership. The struggle continued for several weeks and involved more than 2,000 workers at its height. It ended in victory for the employers and depleted strength for the striking unions. The union of cooks and waiters reportedly lost four-fifths of its estimated prestrike membership of approximately 1,200.[53]

In 1888 a nationwide brewery employers' association, bent upon destroying the young national union of brewery workers, announced that its member firms would thenceforward refuse union recognition. Accordingly, its affiliated San Francisco association canceled the union agreement won by the 1887 strike. The result was the most prolonged, intense battle yet fought by a Bay Area union against an employers' association. An aggressive boycott campaign was pursued for months with the support of thousands of aroused San Francisco workers. Brewery sales declined substantially, as saloons yielded to demands to cease dispensing "scab beer" rather than lose working-class patronage. The boycott finally brought victory in the summer of 1889, when the San Francisco brewers' association formally called off its attempt to break free from the union. The outcome gave new prestige to the local labor movement, for in no other city did the brewery workers survive so well the nationwide employer assault against them.[54]

In late 1888 there were approximately seventy-five unions in San Francisco, with a claimed membership of about 15,000. Unionization still lagged badly in Oakland, where there were only four unions with 5,000 members. A new San Francisco council of longshoremen and seamen, the Wharf and Wave Federation, claimed to represent more than 5,000 maritime workers in 1888. The federation enjoyed a brief existence as the first of a series of organizations that attempted, over the next sixty years, to weld a lasting alliance between Pacific Coast longshore and offshore unions.[55]

Only about one-fourth of the San Francisco unions were affiliated in late 1888 with the Federated Trades Council. Since 1886 many unions had withdrawn, some because they wanted to affiliate only with separate councils of allied crafts, others because they refused to accept the council's authority to levy strike assessments. Better-established craft unions complained that newly formed unions refused to take direction from older organizations, rushed into ill-advised conflicts, and thereby imposed a financial drain upon other labor groups. Even at this early date the "conservative and intelligent leaders" of the older San Francisco unions, and their policy of avoiding strikes whenever possible, were being praised.[56]

San Francisco unions, although not adhering closely to their central body, did strengthen their ties with the national labor movement. At the beginning of the 1880's only a few local organizations were affiliated with national craft unions, but by the close of the decade a substantial proportion of workers, especially in the building and metal trades, were associated with national unions and with the American Federation of Labor. The Federated Trades Council took out an AFL charter in 1888, and its leaders urged AFL affiliation upon all Bay Area unions.[57]

Through 1889 the San Francisco labor movement remained in healthy condition, in an environment of continued economic prosperity. A number of new unions were organized, and the Federated Trades Council tried to create enthusiasm for a renewed drive for the eight-hour day. However, the prevailing atmosphere of labor relations during the year was one of relative calm. It was a calm that was soon to be blown away.

Conflict, Decline, and Revival in the 1890's

The year 1890 ushered in a period characterized in San Francisco by intense struggles between employer associations and unions. This period of conflict demonstrated that even powerful unions were not yet able to match the strength and resources of employers who had learned the lesson of counterorganization. And, by 1890, employers were learning this lesson in a widening range of industries.

In the spring of 1890 labor strife again erupted in the metal trades industry. The Molders' Union, in 1887, had entered into an agreement with the Engineers' and Iron Founders' Association, but recurrent friction led the association to withdraw from the agreement on January 1, 1890. In March, after the union had rejected demands for wage reductions and other conditions that would enable San Francisco foundries to compete more effectively with firms in the East, the association cut the wage rates of foundry employees. The ensuing strike of molders and machinists turned into a stubborn war of attrition. Both antagonists were strong and well organized. The association imported hundreds of craftsmen from the East and hired armed guards to protect them from the violence that soon broke out. Men on both sides were injured, and two strikers were killed. Supported by donations from other unionists, the strikers maintained the battle through 1890 and 1891. It was finally called off in January, 1892, apparently on an informal understanding that strikers would not be discriminated against in rehiring. The exhausting strike and the severe business depression that prevailed after 1892, however, left the metal trades unions virtually impotent until the end of the decade.[58]

As in the metal trades, labor relations in the shoe manufacturing industry were aggravated by the struggle of local firms to survive against Eastern competition. The need to achieve lower costs was largely responsible for the disputes that, from the late 1880's on, repeatedly flared up between shoeworkers and such Bay Area manufacturers as Buckingham & Hecht, Cahn & Nickelsburg, and G. M. Kutz. Early in 1890 the larger manufacturers formed an employers' association and pledged themselves to join in a lockout should a strike be called against any member firm. The first test of the united employer front came in the spring of 1891, when about 200 workers struck against Buckingham & Hecht, charging that the firm had cut wages and hired nonunion men. The association promptly ordered a lockout affecting about 1,000 workers, and the union soon agreed to call off the strike on employer terms. Early in 1892 the association-wide lockout again demonstrated its potency by defeating a strike called against a wage reduction imposed by Cahn & Nickelsburg. Upon ending the lockout, the employers' association required workers seeking reinstatement to disavow union membership. Enough workers complied to leave unionism strong in only one San Francisco shoe factory.[59]

Notwithstanding these defeats, organized labor in San Francisco remained vigorous in the prosperous years of 1890–1891. Almost a dozen new unions were formed in 1890, though few were of significant size or strength. Labor's chief success of the year came in the building trades. On May Day, 1890, after long and careful preparation for support by other AFL national unions, locals of the Carpenters' Union throughout the nation simultaneously launched an effort to enforce the eight-hour day. Contractors in the Bay Area offered only token resistance. The carpenters thus joined other local building tradesmen who had already won the shorter workday.[60]

Some new unions were established in San Francisco in 1891, but the rate of growth was below that of 1889–1890. Industrial conflict, in contrast, increased markedly during the year. Unions encountered stiffer, more thoroughly organized employer resistance. Retail clerks, who had revived their early-closing movement, alarmed shoe and clothing store owners into forming an employers' association. Unions of granite cutters and planing-mill workers failed in strikes for the eight-hour day, against well-organized employers. Strikes were called by unions of boxmakers, longshoremen, coopers, printers, and upholsterers for such goals as higher wages, the nine-hour day, and the union shop. Most of these strikes failed.[61]

The failure of the longshoremen's strike was particularly significant, for it pointed up the chronic difficulty of achieving unity among workers in the maritime industry. Early in 1891 the Coast Seamen's Union and three separate San Francisco unions of longshoremen formed the City Front Labor Council as a second attempt to federate water-front and offshore workers. But creation of the council did not eliminate the perennial jurisdictional squabbling among its affiliates. A struggle among the various longshoremen's unions for preference in hiring, and jealous insistence on the exclusive right to handle certain types of cargo, kept this large and potentially powerful body of workers disunited. Overlapping jurisdictional claims in the work of loading and discharging cargo frequently produced sharp conflicts between longshoremen and sailors. Under these circumstances the unions affiliated with the new council were too suspicious of one another to vest in its leaders the authority to establish unified policies. Thus the council could not prevent one of the longshoremen's unions from striking, against its advice, for an increase in wages in August, 1891. The other council affiliates refused to give support, the strike failed, and the defeated union soon dissolved. Early the next year the seamen, angry over continued jurisdictional strife, rejected a request from a group of striking longshoremen that they discharge cargo only to union men.[62] The City Front Labor Council did not long survive these repeated failures of its members to aid one another in labor disputes.

The Board of Manufacturers and Employers

The development of employer associations and the increase in labor conflicts led employers in 1891 to consolidate their forces. In August firms employing an estimated 40,000 workers formed the Board of Manufacturers and Employers, the first city-wide employers' federation to have a major impact on local labor relations.[63] The board, by publicly proclaiming that it accepted the right of workers to organize, set a verbal precedent followed by almost every organization created in the next fifty years for the purpose of combating Bay Area unions. The board announced that it objected only to the "arbitrary spirit" displayed by unions, and to their indulgence in strikes and boycotts. The board viewed boycotts with especial concern, for under energetic leadership in 1890–1892 the Federated Trades Council organized numerous boycotts against breweries, retail stores, and other establishments involved in labor difficulties.

A few months after the creation of the Board of Manufacturers and Employers, the most bitter of the prolonged conflicts of the 1890's broke out on the San Francisco water front. By 1891 the Coast Seamen's Union had rebuilt its membership from the low ebb after the 1886 defeat and had merged with a separate union of steamship sailors to form the Sailors' Union of the Pacific. This merged organization was led by a thirty-seven-year-old Norwegian, Andrew Furuseth.* Claiming approximately 4,000 members

---

* Furuseth, who devoted almost fifty years of his life to the Sailors' Union, was probably the most singular figure ever to play a major role in San Francisco labor relations. A lifelong bachelor, obsessed by a determination to improve the conditions under which seamen worked, he subsisted on a small salary throughout an almost uniquely selfless career. Adhering rigidly to the AFL philosophy of craft unionism, Furuseth was intensely proud of the sailors' craft and dubious of any benefits to be gained from alliances with onshore workers. Nevertheless, he and other leaders of the Sailors' Union played important parts in guiding the affairs of central labor bodies in San Francisco. Furuseth opposed entry by unions into political movements and was highly suspicious of labor leaders with political ambitions. But he devoted the major efforts of his career, and many years, to lobbying in Washington for federal legislation to end the right of shipowners to imprison sailors for desertion, and otherwise to improve the legal and economic position of American seamen.

Furuseth, who had great respect for the power of shipowners, advocated moving at a gradual pace to achieve moderate economic gains. In later years, his natural caution was overlaid with a pessimism that seemed defeatist to some of his followers. Yet under Furuseth the Sailors' Union engaged in several of the most intensely fought labor conflicts in San Francisco history. He was, moreover, an early proponent of the militant "job action" tactics that at times have been conspicuous features of labor relations in the Pacific Coast maritime industry. After the defeat of the 1886 strike, and in later

by 1891, the Sailors' Union of the Pacific was by far the largest individual labor organization on the West Coast. It was thus prepared to put up tenacious resistance when a new employers' organization, the Shipowners' Association of the Pacific Coast, imposed a drastic wage reduction late in the year.[64] In the ensuing fight the sailors resorted to sudden strikes by the crews of ships ready to sail, desertions at the first port of call by union members who had signed on as nonunion seamen, sabotage of ships, and violence against strikebreakers. This guerrilla warfare continued throughout 1892.

Another lengthy, though less violent, struggle began early in 1892 when a reorganized association of Bay Area brewery owners launched a new drive to free the industry from union regulation. The Board of Manufacturers and Employers, intervening openly for the first time in a major dispute, backed the employer offensive against the brewery workers. With this powerful support, and with the union soon weakened by the depression of the mid-1890's, the brewery owners achieved a substantial success. They discharged and black-listed militant unionists, and held out through the middle years of the decade against strikes and boycotts. The brewery workers set up a large labor-owned coöperative brewery to sell union beer, but, operating at a substantial loss, it survived only a few years.[65]

Despite the frustrating struggles of the seamen and the brewery workers against powerful groups of employers, the San Francisco labor movement did achieve a notable organizational advance. During 1892 the Federated Trades Council appeared in danger of following its predecessors into oblivion. As Walter Macarthur —the Sailors' Union leader serving in 1892 as council president— later described it, the council seemed to have reached an impasse in which it "couldn't grow and wouldn't die." Most of the building trades unions had withdrawn into a separate central body of their own, and what remained of the council was torn by factional strife over the personalities and policies of its leaders, and over the demands of Socialists and others that it support a working-

---

periods of union weakness, Furuseth urged his followers to continue the fight against shipowners by such harassing techniques as systematic slowdowns aboard ship and last-minute refusals to sail.

class political movement. In the fall of 1892, however, labor leaders from Sacramento intervened as mediators in this discouraging situation. Working with Macarthur and other San Francisco union officers, they brought about an agreement to dissolve both the Federated Trades and the Building Trades councils, and form a completely new central body. Thus the San Francisco Labor Council, starting with thirty-four affiliates, came into existence in December, 1892. It has survived continuously from that time to the present.[66]

The Depression of the 1890's

Substantial unemployment had plagued San Francisco in 1892, but in 1893 conditions in the local labor market rapidly worsened. Financial panic in the East and bank closures and business failures across the nation in mid-1893 signaled the arrival of one of the severest depressions in American history. The depression brought to the Bay Area the most prolonged period of unemployment since the late 1870's. One mitigating factor, however, helped prevent a repetition of such demonstrations of jobless as those led in 1877 by Dennis Kearney. In 1892 Congress extended for another ten-year period its prohibition of Chinese immigration. Lacking replenishment from abroad, San Francisco's Chinese population shrank between 1890 and 1900 from about 25,000 to less than 15,000.[67] Unemployed white workers were thus not embittered, as in the 1870's, by growing competition from Orientals for the jobs available. The deep and prolonged depression was a major influence in cutting the percentage rate of population growth in San Francisco during the 1890's to a level lower than that of any census decade except the 1930's. The city's population in 1890–1900 grew from just under 300,000 to about 340,000. The population of Oakland also increased slowly, from less than 50,000 to about 65,000.

The Bay Area labor movement was badly weakened by the depression. Some unions vanished entirely, and almost all suffered heavy membership losses. Few were strong enough to enter into open conflict with employers. In 1893 organizing efforts were at a standstill, and there were no significant labor disputes except the continuing struggles in the shipping and brewery industries. Early in the year the tide of battle turned against the Sailors' Union, as the Board of Manufacturers and Employers intervened in support of the Shipowners' Association. The board's executive secretary revived the control measure that required all seamen to hire through a central shipping office, where their past employment records could be checked. This enabled the association to weed out active unionists, and so to conduct a winning fight through 1893. Late that year there came a climax of violence. In December a dynamite-filled suitcase planted at a boardinghouse for nonunion sailors exploded, killing eight men. Shocked public reaction, and the unfavorable publicity and heavy financial expenses involved in defending a union member tried, but not convicted, for the crime, were among the factors that brought the Sailors' Union to end, temporarily, its struggle against the shipowners. The long conflict and the depression of the 1890's combined to reduce the membership of the union by more than 75 per cent from its prestrike peak.[68]

The battle against the Sailors' Union was the hardest-fought labor dispute in which the Board of Manufacturers and Employers engaged. No other victory gave it so much satisfaction. Although the board's role in the conflicts of 1891–1894 was not well publicized, San Francisco unions bitterly regarded it as providing the chief stimulation and leadership to the battles against labor.[69] The board was not reluctant to claim credit for the weakness of local unions after months of business depression and failing struggles against employer combinations. In an 1894 speech reviewing the board's first three years of activity, its president announced: "The general success of this Association can best be understood by . . . the fact that among the industries of San Francisco there remains but one single union which enforces its rules upon its trade, . . . the Typographical Union." And that union, he declared, had been spared defeat only by the failure of employing printers to organize against it. Pointing out that such action would have come if the union's leadership had not carefully avoided giving provocation, he confidently predicted that "so long as it maintains this conservative and moderate attitude it will retain the control of its trade, but the moment it becomes controlled by hot-heads this Association will be able to destroy its power as easily as it has the power of other unions." [70]

The Pullman Strike of 1894

Local unions remained, through 1894, too shaken by the impact of depression to seek significant economic gains. But a conflict touched off in the East involved the Bay Area that year in its most dramatic labor episode of the decade. In June, 1894, leaders of the American Railway Union, ardently backing a strike by the manufacturing workers of the Pullman Palace Car Company, ordered ARU members out in a nationwide sympathy strike against trains carrying Pullman cars. The ARU, a broad industrial union taking in all workers connected with railroads, irrespective of craft, achieved a surprisingly effective tie-up of train traffic in the Bay Area and other California railway centers. Though strongly opposed by the craft-unionist leaders of the railroad brotherhoods and of the AFL, the ARU strike was highly popular among California workers because here it was directed against the Southern Pacific Railroad, the largest, richest, and most hated corporation in California. The Southern Pacific, by the 1890's, was almost universally believed guilty of such abuses of power as the monopolistic setting of extortionate freight rates and the wholesale purchase of state legislators and railroad commissioners. To thousands of Californians the ARU strike appeared as a blow against a corrupt and vicious corporate power, and large throngs of strike sympathizers readily gathered to help block the movement of trains.[71]

Before the strike was broken, in mid-July, 1894, Oakland and Sacramento underwent three weeks of near-hysteric excitement. Huge mobs of strikers and sympathizers temporarily tied up railway traffic in both cities by seizing control of the railroad yards. Residents of Oakland feared an outbreak of serious violence, as prominent citizens planned a vigilance committee to suppress the mob, and strikers amassed medical supplies and beds for anticipated casualties. Intervention of the military, ordered by President Grover Cleveland, finally ended the strike in California, as elsewhere. Federal troops moved into Sacramento on July 11, and and on July 12 the navy landed marines and sailors in Oakland. Military control soon restored order and train service to both cities, although not until after one striker had been shot to death in a clash between soldiers and a defiant Sacramento crowd.[72]

The 1894 railroad strike gave Bay Area workers an opportunity to participate, directly or vicariously, in a stirring drama in a period otherwise marked by weakness and apathy in labor ranks. Though the strike failed, it was credited with having temporarily increased local union membership. And the enthusiasm aroused by the strike gave evidence of the potentiality of Bay Area labor for effective organized action upon the return of favorable economic circumstances.

The San Francisco Building Trades Council

Business depression continued through 1895, but organized labor in San Francisco showed more signs of life than in 1893–1894. A few new unions were formed, the brewery workers intensified their flagging struggle against nonunion employers, and the printing pressmen felt strong enough to strike one of the largest local firms for lighter work loads and higher wages. The strike, however, dragged on for more than a year without success. For building tradesmen the year 1895 was definitely the turning point of recovery from their weakness of 1893–1894. The painters reorganized, in a rapidly growing union. The several local unions of carpenters, claiming many new members, again began enforcing the eight-hour day. At the same time they instituted a new technique of policing construction jobs, by insisting that contractors hire only those carpenters able to display a working card granted by the union.[73]

While most unions remained comparatively weak during 1896, as depression persisted, the building tradesmen laid a permanent foundation for their growing power. In February, 1896, unions representing about 4,000 workers formally organized the San Francisco Building Trades Council. The council has been in continuous existence ever since, serving to combine the strength and coördinate the efforts of the separate crafts. From the beginning it sought to establish centralized control over labor relations in the industry. In 1896 it adopted two significant policies: that all building tradesmen would be issued their working cards directly from the council, rather than from their respective unions; and that the business agents of the council would police construction jobs to assure enforcement of the union rules of all crafts.[74] These policies shifted authority from individual unions to the council.

Several building trades crafts were organized or reorganized in 1896, and the stronger unions tried to enforce the closed shop on construction jobs. With aggressive confidence, the new Building Trades Council proclaimed that on and after April 1, 1896, no member would work on jobs with men who had no union working cards.[75] But since not all crafts were organized, or affiliated with the council, the building trades lacked the economic power to establish closed-shop conditions universally throughout the industry.

The vigorous unionism among the building tradesmen led in 1896 to several labor disputes, including a violence-ridden strike by the lathers in which a nonunion worker was the victim of a fatal beating. Several union lathers were tried on a charge of murder, but escaped with convictions and light prison sentences for involuntary manslaughter.[76] The largest-scale building trades contest of the year was fought by the painters, who served the Master Painters' Association with demands for the eight-hour day, a wage increase, and the closed shop. During the negotiations, an employer later charged, the union "made this proposition: that if we would accede to their conditions, they would agree to work for no one but the Master Painters, thus driving all others out of the business." [77] If made, this proposal of a collusive combination was declined. In March the painters struck, after the association had balked at the demand for the closed shop. According to union leaders, the strike brought out approximately 1,300 painters and eventually won the closed shop from the large majority of employers. The association, however, insisted that few of its member firms actually settled with the union on that basis.[78]

New Central Bodies

In addition to the building tradesmen, workers in another San Francisco industry made an important advance in the depression year of 1896. The Typographical, Printing Pressmen's, and Bookbinders' unions joined in forming the Allied Printing Trades Council, an organization that has survived to the present day. The new council adopted a union label, to be granted only to firms employing no nonunion men in the crafts affiliated with the council. Labor's political influence proved sufficiently potent in early 1897 to bring passage by the Board of Supervisors of an ordinance requiring that city printing contracts be awarded only to firms entitled to use the new APTC label.[79] This legal discrimination in favor of unionized firms came under repeated attack in future years by various San Francisco employer groups.

While the building trades and printing trades were establishing their central councils in 1896, the San Francisco Labor Council drifted in the doldrums. From 1893 on it had been losing affiliates. Some unions had dissolved, others had transferred to the Building Trades Council, others had lost interest as the depression continued. Able to accomplish little during 1893–1895, the council found itself in 1896 facing a new challenge. Resentful of its policy of eschewing class-conscious political action, several dissident unions coöperated with the local branch of the Socialist Labor Party to set up a rival council, the Central Trades and Labor Alliance. The alliance called for such measures as a federal income tax and government ownership of public utilities, and issued a blanket denunciation of the Labor Council leaders for "compromising with employers . . . bartering your labor leadership for political offices in the gift of capitalist parties." [80] This became a familiar charge against conservative union leaders in later years.

Although the class-conscious Central Trades and Labor Alliance posed a brief threat to the Labor Council in 1896, it gained relatively little support among San Francisco unionists and soon dissolved. The Labor Council, meanwhile, continued to lose strength. In mid-1897 only fifteen unions, with an estimated 4,500 members, still retained affiliation.[81] But at that point the council touched bottom in its long decline. Its membership soon began to rise, slowly at first, then with accelerating speed.

Economic Revival in 1897

The year 1897 marked the end of the severe depression of the 1890's, in the Bay Area as throughout the nation. The discovery of gold in the Klondike territory adjoining Alaska set off at mid-year another gold rush which brought thousands of men to the Pacific Coast en route to the far north. The flow of men and supplies to the gold fields, and the return flow of gold, gave a special stimulus to West Coast commerce. As business began to revive, the rate of population growth of California and the Bay Area accelerated. The twin expansion of industry and population brought a strong demand for new construction, creating a building boom by the close of the century.

This environment of economic growth offered renewed opportunity for labor. Union activity, however, revived sluggishly in 1897–1898. The Labor Council, growing slowly, expanded to only eighteen affiliated unions by mid-1898. Few unions made demands in 1897, and little organizing was carried on among nonunion workers. In 1898, unions still remained generally unaggressive. The San Francisco labor scene was enlivened, however, by a major dispute in the printing industry. In April the Allied Printing Trades Council unions struck book and job printing firms, demanding that the workday be reduced from ten to nine hours. The strike involved more than 400 workers and lasted more than two months before it was called off as a failure.[82]

The most significant labor development of 1898 came in July, when Patrick Henry McCarthy, a carpenter born thirty-five years earlier, in Limerick, Ireland, was elected president of the San Francisco Building Trades Council.[83] The new president had come to stay. For almost a quarter of a century P. H. McCarthy headed the council, establishing a virtually dictatorial personal control of its policies. Under his aggressive direction the council intensified its organizing activities in 1899 among laborers, hod carriers, cement workers, and other groups. Determined to extend his leadership throughout the industry, McCarthy strove to persuade or force every craft into affiliation with the council. From 1898 on, he moved steadily toward the goal of centralized power over the building trades unions.

In 1899 the favorable conditions resulting from more than a year of economic revival brought forth a surge of organizing activity. Especially in the building trades, but also in other industries, new unions were formed at a sharply accelerated pace. Among them were the unions of painters and plumbers in the East Bay, dairy employees and ladies' garment workers in San Francisco, and longshoremen on both sides of the Bay. The San Francisco Labor Council grew to a membership of twenty-one unions by mid-1899 and gained additional affiliates later in the year.[84]

A widening range of unions reached out in 1899 for economic gains. Since 1897 the upturn in business activity and the new inflow of gold from the Klondike had given prices a strong upward push. As living costs went up, more and more organized workers sought to raise their wages. Such efforts were not likely to encounter adamant employer resistance in the midst of rising employment, prices, and profits. The economic upswing had gained further momentum with the outbreak of the Spanish-American War early in 1898, and with the annexation of Hawaii later in the year. San Francisco became the main supply base for the troops engaged in the 1898–1901 fighting in the Philippines, and derived an additional advantage from its position as the chief center of the rapidly expanding Hawaii-mainland trade.

Little overt conflict accompanied the chief advances made by Bay Area unions in 1899. By midyear the brewery workers had regained union-shop conditions in the large majority of local breweries. The Typographical Union quietly won the eight-hour day from the San Francisco daily newspapers. The building trades unions enforced the closed shop on most San Francisco construction jobs. The rapidly rebuilding Sailors' Union, through a successful strike, managed to force wage increases for many of its members employed on coastal sailing vessels. A few small strikes occurred in 1899, mainly over wage issues, in the metal trades, shipbuilding, and several other industries. But the year closed on a sustained note of economic expansion and resurgent union activity without having witnessed a major hard-fought labor dispute in the Bay Area. It was the last peaceful period on the local labor front for years to come.[85]

Chapter II | *The Resurgent*
Labor Movement
1900–1901

As THE NEW CENTURY opened, unions in San Francisco could look back on a fifty-year period during which organization among workers had maintained a continuous, though at times precariously thin, thread of existence. They could look forward to a new era of growing union strength. The cities of the Bay Area were among those expanding most rapidly in the nationwide boom under way by 1900. The ranks of organized labor were filling up in the Bay Area and throughout the nation, as the unions of the AFL experienced a forward surge that expanded their membership from under 300,000 in 1897 to well above 1.5 million by 1904.[1]

The first two years of the century were particularly crucial to the future of unionism. Bay Area labor was fast gaining strength as organization spread at an accelerating pace. But would this new union growth be able to entrench itself solidly and hold fast against employer efforts to uproot it? This was the vital question which was largely to be answered by the end of 1901.

The 1900–1901 course of events in San Francisco hinged to a significant degree upon the factor of timing. In this period the unusually fertile soil which San Francisco provided for unionism was evidenced by the rapidity and the vigor of labor's rebound from its comparative dormancy during the prolonged depression. The speed of its resurgence was of great advantage in that it permitted unionism to spread widely and develop powerful momentum before antiunion employer forces became sufficiently alert to mass for a counterattack. The employer blow, when it came, was thus delivered beyond the time when it would have had maximum effect.

Developments on the San Francisco labor scene in this period moved to an unusually well-defined and dramatic climax—the violent conflict of 1901 in the teaming and maritime industries. This critical episode highlighted the importance of extensive united fronts to both workers and employers, indicating that the struggle for power would not be conducted solely through isolated union-employer contests in individual industries, but in battles between broadly aggregated forces on both sides. By 1900, and in later years, the basic strength of San Francisco unionism was such, indeed, that it could be severely shaken only by an organized body of employers able to draw upon the resources of business firms throughout the city. Antiunion elements rallied a formidable number of businessmen behind a new central body in 1901 and drove far toward their goal of administering a heavy defeat to the rising labor movement. But the employer attack found San Francisco labor joined along a wide front and prepared to fight with firm solidarity.

A Favorable Setting for Union Growth

In the 1900–1910 decade the population of Bay Area cities rose well above the level of the 1890's. The San Francisco population expanded from under 350,000 to slightly more than 415,000, while the combined populations of Oakland, Berkeley, and Alameda leaped from about 95,000 to almost 215,000. The new housing required by this swelling population created a demand for building tradesmen which drew skilled craftsmen to the Bay Area and facilitated the continuing accumulation of power by the unions in the construction industry.

Although organization was on the upswing and unions had developed exceptional strength in a few industries, most notably in the building trades, only a minority of San Francisco wage earners were as yet organized. In the principal East Bay cities— Oakland, Berkeley, and Alameda—an even smaller minority of workers were union members. Conditions in 1900, however, were favorable to union expansion. In addition to the booming economy's rising demand for workers, a number of other factors enhanced organized labor's potentiality for rapid growth in member-ship and strength. These factors were especially apparent in San Francisco. Since the early 1880's a substantial, though fluctuating, amount of union activity had been constantly carried on in San Francisco. In 1900 the local labor movement possessed a firm nucleus of skilled and veteran labor leaders and a small body of unions that had survived for ten, twenty, or more years. Among the older unions there had developed a sense of proud traditions and a militant *esprit de corps* that would furnish inspiration to newly organized groups of workers. Permanently rooted central labor councils had finally been established. San Francisco labor had largely discarded aspirations of reaching distant goals through sweeping political change, and had adopted the AFL policy of relying on trade-union action to achieve gradual economic ad-vance. Unions had learned to use modern techniques both for consolidating union strength and for contending with refractory employers: for example, retention of salaried officers, free to de-vote their full time to organizing efforts and to the inspection of jobs and plants for the maintenance of union conditions; insistence upon the strict union shop and employer acceptance of the union label, as a means of assuring job control by the union; collection of initiation fees, dues, and assessments to finance organizing drives and strikes; support of prolonged strikes from funds sys-tematically raised by other local unions; maintenance of well-publicized boycotts against the products of firms resisting unions; resort to sympathy strikes and secondary boycotts in critical labor disputes; discouragement of strikebreakers, sometimes by peace-ful persuasion, sometimes by intimidation and violence.

Union growth was favored also by certain factors stemming largely from the Bay Area's geographical location. Despite the existence of transcontinental railroads, Bay Area employers still found it difficult and expensive to import replacements for strik-ers, especially in highly skilled crafts. Moreover, the 3,000-mile expanse of continent protected workers in the Bay Area from the flood of Italians, Slavs, and other European immigrants then pour-ing into low-paid jobs in Eastern industries. In 1900 San Fran-cisco's own historic body of cheap labor, the Chinese, was a dwindling threat to the white labor force. Yet the traditional antagonism toward the Chinese was still serving, as in the past, to unite the city's white wage earners. This unifying experience of having long made common cause against the Chinese was an additional factor in preparing San Francisco workers for a strong union movement.

More than one-third of the San Francisco population in 1900 was foreign-born,[2] but this element was predominantly Irish, German, British, and Scandinavian. Unlike the easily exploitable arrivals in the East from southern and eastern Europe, San Francisco's foreign-born workers were highly receptive to unionization. The Irish and the British did not encounter a language barrier, and many British immigrants brought with them the advanced trade-union traditions of their native land. The Germans, like the British, came from a land in which, by 1900, both the trade-union and Socialist movements were appreciably more developed than in the United States. And men of Scandinavian origin furnished exceptional leaders and a high percentage of the membership of the Sailors' Union of the Pacific, the largest and one of the most militant labor organizations on the Pacific Coast.* Moreover, San Francisco's foreign-born workers included a higher proportion of skilled craftsmen than did the largely unskilled European immigrants pouring into Eastern industry. San Francisco shipbuilding firms relied heavily on the special skills of employees of Scotch and English origin. Skilled German craftsmen were particularly numerous in such trades as baking, brewing, and carpentering. In 1900 a few local unions in these trades were, in fact, still made up exclusively or predominantly of Germans.

Several factors on the employer side also contributed to po-

---

* The Sailors' Union was unusually influential in the San Francisco labor movement. In 1887 it began publishing the *Coast Seamen's Journal*, the only union paper existing in San Francisco when the twentieth century opened. The Sailors' Union donated large sums to support strikes by other unions, and by 1900 many of its members had been active in organizing onshore workers and in serving as outstanding leaders of various San Francisco unions and labor councils. One observer, who concluded that the Sailors' Union filled a unique role as a training ground for men who later carried unionism to shoreside workers, estimates that during the years 1889–1900 approximately 10,000 members left the Sailors' Union for other occupations. (Lucile Eaves, *A History of California Labor Legislation* [Berkeley: The University Press, 1910], p. 4.)

tential rapid union growth. Relatively small firms predominated in the industries of the Bay Area. The Southern Pacific Railway was a corporate giant, controlling through its subsidiaries large interests in real estate, street railways, ferry-boat lines, and oil production and refining. The Union Iron Works and the Risdon Iron Works, employing between them several thousand workers, loomed large in the metal trades industry. Firms of substantial size, each with some hundreds of employees, were sprinkled among manufacturing industries producing sugar, oil, cotton cloth, overalls, and several other products. But in the early years of the century Bay Area unions typically dealt with small firms and contended with few individual employers of great size and economic strength. San Francisco stood in sharp contrast to such cities as Pittsburgh, with its steel mills, or, in later years, Detroit, with its automobile plants. The local economy was dominated by no single industry whose employers might, by forceful example, furnish antiunion inspiration to the entire business community.

The expanding unions of 1900 were not at the outset forced to struggle against well-organized, aggressively hostile Bay Area employer associations. Labor's apathy in the long depression of the 1890's had lulled most of the existing employers' associations into inactivity. The San Francisco Board of Manufacturers and Employers had passed from the scene after its antiunion drive of the early 1890's. The Merchants' Association, with about 1,200 member firms, was the leading organization of San Francisco employers in 1900, but officially it followed a hands-off policy in regard to labor problems. There was no local counterpart of the Merchants' and Manufacturers' Association of Los Angeles, by 1900 a well-established organization that for years to come would wage successful battles against organized labor.

Intense antiunion feelings, moreover, do not seem to have been widespread among local employers. Only a minority of Bay Area firms refused to deal with unions. In 1900 organized labor had begun but recently to recover from its depressed condition of the 1890's, and consequently few employers had yet faced insistent demands backed by union strength. The demands of workers just before the turn of the century had stressed reductions in long working hours and amelioration of unpleasant working conditions.

Many employers, basically sympathetic to the justice of these demands and rejoicing in returning prosperity, felt no need to resist union efforts to gain improved conditions.

San Francisco unions benefited from several other environmental factors. The city's heavily working-class population gave the spokesmen of organized labor a potentially weighty influence in local political matters. The general public was sympathetic and tolerant toward unions, and not easily aroused by the inconveniences attendant upon major strikes. No San Francisco newspaper, in 1900, emulated the ardently antiunion *Los Angeles Times* in its bombardment of readers with verbal salvos against labor. The Bay Area labor movement, moreover, had a powerful journalistic ally in the *San Francisco Examiner,* one of the chain of newspapers owned by William Randolph Hearst. Hearst, in 1900, was a liberal Democrat with political ambitions. His papers were then giving such support to organized labor that in 1903, at the urging of local labor leaders, Hearst established in Los Angeles another *Examiner,* to defend labor in journalistic combat with the *Times.*[3]

Organized labor in the Bay Area thus entered the new century under favorable auspices. The rapid union expansion of 1899 accelerated in 1900 and 1901. This wave of union activity stirred employers to reorganize and, in San Francisco, led to crucial tests of strength between unions and employer associations.

Labor's Gains in 1900

In 1900 new unions were being formed and total union membership was mounting rapidly in the Bay Area. At midyear the state Bureau of Labor Statistics, surveying the extent of labor organization in California, listed ninety unions for San Francisco and twenty-four for Alameda County.[4] The number of unions, however, was not an accurate gauge of the number of separate crafts and occupations into which organization had penetrated. The San Francisco total, for example, included half a dozen individual locals of the Carpenters' Union and two or more separate, and sometimes rival, unions among such classes of workers as longshoremen, bakers, barbers, cigar makers, cooks, tailors, painters, and building trades laborers. A large minority of Bay Area unions still had no affiliation with national organizations in their respective trades, and some of these competed for members against locals of AFL unions.

Of the ninety unions in San Francisco in mid-1900, fifty-five responded to a request for membership data, reporting a total membership of more than 12,000. The Bureau of Labor Statistics calculated, therefore, that total union membership was about 20,000 in San Francisco, and about 3,000 in Oakland. These estimates probably exaggerated the number of organized workers, since a higher proportion of the larger than of the smaller unions reported their memberships. The San Francisco total was swelled by inclusion of all members of the coast-wide offshore unions with headquarters in the city. However, unions were growing rapidly during the year; by the end of 1900 union membership may therefore have exceeded the midyear estimates.

The San Francisco Labor Council had thirty-four affiliates by mid-1900, with new unions joining at a rapid rate. The increase in membership enabled the council, early in the year, to make its chief officer, the secretary, a full-time salaried representative. From 1900 on, the successive secretaries of the Labor Council played major negotiating and policy-making roles in San Francisco labor relations, and central labor bodies exerted greatly increased influence within the local union movement. The San Francisco Building Trades Council continued in 1900 to acquire new affiliates and to gain power in its industry. And in early 1900 a solidly established central body was finally organized in Oakland, with an initial membership of six unions. As the Alameda County Central Labor Council, it has ever since been active in the East Bay.[5]

During 1900 the foremost issue in Bay Area labor relations was the length of the workday. Unions in a number of trades demanded shorter hours with no reduction in the daily wage rate. Although many firms acceded with little protest, several labor disputes resulted, including the longest, hardest-fought struggle of 1900—the conflict between the Building Trades Council and Bay Area planing-mill employers.

The Typographical Union renewed its drive for a nine-hour day in the book and job branch of the local printing industry. In contrast with its 1898 strike, the union now achieved general success. In San Francisco more than forty firms were members of the local affiliate of the United Typothetae, the industry's nationwide employers' association. Several members of the Typothetae were subjected to brief strikes or boycotts before an agreement was reached establishing the nine-hour day in the large majority of firms. Several printing firms persisted in their refusal to accept union conditions or use the Allied Printing Trades Council label. The Typographical Union maintained a vigorous boycott campaign against these recalcitrants, with the active support of the San Francisco Labor Council. The secretary of the council in 1900 was an energetic Scandinavian from the Sailors' Union, Ed Rosenberg. Rosenberg and other council leaders contacted customers of nonunion establishments, urging them to transfer their business to firms using the union label. The council did not rely exclusively on persuasion, but proclaimed a boycott against at least one customer who refused to withdraw his trade from a nonunion printing company.[6] Although a few establishments managed to continue operations under nonunion conditions, book and job printing in the Bay Area was, from 1900 on, a highly organized industry in which employers recognized collective bargaining as a firmly established practice.

During the year the two separate San Francisco unions of German and American bakers merged, thus giving one local of the national union jurisdiction over most bakery and confectionery workers. In late 1900 the merged Bakers' Union finally won the six-day week, a goal it had sought for years. In November most bakeries changed over to a sixty-three-hour weekly schedule of thirteen hours on Saturday, ten hours on others days, and no work on Sundays. The establishment of Sunday as a day of rest had unusual symbolic and emotional significance for local bakery workers, and they commemorated it for years afterward. In 1900, in order to extend the six-day week throughout the industry and equalize competitive conditions for their employers, the Bakers' Union set up a separate local with jurisdiction over workers in French and Italian bakeries.[7] However, this effort to organize Latin bakeries—the first of several such efforts in a dozen-year period—made little headway. Latin bakeries continued for years to work exceptionally long hours, thus maintaining a competitive threat disturbing to both the Bakers' Union and the unionized firms.

A new union of skilled upholsterers reported late in the year that almost every San Francisco furniture and mattress firm had cut their hours from nine to eight per day and increased the daily wage rate from $2.75 to $3. Women laundry workers, among whom unionism was now beginning to stir, turned to political efforts to shorten their workday. They induced the Board of Supervisors to pass, in September, an ordinance forbidding steam laundries to operate more than thirteen hours per day. Before the end of the year, however, a court had declared the ordinance unconstitutional.[8]

San Francisco retail clerks moved more successfully toward shorter hours. At midyear the shoe salesmen organized a union which grew rapidly. Soon afterward, several hundred clothing and dry goods store clerks formed a union. Both clerks' unions, through the remainder of 1900, campaigned for a 6 P.M. closing hour every weekday but Saturday, the customary day for late evening shopping. To publicize their demand, they put on several demonstrations in which groups of more than 100 clerks marched in organized formations through downtown San Francisco, chanting "six, six, close at six." Both unions set January 2, 1901, as the target date for institution of the earlier hour. From the beginning of 1901 on, the 6 P.M. closing hour was, in fact, observed by almost all downtown shoe stores and by most other downtown retail stores. The shoe clerks had greater success than others, as their union had organized a larger proportion of its jurisdiction and was to a greater extent made up of skilled specialty salesmen. To give weight to their demands, the shoe clerks adopted a union store card and called for its prominent display in every shoe store observing union conditions. Several widely publicized boycotts were launched against clothing and other stores that refused to adopt the early-closing schedule.[9] After 1900 the unfair list of the Labor Council usually included half a dozen or more retail stores under boycott by clerks' unions.

The Sailors' Union of the Pacific, early in 1900, was surging with new vigor. From about 1,300 in 1899, its membership swelled to almost 3,500 by 1901.[10] Soon the union was debating the question of enforcing a shorter workday, but its leaders were reluctant to engage in what they were certain would be a hard-fought contest with powerful, organized employers. The conservative polices of Andrew Furuseth prevailed, and the sailors decided to postpone their drive for shorter hours until they felt greater confidence in the union's recovered strength.

Late in 1900 a major effort to win a shorter workday was undertaken by electrical workers employed as outside linemen by California telephone and power companies.* After refusal of their demands for the eight-hour day and a $3 daily wage, linemen struck in December against electric power and telephone companies in San Francisco, Los Angeles, and several smaller cities. An estimated 150 to 200 men joined in the San Francisco walkout. The strikers quickly won a signed agreement, fully granting their demands, from the Independent Light & Power Company of San Francisco. It was one of the earliest formal agreements won in the light and power industry by any local of the International Brotherhood of Electrical Workers. But the strike did not achieve such sweeping success against other employers. The San Francisco Gas & Electric Company—one of the firms that later merged to form the present Pacific Gas & Electric—offered its striking linemen a $3 wage, but for a ten-hour day and only after the return of strikers "upon an individual basis, without recognition of the union." [11] The linemen's strike carried over into early 1901, making little headway against strong employer resistance.

Organized workers made efforts in 1900, generally with satisfactory results, to win concessions from employers in a number of other industries. The several unions of longshoremen engaged in sporadic, brief strikes on individual docks in San Francisco and Oakland. The San Francisco longshoremen succeeded in raising the prevailing wage rate to 40 cents, with an overtime rate of 50 cents after nine hours; the small Oakland Longshoremen's Union settled for somewhat lower rates. The separately organized and more highly skilled lumber longshoremen claimed 800 members by mid-1900 and raised their wage rate early in the year to $4 for

---

* Organized workers in the Bay Area later waged some of their longest and most frustrating struggles against public utility companies. But in 1900 an element of competition still existed in the utility field, with several rival street railway companies, gas and electric companies, and telephone companies operating in the area. The firms faced by the electrical linemen were thus not so large and powerful as the merger-created utility corporations that confronted unions in later years.

a nine-hour day. Through voluntary employer action and brief strikes against some firms, the Molders' Union won increases of 25 cents per day for many of its members on both sides of the Bay, thus establishing a union scale of $3.50 for a ten-hour day.[12] Among the newly organized groups which promptly displayed aggressiveness was a union of San Francisco hackmen. Growing in a few weeks to a membership of more than 200, it began a campaign to exclude nonunion hackmen from driving in funeral processions, demanding, in effect, that all funerals be conducted under union-shop conditions. The Hackmen's Union was soon antagonizing a large body of the public and lending a further unhappy feature to funerals by holding up lines of occupied hacks ready to proceed to the cemetery, while union members harangued nonunion drivers, insisting that they immediately join the union or leave the procession. At times groups of union and nonunion hacks drove along separate routes to the cemetery, carrying mourners apprehensive that the hostile factions would engage in battle at the funeral site. The Hackmen's Union showed little concern over the emotional reactions of the bereaved, and announced, as a union tenet, that "a non-union corpse is practically as bad as a living scab." [13]

Prolonged labor disputes broke out during the year in two industries, both of which were long marked by ill will between employers and unionized workers. Early in 1900 employers fired the opening gun in a battle that flared up sporadically for years in the San Francisco ladies' garment industry, which was made up of small firms competing for survival among themselves, against local Chinese firms, and against Eastern garment manufacturers. When unionism appeared in the industry in 1899, in the form of a small organization of relatively skilled cloakmakers, employers viewed it as a potentially serious threat to the maintenance of competitive production costs. Three of the larger firms —M. Siminoff, Meyer Brothers, and Davidson & Company—decided jointly to forestall this threat. In January, 1900, they locked out members of the new union, demanding that they renounce union membership. The action precipitated a yearlong test of endurance. The locked-out cloakmakers drew financial support from other unions, and the Labor Council conducted a major boycott campaign against the three manufacturers, contacting local retail clothing stores and urging their coöperation in the boycott. Several of the retailers became sufficiently convinced of the injustice of the lockout to intervene as mediators, but their attempts at settlement were unsuccessful. The boycott continued, with fair success. The cloakmakers harassed the firms with persistent picketing, despite occasional arrests of pickets. Meanwhile the union grew stronger, widely extending its membership. Since the lockout was clearly not accomplishing its purpose, two of the three employers withdrew from the battle before the year ended and entered agreements to maintain union conditions. The Cloakmakers' Union, having won a substantial victory in its first trial, soon afterward affiliated with the newly formed International Ladies' Garment Workers' Union. Unionism penetrated further into the local garment industry in December, 1900, when a local of the United Garment Workers was organized.[14] It had jurisdiction over the relatively unskilled workers, almost all of them women, employed by firms manufacturing overalls, shirts, and other items of men's work clothing. It grew rapidly and was destined to have a far less strife-torn career than the ILGWU cloakmakers.

There was a less extended, but intense, conflict in the San Francisco shoe manufacturing industry, where local employers also suffered painful competitive pressure from Eastern firms. Early in the year the shoeworkers, disorganized since their strike defeats of the early 1890's, again formed a union. Within a few weeks the union suspected that one of the principal shoe manufacturers, G. M. Kutz, had begun gradually to replace all known union members. To preserve its membership the union raised a wage issue and struck the firm early in April. Again the Labor Council backed the strikers with a boycott. Kutz initially put up determined resistance, refusing negotiations and hiring strikebreakers. The firm also won from a local court a temporary injunction against Labor Council Secretary Ed Rosenberg and others active in the boycott campaign, forbidding them to interfere in any way with the firm's business. This weapon had rarely been used in Bay Area labor disputes, though it was already well known and hated by unions in the East. San Francisco unionists deeply resented the employer's resort to this legal tactic. In early July, however, another court ruled that the union could be enjoined only if its pickets were barring access to the Kutz establishment by means of threats or other forms of intimidation. The court thereupon lifted the injunction, and within a few weeks the firm settled with the union, agreeing to discharge all strikebreakers, rehire strikers at the union scale, and use the union label. This midyear victory was followed in the fall by a brief strike against the large Buckingham & Hecht shoe factory, a strike quickly settled by negotiation.[15] Thus before the close of 1900 the new shoeworkers' union had passed the test of ability to survive conflict with employers.

The Building Trades

Throughout 1900 the president of the San Francisco Building Trades Council, P. H. McCarthy, was busy consolidating the council's power over the affairs of its constituent unions. He tried to fill the offices of the council and its individual unions with men who would be his faithful personal followers. As this group of McCarthy adherents grew, and entrenched itself in power, it was bitterly attacked by opposition factions as the "McCarthy machine."[16] But the sporadic efforts within the building trades to overthrow the "machine" and to develop a more democratic leadership never offered a serious challenge to McCarthy. Only defeat at the hands of organized employers, years later, destroyed his hegemony over the San Francisco building tradesmen.

P. H. McCarthy recognized early the value of publicity in making his leadership effective. Early in 1900 the Building Trades Council began publication of a weekly paper, *Organized Labor*. A leader of the cement workers' union, Olaf A. Tveitmoe,* became the first editor of this new labor journal, thus beginning a career of more than twenty years of service as a journalistic spokesman of the McCarthy regime. In mid-1900 Tveitmoe assumed another major role when, through McCarthy's influence, he was elected secretary of the Building Trades Council,[17] a position he held as long as McCarthy dominated the council. In his dual ca-

---

* Of Norwegian origin, Tveitmoe had come to San Francisco in the late 1890's after a career in Minnesota which included the brief editorship of a small newspaper. He was an effective publicist, with a penchant for caustically ridiculing his opponents. Under Tveitmoe, *Organized Labor* expressed the policies of McCarthy and his associates, and attacked, often in virulent language, both employers and union leaders antagonistic to McCarthy.

pacity as editor and council secretary, Tveitmoe became Mc-Carthy's chief lieutenant and one of the most prominent figures in California labor.

During 1900 McCarthy's control over the building crafts was revealed by two incidents concerning the painters. The council forced a local of the Painters' Union to remove its business agent from office after he had assumed authority reserved to the business agent of the council itself. In addition, the council blocked an effort by a group of German painters to form an exclusively German local of the Painters' Union. The council bluntly warned the group that it would refuse to issue the council's quarterly working card to members of the proposed new local and would thereby cut them off from employment at their craft in San Francisco. Much of the resentment engendered by the exercise of such strict authority was, however, allayed by the council's sweeping success in establishing union power in the industry.[18]

Organization expanded during 1900 among building trades workers on both sides of the Bay. Oakland was experiencing the most rapid union growth in its history, much of it in the building trades. A few Oakland building crafts won wage increases early in 1900. By midyear the San Francisco Building Trades Council had grown to include twenty-eight member unions, and claimed a total membership of about 10,000. Several of the council unions achieved gains peacefully. Prominent among them was the Electrical Workers' Union, which raised its daily wage rate to $3 and established an eight-hour day. The marble cutters were forced to strike briefly at midyear in order to win a higher wage scale, but until August no serious dispute appeared in the building industry.[19]

The Millmen's Lockout-Strike

By July, 1900, the building trades councils in both San Francisco and Alameda County had proclaimed that from August 13 they would enforce the eight-hour day for all their affiliated unions. Only a few crafts were still working more than eight hours a day. Of these, the most important group, and the only one to meet significant employer resistance, was that of the millmen employed in Bay Area planing mills. The refusal of planing-mill owners to accept the council's unilateral establishment of the eight-hour day brought on the greatest conflict of the year between organized employers and unions. Its outcome demonstrated the effectiveness of the Building Trades Council's centralized power and thorough organization against a group of employers who failed similarly to unify the construction industry. Building trades employers, though comparatively well organized in associations of general contractors, of specialized contractors, and of supply firms,[20] lacked a central organization equivalent to the Building Trades Council, with authority to lay down policies binding upon firms in every branch of the industry.

The planing mills met the challenge of the council head on. In San Francisco, twenty-six firms were banded together in the Planing Mill Owners' Association, headed by a prominent citizen, William H. Crocker. The association made no effort to negotiate with the council. Instead it waited until August 11, two days in advance of the council's announced date for enforcing the eight-hour day, and then voted to lock out all union millmen on August 13. Following the leadership of San Francisco employers, planing mills shut down throughout Alameda County and in Santa Clara County, to the south of San Francisco. The conflict involved the largest number of workers for the longest period, and had the greatest impact on construction activity, of any labor dispute arising in the Bay Area building industry before the 1920's. In San Francisco approximately 1,000 millmen—members of carpenters' locals—were locked out. Throughout the Bay Area thousands of millmen and other workers were idled by the lockout and the consequent disruption of building operations. A few of the many planing mills not members of the association accepted the eight-hour day and maintained production, but contractors faced a crippling shortage of finished lumber.[21]

As the conflict continued, the chief threat to the Building Trades Council was the possible intervention by contractors in support of the Planing Mill Owners' Association. The association, early in the dispute, proclaimed an open-shop policy and brushed aside suggestions that it negotiate or accept arbitration. It then strove to rally all other employers in the industry to join in the struggle, pleading that this was the critical moment for closing ranks in a common cause. Under the leadership of William H. Crocker, the association attempted to form a new central organization that would bring all contractors together in a declaration for the open shop and a joint effort to throw off the strict closed-shop conditions imposed by the building crafts. Crocker, however, found himself outmatched by McCarthy, who forbade members of all crafts to work on any construction projects using finished lumber from planing mills not observing the eight-hour day. At the same time McCarthy increased the output of "fair" millwork by inducing the Bay Area mills that had accepted the eight-hour day to put on extra shifts and operate around the clock. He made a special effort to ensure that the large general contractors, the most dangerous potential leaders of an antiunion drive, received the millwork required to complete their contracts on schedule.[22] By this careful attention to their needs, and by threatening that any alliance with the Planing Mill Owners' Association would bring on a strike paralyzing all construction, he kept the contractors neutral. Planing-mill owners found them unreceptive to proposals for shutting down the entire industry in order to save the planing mills from the eight-hour day long accepted by other building trades employers.

With the passing months, the scales of victory swung toward the Building Trades Council. An increasing supply of "fair" millwork appeared on the local market as individual mills broke away from their fellow employers to accept the eight-hour day. The scales were tipped sharply in December, 1900, when production began to flow from a large new planing mill built and owned by the Building Trades Council. The mill, capitalized at $100,000, was tangible evidence of the financial strength of the organized building crafts. It was built largely with funds contributed by members of the council, although the national carpenters' union supplied $40,000 to assist its Bay Area millmen's locals in their prolonged fight. Establishment of this mill, the second largest in San Francisco, soon persuaded the Planing Mill Owners' Association to end the contest. In February, 1901, the association and the Building Trades Council entered into a formal agreement granting the eight-hour day and providing for the union shop after a six-month period in which all present employees would be accepted into union membership. All disputes arising under the agreement, it was stipulated, were to be settled by a permanent joint committee of representatives from the council and the association, with arbitration as a final resort. Following this agreement the council sold its planing mill, at cost, to the employers. The most interesting provision of the agreement was one that made it especially palatable to the employers. Since the beginning of the lockout, seven months before, McCarthy had held out to the planing-mill owners a standing offer of protection against outside competition in return for their acceptance of shorter hours and the union shop. He promised that all council unions would refuse to work with material from planing mills not operating under wage and hour conditions equal to those prevailing in San Francisco. This protective guarantee was formally incorporated into the agreement. In effect, it established a monopolistic control of the local market. From 1901 on, very little finished lumber entered the Bay Area from planing mills elsewhere, as few of them matched local union conditions. The 1901 agreement also provided that all mill products used in San Francisco construction must bear the union stamp. Accordingly, any contractor importing finished lumber from outside nonunion mills was required to submit the lumber—for a charge—to a token processing by a local mill, in which it received the union stamp and underwent a metamorphosis from "unfair" to "fair." [23]

Frederick L. Ryan, the chief historian of the San Francisco Building Trades Council, credits McCarthy with having ingeniously established the basis for much of the council's future success by formulating this collusive agreement with the Planing Mill Owners' Association. The agreement joined the two parties in a mutually advantageous alliance exercising joint control over the principal building material required by contractors. It gave the association a vested interest in the continuance of the council's power, thus reducing the likelihood of its coöperating in any future antiunion campaign. Other planing mills were quick to sign the agreement; the association's membership rapidly expanded to more than sixty firms, including almost every mill in San Francisco.[24] Most of the mills in Oakland and other cities around the Bay also accepted union conditions and gained protection from outside competition. A few mills, which continued to defy unionization, were subjected for years to boycotts and sporadic organizing efforts.

The millmen's lockout was the only major effort to establish open-shop conditions by any large organized group of San Francisco building trades employers before the 1920's. The overwhelming union victory enhanced employer respect for the Building Trades Council's combative ability and, together with the amicable *rapprochement* reached by the opponents, discouraged future attacks upon it. From 1901 on, the large majority of employers in the local building industry accepted with little overt resentment the closed-shop conditions and high wage levels enforced by the council. Operating in a local market almost entirely insulated from outside competition, they were usually able to pass on to their customers any resulting increases in construction costs.

P. H. McCarthy thoroughly enjoyed his power as the single figure dominating labor relations in the building trades. But once having achieved dictatorial authority, he was careful not to overplay his hand. He adopted a policy of moderation in his dealings with employers, and kept each building craft under tight rein, interposing the council's centralized power against any union attempting to win gains which he considered excessive or ill timed. The antithesis of the militantly class-conscious labor leader, McCarthy took into account the economic problems and needs of employers and maintained close personal relationships with several leading contractors. Although various groups of employers at times became restive under union conditions, McCarthy countenanced no provocations sufficient to unite them in a general uprising that might have swept away his power. Many years elapsed before building trades employers combined to overthrow McCarthy, and even then their stimulus came from other San Francisco employer organizations, rather than from any provocatory change in McCarthy's policies.

Split in the San Francisco Labor Movement

In the months following the victorious conclusion of the millmen's dispute, several building trades unions peacefully enforced wage increases, and a few new affiliates of the Building Trades Council won the eight-hour day. The minimum wage rate for journeymen of any skilled craft edged up toward $4 per day. By mid-1901 the council had grown to thirty-six affiliated unions, and claimed a total membership of about 15,000. Thereafter few men could find employment in the San Francisco building industry without possession of the council's working card.[25]

The council had established union power to an extent unmatched in any other local industry, and its members were highly conscious of the marked superiority of their conditions to those of other workers. The building craftsmen's pride, often tinged with contempt, in the contrast between their economic position and that of their less fortunate fellow workers was partly responsible for their growing alienation from the rest of organized labor in San Francisco. Since the beginning of their revival in the mid-1890's, the building trades unions had tended to withdraw into a parochial concern with the affairs of their own industry. Through P. H. McCarthy's ambitions and policies this separatist tendency developed into an open break in 1901, when the Building Trades Council forbade its unions to hold membership in the San Francisco Labor Council.[26] The immediate cause was a trivial dispute that should have been amenable to easy settlement between the two councils. But if this issue had not served McCarthy as an excuse, he would soon have found another. Ambitious to destroy any allegiance of building industry workers which might conflict with his own authority, and untroubled by idealistic impulses to create a united movement for labor's general economic betterment, McCarthy wanted to eliminate all influence of the Labor Council over building trades unions still interested in local labor unity. He demanded that his followers be uncontaminated by loyalty to any central body of unions not confined entirely to the building industry.

McCarthy likewise resisted any encroachment upon his authority by the national leadership of either the building trades unions or the AFL. Intent upon carving out a feudal principality within the American labor movement, he insisted that San Francisco locals accept complete guidance from the Building Trades Council rather than from their respective national unions. For years after 1901 the council's membership included almost a dozen strictly local unions, having no AFL affiliations, although most of these were comparatively small organizations of workers in minor trades. McCarthy found such unions easier to control than locals of powerful national unions like that of the carpenters. According to his opponents, McCarthy also nursed for several years the ambition to induce all building trades unions in California to secede from their national organizations and affiliate exclusively with a state-wide body led by himself.[27]

McCarthy's isolationism also influenced the attitude of San Francisco building trades unions toward building craftsmen migrating to this high-wage area. After 1900, except at times of acute labor shortage, most of these unions accepted few men into full membership by transfer from union locals elsewhere. Newcomers typically worked only under temporary permits when extra work was available, with the permanent core of job opportunities reserved to the self-styled "home-guard." [28]

By early 1901, then, the Building Trades Council had firmly established its power and had emerged the victor in a major contest with employers. A more exhausting test of strength, fought on a far wider front, was about to confront thousands of San Francisco workers in other trades, where unionism had not yet proved its ability to survive. During the 1900–1901 millmen's conflict, other Bay Area unions had supported the council's cause with much enthusiasm and with some financial contributions. Even before that conflict ended, however, McCarthy had served notice in the pages of *Organized Labor* that building tradesmen must isolate themselves from "the inevitable disastrous results of foreign interferences, influences, or entangling alliances." [29] Then came the open split with the Labor Council. Unions under the leadership of the latter were soon waging a desperate battle against strongly organized employers, but they received neither support nor sympathy from the Building Trades Council.

The Teamsters' Union

On a Saturday night early in August, 1900, there occurred an event of especial import both for the coming 1901 struggle between San Francisco employers and unions and for the future course of local labor relations. A group of team drivers met to form the Teamsters' Union, which later became the largest and most powerful individual labor organization in San Francisco.[30] From the outset the leaders of the teamsters were Mike Casey and John P. McLaughlin, who served continuously for decades and attained exceptional prestige and influence not only among unionists but also among employers. Mike Casey, like many members of the new organization a native of Ireland, was in command of the Teamsters' Union from 1900 until his death more than thirty-five years later. In his long career Casey possessed greater power within the Bay Area union movement than any other labor leader with the probable exception of P. H. McCarthy.

The new union, with an initial membership of less than fifty drivers, was quickly tested. On Labor Day, 1900, McNab & Smith, one of the largest San Francisco draying firms, discharged several drivers who refused to quit the union. Thereupon an overwhelming majority of the almost 100 drivers employed by the firm answered the union's call for a strike. Taken by surprise, McNab & Smith did an about-face and reinstated the discharged unionists after a strike of only one day. In the wake of this easy victory came one of the most explosive individual union expansions ever seen in San Francisco. By mid-September, 1900, approximately 1,200 men had joined the Teamsters' Union.[31] They had strong incentives to do so. Team drivers were among the most overworked men in San Francisco, frequently putting in twelve or more hours per day on the job, seven days per week, at varying wages set by employers in a highly competitive field.

Its strength bolstered by this influx of members, the Teamsters' Union in mid-September circularized employers in the draying industry with demands for improved and standardized conditions. The employers proved quite receptive to this overture. Early in 1900 many of them, long disturbed by the industry's rigorous price competition, had formed the San Francisco Draymen's Association. The association hoped to bring in all drayage firms so that it could set up an effective industry-wide code stabilizing prices and other terms of competition. Price stabilization entailed cost stabilization, and, with labor constituting perhaps 75 per cent of drayage costs, the association favored uniform wage and hour conditions. It soon recognized in the Teamster's Union a useful agency for enforcing standardized labor costs upon all firms. Thus on October 1, 1900, after only brief negotiation, the Draymen's Association signed a detailed formal agreement with the union.[32]

Like the agreement in the planing-mill industry, the drayage contract set up a collusive partnership designed to handicap competitors outside the employers' organization. The union received a standard daily wage for a twelve-hour day, and overtime pay for work on Sundays, holidays, or after 6 P.M. It also won a stipulation that Draymen's Association members would employ only members of the union, and would give no assistance or coöperation to public drayage firms employing nonunion men. In return the Teamsters' Union agreed that its members would not work for any drayage firm refusing to join the association or for a wage lower than that set forth in the contract.[33] The agreement thus gave the Drayman's Association a strong labor ally which could force employers to join the association.

Apparently the Teamsters' Union willingly accepted the collusive features of this agreement. Only after the union had become locked in deadly battle with the Draymen's Association, almost a year later, did its leaders air charges that the association had attempted to use the union improperly as a means of restraining competition. Mike Casey and John McLaughlin then accused the association of falsely assuring them at the time of the agreement that it included 80 per cent of the city's draying firms, whereas, they claimed, it included at most 60 per cent. The Teamsters' Union soon found it had promised more than it had intended in agreeing not to work for nonmember employers. With the union's help the association did sign up new members, but Casey and McLaughlin, by their own account, were reluctant to accede to its demands for strikes against nonmember firms. The association's actual goal, they charged, had been the destruction of small firms remaining outside the organization.[34] Despite this denunciation voiced during the heat of the 1901 conflict, the Teamsters' Union and the Draymen's Association were tied together by a mutual self-interest in stabilizing competition within the industry. This interest survived their 1901 encounter and reasserted itself rapidly.

The City Front Federation

Developments on the San Francisco water front in late 1900 and early 1901 proved of decisive importance in the impending general battle between employers and unions. Throughout 1900 the reinvigorated Sailors' Union had attempted to persuade the Shipowners' Association to enter negotiations. Although the employers were not yet interested in reaching an accord, the union made progress in another direction. In the fall of 1900 it joined with its

perennial antagonists, the longshoremen, in an agreement deline-
ating lines of jurisdiction in cargo handling. Conflict of jurisdiction had been the chief barrier to harmony between the parties,
but the pact went beyond the settlement of this issue. It established a positive policy of mutual assistance by providing that
members of these unions would neither receive cargo from, nor
discharge cargo to, nonunion workers. Although neither party
apparently made a thoroughgoing effort to enforce the agreement, the two groups saw the possibility of greater strength
through closer coöperation.[35]

This awareness of the potential benefits of alliance achieved
meaningful fruition early in 1901 with the formation of the City
Front Federation. Like its predecessors, the federation was a
central body embracing unions of onshore and offshore workers,
but, unlike them, it was a body with formal centralized authority.
Although the creation of the federation came several months before the outbreak of serious industrial strife in San Francisco, its
leaders had prepared for the possibility of an all-out battle with
employers. The constitution of the federation authorized its president to order a vote of all member unions "when trouble of
such a nature arises that it may be necessary to order a general
strike." [36] An affirmative vote by a two-thirds majority of the
unions empowered the federation to order all affiliates out on
strike and to expel those refusing to obey. Water-front workers
possessed at last an organization capable of mobilizing swift,
united action in support of any affiliate involved in a clash with
employers.

The City Front Federation rapidly became a powerful force.
By the summer of 1901 it claimed more than 13,000 members in
fourteen affiliated unions and had amassed a treasury of $250,000.
Its membership was drawn from a wide range of occupations.
The essential basis of the federation's power over transportation
was provided by its largest affiliates, the unions of sailors, longshoremen, and teamsters. The coast-wide Sailors' Union, which
was claiming 5,000 members by the middle of 1901, made up
substantially more than a third of the federation's membership.
Four separate unions of longshoremen totaled an estimated 3,000
members. The Teamsters' Union, now expanded to about 1,800
members, controlled the third major group of organized workers

through whose hands San Francisco water-borne commerce passed. In addition the federation's affiliates included the union of marine firemen; a recently organized union of ship clerks, employed in checking cargo handled on the docks; a large new union of porters, packers, and warehousemen working in packing houses and warehouses adjoining the water front; a separate teamsters' union of coal wagon drivers; and several unions of ship repair craftsmen and harbor workers.[37]

Through the affiliation of the Teamsters' Union the federation had acquired unified control over the flow of commerce in and out of San Francisco. The teamsters occupied an invaluable strategic position. San Francisco, at the northern tip of a peninsula, then had no bridge connections with the East Bay and only one circuitous railway connection with the interior, the Southern Pacific line that ran north and south along the peninsula. The city was unusually dependent upon water transportation, and upon the drivers of wagons that hauled goods to and from its docks. An effective alliance between teamsters and the other chief groups of workers in the field of transportation and distribution —seamen, longshoremen, warehousemen—thus possessed a formidable power to choke off the city's economic life.

1901: The Year of Decisive Battle

The year 1901, though destined to rock San Francisco with industrial conflict on an unprecedented scale, opened quietly. The only significant labor dispute, the millmen's prolonged contest, was drawing swiftly to its close. Business conditions were excellent, organization was continuing to spread rapidly among workers, and employers generally offered little resistance to moderate union demands. The Labor Council was growing. It jumped from thirty-four affiliates in mid-1900 to ninety in July, 1901, with a total membership estimated at above 25,000.[38] With the claimed 15,000 Building Trades Council members and with unionists affiliated to neither council, organized labor in San Francisco could boast of approaching a membership of well above 40,000. Although union estimates tended toward exaggeration, union membership had undoubtedly reached an exceptional level for a city of somewhat more than 350,000 population.

Since the early 1890's resentment against the AFL had occasionally flared up among Bay Area unionists, who believed that the federation was neglecting the labor movement on the West Coast. At one period in the 1890's, in fact, many Bay Area unions had supported a major, though unsuccessful, attempt to form a Pacific Coast federation of labor that would be independent of the AFL. With the turn-of-the-century boom, however, the leaders of the AFL and of a number of national unions drew upon their growing financial resources to send full-time organizers to the West. In January, 1901, Jefferson D. Pierce, the first AFL organizer assigned to the Pacific Coast, arrived in San Francisco.[39] Pierce, who had just completed a brief period of organizing work in Los Angeles, planned to remain a few months in the Bay Area before moving on to the cities of the Pacific Northwest. But labor battles disrupted his plans, and he remained in San Francisco during the spring and summer of 1901.

In San Francisco, Pierce coöperated closely with Ed Rosenberg and other Labor Council leaders in giving added impetus to the drive for increasing union membership. In addition, he worked to bring all local unions into affiliation with their respective national organizations. Workers organized in occupations or industries over which no national union claimed jurisdiction were placed in "federal" labor unions, local organizations holding charters directly from the AFL and under supervision of the national AFL leadership. By the end of 1901 about two dozen such federal unions were affiliated with the Labor Council. Most of them were composed of relatively unskilled workers, and none possessed the prestige and financial backing that stemmed from connection with a powerful nationwide trade union.* Pierce and the Labor Council leaders, by encouraging all workers to organize, irre-

---

* The federal unions were the neglected stepchildren of the American labor movement. Existing in the interstices between the jurisdictional borders charted by national unions, they were, in the view of many advocates of strict craft unionism, of dubious legitimacy in a labor movement organized along craft lines. The craft-conscious leaders of the AFL had neither the will nor the staff and funds to give substantial support to individual federal unions engaged in struggles with strong employers. The typical federal union was thus a relatively weak, isolated organization, often lightly regarded by the craft unions of its locality. Unions in the recognized trades were prone to be skeptical of the judgment and the sense of responsibility possessed by leaders of federal unions, and frequently attempted to keep them under unusually close control by local central councils. Despite such handicaps, a number of these unions in San Francisco managed to attain strength and respect, and to maintain a stable existence for years.

spective of occupation, helped to make San Francisco preëminent among major American cities in the degree of unionization among less skilled workers. Both federal unions and locals of national unions were formed among such relatively unskilled groups as longshoremen, warehousemen, tannery workers, wooden box makers, wagon drivers in general and specialty teaming, stablemen, waiters, common laborers, women workers in laundries and garment manufacturing, factory production workers, milkers, and helpers in the skilled trades.

P. H. McCarthy and Olaf Tveitmoe, after the Building Trades Council openly broke with the Labor Council early in 1901, publicly scorned such efforts to organize the less skilled. With their own skilled craft unions well established, they saw no advantage in stirring up union sentiment among unskilled, easily replaceable workers. Accordingly, late in April the Building Trades Council "met in special session . . . and solemnly denounced Secretary Rosenberg and Organizer Pierce." [40] By the summer of 1901 the council was assigning blame for the increasingly serious labor conflict in San Francisco to the formation of new and impetuously led unions. In *Organized Labor* Olaf Tveitmoe exercised his talent for caustic wit as he reviewed the Labor Council's policies:

> Unions were formed—that is, very few of them were trade unions, but there were many, many unions of divers occupations and callings. . . . The Labor Council gathered under its wings a most varied collection of eggs and hatched some curious ducklings and labeled them trade unions.[41]

Upon alleged rash demands and strikes by these "curious ducklings" Tveitmoe affixed the chief responsibility for provoking employers into organized antiunion activity.

Later on there were complaints from other sources, chiefly the skilled metal trades crafts, that the new unions, by improperly rushing forward with demands, had prejudiced the carefully prepared plans of older unions to seek concessions from employers. Experienced unionists felt that demands should be advanced cautiously, in order to avoid arousing the sleeping giant of employer antiunion belligerence. When this belligerence materialized in 1901, many unionists held the actions of newly formed organizations accountable for its emergence. But the evidence does not indicate such actions were in fact responsible for the employer counterattack. Organization was making swift headway among the city's workers, and in its wake numerous demands, considered or ill considered, were inevitable. The growing strength of unionism was itself the primary force stimulating the formation of a new central employers' association. This new organization was already active by May, 1901, when the first major strike was called by one of the more recently organized unions.

Before the eruption of the major conflicts of 1901, a variety of workers made advances. In January about 2,000 white women laundry workers formed a union, and in March won a ten-hour day and increased wages from most of the San Francisco steam laundries. In the late spring a new union of butchers persuaded most retail meat markets to adopt shorter working hours. A specialty teaming union of building material teamsters struck in February, after rejection of demands for improved wages and hours and for abolition of a requirement that drivers live in boardinghouses operated by some of the large contractors. The Building Trades Council gave neither approval nor support to the strike, but Labor Council leaders helped the union negotiate a favorable settlement. The teamsters won the freedom to board where they pleased and a uniform $2.50 wage for a twelve-hour day—a great improvement upon their former prevailing daily wage of about $1.75 for fourteen or more hours of work.[42]

Members of several metal trades crafts called brief strikes against a few individual firms before winning minor improvements in working conditions. Retail clerks faced continuing opposition to early closing from some stores, and a court injunction, which they largely disregarded, forbidding them to pursue a boycott against two nonunion firms. But for the most part, according to labor spokesmen, San Francisco employers in early 1901 gave generous consideration to their employees' requests for shorter hours and improved conditions. Many frankly assured union leaders that they had little objection to granting reasonable improvements, "provided the trade-unions were sufficiently well-organized to insure the acquiescence of all employers in a given trade."[43]

The Employers' Association

The first hint of the approaching general struggle came in April. On the first of that month, fifty to seventy-five members of a small, veteran union of metal polishers struck in about ten San Francisco shops, demanding that their workday be cut from ten to eight hours. Several of the shops, although reportedly willing to grant the demand, were intimidated by threats that supplies would be cut off from any firm accepting the eight-hour day.[44] They continued to resist as rumors spread that a powerful new employers' association, similar to the Board of Manufacturers and Employers of the early 1890's, had been secretly created to block further surrender by business firms to union demands.

The Employers' Association of San Francisco had, in fact, been formed in April, although it did not openly intervene in local labor relations until May. From the start the association maintained unusual secrecy concerning its finances, membership, and policies. Most of the information later published concerning it was ferreted out by reporters on William R. Hearst's prounion *San Francisco Examiner*. The association's leaders and its membership were predominantly drawn from among wholesale merchants, larger retail merchants, and manufacturers in certain industries, including consumer goods industries. Both merchants and consumer goods manufacturers were by now wary of the boycott, an increasingly powerful weapon in labor's armory. The leaders of the Employers' Association recognized, moreover, that some member firms were less prepared than others to withstand boycotts, and under union pressure might desert the association, seriously splitting the employer ranks. Thus, to assure unity in the conflicts to come, the association protected its members by keeping their identity a closely guarded secret. When the association first attracted widespread public attention in early May, it was visible only in the form of its attorney and authorized spokesman, M. F. Michael. To the press Michael modestly acknowledged that the organization included "all the leading merchants in all branches of industry," but that their names were to be temporarily withheld.[45] Michael described the association as governed by a five-man executive committee whose policies and decisions would be announced only through himself.

The secrecy that enveloped the Employers' Association helped to create a popular image of a mysterious agency of unknown, but awesome, power. The association actually embraced only a small minority of San Francisco employers, although it unquestionably possessed exceptional strength. Its membership contained a high proportion of large, influential employers, who gave it impressive financial support. Reportedly the association grew from a nucleus of fifty militant employers, each of whom, in April, 1901, pledged $1,000 to the organization. As new members joined they were required to post bonds as guarantees of their observance of the policies laid down by the association. Early in May association funds were estimated to have reached $150,000. By late summer union leaders locked in combat with the association believed that it had raised from $350,000 to $500,000 to support antiunion activities. Although its membership was estimated at but 300 to 400, the association exercised a potent influence upon a much larger number of firms. Its goal was to serve as a "peak" association, a top policy-making body giving firm direction to subsidiary employers' associations in individual industries. It made appreciable progress toward this goal. By early May, after becoming involved in labor disputes, the Restaurant Keepers' Association and the Carriage Makers' Association announced that they would turn to the Employers' Association, "which will speak for publication through Mr. Michael," for decisions on any labor relations issues arising within their own industries but deemed to affect the common interests of all employers. Soon other groups of employers were similarly acknowledging the authority of the association. Over its own member firms it exercised direct, centralized control, its bylaws specifying that no member could grant a union demand or settle any labor dispute without the express consent of the association's executive committee.[46]

Spreading Industrial Conflict

In May the Employers' Association found its opportunity for action. It intervened almost simultaneously in two industries. On May Day, then a traditional date for launching union efforts to win major gains, the recently formed union of cooks and waiters called an industry-wide restaurant strike in support of sweeping demands which included one day of rest per week, a ten-hour day, the union shop, and display of the union card by all restaurants. The strike brought out more than 1,000 workers, by far the largest number yet involved in a 1901 dispute. A large number of the smaller restaurants and cafés, primarily those with a predominantly working-class clientele, acceded to the union demands. But under the leadership of Mathias Johnson, owner of a well-known restaurant, many of the larger establishments formed the Restaurant Keepers' Association and began working closely with the Employers' Association to defeat the strike.[47] Though the Employers' Association would almost certainly have intervened in this dispute, irrespective of the issues, it was especially spurred into action by the demand for the union shop. The association, via its spokesman, Michael, never offered the public a clear and complete exposition of its principles. However, in a manner typical of major San Francisco employer organizations formed to resist unions, it repeatedly emphasized that it accepted the right of labor to organize, but was unalterably opposed to the union shop.

The union-shop issue helped arouse the Employers' Association, at the same time, to extend its authority over another industry. According to Labor Council leaders, the Carriage Makers' Association, on May 1, had willingly agreed with the three craft unions employed in San Francisco carriage shops to cut hours from ten to nine per day and employ none but union members. The Employers' Association immediately objected and warned that supplies would be shut off from every carriage shop honoring the agreement. This brought a quick repudiation of the agreement by the Carriage Makers' Association and a consequent strike of about 500 workers on May 8. Within a few days several small carriage shops had settled with the unions, only to find, as had been threatened, that their suppliers refused to accept their orders.[48]

The restaurant strikes, meanwhile, had led to sympathy walkouts of almost 200 bakers and bakery wagon drivers against individual bakeries believed to be denying supplies to the restaurants that granted union conditions. By the middle of May almost 2,000 cooks, waiters, carriage workers, bakery employees, and metal polishers were on strike in San Francisco, and a long-threatened industry-wide strike was looming in the metal trades. Tension had mounted sharply since May 1, and some employers were already considering a general showdown battle with organized labor. On May 13 the *Argonaut*, a conservative weekly journal, warned labor that employers were now organized as never before, that thousands of soldiers returning from the Philippines for discharge were potential strikebreakers, and that, should the unions dare to call a general strike, it would be "disastrous for them." By then the bakery workers' sympathy strike and the evident intention of the Employers' Association to invoke economic sanctions against firms granting strikers' demands had impelled Labor Council leaders to seek a general understanding with the association, in an effort to confine the growing conflict. The association, however, rejected the council's overtures, announcing through M. F. Michael that it refused to enter into discussions with union representatives.[49]

The Metal Trades Strike

On May 20 another strike broke out in San Francisco. For months the International Association of Machinists had been organizing its trade and building a strike fund in preparation for a nationwide attempt, scheduled for May Day, 1901, to win the nine-hour day. In San Francisco, with the aid of Russel I. Wisler, an organizer for the international union, the Machinists' Union had multiplied its membership severalfold during the winter and spring of 1901. By May it was the largest union in the metal trades, with a claimed membership of more than 1,500.[50] Organization had also progressed among other metal trades workers. In March the industry's unions revived their central body, the Iron Trades Council. The council gave added stimulus to efforts to organize all metal tradesmen, and its member unions determined to participate in the machinists' drive to reduce working hours from ten to nine per day.

The International Association of Machinists had hoped for a peaceful establishment of the shorter day. In 1900 it had amicably reached an agreement with the National Metal Trades Association, comprising a large proportion of the industry's chief firms throughout the East. By early 1901, however, the NMTA had become a belligerent advocate of the open shop, and refused to recognize or bargain with the union after the expiration of the 1900 agreement. In a final effort to negotiate a settlement, the machinists let pass their original May Day deadline for enforcement of the nine-hour day. The effort failed, and on May 20 their nationwide strike began. It brought out the largest number of men involved in an American labor dispute since the 1894 Pullman strike. In San Francisco it added 4,000 or 5,000 workers to the approximately 2,000 already on strike, and several hundred workers in the small East Bay metal trades industry also struck. Fourteen unions of machinists, molders, boilermakers, blacksmiths, patternmakers, and their helpers and apprentices joined in the strike.[51] Shipyards, foundries, machine shops, and other metal trades firms were paralyzed. Walter Macarthur exulted that "for the first time in many years they have succeeded in tying up the local works, including that notorious nest of scabbery, the Union Iron Works." [52] But San Francisco employers, though not affiliated with the National Metal Trades Association, put up a determined, organized resistance. They began to import strikebreakers from the East and settled down to a test of endurance. Requiring little aid from the Employers' Association, the metal trades firms fought their own battle with the unions. The strike in this industry, although it continued for months, was thus largely independent of the general conflict between the Employers' Association and San Francisco labor.

Summer of Continuing Struggle

Although the scope of industrial dispute broadened greatly as the summer advanced, the strike in the carriage industry was settled quickly. The Teamsters' Union became involved for the first time in the city's industrial turmoil, thereby demonstrating that its policy would be of critical influence in any general battle between organized employers and organized labor in San Francisco. In mid-May teamster leaders threatened to call out on strike the drivers of firms continuing to refuse supplies to carriage shops that had granted the nine-hour day. This threat induced the Carriage Makers' Association to reopen negotiations with the strikers and on May 22 the strike ended. The association, though accepting the nine-hour day, refused to sign a formal contract.[53] The settlement, giving the carriage workers no written guarantee of union-shop conditions or union recognition, was widely viewed as an employer victory. But the Employers' Association had seen a negotiated settlement forced by the Teamsters' Union, whose power, if left uncurbed, might impede the campaign to free San Francisco employers from the necessity of dealing with unions.

In June the restaurant strike led to conflict in another branch of the provision trades. Union spokesmen claimed that a threatened walkout by the Butchers' Union early in the strike had ended a refusal of wholesale meat firms to sell to some 200 small restaurants and cafés displaying the union house card. But in June the Wholesale Butchers' Association, led by Miller & Lux and the Western Meat Company, banned all sales to retail meat markets displaying the union card. On June 13 the Butchers' Union called a strike to force a lifting of this ban. More than 1,000 butchers reportedly answered the call, but the strikers' ranks soon melted away. The strike lacked proper organization, the butchers had no strike fund, and the inexperienced new union proved unable to maintain its determination and morale. On June 17, after only three days, the union called off its strike, promising that its members would work alongside nonunion butchers and forego display of the union card. On July 1 the Wholesale Butchers' Association forbade retail meat markets to sell to restaurants showing the union card. The wholesalers supplied the retailers with lists of such establishments, and within a short time the inability to buy meat had forced many restaurants to take down the cards.[54]

San Francisco, in the early summer of 1901, was thus witnessing an effective display of power by organized employers. In June a score of small metal trades employers agreed to accept the nine-hour day. But, when subjected to a suppliers' boycott, almost all speedily repudiated their agreement. In July the small metal polishers' union called off its strike. Some of its members had won the nine-hour day, but most returned to work on the original ten-hour schedule. The young Garment Workers' Union was by then badly demoralized. During the winter and early spring it had grown to well above 1,000 members, most of whom were semiskilled women workers. But rumors at the large work-clothing factories of Levi Strauss and Neustadter Brothers, both believed to be active in the Employers' Association, that all union members were to be discharged led to wholesale desertions which endangered the union's survival.[55]

The Teamsters' Lockout

In mid-July the restaurant and metal trades strikes were still under way, though showing little promise of union victory. But for almost a month no union had challenged the increasingly feared power of the Employers' Association. At this point the members of the Epworth League arrived in San Francisco to hold their 1901 convention and, unwittingly, touched off an explosion on the labor front. The Morton Special Delivery Company, a nonunion draying firm which did not belong to the Draymen's Association, had contracted with the Epworth League to handle the baggage of its conventioners. Morton had subcontracted part of the task to a unionized firm, a member of the association. This agreement flatly violated the Draymen's Association policy of noncoöperation with firms refusing to join it or conform to its measures for regulating competition. Upon learning of the subcontract, Mike Casey, head of the Teamsters' Union, reminded the association that its own bylaws forbade any member to furnish extra teams or drivers to a nonmember firm, and that its agreement with the union called for union drivers to reject employment by nonmember firms. Moreover, the Morton Special Delivery Company was a vigorous opponent of the Teamsters' Union, and, Casey warned, the union's members would refuse to work indirectly for Morton by handling baggage of the Epworth League. In effect Casey proscribed the baggage as "hot cargo," to be touched by no union teamster.[56]

The Draymen's Association could easily have accepted Casey's objections while fully adhering to its own policies. But by July the relationship between the association and the Teamsters' Union was no longer amicable; tension had developed since the advent of the Employers' Association in April. By the late spring the draymen were giving a cold reception to union proposals for minor improvements in their agreement,[57] and subsequent victories by the Employers' Association had hardened their resolve to take a firm line with the union.

Both sides had become aware by mid-July that the Teamsters' Union was a prominent bulwark of local labor power to which no challenge had yet been presented. Mike Casey's designation of the Epworth League baggage as "hot cargo" gave the Draymen's Association an issue upon which to base such a challenge. And pressure from the Employers' Association helped decide them in favor of taking a combative stand. On July 15 prominent businessmen filed articles of incorporation for a new drayage firm. Three of the incorporators were large wholesale merchants, and all were reported to be among the leaders of the Employers' Association. The proposed establishment of a new firm was a quiet warning to members of the Draymen's Association that compromise with the Teamsters' Union might result in a shift of their chief customers to drayage firms that conformed to open-shop policies.[58]

On the following day, July 16, the situation came to a head. The firm holding the contract with the Morton Special Delivery Company ordered its union drivers to haul the Epworth League baggage. The order was given with the approval of the executive committee of the Draymen's Association. The Teamsters' Union, now facing its challenge from organized employers, had an important decision to make. Its refusal to meet the challenge might seriously demoralize much of the city's union membership, already shaken by the recent successes of the Employers' Association. Also, a retreat would certainly encourage the association to attempt further inroads upon union strength. Accordingly, on July 16, Casey instructed the drivers to defy the orders to handle the baggage. Almost a dozen drivers who followed his orders were promptly discharged, and San Francisco's epic conflict of 1901 was under way.[59]

In the next few days several members of the Draymen's Association joined in the battle, ordering their drivers to handle Epworth League baggage and discharging them upon refusal. Most association firms, however, did not want a clash with their employees. A large majority of them voted not to endorse the executive committee's approval of the contract between the Morton Special Delivery Company and a member firm. But the association members, apparently under pressure from their own leaders and from the Employers' Association, soon changed their tune. On July 19 they voted overwhelmingly to vest in the executive committee full authority to determine the proper policy in regard to the Teamsters' Union. The committee, in turn, conferred with M. F. Michael of the Employers' Association. On July 20, consequently, orders were issued for each drayage firm, one after another, to command its drivers to handle Epworth League baggage. Few drivers obeyed. A systematic, progressive lockout of men loyal to the Teamsters' Union therefore began.[60]

By July 24 about 1,300 teamsters had been locked out, and drayage firms were busily hiring nonunion replacements. Thus far the Teamsters' Union had retaliated chiefly by calling on strike all drivers engaged in hauling hay and feed to the stables of association members. But its leaders, now seeing the lockout as an attack on the union's very existence, decided to make an all-out effort to disrupt vulnerable areas of the city's economy. Economic punishment of outside parties, they reasoned, would bring pressure from small merchants and other affected businessmen upon the Employers' and Draymen's associations to end their battle against the teamsters. On July 25 the union therefore ordered a walkout by every employed member. The Oakland Teamsters' Union gave full coöperation by simultaneously calling out on strike members engaged in hauling goods, via transbay ferries, to San Francisco. This enlargement of the conflict particularly injured produce merchants, retail grocers and other store owners, and building contractors. Perishable foods began to spoil on docks and in warehouses as almost 100 fruit and vegetable teamsters struck. Lumberyard drivers walked out, halting deliveries to planing mills and to building sites. As expected, the interruption of vital services quickly created sentiment among San Francisco businessmen and the general public for an end to the battle.[61]

During the final week of July prominent citizens made futile attempts to bring about a settlement. Mayor James D. Phelan presided over conferences between businessmen and union officers. Mike Casey, Andrew Furuseth, Ed Rosenberg, and other representatives of the teamsters, the City Front Federation, and the Labor Council, met with George Newhall, president of the Chamber of Commerce, and with spokesmen for produce merchants and other employers. But only the Employers' Association, to whom the Draymen's Association had now clearly relinquished authority, was competent to settle the dispute. And the Employers' Association refused to compromise its principles by entering into discussions with union representatives. Its board of directors, however, did condescend to meet separately with Mayor Phelan on July 29. Phelan sent the strike leaders a message conveying the association's only terms of settlement: reinstatement of the locked-out and striking teamsters upon a promise that they would not in the future participate in sympathetic strikes.[62]

The Teamsters' Union could hardly have accepted at any time such a curt offer, extended only through an intermediary. But San Francisco labor leadership was stiffening its determination to give battle to the Employers' Association. The leaders of the Labor Council and the City Front Federation had initially counseled all unions against involvement in the teamsters' dispute while mediation efforts were under way. The Bottlers' Union, nevertheless, called a walkout of its members at one beer-bottling firm, in a refusal to handle "hot" beer delivered by strikebreaking teamsters. The organized employers retaliated on July 26, when fourteen of the fifteen member firms of the Bottlers' Protective Association posted this ultimatum:

All union employees will please step into the office this evening to be paid off in full. . . . Any of our employees who desire to come to work tomorrow morning . . . may do so, but with the distinct understanding . . . that we are . . . recognizing no more labor organizations.[63]

By July 29 almost 200 employees of these fourteen bottling firms were locked out or on strike. Meanwhile a number of other firms had discharged their porters, packers, and warehousemen for refusing to load or unload wagons driven by strikebreaking teamsters. Late in July box manufacturers joined in the assault against unionism, presenting for their workers' signatures a pledge that, in consideration of a promise to grant within six months a nine-hour day at a $2 daily wage, the signing employee would give up present union membership and would join no union in the future. The resulting lockout-strike closed the city's principal boxmaking plants.[64]

As industrial conflicts spread, San Francisco unionists developed strong animosity toward local governmental authorities. On July 26 Judge M. C. Sloss had granted Mathias Johnson, head of the Restaurant Keepers' Association, an injunction against picketing by the Cooks' and Waiters' Union, now on strike for almost three months. Still unaccustomed to the use of injunctions, local labor leaders were angrily aroused by Sloss's restraining order. They were even more infuriated by the policy of Mayor Phelan who, while trying to mediate in the teamsters' dispute, was simultaneously helping employers to maintain operations. Within a week after the lockout began, Phelan had placed almost 200 extra policemen on duty in downtown San Francisco to protect nonunion teamsters against strikers and their sympathizers. Union spokesmen charged that these policemen, many of whom had been assigned to ride as guards on wagons driven by strikebreakers, were helping to unload wagons and were acting as guides to drivers unfamiliar with San Francisco. Despite Phelan's protestations of his duty to maintain law and order, workers believed that their city government had thrown its resources into a battle against them. On July 28 the Typographical Union passed resolutions demanding efforts to discover the identity of Employers' Association members, so that "a commercial, social, and political" boycott could be proclaimed against them. And it called upon unions to elect city officials who would play fair in future labor disputes.[65]

As July neared its close, San Francisco labor leaders faced a critical decision. The Employers' Association, confident after its earlier successes, was now menacing the existence of a union vital to the strength of the local labor movement—the Teamsters' Union. Organized employers were waging effective battle against metal tradesmen, cooks, waiters, bottlers, boxmakers, and warehousemen. Unionists were convinced that the defeat of these workers, especially of the teamsters, would spur employers on to attack other groups. They had bitter memories of the Board of Manufacturers and Employers, created ten years before, and of its sternly fought campaign to render unions impotent. Organized labor had finally recovered from the crippled condition caused by the board's assault and the long depression of the 1890's, but now another "peak" employers' organization was threatening its suppression. Determined not to allow the Employers' Association to drive labor back to its disorganized state of the early 1890's, leaders of the Labor Council and the City Front Federation met to discuss the use of labor's ultimate weapon, the general strike.

The City Front Federation Strike

After thorough consideration, labor leaders rejected proposals for a full-scale general strike. With a large proportion of the San Francisco labor force still unorganized, and with the building trades unions certain to stand aloof, a call for such a strike was unlikely to succeed. There were no financial resources to support thousands of striking workers, and economic hardship was certain to force early and heavy desertions. Union leaders therefore decided to call out only the unions in the City Front Federation, which were strategically located to inflict maximum damage upon Bay Area commerce. Functioning as shock troops in labor's battle, the City Front strikers could draw substantial financial support from unions whose members remained at work. Weak, unreliably disciplined unions could thus be assigned a useful but limited role in the conflict, while the City Front Federation attacked the San Francisco transportation and distribution system. The federation's strike was intended to achieve the basic aim of the proposed general strike: to mete out such economic punishment to belligerent employers, neutral employers, and the public alike that irresistible pressure would be placed upon the Employers' Association to negotiate a quick settlement with organized labor.

Delegates from the member unions of the City Front Federation met on the night of July 29, 1901, while the unions assembled separately in membership meetings to receive the expected strike order. In tense excitement, almost 2,000 members of the Teamsters' Union stood by to await the news that their fellow affiliates of the federation were joining them on strike.[66] At the headquarters of the Sailors' Union, more than 300 sailors were informed by Andrew Furuseth that the "employers are determined to wipe out labor unions one after another. . . . There is no other way of having peace in this city except by fighting for it."[67] Federation members felt that they were standing on the threshold of a battle that would decisively influence the future of organized labor in San Francisco. Walter Macarthur went further, proclaiming that the "City Front Federation of San Francisco now holds in its hands the fortunes of the labor movement of the Pacific Coast." [68] Shortly before midnight the delegates returned to their respective unions and announced that the strike had been declared. The all-out battle against the Employers' Association was under way.

On the morning of July 30 the normally bustling San Francisco water front was quiet, as thousands of sailors, marine firemen, longshoremen, warehousemen, coalyard teamsters, and other workers in the City Front Federation left their jobs. Only the Ship Clerks' Union failed to obey the strike call. As white-collar workers, its members were unwilling to resort to so crude a weapon as the strike, and the union left the federation and soon dissolved. Other unions not affiliated with the City Front Federation, however, called out their members in order further to disrupt the Bay Area economy. The Building Material Teamsters' Union, almost 500 strong, joined in the strike, thereby crippling San Francisco building operations. Directly across the Bay, longshoremen struck along the Oakland water front. At the small port towns of Crockett and Port Costa, on the northeast arm of the Bay, the Crockett Warehousemen's Union struck. Its action was particularly damaging to the wheat farmers of California's interior valleys, for the seasonal movement of wheat to Port Costa warehouses, to await shipment abroad, was just commencing. By blocking access to storage facilities, the warehousemen's strike threatened farmers with spoilage of their crops.[69] The San Francisco harbor, meanwhile, was crowded with idle ships. As vessels arrived the union members among their sailors, firemen, cooks, and stewards joined in the City Front Federation strike, leaving the ships immobilized.

At the outset optimism ran high among the strike leaders: Andrew Furuseth, chairman of the strike committee; his lieutenants from the Sailors' Union, Walter Macarthur and John Kean; Mike Casey and John McLaughlin of the Teamsters' Union; Ed Rosenberg and Walter Goff, the chief officers of the Labor Council. They were confident that labor's devastating attack upon Bay Area commerce would force the Employers' Association to sue quickly for peace.[70] The federation strike brought to 15,000 or more the total number of workers on strike or locked out in San

Francisco, and the employers were believed incapable of long withstanding this mass depletion of their labor force.

It was soon evident, however, that the test of endurance would disrupt the local economy for days to come. As expected, the strike redoubled the mediation efforts of outside parties: Mayor Phelan; the San Francisco Board of Supervisors; leaders of the Retail Grocers' Association; and spokesmen for civic organizations, for retailers and other small business groups, and for farmers. But the Employers' Association declined the services of all mediators and threw its funds and energy into the huge task of recruiting men to replace the strikers. Bulletin boards at San Francisco's army base, the Presidio, were covered with notices offering employment to soldiers returning from the Philippines. Employers' agents hired youths from farms and small towns throughout the interior. Students at the University of California and at Stanford were recruited as strikebreakers. For the first time in a Bay Area industrial conflict, employers imported large numbers of Negroes from the Middle West. Discouraged from membership by virtually every union of the AFL, Negroes had little incentive to refrain from strikebreaking against men who did not welcome them into the American labor movement. From the outset the strike did not effect a complete shutdown of activity on the docks. The association now began to add new recruits to the small force of workers who had remained on the job. For protection, strikebreakers were housed and fed aboard ships anchored off the piers, and the water front was put under heavy police patrol.[71]

As the strike went on, unionists protested the employers' refusal to negotiate and their use of strikebreakers. The motives and policies of the Employers' Association came under continuous attack in the pages of the *Coast Seamen's Journal.* The San Francisco Labor Council wrote to Benjamin Ide Wheeler, president of the University of California, denouncing the university's "scholars of the amateur stevedore type . . . who took the places of honest workingmen in Oakland."[72] Turning to more direct action, strikers and their sympathizers staged demonstrations against strikebreaking teamsters and their police guards—minor episodes that allowed Olaf Tveitmoe, in *Organized Labor,* to scoff at the early reports of violence in the daily press. "If labor unions believed in violence," Tveitmoe reminded employers, "they would not herd together as a mob does and throw a few bricks or rotten eggs. . . ." [73]

But strike violence increased with the continued successful use of strikebreakers. At train stations and at the San Francisco ferry building, union men fought with arriving strikebreakers. Along the water front strikers attacked nonunion men working as sailors and longshoremen. In San Francisco streets, the police used their clubs against men who were throwing rocks at "scab" wagons and attempting to drag the drivers from their seats. The strikebreakers fought back. By the middle of August one striker was dead of gunshot wounds, and on both sides the toll of injured was mounting. All the daily newspapers except Hearst's *Examiner* played up the incidents of violence in order to mobilize public opinion against the strikers. As early as August 10 George Newhall, president of the Chamber of Commerce and city police commissioner, demanded that Mayor Phelan ask for state militia to maintain order, if the city lacked sufficient funds to hire additional policemen. Employers were eager to have troops brought in to ensure the movement of goods. Governor Henry T. Gage, however, showed no sympathy for the aims of the Employers' Association. Coming to San Francisco early in August in a futile effort at mediation, Gage spent several weeks personally observing local conditions. As the battle continued through August and into September, he turned a deaf ear to employers' repeated appeals for state militia, insisting that the disorder was not sufficient to warrant state intervention.[74] His refusal to abandon an ostensibly neutral position proved invaluable to the striking unions.

During August and September there was no progress toward settlement. The Employers' Association stood firmly against compromise, and labor leaders sponsored enthusiastic mass meetings and parades to inspire their followers. On Labor Day, 1901, the largest parade ever staged by San Francisco labor moved through the streets, with the striking City Front Federation unions prominent in the line of march. Labor Council leaders claimed that 20,000 workers had taken part. Employers, though cutting this estimate in half, were still impressed by the show of union strength. To prevent serious rioting, they kept their strikebreaker-manned wagons off the streets on Labor Day. Labor's display of solidarity was marred by the absence of the building tradesmen. The City Front strike had idled many construction workers by interfering with the flow of lumber from the Pacific Northwest. The strike of building material teamsters impeded the movement of other supplies to construction sites. Late in August P. H. McCarthy partially alleviated the supply problem by organizing a new material teamsters' union, which the Building Trades Council kept from affiliating with the national teamsters' organization. To the Labor Council the 1901 strike was a desperate battle for union survival, but to the Building Trades Council it was a source of financial loss. McCarthy gave no aid to the strikers and, according to his later account, was outraged when the *Examiner* proposed that he call his unions out in a supporting strike.[75]

While the strike was inflicting painful losses on San Francisco business, the Labor Council was boycotting vulnerable members of the Employers' Association. Each week the council distributed thousands of circulars publicizing the names of firms under boycott. At mass meetings in nearby small towns, the council's agents exhorted labor sympathizers to order no goods from these firms. For greater effectiveness, the boycott was concentrated against certain firms reputed to be vigorous supporters of the association: the Emporium, the city's largest department store; Cahn & Nickelsburg, shoe manufacturers; Levi Strauss and Neustadter Brothers, garment manufacturers; John Rapp & Son, leader of the beer bottlers' association; and several other companies dealing in consumer goods. The antiunion battle of the Employers' Association unintentionally aided labor's boycott drive. In mid-August a group of about 150 small retailers denounced the withholding of supplies from union-shop firms, and threatened to boycott association members. Other employers who suffered from the destructive conflict began to express open hostility to the association. In turn, association members and sympathizers launched a counterboycott against labor's ally, the *San Francisco Examiner*. Late in September, representatives of the Merchants' Association, the Shipowners' Association, the Board of Trade, and other business organizations called for withdrawal of all advertising from that newspaper. But during the strike the *Examiner* had increased its circulation among the working class, and businessmen could not long be restrained from advertising in so valuable a medium. Within a few weeks the *Examiner* boycott had collapsed.[76]

The havoc wrought upon the Bay Area economy by the prolonged conflict brought repeated and frantic efforts at mediation, none of which found the Employers' Association receptive. Owing to the shortage of longshoremen and teamsters, goods piled up on the San Francisco docks and unloaded freight cars began to congest the Southern Pacific Railroad yards. At the end of August unionists claimed that only about 800 men were working on the water front, and that almost 200 ships were tied up in the harbor. Interruption of the inflow of fruits and vegetables forced the canning industry to lay off hundreds of workers at the height of the season, and temporarily shut down the local plant of the American Can Company. Dire warnings were proclaimed that labor strife would drive canning and other industries from San Francisco and arrest the city's growth. California farmers, threatened with spoilage of their crops, sent emissaries to San Francisco to demand that their vital "road to market" be kept open. But the farmers met the same frustration as others who attempted to mediate a settlement. Andrew Furuseth, spokesman for the strikers, referred them to the Employers' Association as the only agency empowered to end the conflict, and the association blandly informed them that there was obviously nothing it could do to bring the strikers back to work.[77]

Shortly after the strike began, the Employers' Association had offered a settlement through Mayor Phelan. The offer simply set forth terms of union surrender, demanding that union members pledge themselves not to "attempt to compel a fellow-employee . . . to join a labor union," nor, "directly or indirectly, [to] engage in or support any sympathetic strike or boycott."[78] Sympathetic strikes and boycotts were anathema to employers, who preferred contests with isolated unions and who were, moreover, sincerely outraged when workers with no grievances of their own refused to cross picket lines, handle "hot cargo," or purchase boycotted products. Such tactics, they felt, were not legitimate union weapons.

The Employers' Association rejected all suggestions by Mayor Phelan and other mediators that it alter the settlement terms offered to the strikers. Its representatives met on several occasions with Phelan, but alienated public opinion by refusing to accept as mediators a special committee of the Board of Supervisors. The association asked that mediation efforts cease, announcing that the "principle involved in this strike may be surrendered, but it cannot be compromised." [79] This "principle," however, was not explicitly described. One student of the 1901 struggle has argued that "neither the public nor the press, nor indeed the parties themselves, had a clear conception of the causes and objects of the strike." [80] Certainly neither side had publicized terms under which it could reasonably hope to bring the struggle to an end. But whatever their initial intentions and expectations, both sides realized that they were locked in mortal combat whose outcome would determine whether the striking unions would retain any significant degree of power.

The Chamber of Commerce and the Merchants' Association gave tacit support to the Employers' Association, whose membership, of course, overlapped heavily with theirs. In mid-August Mayor Phelan reported to the Labor Council that the directors of the Chamber of Commerce, when asked to attempt mediation, "promptly and formally refused to discuss the subject . . . as they preferred to remain in ignorance." [81] Early in September the Merchants' Association held a special meeting, with about half of its 1,300 members attending, to consider the situation. Its chief officers, Frank J. Symmes and F. W. Dohrmann, denounced the union shop and the actions of the Teamsters' Union. Symmes was an executive of a large metal trades firm, and Dohrmann held a large interest in the Emporium. Despite the protests of some members, the meeting voted not to hear the contents of a letter sent from the Teamsters' Union, and not to set up a committee to mediate a strike settlement "through mutual concessions." [82]

Growing economic losses and the restiveness of the Draymen's Association did, however, force the Employers' Association to retreat slightly from its adamant stand against negotiation. In early September its leaders bowed to the draymen's insistence that they be allowed to discuss a settlement with their striking employees. The ensuing discussions, however, bore no results. According to teamster leaders, the draymen were operating at only one-third of their normal business volume and were anxious to end the strike. But the Employers' Association refused to countenance genuine collective bargaining and forced the draymen to continue the struggle. To encourage the reluctant draymen, the Teamsters' Union charged, the association paid them substantial subsidies to make up the losses incurred from the strike.[83]

The costs of battle weighed heavily upon both sides, but it soon became evident that the unions were nearer exhaustion than the amply financed employers. Early in September the Cooks' and Waiters' Union, on strike for four months, allowed its members to return to work under the conditions prevailing. The union had lost substantially in membership, but remained a potentially powerful force. Viewing the strike failure as a temporary setback, it continued to boycott certain antiunion restaurants and started to rebuild its strength. The Oakland longshoremen, after several vacillations between joining and abandoning the City Front strike, returned to work permanently in early September. At Port Costa, late in September, farmers gathered enough nonunion workers to disperse pickets of the Crockett Warehousemen's Union and resume the warehousing and shipping of the wheat crop.[84] In San Francisco the number of strikebreaking teamsters and longshoremen continued to increase, under heavy police protection. By the end of September employers claimed that the movement of goods on the water front was nearing its prestrike level.

Although unions disputed all claims that business activity was returning to normal volume, employer spokesmen cited an increase in strike violence as a sign that unionists were growing desperate. A change in policy by Mayor Phelan also contributed to the stepped-up violence. In August Phelan informed the Labor Council that the city policemen assigned to guard nonunion wagon drivers were being replaced by employer-hired guards, and announced that almost 250 such private guards had been deputized as special policemen. Of these, three-fourths had been hired by the Employers' Association through the Curtin Detective Agency, and the rest by McNab & Smith, the city's largest drayage firm. Union members looked upon private detective agencies as their traditional enemies, and denounced the special police as "Pinkertons." Their distrust of the city administration was heightened because the Board of Police Commissioners was headed by George Newhall, president of the Chamber of Commerce and supposedly a key supporter of the Employers' Association.[85]

Incidents of serious violence became increasingly common. Strikers and their sympathizers were more easily stirred to assaults on "Pinkertons" than upon the regular city police, and the special police were less restrained in retaliating. Employers charged that striking teamsters dragged nonunion drivers from wagons and fractured their arms, with the intent to leave them permanently crippled. On occasion, mounted police struggled with large mobs attacking wagons in downtown streets.[86]

Violence also flared up along the water front, where union pickets were "learning to keep clear of the policemen's clubs and yet watch the scabs." [87] Men going to the water front with union permission carried passes signed by Andrew Furuseth, chairman of the City Front strike committee, and entitling the bearer to "courteous treatment." "This Scandinavian dictator of ours," said the *Argonaut*, "wants his Scandinavian scum to be permitted . . . to beat American citizens into a bloody pulp with slung shots and bludgeons." [88] The city police maintained heavy patrols on the water front and in late September began to make blanket arrests of men found there after dark. On some nights water-front patrols arrested more than 100 men, chiefly members of the Sailors' Union, and jailed them until the following morning. This practice intensified the anger of unionists, who charged that the police were under orders not only to arrest but to use their clubs upon union men encountered on the water front after dark.[89]

Employers, for different reasons, were not entirely satisfied with their local government. Late in August Frank J. Symmes, Employers' Association leader and foreman of the grand jury, threatened an investigation of the city's police court judges. These judges, as elective officials, were highly aware of the labor vote. Of the strikers brought before them on charges of violence in 1901, few received more than nominal punishment. Employers thus denounced the police courts as sabotaging the efforts to restore law and order.[90]

By the end of September the City Front strike had brought San Francisco two months of violent industrial conflict, during which two strikebreakers and two strikers had been killed, and several hundred men had been injured, some quite seriously. Tension gripped the city. Employers urged the formation of a new vigilance committee, and the Employers' Association made plans to raise a $200,000 fund to enable the city to hire extra policemen. Just before the month ended, another incident of violence heightened public fear of increasingly serious disorder. On the night of September 28 a brawl erupted in downtown San Francisco between a small group of special policemen and a crowd of unionists. Almost a dozen men received minor gunshot wounds or injuries before police broke up the fighting.[91]

Four days later, on October 2, Governor Henry T. Gage came once again to San Francisco. By then the flow of goods across the docks was estimated at one-half to three-fourths or more of normal volume. Despite strike violence employers were slowly, and at heavy cost, restoring adequate transportation and distribution services. The strikers had little reason to expect ultimate victory. Governor Gage, however, was determined to end the strike. After meeting with representatives of the Draymen's Association, he summoned leaders of the Teamsters' Union and of the City Front Federation to the meeting.[92] An hour later, Gage made a surprising announcement. "I am authorized by officers of both contending parties," he told the press, "to declare the teamsters' strike and all collateral . . . strikes or lockouts . . . at an end, which I hereby do." [93] The news spread rapidly through San Francisco. Crowds gathered before bulletin boards at newspaper offices read that the conflict was over, then rushed away to inform families and friends.[94] San Francisco citizens, who had suffered through two months of destructive conflict, could again look forward to industrial peace.

Aftermath of the 1901 Strike Settlement

No details of the terms of settlement or of the means by which Governor Gage had achieved them were made public. Years later a member of the Teamsters' Union stated that Gage had simply issued an ultimatum that, unless the battle ended at once, he would declare San Francisco under martial law. By the same account, this solution was suggested by Gage's friend and political supporter, Father Peter C. Yorke, a San Francisco priest. Throughout the strike Father Yorke had aided the Teamsters' Union, a large proportion of whose members were, like himself, Irish-born Roman Catholics. He had advised Mike Casey concerning strike strategy, written public statements issued by teamster leaders, defended the strikers in articles in the *Examiner,* and inspirited their mass meetings with denunciations of the "union of rich men" which was attempting to destroy the "unions of the poor men." [95]

Whether or not prompted by Father Yorke, Governor Gage's intervention was favorable to the striking unions. Immediately after the settlement the Labor Council assured the public that "a general strike of all workers has been averted." [96] But it is more probable that labor's resources were nearing the point of exhaustion, and that the unions would eventually have called off the strike in defeat. But Governor Gage's intervention may also have been welcomed by the Draymen's Association, which had never displayed great enthusiasm for the battle against the teamsters. The draymen may well have found the pressure applied by Gage a ready excuse for abandoning the policy, imposed by the Employers' Association, of no compromise with unionism. Significantly, no official representative of the Employers' Association was present at the October 2 meeting which made the settlement.

Those involved in the negotiations stated that the terms of settlement must remain secret unless Governor Gage chose to make them public. But events demonstrated that the agreement stipulated that employers take back, without discrimination and at prestrike wages and conditions, the striking members of the City Front Federation unions. The strikers were given no assurance of a union shop or other formal guarantees of union security, and no promise that strikebreakers would be discharged. The Labor Council called off all boycotts levied in support of the strike, and employers soon began to sell supplies to firms granting the nine-hour day to the striking metal tradesmen. Unionized restaurants again displayed union house cards without fear of a suppliers' boycott.[97]

Many unionists were suspicious of a settlement that sent them back to work alongside nonunion men. City Front Federation leaders brought Father Yorke to meetings of teamsters, longshoremen, sailors, and marine firemen to help persuade these workers of the wisdom of returning to work now and postponing to a more propitious time insistence upon the union shop. Labor leaders admitted that the strike had not achieved "all that was hoped for." [98] Superficially, the Teamsters' Union had received a setback. Its members returned to their jobs under agreement to work with nonunion men, whereas formerly they had possessed union-shop conditions.

It was the Employers' Association, however, that suffered real defeat in the 1901 battle. Dedicated to rendering unions impotent to enforce demands upon employers, it had rejected collective bargaining, opposed negotiations with labor leaders, and insisted that strikes be fought uncompromisingly to a finish. Now, after months of costly struggle, the battle with organized labor had ended in a stalemate. Employers had made a settlement by direct negotiation with union leaders. The City Front Federation members, the Oakland teamsters, and the boxmakers had returned to work with their organizations unbroken. The Labor Council's membership, during the conflict, had grown from ninety to ninety-eight affiliated unions.[99] The striking unions had turned the association's campaign into a debacle. Many of its members, willing to support it only in victory, abandoned the organization. Others left to avoid provoking further boycotts by unions, which had indicated that they were in San Francisco to stay. After its frustrating contest with the City Front Federation, the Employers' Association played no significant role in local labor relations. By 1902 the association was scarcely heard of, and by 1903 it was defunct.

The failure of the Employers' Association stemmed in part from the disinclination of many San Francisco employers to battle on principle against organized labor. Many employers involved in the industrial conflict of 1901 philosophically regarded the outcome as a signal to accept bargaining relationships with their organized workers. Water-front employers, in order to mollify union longshoremen, retained few, if any, of the Negroes imported to work on the docks. Draying firms soon discharged most of the strikebreakers who had remained at work after the strike settlement. In the fall of 1902 the Draymen's Association again entered into a formal contract with the Teamsters' Union, reëstablishing a relationship that has lasted without a strike or a lockout to the present day.[100] Charles Lee Tilden, president of the Draymen's

Association, had announced at the outset of the 1901 dispute that "I am going to do this hauling if I have to get on a box with a shotgun and drive the team myself." [101] After 1901, however, Tilden developed close and friendly relations with Mike Casey, head of the Teamsters' Union. The two men, in personal negotiations year after year, informally settled the main details of the contracts renewed annually between their respective organizations. Casey, despite his leadership of a violent strike, soon acquired a reputation among businessmen as a conservative and responsible labor leader. The Teamsters' Union, key target of the Employers' Association, became one of the most respected unions in the city, both for its power and for its moderate leadership.

The Sailors' Union also found employers receptive to collective bargaining. Before the City Front strike the union had seemed to be within reach of its long-sought goal of acceptance by shipowners. In the spring of 1901 many firms were apparently willing to relax their hostility to unionism. Shipowners met amicably on several occasions with representatives of the sailors and the marine firemen to discuss the possibility of an agreement. In May the Sailors' Union won its first contract; the Pacific Coast Steamship Company, important in the coastwise trade, accepted a one-year closed-shop agreement under which its sailors were to be furnished by the union. By June the sailors reported most employers willing to enter agreements establishing standard hours and wages, but still resisting the demand for the closed shop. According to union leaders, the Shipowners' Association had offered to accept the closed shop in return for the sailors' refusal to work for nonmembers of the association. The Sailors' Union, however, voted against so collusive an arrangement. In July, when it obeyed the City Front Federation strike call, the union sacrificed its hopes for an early favorable outcome of its 1901 negotiations and jeopardized its new friendly relationships with employers. Shipowners resented this sympathy strike, and the Pacific Coast Steamship Company filed a damage suit against the Sailors' Union for breach of contract. But resentment quickly faded upon the strike's conclusion. Under a new president, James M. Rolph, who fully accepted the principle of collective bargaining, the Shipowners' Association again entered negotiations with the sailors late in 1901. In April, 1902, the two organizations signed their first formal contract. Though not specifying the closed shop, it gave each ship captain the option of hiring sailors exclusively through the union, if he should so desire. It covered the majority of ships in the coastwise sailing trade and founded a bargaining relationship which survived for years.[102]

The cooks and waiters, whose 1901 strike for a day of rest each week had failed, reported in the spring of 1902 that numerous restaurants were individually accepting union conditions and a six-day week. In May the Restaurant Keepers' Association quietly accepted the six-day week, though it still refused to bargain with labor organizations. In the same month the wooden box manufacturing firms, which in 1901 had attempted to destroy the Boxmakers' Union, granted their employees the nine-hour day. Of the unions involved in the important 1901 conflicts, only that of the porters, packers, and warehousemen failed to maintain or rebuild its strength. It eventually dissolved, leaving an important sector of San Francisco industry unorganized.[103]

Unsettled Disputes

When the City Front strike ended, the conflicts in the metal trades and beer-bottling industries were still unsettled. The strike of the Iron Trades Council unions was disciplined and well financed. Funds sent by national organizations were supplemented by more than $40,000 raised by the Labor Council. The Iron Trades Council, nevertheless, finally bowed to the employers' greater endurance, and in March, 1902, called off the strike. Although claiming that more than 1,000 union members had won the nine-hour day, the council admitted that about 2,500 men employed by Union, Risdon, and other large metal trades firms were returning to work under prestrike conditions.[104]

As a face-saving excuse for giving up the struggle, union leaders cited their hopes that the National Civic Federation would induce local employers to grant concessions. The federation was composed of prominent industrialists, labor leaders, clergymen, and other citizens interested in the establishment of harmonious labor relations. The executive committee of its industrial department, which was responsible for settling labor disputes, included two San Franciscans: Walter Macarthur of the Sailors' Union, and Julius Kruttschnitt, soon to become president of the Southern Pacific Railroad. The National Civic Federation delegated Macarthur to settle the metal trades conflict. After Macarthur ascertained that a number of employers would reinstate strikers, the Iron Trades Council ended the struggle. Macarthur then induced Henry T. Scott, head of the Union Iron Works, to promise that his company would submit wage and hour issues to arbitration by the National Civic Federation if the two leading shipbuilding firms of the East Coast did likewise.[105] The proviso revealed the concern of San Francisco metal trades employers over maintaining their competitive cost position relative to firms elsewhere. But nothing more came of the arbitration proposal. The Union Iron Works, along with the majority of metal trades firms, continued to maintain a ten-hour day.

After settlement of the City Front strike, the Labor Council had advised the locked-out members of the Bottlers' Union to accept reinstatement offered by their employers, but the union refused to end the struggle until the firms agreed to closed-shop conditions. Because of its recalcitrant attitude, the national brewery workers' organization revoked the union's charter and formed a new local of men loyal to the national leadership. By June, 1902, the new Bottlers' Union had signed union-shop contracts with more than a dozen firms in San Francisco, the East Bay cities, and San Jose, including two firms that had broken away from the Bottlers' Protective Association. In succeeding months several more firms left the association, reportedly after expiration of a period during which a separate settlement with the union required forfeiture of a $1,000 bond. The bottlers permitted firms that ceased resistance to use the union label, a valued aid in selling beer to workingmen, and imposed a boycott on firms that continued to resist. Throughout 1902 the union concentrated its boycott against the firm of John Rapp, president of the Bottlers' Protective Association.* Finally, in February, 1903, Rapp and the four other firms remaining in the association made their peace

* Another brewery was also boycotted for some months, but the boycott was levied by the Building Trades Council. P. H. McCarthy and his associates, seizing an opportunity to antagonize the Labor Council, took under their patronage the remains of the original bottlers' union. Proclaiming this dissident group the only legitimate bottlers' organization, the Building Trades Council called on its members to boycott the Enterprise Brewery, one of the first firms to sign a contract with the new Bottlers' Union. This anomalous boycott of a union-shop firm served to widen the split between the building trades and other San Francisco unions. (*Labor Clarion,* April 11, 1902.)

with labor, signing union-shop contracts covering bottlers and wagon drivers. All branches of the Bay Area brewing industry thus became thoroughly unionized.[106]

The Union Labor Party

A political development stemming from the 1901 strike was the emergence of a political organization professing to represent the interests of workers and capitalizing on their resentment over the conduct of Mayor Phelan and other city officials during the strike. Throughout the 1901 struggle, workers felt more and more strongly that they were being persecuted by an employer-controlled city administration. They asserted that the police had, without provocation, brutally clubbed scores of workingmen. Labor leaders denounced the special police as "mercenaries clothed with police power," including "men lately released from San Quentin, . . . opium fiends, . . . other dregs of society." [107] Some weeks before the teamsters' strike began, a number of politically inclined labor leaders had explored the possibility of creating a labor party. As industrial conflict spread, unions developed increasing interest in the proposed new political body, the Union Labor Party.

On September 5, 1901, delegates from almost seventy unions met in the party's first convention and nominated a slate of unionists for the coming city elections. For mayor the convention chose Eugene Schmitz, president of the Musicians' Union and a popular local orchestra leader. Schmitz was a handsome, genial, and colorful candidate who appealed to the delegates as a potential vote winner. Yet his selection indicated that the new party would only nominally represent labor. Far from being a dedicated union leader, Schmitz had shown little concern with the problems of the labor movement. He had acquired business interests of his own and, like other leaders of the Union Labor Party, offered no program of reforms that would significantly benefit labor's economic position.[108]

Schmitz owed his nomination largely to the efforts of his personal attorney, Abraham Ruef. Ruef, a young lawyer with a growing reputation for shrewdness, was ambitious to become a dominant power in California politics. Earlier in 1901 he had enlisted a group of men, including Schmitz and several other union officials, in an unsuccessful effort to capture control of the Republican Party in San Francisco.[109] After this effort failed, Ruef turned to the proposed new labor party as a promising arena. Selecting the pliant, personable Schmitz as an ideal figurehead, Ruef worked to promote his nomination. When the Union Labor Party named labor's ostensible candidate, it was naming Ruef's candidate.

The incumbent administration of Mayor Phelan was Democratic. In 1901 P. H. McCarthy, who possessed a ready talent for identification with the party currently in power, was an avowed Democrat. His political support had been rewarded with political appointment; the mayor had named him a member of the city's board of civil service commissioners. Accordingly the Building Trades Council, under McCarthy's influence, vociferously opposed the Union Labor Party in the 1901 campaign. The Labor Council officially took a hands-off position. Adhering to traditional AFL policy against labor's identification with any political party, the council voted down a resolution calling for endorsement of the ULP. Most unionists, however, welcomed the opportunity to vent their anger against Phelan's administration by voting for a candidate pledged to governmental fairness in labor disputes. The result was that the November, 1901, election brought Schmitz victory, by a plurality, over his Democratic and Republican opponents.[110] San Francisco labor thus entered the year 1902 triumphantly, under a new mayor elected by labor's vote. Though conservative, self-seeking, and largely dominated by Ruef, Mayor Schmitz could nevertheless be relied upon to support unions in their conflicts with employers.

The Close of 1901

At the end of 1901 organized labor in San Francisco was in healthy condition. It had emerged intact from a battle that had threatened to set back for years the progress of the union movement. Significantly, the battle had gravitated to the water front; the City Front Federation had carried the burden of the fight against the Employers' Association. A pattern had thus been set, for in later years the maritime industry again stood out as the center of the most vital—and most violent—conflict. Critical struggles between employers and unions at key turning points in

Bay Area labor history revealed a persistent tendency to converge upon the water front, across which passed so much of the commerce essential to the area's economy. For years to come a major alteration in the union-employer balance of power in the maritime industry provided the best single indicator of a significant shift in power relationships in local industry.

Despite the seeming neutrality of the settlement, the outcome of the City Front strike of 1901 was an impressive victory for San Francisco labor. The strike had been called to break up an employer offensive potentially menacing all unions in the city, and had succeeded thoroughly. The salient feature of the strike was that for the first time teamsters, longshoremen, and seamen joined in a common battle under unified command. When the strike ended, Labor Council leaders exhorted these workers to maintain their close bonds, rejoicing that the federation had "succeeded perfectly in demonstrating its working capacity as a combination." [111]

Yet the strike brought into play forces that crippled future capacity for unified action. Demonstrating to employers the destructive power of a joint strike by strong unions, it stimulated them to seek safeguards against repetition of such an episode. Thus when the Shipowners' Association, early in 1902, first granted formal union recognition to the sailors, it induced them to stipulate in the contract that the "Sailors' Union is not in favor of sympathetic strikes." [112] Despite protests from other affiliates of the City Front Federation, the Sailors' Union continued to honor the restrictive stipulation.

Moreover, the Teamsters' Union, for whose preservation the federation had called its 1901 strike, soon came to a tacit disavowal of sympathy strikes. Although receiving frequent requests not to haul to and from strike-bound establishments, the union was reluctant to jeopardize its relationship with the Draymen's Association. The violence and the privations of the 1901 struggle had made a deep impression on Mike Casey, the teamsters' leader. Casey was never again willing to allow his followers to participate in so bitter and general a conflict.

The City Front Federation maintained existence for some years, but its affiliates, unwilling to disturb their individual contractual relationships with employers, lost enthusiasm for joint action. Unity was further weakened by the reëmergence of suspicions and jurisdictional jealousies between seamen and longshoremen. Ironically, the 1901 strike, in which the federation proved an invaluable asset to the local union movement, was its first and last strong action. Not until 1934, at another time of crisis for San Francisco labor, did teamsters, longshoremen, and seamen unite once more in effective battle against employers.

| *Chapter III* | *Collective Bargaining Relationships 1902–1903* |

IN THE YEARS immediately following its test of strength in 1901, the Bay Area labor movement was vigorous and healthy. Population was rising rapidly on both sides of the Bay. In San Francisco the early years of the decade brought an especially high rate of expansion. In 1905 the Chamber of Commerce estimated the San Francisco population at 450,000, well above the 1910 figure of about 415,000 to which the city had rebuilt itself after the 1906 earthquake. Coincident with the population upsurge came increased construction activity, marked expansion in public utility services, and growth in the volume of shipping and trade. The active demand for both skilled and unskilled labor eased the task of extending unionization on all levels. Bay Area union membership continued to rise in the early part of the decade, though at a slower rate than in the 1899–1901 period. Nationwide, as in the Bay Area, the unions of the AFL were still experiencing their turn-of-the-century boom. AFL membership more than quintupled during 1897–1904, before leveling off to hover around 1.5 million for the remainder of the 1900–1910 decade.[1]

The years 1902–1903 were essentially a period of union expansion and consolidation. Labor was free from major employer attack. It enjoyed an interlude between the onslaught of the Employers' Association in 1901 and an antiunion campaign in 1904. The unions thus had time, in a continuing favorable economic environment and in the absence of militant, organized employer hostility, to develop stable bargaining relationships and accustom employers to the idea of dealing with labor organizations.

This was, indeed, the first period in which collective bargaining was permanently established, on an extensive scale, in San Francisco. During 1900–1901 doubt existed whether the emerging union-employer relationships would long survive, but by the end of 1903 these relationships, in many industries, had become relatively settled. The collective bargaining structure that took shape in these years was varied in composition. Already prominent, however, was a characteristic feature of San Francisco labor relations: multiemployer bargaining, with master contracts either industry-wide in scope, or establishing the terms accepted as standard throughout the industry. Labor organization, comparatively far advanced in San Francisco, led to the early and outstanding development of employers' associations which gave firms greater bargaining power in negotiations with strong unions.

In 1902–1903 San Francisco first acquired its reputation as America's "closed-shop city." Though exaggerated, this description reflected a significant aspect of the local labor movement. Unionism in San Francisco was not confined to the skilled workers of the traditional, recognized crafts, but, to a greater extent than in any other leading metropolitan area, it embraced a variety of less skilled groups. The continuing growth of new unions in 1902–1903, after the upsurge of 1899–1901, made it evident that the San Francisco labor movement would be exceptionally broad-based. To observers accustomed to conventional craft unionism it could easily give an impression of virtually total organization, for it included such uncommon unions as those of dishwashers and kitchen helpers, gasworkers, milkers, laundry workers, miscellaneous women factory workers, poultry dressers, and grave-diggers.

Popular acceptance of this stereotype of the "closed-shop city" carried with it a related development, also well publicized. This was the alarmist, hand-wringing description of San Francisco as a "problem" area desperately in need of redemption from the economic and political thralldom imposed by unrestrained unionism. Though far removed from the main concentration of industry and population in the East, San Francisco had gained nationwide attention by the end of 1903 as a source of vexation to American business leaders determined to render organized labor impotent throughout the country. It was a focus for the resentment of open-shop advocates frustrated by the seeming invulnerability of this Pacific Coast outpost of union strength.

Young and Flourishing Unionism

The San Francisco labor movement, in the early years of the new century, demonstrated an exhilaration that it may have since recaptured, if at all, only in the mid-1930's. It had passed through its 1901 ordeal into an era of unprecedented opportunity. New unions springing up throughout local industry were finding employers evidently willing to accept their existence. Though the San Francisco labor movement had its veterans, most of its leaders were young men, typically heading freshly formed unions and enthusiastic over the vistas opening up for organized labor and for their own careers. Many of them eventually pursued personal business and political ambitions, but initially they devoted their energies to the rapid build-up of union strength in San Francisco.

In an action indicative of the solid basis of the new union growth, the Labor Council, in February, 1902, established a weekly journal, the *Labor Clarion*. Through the early years of the decade the paper enjoyed the services of an articulate and conscientious editor, J. J. O'Neill, who gave much of its space to periodic reports of individual unions. These reports announced membership increases, economic gains, and plans for future achievements. Not until three decades later, under Franklin D. Roosevelt's first New Deal administration, was there a comparable surge of organization among San Francisco workers. Then, however, much of the youthful expectancy and sometimes ingenuous enthusiasm characterizing the new unionism of the earlier period was missing.

The Labor Council, at the end of the 1901 conflict, comprised 98 member unions. By the spring of 1903 the council had expanded to almost 130 affiliates, more than two-thirds of the number of unions in San Francisco. About 35 unions were then members of the Building Trades Council. Outside the two councils there existed a few independent unions unconnected with any national labor organization, a small minority of AFL unions abstaining from local affiliation, and a number of locals of the national railroad unions. By the Labor Council's own estimates, its total membership had grown less rapidly than the number of its affiliates. It claimed 30,000 members in 1903, a plausible figure only moderately above its almost certainly exaggerated estimates of 1901.[2] Adding to this the more than 15,000 members of the Building Trades Council unions, and the membership of the unaffiliated unions, the number of organized workers in San Francisco in 1903 was nearing 50,000.

By mid-1902 the Labor Council was proudly claiming that San Francisco was the most thoroughly unionized city in America. On Labor Day that year the local unions turned out in a parade matched in numbers only by the unionists of New York City. Led by Mike Casey and P. H. McCarthy, the thousands of workers marching through downtown San Francisco impressed even unsympathetic journalists. The *Examiner* reminded employers that they had witnessed a "peaceful exhibition of power," a warning demonstration to any who might still be nursing hopes of a renewed onslaught against labor.[3] Father Peter Yorke, delivering the traditional Labor Day oration, exulted to his enthusiastic audience that, as the parade passed by, "the only use the police had for their clubs was to raise them to their foreheads in salute." [4] In the eyes of San Francisco unionists, their labor movement had come far since the tense months of 1901.

Organizing on a Broad Front

Much of the Labor Council's increase in the number of affiliates in 1902–1903 stemmed from its policy of extending unionization to every organizable group of workers—though with the usual exclusions of all Orientals and most Negroes. In addition there were spontaneous bursts of self-organization among workers outside the traditional crafts. The strong and successful unionism among skilled craftsmen stimulated the organization of such weaker groups as women and unskilled factory production workers. Leaders of the Labor Council and of established unions assisted these new recruits in organizing and in negotiating with employers, and gave them the benefit of experienced counsel. Officers of the older unions were sometimes doubtful of the prudence with which the new organizations would conduct their

own affairs and fearful that they would recklessly embroil themselves in disputes. But when a new union of relatively unskilled
workers, after heeding Labor Council advice, still found it impossible to avoid a serious conflict, it could generally rely upon
the better-established organizations for help. Such help came in
the form of boycotts, financial aid, efforts at mediation, and, occasionally, sympathy strikes. The knowledge of this potential backing encouraged young, otherwise weak unions to take a firmer
stand in presenting council-approved demands to employers.

During 1902–1903 a wide variety of relatively unskilled workers were organized into newly chartered unions. A Gas Workers'
Union, the first of its kind in the nation and one of the few self-
styled "industrial" unions in the Bay Area, built a substantial
organization among "laborers, semiskilled, and skilled mechanics"
employed by public utility corporations in both San Francisco
and the East Bay. Late in 1902 appeared the Miscellaneous
Culinary Employees' Union, another organization first developed
in San Francisco.[5] Composed of dishwashers and other kitchen
helpers, it joined with the more skilled unions of cooks and
waiters in a working alliance that has lasted to the present day.
Factory production workers, a large proportion of them women,
flocked to new unions formed within individual manufacturing
industries. A few of these factory and plant unions received
charters from national labor organizations, but most of them were
federal unions. Prominent among them were the unions of Paper
Box Workers; Bindery Women; Glove Makers; Sugar Workers;
Cloth Hat and Cap Makers; Can Makers; Soap, Soda and Candle
Workers; Burlap and Cotton Bag Workers; Wire Workers; Soda
and Mineral Water Bottlers; Flour and Cereal Mill Employees;
Paint, Lead and Oil Workers; Rope and Cordage Workers; and
Wine and Liquor Workers. The majority of these unions enrolled
a large proportion of the production workers in their respective
industries. However, as San Francisco was a city of predominantly
small-scale, light manufacturing industry, few of them had more
than 500 members. Despite their easy initial growth, not all of
them survived beyond the early years of the decade.

The expansion of unionism in San Francisco in 1902–1903 also
stimulated organization among workers in the service industries
and other occupations. Typically small, and chartered by the

AFL as federal unions, the organizations formed among such workers rarely developed strong bargaining power. Among them were the new unions of Wool Sorters, Elevator Operators, Dyers and Cleaners, Janitors, Newswriters, Salesladies, Cemetery Employees, Bootblacks, Oyster Workers, and Fish Cleaners. Officers of the Labor Council gave generously of their time and energy to these frail organizations, though building trades leaders and other tradition-bound craft unionists looked askance at the welcoming of such fringe groups into the trade-union movement. When the Poultry and Game Dressers' Union received its charter, P. H. McCarthy found a contemptuously alliterative symbol to characterize all the new unions of unskilled workers. With great amusement he scoffed at the visionary efforts of Labor Council leaders, which produced only ludicrous organizations of "chicken-pickers." [6]

Employer Response to Rising Unionism

San Francisco labor relations in 1902–1903 indicate that the 1901 Employers' Association had failed to solidify employers' antagonism to organized labor. From the outset many employers had been indifferent or openly unsympathetic to the association's policies. Others, though originally supporting the association, found the stalemated 1901 struggle disillusioning. Dismayed at the costliness of the effort that would clearly be required to uproot local unionism, they were far from eager to see the city's economic life disrupted again. During 1902–1903 no new central organization arose to enlist San Francisco employers in another antiunion crusade. And only infrequently did an employer refuse on principle to meet with union representatives. Even firms that initially brushed aside union requests for meetings quickly abandoned this attitude after threatened or brief strikes. During this period many of the San Francisco employers were willing to experiment with collective bargaining. Some unions won written contracts from individual firms or employer associations, providing for annual renewal by negotiation. Others accepted verbal agreements or "understandings" that employers would maintain certain terms of employment for a specified period, or until either party gave notice of desired change. Still others, though not seeking a bargaining relationship, settled for employer observance—either by tacit acquiescence or after informal discussions—of announced union hours, wage scales, or other conditions.

Negotiations in these early years were brief and confined to a relatively small number of issues. Bargaining centered upon the basic questions of wages, hours, overtime rates, union security, and working conditions. Some unions, especially in the skilled crafts, bargained occasionally over apprenticeship regulations, jurisdictional rights, and work methods. A few agreements embodied procedures for the handling of grievances, and some negotiations took up such questions as compulsory use of the union label or the functions of union shop committees. In the early 1900's, however, union and employer representatives did not wrestle at the bargaining table to produce long, detailed contracts covering seniority rights, pension plans, health and welfare plans, paid vacations, layoff and rehiring procedures, the use of time-study and job evaluation techniques, incentive pay, work norms, and other technical issues. Formal written contracts usually consisted of a few brief paragraphs, and rarely ran beyond one type-written page in length. Their negotiation did not require the services of highly skilled specialists such as lawyers or technical advisers. Bargaining was comparatively straightforward and unsophisticated, and the parties were less intent on arriving at a compromise than are their present-day counterparts. Unions were less likely to inflate their demands, and employers to minimize their offers, in order to establish strategic positions between which a bargain would eventually be struck. Furthermore, unions made demands then with much less periodic regularity than in later years. But when a union concluded that the time had come to insist upon a decrease in the workday, or an increase in the wage rate, it was extremely reluctant to retreat from its original demand. Nevertheless, the desires of both parties to avert open conflict made compromise a common, if unanticipated, outcome.

Most San Francisco unions, as a matter of course, assumed the union shop as their goal. To some unions the term "union recognition" automatically denoted a union shop. And employers were apparently less concerned than in later years over the distinction between recognition and the full union shop. They seem to have felt no powerful compulsion to defend the principle enunciated in later crusades for the "open shop" and the "right to work." San Francisco unions did not usually insist upon formal, written guarantees of union security. Many accepted verbal "understandings" that a union shop would be maintained; others made no explicit agreement covering this issue, but tried to maintain union-shop conditions by persuading reluctant employees to join the union, or, occasionally, by threatening strikes against firms that refused to discharge nonunion workers. Almost all such threats, however, were directed at small firms. Rarely in the 1900–1910 decade did a union strike against a major employer for the union shop, unless the employer also resisted wage and other demands. When a small employer faced a strike threat over his continued employment of nonunion workers, Labor Council officers attempted to settle the dispute. They often induced the workers to become union members, or the employer to require union membership of his employees. In some instances they persuaded unions to relinquish union-shop demands as unwise or premature, or to accept employees into membership and cease pressuring an employer to replace them with present members of the union.

Organization among Employers

In the early 1900's multiemployer bargaining was already a common feature of local labor relations. Among the industries in which employers' organizations dealt with labor problems were general drayage, shipping, building, newspaper publishing, book and job printing, baking, brewing, meat wholesaling and retailing, milk retailing, restaurant service, ladies' cloak manufacturing, leather tanning, laundry service, glove manufacturing, paper box manufacturing, public stable and carriage rental service, horseshoeing, and carriage manufacturing. Employers' associations varied considerably in form, life span, and influence. Some groups —for example, draymen, milk dealers, laundry owners—entered into and maintained permanent industry-wide bargaining relationships with unions. Others, more loosely organized, came together chiefly to deal with pressing union demands or threatened strikes. Although most associations of this category did make collective bargaining agreements with unions, the ties established were not of long duration. Within a few years a labor dispute, lack of cohesion within the employer group, or a decline in union strength brought such relationships to an end, though industry-wide bargaining frequently reappeared later. Among the early employer associations of this type were those of restaurant proprietors, stable owners, retail butchers, and manufacturers in most of the industries not organized by strong craft unions.

By comparison with modern employer associations, these early San Francisco organizations usually limited their operations to periodic labor negotiations. Few of them hired staff employees. Fewer still policed their members' observance of contracts or provided for systematic consultation with union representatives on problems that might arise during the life of a contract. Associations were relatively informal, maintained only a loose discipline over their members, and frequently comprised only a minority of firms within an industry. Most of the associations, however, functioned with enough unity and included enough employers to establish their negotiated terms of employment as generally observed industry-wide patterns. Industry-wide bargaining had not yet become institutionalized, but it was an effective force in San Francisco industrial relations.

Union-Employer Stabilization of Competition

In addition to prosperity, another important factor contributed to the growth of collective bargaining. Employers saw that a union relationship could help to stabilize or restrict competition, particularly in industries confined to the local market. In 1900–1901 the Draymen's Association, the Planing Mill Owners' Association, and the Shipowners' Association had demonstrated their interest in unions as potential allies in standardizing wages and prices, discouraging outside competitors, or preventing competent craftsmen from working for nonmembers of an industry association. In 1902–1903, the Master Masons' Association and the Master Plasterers' Association showed substantial evidence of having made informal agreements with unions which largely cut off the supply of union bricklayers and plasterers to nonmember employers. Both the Carriage Makers' Association and the Master Horseshoers' Association persuaded unions to enter agreements to refuse employment offered by nonmember firms.[7]

A few union-employer agreements involved price fixing. Early in 1902 the Hackmen's Union made an agreement with the Stable and Carriage Owners' Association, raising wages and explicitly providing for an increase in the rental rates of hacks driven in funeral processions. The Milkdrivers' Union aroused adverse publicity and serious concern in 1902–1903 because of its alleged collusion with employers to raise the price of milk. The union successfully built up its organization through 1902 and late in the year won its first industry-wide contract with the Dairymen's Association. The contract reduced the workday to ten hours and raised wages sharply; it was accompanied by a substantial increase in the retail price of milk. In a barrage of protest the union and the association were denounced for callous disregard of consumer interests, and the union was accused of having pledged itself to strike against any milk dealer who failed to maintain prices at the higher level. Though the Milkdrivers' Union denied the accusations of price fixing, it is probable that the bargaining relationship maintained since 1902 between the union and the organized San Francisco milk dealers was originally based in part upon a joint effort to control local milk prices. The union's leader, Alexander Dijeau, soon acquired a dubious reputation within the Bay Area labor movement. Recurring charges of price-fixing agreements were raised against him, along with accusations of unethical activities directed against other unions and union leaders. In 1905, when the Street Carmen's Union organized a cooperative dairy to supply milk cheaply to members of its own and other organizations, it was forced to ask Labor Council intervention against continued harassment by the Milkdrivers' Union. Dijeau, apparently by arrangement with commercial milk dealers, made strenuous efforts to block this challenge to their control of the market.[8]

Some employers claimed that they fought against forced increases in prices. Late in 1902 the Stable and Carriage Owners' Association, most of whose members resisted the organizing drive of the new Stablemen's Union, protested that the union demand for a 25 per cent wage increase would necessitate price increases. The association went so far as to demand that the Labor Council examine its member firms' books as proof of inability to raise wages, but most of the firms soon acceded to the new union scale, increasing wages from $2 to $2.50 for a twelve-hour day. The Owl Drugstore chain, under boycott by the Drug Clerks' Union and the local labor movement, also appealed to the public. It repeatedly charged, over union denials, that the Retail Druggists' Association was supporting the boycott because Owl Drug had refused to coöperate in the association's price-fixing policies.[9]

From the outset Labor Council leaders strongly condemned union-employer collusion to fix prices or injure firms not members of employer associations. Especially after the unfavorable publicity over the rise in milk prices, the council became fearful that the labor movement would bear the onus for increases in the cost of living. In December, 1902, the *Labor Clarion* exhorted unions to resist the "tendency recently developed here on the part of organized employers to enlist the cooperation of organized labor in movements to raise the price of their products." [10] Such coöperation, the *Clarion* warned, would prejudice the cause of unionism. In contrast to the Building Trades Council, which officially opposed collusive agreements but did little to stop them, the Labor Council strove to persuade several unions to abandon such agreements. In 1903 council leaders failed to deter the Horseshoers' Union from a strike against a firm expelled from the Master Horseshoers' Association for lowering prices below a prescribed level. By honoring its pledge not to work for non-member firms, the union enabled the association to punish employers who introduced price competition. Late in 1903 the Labor Council, after vainly protesting the carriage workers' collusive agreement with the Carriage Makers' Association, voted to send a formal complaint to the AFL against San Francisco unions that had entered into such agreements.[11]

Despite the concern aroused, price fixing and other aspects of collusive union-employer agreements affected only a small segment of San Francisco industry. More important to union acceptance was recognition by employers that a well-established union, by standardizing terms of employment throughout an industry, helped raise a legitimate barrier against severe price and service competition. Most employers were ready to bargain with unions that could promise maintenance of uniform wages and hours for substantially all major competitors. Unions active in industries limited to the local market therefore met less employer resistance than unions that could not assure San Francisco firms of cost parity with outside competitors. In 1903 San Francisco cracker bakeries granted the Cracker Bakers' Union a 50 cents per day wage increase only on the understanding that the Bakery Workers' International Union would launch a campaign to unionize all cracker bakeries on the West Coast. The Stable and Carriage Owners' Association, in its 1902 effort to avoid a wage increase, sent the Labor Council a list of more than thirty stables which, it complained, the Stablemen's Union had failed to organize. Several unions in 1902–1903 reported that employers had withdrawn their initial acceptance of wage or hour demands upon union failure to impose the terms upon certain competitors.[12]

Caution and Conservatism

Despite their growing strength, San Francisco unions advanced cautiously in the early 1900's. Union after union explicitly described itself as "conservative" in its policies. Then as now, unions followed Samuel Gompers' dictum that labor's aim was "more, more and more," but they waited longer intervals than present-day unions do between successive increments of "more." The powerful Teamsters' and Sailors' unions, for example, demanded no significant wage increases until almost five years after entering into their 1902 agreements. In the midst of prosperity labor looked back uneasily to the depressed 1890's, apprehensive that newly won gains might be swept away by a return of business depression and unemployment. Veteran unionists frequently warned labor to "go slow," to follow "conservative methods," to avoid extreme demands that could provoke San Francisco employers to another assault upon unionism. They urged unions to tighten discipline, build up their treasuries, and entrench themselves against the next downturn in business conditions. "These are days of peace and prosperity," the *Labor Clarion* proclaimed in 1903, "the days when we should prepare for war and adversity."[13] New unions were repeatedly warned that they would face their first real test of survival when employers took advantage of the next depression "to teach the horny-handed their proper place."[14]

The Labor Council urged its affiliates to follow conservative policies. Most unions gave the council advance notice of their demands and of proposed action to enforce them, and council officers made use of this opportunity to intervene in situations threatening open conflict. They induced unions to postpone strikes, persuaded employers to be more conciliatory, and worked to create a bargaining atmosphere leading to peaceful settlement. When employers refused to yield, the council frequently persuaded unions into temporary strategic retreats. In 1902, for example, council leaders advised the culinary unions not to insist upon formal signed contracts from restaurant owners who otherwise observed union conditions.[15] In 1903 they induced the Carmen's Union to give up its proposed strike for the union shop. Recognizing the council as an advocate of a gradual and conciliatory approach, many employers appealed to the central body when confronted by union demands they felt were unreasonable.

Council leaders often extracted from employers concessions stubbornly refused to individual union representatives. Their greater finesse and experience in bargaining, and their prominent and respected positions as labor spokesmen, made their assistance particularly valuable to weaker unions of less skilled workers. Although well-established unions usually called on the Labor Council only in the later stages of deadlocked negotiations, newer and weaker organizations relied upon its officers to present grievances to employers, negotiate agreements, and give needed advice.

"The Labor Council is essentially an instrument of peace," its spokesmen proclaimed to San Francisco employers.[16] Unquestionably council leaders tried to avoid strikes, which often placed a heavy financial strain upon the labor movement and irritated employers. Moreover, the loss of a prolonged strike might mean permanent replacement of strikers by nonunion workers and might even destroy the union. Council spokesmen vehemently opposed the tendency to rush into strikes without careful planning, in the expectation that other unions would provide financial support or call sympathy strikes. Early in 1903 the *Labor Clarion* warned against "radical action on the part of unions with empty treasuries," and later in the year praised the Teamsters' and Sailors' unions for refusing to cut off transportation facilities from several strike-bound firms.[17] San Francisco labor leadership preferred localized conflicts to sympathy strikes and secondary boycotts which might occasion an unwelcome repetition of the 1901 struggle.

The gradualist and conservative policies of the San Francisco labor movement in the early 1900's made it easy for employers to tolerate a collective bargaining relationship. Union leaders, adhering to the AFL philosophy of "business unionism," worked patiently to achieve reasonable economic gains. The strong Irish-Catholic flavor of local union officialdom and the tendency for prominent unionists to seek personal political careers may well have reinforced the labor movement's conservatism. An appreciable minority of union members did show enthusiasm for Socialist and other doctrines emphasizing the class struggle, but rarely did a militantly class-conscious unionist rise to prominence as a San Francisco labor leader. The city's labor journals, moreover, followed a moderate and, by later standards, surprisingly objective editorial policy, eschewing violent attacks upon employers' motives or actions and emphasizing the opportunities for harmonious, coöperative union-employer relations.

Continued Union Advance

Many San Francisco unions, both old and new, bettered their economic positions in 1902–1903, usually through negotiation. Most skilled craftsmen's unions and other comparatively well-established organizations met little open antagonism from employers. The offshore unions of sailors, marine firemen, and marine cooks and stewards extended the bargaining relationship between sailors and shipowners which began in 1902 by entering into a joint contract in 1903 with the Steam-Schooner Managers' Association, composed of firms transporting lumber and general freight and headed by Captain Robert Dollar, a prominent figure in West Coast shipping. The contract specified union-shop conditions, but repeated the 1902 stipulation that the unions were "not in favor of sympathetic strikes." [18] It thus delivered another blow to the potential unity of the City Front Federation in moments of future crisis.

A labor conflict arising in 1903 demonstrated the anxiety of the Sailors' Union leadership to safeguard the recently won acceptance by employers. At the small, isolated lumber-mill town of Fort Bragg, on the northern California coast, a new federal union of lumber workers carried on for months a futile strike for recognition by the large Union Lumber Company. San Francisco unions in both the Labor Council and the Building Trades Council generously supported the strike, for the Union Lumber Company operated in San Francisco one of the Bay Area's few nonunion planing mills. The City Front Federation began to picket the employment agency of Murray & Ready—"the headquarters of 'scabs' in this town"—which was recruiting strikebreakers for Fort Bragg. Agitation arose within the federation for a strike against the handling of shipments coming by sea from the Union Lumber Company. But the Sailors' Union, obligated by its contract with the Steam-Schooner Managers' Association to furnish sailors to the lumber schooners of the Union Lumber Company, an association member, refused all requests of the Fort Bragg lumber workers for a sympathy strike. It feared that a coast-wide lockout of union sailors would result. "Organized labor of San Francisco cannot at this time afford to put all its eggs into one basket," the union's leaders argued. When sailors walked out in a wildcat strike from a ship loading strikebreakers destined for Fort Bragg, Andrew Furuseth furnished a new union crew despite cries of protest, which included loud expressions of righteous indignation from P. H. McCarthy.[19] The Sailors' Union observed its contract, and the Fort Bragg lumber strike ended in defeat.

In 1903 the offshore unions won their first agreement from the Oceanic Steamship Company, a transpacific passenger line owned by John D. Spreckels, a wealthy San Francisco citizen. Spreckels had stated earlier that expenses incurred in the 1901 strike were chiefly responsible for the more than $200,000 net loss reported by Oceanic in that year;[20] after 1901 Spreckels showed a general willingness to accept unions. He also bargained with the organized workers employed by the *San Francisco Call* and the Western Sugar Refinery, enterprises under his control.

Early in 1903 the Typographical Union signed a two-year agreement providing for a gradual reduction in the workday from nine to eight hours by January, 1905, and an increase from $18.50 to $20 in the weekly wages of journeymen printers employed in book and job printing concerns. The Pressmen's Union shortly accepted an employer offer of a similar contract. These long-term agreements, products of one of the most settled bargaining relationships in San Francisco, extended the eight-hour day to all branches of the local printing industry. The Bookbinders' Union took a step toward industrial unionism in 1902 by establishing an auxiliary Bindery Women's Union. The new union organized more than 200 relatively unskilled workers and in mid-1903 went on strike, after employers had refused demands for a $10 weekly wage for workers with several years of experience. With the encouragement and financial aid of other Allied Printing Trades Council unions, the women remained on strike for a month before compromising on a $9 weekly wage.[21]

In the newspaper branch of the printing trades, early in 1902, the San Francisco Newspaper Publishers' Association entered into a contract with the new Mailers' Union, providing the industry's standard forty-eight-hour week and a substantial wage increase. The Newswriters' Union, however, formed late in the same year and soon claiming to have organized two-thirds of the city's reporters, met a different reception. In February, 1903, it reported to the Labor Council that two of its leaders had been discharged and that M. H. de Young, publisher of the *Chronicle*, had warned his employees that members of the Newspaper Publishers' Association would discharge all reporters who joined the union.[22] Leaders of the Labor Council and the Typographical Union, along with Father Peter Yorke, the Roman Catholic priest, represented the newswriters in meetings with individual newspaper owners. The wholesale discharge of unionized reporters did not materialize, but the Newswriters' Union made no headway. Though chartered as a local of the International Typographical Union, it could not expect sympathy strikes or observance of picket lines from its fellow printing trades unions, which scrupulously observed the contracts they had made with employers. With nothing more than the "moral support" freely offered by printing tradesmen, the Newswriters' Union lacked the economic pressure to win recognition from employers, and soon dissolved.

In the metal trades, the Bay Area employers who had withstood the 1901 strike for the nine-hour day soon bowed to the industry's nationwide trend. Beginning in mid-1902, firm after firm adopted the shorter day, and in the spring of 1903 the last recalcitrants yielded. In March the Risdon Iron Works announced the nine-hour day, accompanied by a wage increase, for its more than 1,000 workers. Within a few days the Union Iron Works *—now controlled by an Eastern shipbuilding trust—announced identical terms.[23]

In 1902–1903 metal trades employers preferred to improve workers' conditions unilaterally, rather than by negotiations with their organized workers. They had yet to grant formal union recognition or accept collective bargaining. The metal trades unions, however, felt no strong compulsion to fight for immediate formal guarantees of union security. Working under improved wages and hours, and thoroughly enough organized to maintain virtually union-shop conditions among skilled journeymen, the metal tradesmen made no plans for an early advance beyond the *status quo.*

Culinary and Provision Trades Unions

By mid-1902 the culinary workers were organized in three separate unions: the Cooks' Union, the Waiters' Union, and the Miscellaneous Culinary Employees' Union. The three organizations maintained close coördination and among them claimed a total membership of well above 2,000. Their impressive gains through 1902 finally led their former antagonist, the Restaurant Keepers' Association, to alter its opposition to collective bargaining, and in December it signed a formal one-year contract with the unions. Drawn up in unusual detail for this period, the contract provided for a union shop, a minimum weekly wage rate for each category of worker, a six-day week, an eleven-hour day for waiters, a twelve-hour day for cooks, optional display by restaurants of the union card, and arbitration of disputes arising under the agreement. The contract named Mayor Eugene Schmitz as arbitrator. Schmitz, whose influence as a mediator had helped bring the parties into the agreement, had evidently impressed the em-

* The Machinists' Union complained sporadically through 1902 that the Union Iron Works and other large firms were importing skilled men from the East and harassing union members with discriminatory layoffs and other tactics. But the machinists, who admitted losing a third of their members in the 1901–1902 strike, nevertheless rebuilt their union in 1902–1903 to a claimed membership of more than 1,500. (*Labor Clarion,* 1902 *passim;* Jan. 8, 1904.)

ployers as impartial. Covering most of the city's major restaurants, this contract established an industry-wide pattern and represented a major union achievement. It did not, however, end labor conflict in the restaurant industry. The culinary unions continued to meet resistance from a minority of the principal restaurants. Concentrating their efforts on one or two hostile employers at a time, the unions engaged in an almost continual series of disputes with individual restaurants. As pickets they employed sandwich men wearing boards emblazoned with the warning "Unfair!" In 1903 prolonged picketing and boycotts forced union conditions upon several large restaurants.[24]

Other provision trades unions came to terms with employers in 1902–1903. In mid-1902, after a year of strained relations, the Bakers' Union reopened negotiations with the organized bakery owners. The two local associations of master bakers soon agreed to establish new minimum weekly wage rates and to continue the prevailing sixty-three-hour week. In 1903 the employers acceded to union demands for a sixty-hour week and freedom for all workers to choose their own living quarters instead of boarding at their employers' establishments, a long-standing practice in this industry. The Bakery Drivers' Union, late in 1902, also won union-shop conditions and an increase to $16 in the minimum weekly wage for a sixty-hour week. By these agreements, the bakers and bakery drivers established a lasting and almost industry-wide relationship with the two master bakers' associations. They thus approached the post-1902 conditions in the brewing industry, where contracts between employer associations and unions covered virtually every brewery and beer-bottling establishment in San Francisco and Oakland. But there was still a wide differential, for the brewers and the bottlers had won the eight-hour day in 1901, and journeymen brewers earned $20 a week, one of the highest union wage scales prevailing outside the building trades.[25]

The Butchers' Union regained its strength more slowly. Through 1902 it reported a gradual, steady increase in the number of unionized retail meat markets, though threats of withdrawal of supplies by wholesalers still prevented the markets from displaying union cards. By the spring of 1903 the list of unionized meat markets had grown to approximately 175, and the Butchers'

Union had signed contracts with several large sausage-making firms. Later in the year it coöperated with the Oakland Butchers' Union in organizing the cattle and sheep butchers employed in slaughterhouses on both sides of the Bay. A negotiated agreement reached in November, 1903, included all San Francisco slaughterhouses except Miller & Lux. In the fall of 1903 the union felt strong enough to demand an increase in wages from retail meat markets. By the end of the year, despite substantial resistance, the Butchers' Union claimed that a large majority of the markets had accepted the new scale.[26]

A significant feature of the San Francisco labor scene in the early 1900's was the development of central councils to facilitate consultation and coöperation among closely related unions. This was a noteworthy step toward the industry-wide unity of action advocated by proponents of industrial unionism. In addition to the Allied Printing Trades Council and the Iron Trades Council, there arose such new organizations as the Allied Provision Trades Council, the Joint Council of Team Drivers, the District Council of Retail Clerks, and the Packing Trades Council.[27] These councils established closer liaison between San Francisco unions and other Bay Area unions in their respective industries, and assisted the joint pursuit of boycotts and other economic action against recalcitrant employers. In the provision trades, for example, the Milkdrivers' Union sometimes threatened to cut off milk deliveries to nonunion restaurants, or the Bakers' Union occasionally refused to bake with nonunion milk.

Unions among Factory and Noncraft Workers

A distinctive aspect of San Francisco unionism was its inclusion of large numbers of unskilled and semiskilled workers, whose bargaining power was inherently weaker than that of recognized crafts, and whose organizations were aided and protected by the well-established unions. On the whole, the newly formed San Francisco unions of noncraft workers enjoyed good relations with employers during 1902–1903. Many of them recorded gains in wages and hours. Some won explicit recognition and agreements; others achieved passive acceptance by employers and informal acknowledgment of their existence. Few found their efforts completely ineffective.

An outstanding example of successful organization among the comparatively unskilled was the union of San Francisco steam laundry workers. This predominantly women's union improved the position it had established for itself in 1900–1901. In the spring of 1902 it negotiated with the organized employers an agreement providing the ten-hour day, a union shop, and wage increases for some categories of workers. The agreement covered virtually all its 1,500 to 2,000 members. The union was one of the largest in San Francisco and by far the largest organization of laundry workers in the nation. In 1903, after a threatened strike, it won a new contract providing a nine-hour day but not the wage increase demanded. A new union of laundry drivers also reached agreement with employers during 1902–1903. From the early 1900's on, these two unions of drivers and inside workers maintained a generally cordial bargaining relationship with the local laundry employers' associations. The mutual interest of steam laundry owners and their employees in fighting the competitive threat of Chinese and Japanese hand laundries was a major incentive toward the maintenance of their relationship. By contrast, an AFL federal union of dry-cleaning plant employees, formed in 1903, was unable to duplicate the success of the laundry workers. After reaching informal agreements with several dry-cleaning firms, it encountered inflexible opposition from the firm of F. Thomas Parisian, the largest local employer. The union could not maintain its foothold, and dissolved not long afterward.[28]

The industrially organized gas workers amicably negotiated terms with public utilities on both sides of the Bay. In September, 1902, John A. Britton, president of the Oakland Gas, Light & Heat Company, met with East Bay union representatives and accepted their proposed schedule of wages, ranging from $2 to more than $3 per day for different classes of workers. Britton confirmed his acceptance in a warm letter. "I need hardly tell you," he wrote, "that I am in sympathy with the efforts of the laboring classes to obtain just return for services rendered. . . . I will be at all times ready and willing to listen to any plea of the men in my employ. . . ."[29] The San Francisco union, early in 1903, won the four local gas plants to an agreement providing a nine-hour day and a minimum wage of $2.25 for its least skilled members. By 1903 Bay Area gas workers had thus followed the skilled linemen of the International Brotherhood of Electrical Workers in achieving collective bargaining in the public utility industry. The IBEW linemen, by then, had negotiated a wage of $3.50 for the eight-hour day and could claim almost industry-wide union-shop conditions in San Francisco and the East Bay.[30]

A marked shift in employer attitudes assisted the San Francisco local of the United Garment Workers, consisting almost entirely of women employed in work-clothing factories, to recover from the demoralization brought on it in 1901 by the Employers' Association. In 1902, after a long boycott, a number of Bay Area work-clothing manufacturers decided that their products would sell more readily to workingmen if they bore the UGW union label. In March the large firm of Heynemann & Company requested permission to use the label, and in return signed a contract assuring union-shop conditions. In quick succession several other firms followed suit. In April the *Labor Clarion* announced "great rejoicing among the union men of San Francisco" upon the union's signing of its first agreement with the firm of Neustadter Brothers, one of the largest clothing factories west of St. Louis. Neustadter instructed its more than 500 workers to join the union and reportedly paid their initiation fees as a gesture of good will. Neustadter's action was especially symbolic of the post-1901 shift toward employer acceptance of unionism. The firm had earlier been a leading supporter of the Employers' Association, and its about-face was hailed as signaling an early death for that organization. By the end of 1903 the Garment Workers' Union had contracts covering most Bay Area work-clothing factories, although it proved unable to organize the firm of Levi Strauss. This firm held out for years against boycotts, successfully marketing its overalls, "levis," and other products. The unionized firms, however, did not find their new collective bargaining relationship uncomfortable, for the union made few demands and did not attempt to advance wages to a level threatening the San Francisco manufacturers' competitive cost position.[31]

Union-employer relationships were not equally peaceful in other clothing manufacturing industries. In the highly competitive ladies' garment industry the Cloakmakers' Union increased its membership in 1902–1903, largely by organizing women workers, and induced several cloak manufacturing shops to adopt the

ILGWU label. After sporadic disputes with individual shops, the union reached an agreement in October, 1903, covering about 300 members employed in a majority of the establishments. The employers, organized into the Cloak Manufacturers and Ladies' Tailors Protective Association, agreed to a union shop and a two-hour reduction in the workweek.[32] But the agreement did not end the mutual suspicion and petty disputes that had characterized labor relations in this industry since 1900. The agreement, in fact, was extremely short-lived.

A new union formed in 1902 among glove manufacturing workers soon included more than 400 members, most of them women, and reported that several firms had accepted its label. In March, 1903, it struck the member firms of the Glove Manufacturers' Association, charging that they had failed to put into effect a higher wage scale agreed upon in negotiations with union and Labor Council representatives. With financial support from Labor Council unions, the Glove Workers' Union maintained picket lines for almost two months, while the association refused all negotiations. The intervention of Mayor Schmitz as a mediator helped end the dispute, in May, with a compromise settlement. The strike reduced union membership and strength in several firms, however, and the union was unable to enforce the terms of settlement in these establishments.[33]

The early 1900's were years of temporary union success and comparative peace in the local shoe manufacturing industry. Several brief strikes occurred in 1902–1903 at individual firms, but the only major conflict came in November, 1902, when approximately 200 workers, a third of them women, struck the Buckingham & Hecht factory for a wage increase and reinstatement of a discharged union member. Within two weeks the firm granted the strikers' demands and agreed to use the union label. As with work-clothing manufacturers, the label proved a potent force in bringing the shoe industry employers to readier acceptance of the union. At the end of 1902 the Shoemakers' Union reported use of its label by every manufacturer in San Francisco. In the spring of 1903 the manufacturers agreed to a formal wage arbitration, which awarded an industry-wide 10 per cent wage increase to the highly skilled shoe cutters, organized into a separate local.[34]

Employers in other manufacturing industries faced demands

from relatively unskilled workers, most of them organized in AFL federal unions. The Boxmakers' Union, through brief strikes in 1902 and 1903, won a higher minimum daily wage for its more than 400 members, over protests by employers that they would be unable to meet the competition of Pacific Northwest wooden box manufacturers. Employers offered little resistance to a brief 1902 strike of the new Paper Box Workers' Union and quickly conceded a higher piece-rate scale to more than 200 strikers, most of them women. The Sugar Workers' Union, within a few weeks after its formation late in 1902, brought more than 400 workers out on strike at the Western Sugar Refinery, in protest against the alleged discharge of dozens of union members. John D. Spreckels, head of the firm, denied any policy of anti-union discrimination and settled the dispute almost immediately. He called back laid-off workers, negotiated an increase in wages, and established an amicable bargaining relationship with the union.[35] Other manufacturing unions that engaged in strikes in 1902–1903, with a mixture of success and failure, included the unions of Capmakers, Tannery Workers, Soap Workers, Can Makers, Wire Workers, Burlap and Cotton Bag Workers, Leather Workers, and Wool Sorters. Most of the strikes were brief ones called in support of wage and hour demands and settled by informal negotiations. In the briefer disputes, strikers usually won concessions ranging from the merely nominal to virtually their full demands. In the few prolonged conflicts, however, unions found that determined employers could be formidable opponents.

The Northern California Tannery Strike

The Bay Area's longest and costliest 1902 strike indicated that organized employers with substantial financial resources still enjoyed a telling advantage over even well-supported unions. In the summer of 1902 northern California unions of tannery workers demanded a minimum daily wage of $2 and a reduction from ten to nine hours in the workday. A number of tanneries offered to grant the demands on the condition that two large local firms be persuaded to accept. Although these two firms—Kullman, Salz & Company, and Frank Brothers—joined with other members of the California Tanners' Association in a conference with union representatives, no agreement was reached. Consequently, on August 1, approximately 700 tannery workers walked out on strike in San Francisco and in other towns near the Bay. Several of the smaller San Francisco tanneries, employing about 100 workers, immediately conceded the demands, but for the rest of the strikers the contest continued until the end of the year. The California Tanners' Association made no offer of acceptable terms, and by late September labor spokesmen were describing the struggle as a "fight to the finish." The San Francisco Labor Council collected almost $20,000 from Bay Area unions for the striking tanners, and persuaded the AFL to place the tanneries on its unfair list. Eastern unions of shoe workers and other leather workers promised to support a nationwide secondary boycott against them.[36]

Although the strike was well financed and well organized, it failed to break down the resistance of employers, who imported strikebreakers from the East and thus kept their tanneries in production despite heavy picketing. At Benicia, a small community on the northeastern reaches of the Bay, the firm of Kullman, Salz & Company brought in large numbers of Greek workers, housed them in its tannery under armed guards, and obtained a drastic court injunction which temporarily cleared the streets of pickets. Feeling was sharply intensified on December 14, 1902, when a Benicia citizen, uninvolved in the strike, was shot to death in a flurry of random gunfire by allegedly drunken strikebreakers. Disregarding demands from Benicia officials and citizens for immediate expulsion of the strikebreakers, Kullman, Salz maintained production and by the spring of 1903 had defeated the strike. In San Francisco, and at the Frank Brothers tannery in Redwood City, a few miles down the Peninsula, the strike was called off in January, 1903, after employers agreed to establish a 9½-hour day. Nevertheless, the strike was essentially a union defeat. The local at Redwood City soon dissolved, and the tannery workers in San Francisco did not again offer a determined challenge to their employers.[37]

The United Railroads and the Streetcar Employees

In 1901 a new union had been furtively organized among San Francisco streetcar men, who were described by union leaders, with little exaggeration, as having long worked in "abject servility" under a "perfect system of espionage." [38] When E. P. Vining, manager of the Market Street Railway, heard about the new organization, he ordered temporary layoffs of several of its leaders, including its president, Richard Cornelius. Organizing continued, however, despite additional layoffs of union members. Early in 1902 an Eastern syndicate purchased control of the Market Street Railway and merged it into a new subsidiary, the United Railroads Company of San Francisco.[39] The United Railroads retained Vining as general manager and inherited his feud with the Carmen's Union.

As discharges of union members continued in the spring of 1902, pressure for a strike grew stronger. Although the union had organized only a minority of the carmen, it was eager for militant action. Labor Council leaders were increasingly apprehensive that the street railway dispute might become "another sanguinary labor contest." They saw no hope for a successful strike and made an anxious effort to persuade the union to postpone action. In mid-April Mayor Schmitz joined in this effort. He tried unsuccessfully to induce Vining to meet with Cornelius and other union leaders, who had demanded the reinstatement of thirty-five union members and a reduction in working hours from 11½ to 10 per day.[40] With Vining still refusing negotiations, the union discarded the Labor Council's waiting policy. At 6:30 P.M. on Saturday night, April 19, with no prior warning, its members abandoned their cars in the downtown business district, blocking the tracks and effectively tying up traffic. Nonunion carmen joined enthusiastically in this surprise strike. As the astonished Walter Macarthur described it, "it appears that the street carmen's idea was to strike, and organize afterward. This is just what they did . . . in open defiance of all the rules." [41] More than 2,000 United Railroads employees were soon off the job, as the strike spread contagiously to "paralyze a corporation previously esteemed impregnable." [42]

Vining initially attempted to meet the strike head on, thereby giving Mayor Schmitz his first opportunity to become the hero of San Francisco labor. When Vining began hiring special police from the Curtin Detective Agency to ride as armed guards on the cars, Schmitz refused the guards permits to carry weapons. Deprived of special police protection, the United Railroads also faced a hostile public. This strike was almost unique among major San Francisco labor conflicts in receiving solid support from the daily newspapers. They expressed the public's sympathy with the demands of the streetcar men, who had for years worked long hours under conditions of exceptional nervous and physical strain. This public sympathy, shared indeed by most local employers, was a major force in bringing the strikers an early victory. Acting on instructions from his company's Eastern headquarters, Vining negotiated terms which the union accepted on April 26, only one week after the strike began. Although the union had not won formal recognition, it had achieved a signed agreement pledging no discrimination against its members and obligating management to meet with union grievance committees. The United Railroads also agreed to reduce the workday to ten hours within a fourteen-hour period, to maintain the daily wage of $2.50, and to rehire discharged union members.[43] Immediately after the strike the company discharged Vining as manager, apparently with the intention to begin a new phase of harmonious relations with its employees.

The Building Trades

As organization continued to spread among San Francisco workers in the early 1900's, the Building Trades Council maintained its preponderance of power over the less centrally organized employers. Its 1901 constitution announced that "the Building Trades Council controls the building industry from the foundation to the roof, inclusive, and [in a warning to the Labor Council] it will tolerate no interference from any miscellaneous central body or organization." [44] From the early 1900's to the 1920's there was little change in the council's position, despite sporadic efforts to weld employers into an effective united front.

In the fall of 1902 fourteen specialty trades employers' associations formed the Affiliated Building Contractors, a central association intended to serve as a counterpart of the Building Trades Council. The new association, however, neither established a bargaining relationship with the council nor rallied general support behind various specialty contractors' groups faced with union demands, and by mid-1903 it was defunct. Resistance to union demands was left to individual employers' associations, each of which dealt singly with its labor problems. Thus isolated, these employer groups could do little to prevent unilateral establishment by unions of new wage scales or other conditions. The only battle fought by a specialty contractors' association in 1902–1903 ended in union victory. The Master Masons' Association, after a lockout-strike lasting seven weeks early in 1903, granted the increased wage scale of $6 per day demanded by the Bricklayers' Union. The union, in return, promised that its members would help to control competition by working only for "legitimate" master masons.[45]

Building contractors, protected from outside competition and able to pass increased costs on to their customers, were not powerfully motivated to form a central employers' organization. Nor did the Building Trades Council, under P. H. McCarthy's leadership, provoke them to such action, though it did on occasion humble them. For example, for a short time in the early 1900's the council imposed fines upon firms charged with violating union rules. McCarthy also spurned employer demands for formal contracts for specific periods of time, for he saw no reason for the unions to bind themselves to observe negotiated terms of employment until a distant contract expiration date. In addition, McCarthy ruled that council officers would discuss labor issues only with individual specialty employer associations, and would not negotiate with a central employers' organization.[46]

Employers, nevertheless, enjoyed certain advantages from McCarthy's control over the building trades unions. Although opposed to termination dates for contracts, the Building Trades Council did require each union to give employers ninety days' notice of intention to change working conditions. Furthermore, it stood ready to confer with employers who raised objections. If convinced of the undesirability of a proposed change, the council urged the union to withdraw its demands. In McCarthy employers found a single, reliable seat of union authority and a conservative leader considerably more palatable to them than officers of individual unions. As several contractors expressed it in early 1904, they preferred to deal with one "big boss" rather than with "a hundred walking delegates." The council's authority over its affiliated unions also enabled it to resolve jurisdictional disputes, which particularly plagued the building industry. Under Mc-Carthy's regime such disputes caused fewer strikes in San Francisco than in any other major city in the nation.[47] McCarthy used his power swiftly and drastically against unions that flouted the council's jurisdictional decisions.[*]

San Francisco building trades employers, by comparison with those in most large cities, also faced fewer strikes for economic gains, partly because of their reluctance to engage in an uneven battle with strong unions, but also because of the council's domination of its affiliates. Under McCarthy's leadership the council adjusted all disputes involving more than one trade or more than one construction job. In such disputes no union could strike without council sanction. In 1904, moreover, the council ruled that no business agent elected by a member union could hold office without its approval.[48] It thus reserved the position of business agent in member unions for men of demonstrable loyalty to McCarthy, and kept out individuals not conforming to the "business-unionist" mold. Through its centralized power the council was able to keep union demands within limits tolerable to employers. As the turn-of-the-century boom died away, in 1903, the council gave a demonstration of its conservative wage policy. In terms calculated to aggravate Labor Council leaders, it announced that the "Building Trades Council, acting as the safety brake on the local labor movement, . . . will absolutely refuse to sanction . . ." any further increase in wages until warranted by improved business conditions.[49] This decision was generally enforced, although the sheet metal workers defied council expulsion later that year,

---

[*] An outstanding example of McCarthy's methods occurred in the winter of 1913–14, when the Plasterers' Union went on a city-wide strike in protest against the Building Trades Council's award to the carpenters of certain work on a major construction project. The council promptly voted to expel the plasterers, and McCarthy, in alliance with the General Contractors' Association, formed a new union composed largely of plasterers imported into San Francisco. The Contractors' Association instructed its members to cancel their contracts with any firms in the Master Plasterers' Association, which refused to hire exclusively through McCarthy's new union. Under the joint pressure of council and employers, the striking Plasterers' Union shortly abandoned its jurisdictional claim, made its peace with the council, and returned to work. (*Daily News*, Dec. 18, 19, 24, 1913; Frederick L. Ryan, *Industrial Relations in the San Francisco Building Trades* [Norman: University of Oklahoma Press, 1936], p. 73.)

won a brief strike raising their wage rate to $4.50 per day, and then gained readmittance to the council.[50]

The chief challenge to McCarthy's authority in the early 1900's came from several locals of the Carpenters' Union, which retained affiliation with the Labor Council and braved the consequences of expulsion from the Building Trades Council. They maintained their membership and morale in the face of recurrent attempts by the McCarthy regime to drive their members out of the local construction industry. In 1904 the council readmitted the carpenters' locals despite their continued membership in the Labor Council. Weaker unions and individual workers who defied McCarthy's leadership were less fortunate. Withdrawal of the Building Trades Council working card was a harsh punishment readily available for the discipline of rebellious workers, and more than a few men, after incurring the council's displeasure, found themselves forced to leave San Francisco to find work at their crafts.[51]

San Francisco: "Closed-Shop City"

Its vigorous union movement of the early 1900's soon brought San Francisco nationwide attention as the leading stronghold of organized labor. The National Association of Manufacturers and other employer groups described San Francisco as a city where employers spinelessly accepted dictation from union leaders and lived under a labor government. Embarrassed local businessmen felt called upon to apologize for their city or to tender hopeful assurances that union power would soon be curtailed. Journalists described the San Francisco labor and political situation in the pages of nationally circulated magazines. Conditions in San Francisco were denounced as frightening new investment away from the city and forcing already established firms to seek a less hostile environment. In the 1903 mayoralty campaign local business interests, joined by Building Trades Council leaders, charged that continuance of the Union Labor Party administration would block the city's growth. The journal of the National Association of Manufacturers proclaimed that investors were unwilling to undertake industrial construction projects in San Francisco because of the high wage levels, and that the Union Iron Works had recently lost a government contract worth several million dollars because of the fear that labor disputes would delay completion.

A leading journalist of the muckraking school described San Francisco as virtually closed to workers without union cards, its sidewalks as encumbered with union pickets and sandwich men, and its police court judges as summarily dismissing cases of unionists arrested for violence in labor disputes, and he warned that employers would soon revolt against the intolerable union domination.[52]

San Francisco labor leaders tried to counteract this picture of their city. "It may be confessed," wrote Walter Macarthur in 1904, "that the sandwichman is not beautiful to look upon, neither are the tones in which he hails the passers-by grateful to ears attuned to sweet sounds." [53] He noted, however, that at any given time "the sandwichman represents but two or three unions out of some two hundred unions" in San Francisco. In 1903 Labor Council spokesmen denied a story that unionism was so widespread that even the sandwich men hired for picket duty had formed a union and walked out in a strike that doubled their wages. Union leaders pointed out that almost every illustration of union domination was drawn from the building industry. Complaints of union dictatorship, moreover, came less from the employers in that industry than from outside observers. Union leaders argued that the conservative San Francisco labor movement represented no threat to the city's peace or prosperity. They did not, however, object to the description of San Francisco as a "closed-shop city." In May, 1903, the *Labor Clarion* reported that the task of organization was virtually complete, among unskilled as well as skilled workers.[54]

San Francisco had indeed experienced a prodigious union growth since the mid-1890's. Yet organized labor was by no means solidly entrenched throughout the local economy. White-collar workers in banks, insurance companies, and other offices were untouched by unionism. Although many of the clerks in specialty shoe stores, drugstores, the smaller clothing stores, and a few grocery stores were organized, their unions were largely concerned with closing hours. Among the employees of such large department stores as the Emporium, however, unionism had won a foothold only among the retail delivery drivers. No significant degree of organization existed among janitors, elevator operators, chambermaids, and other building service employees. Dry-cleaning industry workers were largely unorganized. No strong union was active in warehousing, a key sector of the San Francisco economy. In the communications industry, electrical linemen's unions had attained strength despite employer opposition, but effective organizations had not developed among telegraphers and telephone operators. Unionism had not spread to the seasonal workers employed by fruit and vegetable canneries. Unions of production workers had sprung up in many local manufacturing industries, but their ability to survive in times of economic depression was doubtful. Workers were still unorganized in many manufacturing establishments, and even unions that had been successfully established did not yet approach full organization. Such leading firms as Levi Strauss and Gantner & Mattern in the garment industries remained nonunion; the culinary unions had to contend with unorganized hotels and restaurants; and unions like those of butchers, glovemakers, and stablemen met stubborn resistance in their campaigns to organize their jurisdictions. In the metal trades industry the skilled craft unions were well established, but newer organizations of machine hands and journeymen's helpers were still striving to build up their memberships and attain bargaining power. Even in the building trades, the Union Lumber Company's adherence to the open shop in its San Francisco planing mill demonstrated the possibility of defying the most impressive aggregation of union power in the city.

San Francisco was thus far from completely unionized, and even further from the status of a closed-shop city. But the term remained a popular stereotype, and the concept was strengthened by the reëlection of Mayor Schmitz in 1903 despite charges that he and Abe Ruef were running "a government of graft, for graft, by grafters," [55] and despite the Building Trades Council opposition organized by P. H. McCarthy, who was now a Republican. Schmitz's protection of the United Railroads strikers in 1902 and his mediation of several labor disputes helped him to retain the labor vote, as did also a newspaper campaign which portrayed the election as a struggle between capital and labor and called upon all responsible citizens to rid San Francisco of its union government. Although outsiders feared that San Francisco was in the grip of a radical labor government, knowledgeable men with a closer view of the city's political scene felt no such apprehension. The Union Labor Party won only two of the eighteen seats on the Board of Supervisors,[56] and in 1904 James D. Phelan, the former mayor, amusedly reminded a large Merchants' Association audience that fears of Schmitz's radicalism could be dismissed:

> Once upon a time there was an election, the result of which affrighted the conservative businessmen . . . who were greatly alarmed, lest it be anarchistic, until the banner of the administration was unfurled, and then what seemed at first to be the red flag of anarchy turned out to be the red flag of the auctioneer.[57]

By 1903 the ULP was a conventional political machine controlled by Abe Ruef, Schmitz, and their associates. Many of these associates were heads of minor unions or were otherwise connected with the labor movement. The party, however, had alienated the prominent labor leaders who had enthusiastically supported it in 1901. They had been disillusioned by Ruef's domination of the party and by Schmitz's appointment of Ruef's cronies, rather than of genuine labor representatives, to boards and commissions. One of the few union men appointed was Mike Casey, who was named to head the Board of Public Works. The board was in charge of street construction and maintenance, and also ruled on applications for permits to build railroad spur tracks which minimized the dependence of business firms on drayage services. Casey was thus in a strategic position to watch over the mutual interests of employing draymen and union teamsters in the local hauling industry. Casey, nevertheless, soon rebelled against the control of the ULP by Ruef and his coterie, and before the 1903 campaign he and other labor leaders tried, unsuccessfully, to purge the party of its leadership. From 1902 on, many San Francisco officers were involved in politics. The trend alarmed Father Peter Yorke and other exponents of a united labor movement, who warned that political ambition would lead to neglect of union duties and would weaken organized labor by increasing factionalism.[58]

Organized Labor in the East Bay

The East Bay's wave of unionization in the early 1900's fell far short of that in San Francisco. In Oakland, Berkeley, and Alameda, with a combined population of almost 100,000 in 1900, total union membership, exclusive of the railroad brotherhoods, increased during 1899–1903 to approximately 5,000 to 7,000.[59] At least half of this membership was in the building trades unions. San Francisco, whose population was about 350,000 in 1900, was in sharp contrast, for its union membership grew to well above 40,000 in the same period.

Oakland and the smaller East Bay cities provided less fertile soil for union growth. A larger proportion of the working population was of the white-collar class, supplying a heavy flow of commuters to offices across the Bay. East Bay unions also lacked the favorable context of a heavily working-class community with long union traditions. Moreover, as the East Bay population was growing at a relatively faster rate than that of San Francisco, unions faced the problem—seen in a more acute form in Los Angeles—of organizing amidst a continuing influx of migrants, most of whom lacked previous union experience. East Bay unions, furthermore, dealt with local government officials less influenced by the labor vote. The Oakland Union Labor Party nominated a candidate for mayor in 1903, but was unable to elect him.[60]

By comparison with San Francisco, the East Bay labor movement lacked a large nucleus of veteran leaders, and the stimulus of successful campaigns by large and powerful unions. Bay Area industrial and commercial activity was chiefly concentrated in San Francisco, and the comparatively small industries of the East Bay did not employ large numbers of already organized workers who would help spread the contagion of unionism. The band-wagon effect and the principle of success begetting success were unable to operate as strongly among East Bay as among San Francisco workers. Small industries, moreover, posed a difficult organizing problem. Workers were less accessible to organizers because they were scattered in smaller groups throughout an industry and were personally closer to their employers. In some occupations and crafts there were too few workers to form unions large enough to maintain a full-time salaried officer and thus gain the benefits of continuous, experienced leadership. Because its affiliates were small, the Alameda County Central Labor Council lacked the funds to support a full-time staff and organizing and publicity activities comparable to those of the San Francisco Labor Council.[61] Nor could the Alameda County Council raise heavy financial contributions for unions involved in strikes or lockouts.

In some trades San Francisco unions assisted East Bay workers in organizing, led the way for improvements in wages and other conditions, and gave financial support in struggles with employers. Comparatively close liaison existed between San Francisco and East Bay unions of building tradesmen, printing tradesmen, metal tradesmen, teamsters, laundry workers, and butchers. The lack of rapid transportation facilities across the Bay, however, and the tendency of San Francisco labor leaders to concentrate on their own problems, prevented the spread into the East Bay of the surging force of unionization in San Francisco.

The disparity between the labor movements on opposite sides of the Bay was reflected in the amount of industrial conflict they experienced. The California Bureau of Labor Statistics recorded almost ninety strikes and lockouts in San Francisco in the 1902–1905 period. In the same period it listed only about a dozen in the East Bay, almost all quite brief and together involving only a fraction of the number of workers idled by the San Francisco disputes.[62] The absence of serious industrial conflict in the East Bay indicates not only a smaller number of organized workers, but also a lack of confidence in the ability to enforce demands by militant action.

The building trades and the printing trades were well organized in the East Bay in the early 1900's, and were generally successful in establishing union wage scales and conditions. The Oakland Typographical Union peacefully won a wage increase in the winter of 1902. A strike of several hundred carpenters in mid-1903 enforced a higher union scale.[63] There was also a substantial degree of organization among skilled metal tradesmen, teamsters, lumber longshoremen, laundry workers, streetcar employees, and workers in the culinary and provision trades, and most of their unions have survived continuously to the present. East Bay unions were typically smaller than their San Francisco counterparts, had organized their jurisdictions less thoroughly, and had entered into fewer contractual relationships with employers. Collective bargaining was less well established in the East Bay, where there had been no widespread development of employer associations. Most East Bay firms dealt individually with labor problems, and felt little need to band together to oppose powerful unions.

The early 1900's witnessed a limited spread of unionization among less skilled and factory workers in the East Bay. With aid from San Francisco, the Oakland Laundry Workers' Union built a membership of several hundred and established the nine-hour day in 1903. A new Stablemen's Union tried to organize Oakland stables in 1902–1903, but even with generous financial assistance from the San Francisco union made little progress against resisting employers. Retail clerks formed a small union which maintained a continuous, if unaggressive, existence. A weak, short-lived union was chartered in 1903 among the unskilled workers of Oakland's large California Cotton Mills factory, a plant that long resisted unionization. Another large plant that remained nonunion for years, the Standard Oil refinery at Point Richmond, experienced a minor encounter with organized labor in 1902. Bay Area unions of coopers demanded a boycott against Standard Oil when the firm ignored demands that its barrels be made under union conditions. At the small rolling mill of the Judson Manufacturing Company in Emeryville, a suburb of Oakland, more than 100 organized steelworkers struck in mid-1903, winning a partial limitation of a proposed wage cut.[64] New, small unions were active also among workers in East Bay wooden box plants, work-clothing factories, and potteries. Unions of unskilled and factory workers, however, contributed much less to the size and vigor of the labor movement than in San Francisco.

Increased Tension in 1903

San Francisco union-employer relations were comparatively peaceful in 1902, although occasional strikes, picketing, and boycotts reminded the community that a strong labor movement existed. In 1903 the level of industrial conflict rose, partly because the economic environment changed. For several years the steady rise in prices had stimulated workers to organize to win higher wages, and had lessened employer resistance to wage increases. By the end of 1902, however, prices had leveled off, and the turn-of-the-century boom had given way to a slight recession. The Building Trades Council recognized this change in its May, 1903, attempt to impose a moratorium on wage demands. Employers were less yielding to upward pressures on their operating costs, as a number of San Francisco unions discovered.

Another factor that influenced employer attitudes in 1903 was the emergence of nationwide antiunion campaigns. Previously groups like the National Metal Trades Association had fought organized labor in their respective industries, but there had been no effort to rally employers throughout American industry behind an open-shop program. In the spring of 1903 the National Association of Manufacturers took its first strong public stand on the labor question by firmly condemning the "closed shop." David M. Parry, the NAM's president, became the guiding spirit of the resulting open-shop movement which soon spread from the East to California. Parry brought a missionary zeal to the movement and helped supply it with a rationale that made adherence to the open shop an almost religious principle for a large proportion of American employers. The NAM's membership grew rapidly in 1903 and the years immediately following, as employers eagerly responded to the call for resistance to the rising unionism of the early 1900's. Concurrently, the vigorous growth of the AFL gave way after 1904 to virtual stagnation, a change attributed in large part to the open-shop movement.[65]

In October, 1903, Parry formed the Citizens' Industrial Association to organize employers across the nation into local open-shop groups. By that time branches of a loosely coördinated open-shop organization, with the innocuous title of Citizens' Alliance, existed in many cities.[66] Although a branch of the Citizens' Alliance appeared in San Francisco in the winter of 1903–04, until late in 1903 San Francisco workers were not apprehensive about the national open-shop movement. Most of the industrial conflicts of the year stemmed from economic issues, rather than from employers' refusals to deal with labor organizations.

The 1903 dispute that most alarmed the public came early in the year and did not reach the point of open conflict. In March, 1903, as the 1902 agreement between the United Railroads and the Street Carmen's Union neared expiration, the union demanded the nine-hour day, a wage increase to $3 per day, and the union shop. By then relations between the United Railroads and its employers had become strained. Fearing the systematic replacement of union by nonunion men, Richard Cornelius and other leaders charged that the company had begun hiring an unwarranted number of new trainees. This intensified their insistence on a full union-shop contract, which the United Railroads refused to concede. For several weeks San Franciscans feared a violent conflict, as the carmen threatened to strike and the company stocked its carbarns with food and cots in preparation for housing strikebreakers. The Labor Council urged the union to confine its demands to "clear-cut issues of wages and hours," warning that the public would not sympathize with a strike for the union shop. Finally the United Railroads offered to arbitrate all issues but management's right to hire and fire without union restriction, and the carmen reluctantly agreed.[67]

The arbitration proceedings were of unusual length, formality, and expense for this early period. Both parties retained legal counsel and called witnesses to give expert testimony concerning the increased cost of living upon which the carmen based their wage demands. William D. Mahon, national president of the Amalgamated Association of Street Railway Employees; Patrick Calhoun, president of the United Railroads; and Oscar Straus, a prominent figure in the National Civic Federation, constituted the arbitration board. As all three were located in the East, transcripts of San Francisco hearings were forwarded to New York City, where the board held additional direct hearings. In November, 1903, the board's award finally arrived in San Francisco. It provided a grievance procedure and awarded a compromise retroactive wage increase, but left unchanged the carmen's grueling workday of ten hours within a fourteen-hour period.[68] The union protested the award, and soon made plans to renew its demands in the spring of 1904.

In the middle of the year a series of sharp conflicts involved unskilled factory workers employed by branch plants of Eastern firms. In May the Wire Workers' Union demanded the nine-hour day from the local plant of the American Steel & Wire Company. Known as the "Wire Trust," this company maintained the ten-hour day in its numerous plants throughout the country. Its reaction to the demand for shorter hours was to shut down the San Francisco plant on May 23, locking out almost 150 men. A week later the Can Makers' Union also struck for the nine-hour day, calling out more than 1,000 employees, included several hundred women, of the American Can Company—the "Can Trust." The strike paralyzed the company's operations at the height of the canning season. On June 8 about 200 members of the Bag Workers' Union, most of them women, struck for a 10 per cent wage increase at three bag manufacturing plants. The local plant of the Gulf Bag Company, an Eastern firm, took the lead in resisting this strike and won a federal court injunction against picketing.[69]

The results of these conflicts were, in the main, disappointing to the unions. Several of the contests illustrated the difficulty of successfully challenging employers of substantial size who were intent upon resisting demands and who had the financial strength to weather temporary shutdowns and recruit strikebreakers. Despite intensive picketing, the American Steel & Wire Company reopened its gates within a month, restoring production with imported strikebreakers housed inside the plant. The Wire Workers' Union was virtually destroyed by the ensuing months of futile struggle; early in 1904 the Machinists' Union, whose members had also been locked out by the Wire Trust, wrote the conflict off as a loss. The Can Makers' Union was more fortunate in its dispute with the Can Trust. Anxious to resume operations before the canning season ended, the American Can Company yielded to Labor Council persuasion and reached agreement with the union. It promised to institute the nine-hour day in January, 1904, and not to discriminate against union members, but it gave no other guarantee of union security. By early 1904 tension had again risen over the continued hiring of nonunion workers. The Bag Workers' Union, after two months of striking, claimed a compromise wage settlement with one of the firms involved in the dispute, but won no concessions from the other two. Although the union survived the strike, it disappeared within a few years.[70]

On June 23 several hundred electrical linemen in San Francisco struck against the Pacific States Telephone & Telegraph Company as part of a system-wide strike covering five Western states. The linemen's strike had a dual purpose: first, to support southern California linemen who had struck early in May, 1903, and, second, to win from the Pacific States Telephone & Telegraph Company the wages and conditions previously gained by electrical linemen from almost all public utilities in the Bay Area. In June the Western Conference formed by linemen's unions of the Pacific States system demanded a system-wide contract embodying a union shop, apprenticeship regulations, and wages of $3.50 for an eight-hour day. When these demands were rejected after brief negotiations, the Western Conference ordered a strike of telephone linemen throughout five states. John J. Sabin, president of Pacific States, refused to offer any proposal for settlement or to negotiate. From late June to early October the struggle continued in an atmosphere of bitter animosity. The strikers derided their antagonist as "nothing-to-say Sabin." The company was flooded with requests to remove its telephones from union offices and the homes of union members. In San Francisco the Hackmen's Union voted to cease patronizing any saloon, restaurant, or store with a telephone on its premises. Other unions warned that members using telephones would be fined. The Labor Council called for municipal ownership of the telephone system. Mayor Schmitz tried repeatedly to induce Sabin to meet union representatives, and the city administration rejected the company's request that its strikebreakers be given permits to carry concealed weapons for self-protection.[71]

The striking linemen in San Francisco maintained high morale. The Labor Council supported them financially, hoping to prevent their defeat by the Western subsidiary of the antiunion Bell Telephone System. Victory for the telephone company, it was argued, would show other employers that striking unions could be starved into submission. In August, 1903, Sabin, who had relaxed his opposition to negotiation, offered to meet with a committee of San Francisco linemen to reach a settlement for that city alone. But the linemen, who insisted on a system-wide contract, refused the offer, and it was not until October that the dispute was ended through the intervention of F. J. McNulty, national president of the International Brotherhood of Electrical Workers. Neither party revealed the terms of the settlement, but the strike was called off throughout the system. By November, according to IBEW leaders, all striking linemen had been reinstated and the telephone company was amicably observing the agreement.[72] The strike, although not establishing a settled, system-wide bargaining relationship between the IBEW and Pacific States Telephone &

Telegraph, at least brought tacit recognition to local linemen's unions where, as in San Francisco, they remained strong.

In mid-November, 1903, several hundred members of the Paper Box Workers' Union, chiefly composed of women, struck for higher wages at eight plants. In 1902 the union had easily won a wage increase by striking, but now employer resistance had hardened. Within two weeks the strike was called off, having failed to achieve its goal. The union claimed a satisfactory settlement, but this strike was its last militant effort to force concessions from paper box manufacturers.[73]

Renewed Open-Shop Campaign

Local labor leaders had been aware through 1903 of the nationwide growth of open-shop sentiment among employers. During the summer they had raised funds for San Jose unionists engaged in conflict with a recently formed branch of the Citizens' Alliance. The first aggressive employer action in San Francisco, however, came on November 23, 1903, when five cloak manufacturers locked out approximately 100 members of the ILGWU Cloakmakers' Union. Members of the Cloak Manufacturers' Association had agreed a month earlier to a two-hour reduction of working hours on Saturday, but had soon begun to chafe under the agreement. When the union refused to alter the terms, the cloak manufacturers announced a one-hour increase, without compensation, in the Saturday workday. Workers defied this notice, and the lockout began. Within a few days eight firms, employing several hundred men and women, were shut down. At this point Morris Siminoff, a leading antiunion cloak manufacturer, returned to San Francisco from New York City, bringing with him strikebreakers recruited in the East. Since mid-October about fifty union members, one-third of Siminoff's working force, had been on strike in an effort to establish union conditions. Union spokesmen alleged that Siminoff, while in New York, had consulted David M. Parry, leader of the national open-shop movement, and had instigated the local lockout in order to substitute the Eastern piece-rate wage system for the daily wage system prevailing in San Francisco.[74]

On December 7 more than 600 culinary workers were locked out by members of the Restaurant Keepers' Association. In October the association had formally notified the culinary unions that it was nullifying, effective immediately, the union-shop clause in the restaurant industry master contract due to expire in January, 1904, and in November it refused to enter negotiations for contract renewal. The culinary unions then began signing restaurants individually to one-year extensions of the contract, asking no change in terms of employment. On Friday, December 4, the culinary workers struck against a restaurant that had refused to renew the agreement. The association immediately announced a lockout by all members, to become effective on Monday, December 7, if the strikers had not returned. Over the week end the association rejected union requests for negotiations, and on Monday the threatened lockout commenced. Almost forty of the seventy restaurants in the association closed down.[75]

The labor disputes in the cloak manufacturing and restaurant industries led San Francisco's conservative weekly, the *Argonaut*, to comment: "It begins to look as if the long-rumored determination of the employers in this city to stoutly resist all union demands might bear fruit." [76] At the same time there were reports of efforts, half-veiled by an atmosphere of secrecy, to create a local branch of the Citizens' Alliance. According to statements leaked by its promoters, the new open-shop organization was rapidly enrolling hundreds of San Francisco employers and was amassing a fund of $500,000 for a battle against organized labor.[77] The nationwide open-shop campaign had reached San Francisco.

A branch of the Citizens' Alliance was indeed forming, and preparing for conflict with local unions. The lockout by the Restaurant Keepers' Association, however, proved to be an inadequately organized and premature fight for the open shop. From the outset the association members failed to hold together. Within a few days more than half of the restaurants initially obeying the lockout order had reopened under union conditions. Other restaurants followed suit, and on December 14, one week after the lockout began, the association was ready to negotiate. A hasty truce brought the culinary workers back to their jobs. Then, late in December, the Restaurant Keepers' Association signed a new one-year master agreement * reducing daily working hours to nine

* The agreement did not, however, cover the large restaurant of Mathias Johnson, who had led the Restaurant Keepers' Association through the 1901

for waitresses and to ten within a fourteen-hour period for most waiters.[78]

In the cloak industry dispute, meanwhile, employers maintained their unity. The conflict continued unabated into 1904, amidst increasing rumors of a forthcoming open-shop offensive throughout San Francisco industry. The Cloak Manufacturers' Association, however, decided not to lead the way in such an offensive. In February, 1904, it signed an agreement ending the lockouts and strikes at all shops, including that of Morris Siminoff. The agreement apparently established the longer workweek demanded by the employers, in return for assurances that all workers hired during the dispute would be required to join the union and that the union shop would be maintained. But the contract did not allay union-employer hostility in this highly competitive industry. From the first week of their return to work, union cloakmakers complained that employers were violating the contract terms. By late spring the union was again picketing Siminoff's firm, charging that he had reinstituted piecework and had taken back only a few of the strikers. Later in 1904 the union called for boycotts against several other firms and protested that systematic harassment by employers was driving many of its members out of the industry.[79]

End of an Interlude

Though comparatively few San Francisco workers were involved in strikes and lockouts at the close of 1903, there was uneasiness over the possibility of major industrial conflict soon to come. The period 1902–1903 had begun in the wake of the open-shop battle of 1901, and it concluded amid signs of an impending new drive for the open shop. In the interim, however, the labor movement had expanded in scope and in strength. At the beginning of 1904

---

strike of culinary workers. As president of the association, Johnson struggled vainly to keep its members united in this 1903 battle for open-shop conditions. Refusing to accept defeat, he resigned from the association and continued for months to operate San Francisco's most widely publicized and heavily picketed open-shop restaurant. Behind its main window, Johnson piled a heap of gold coins and erected a sign defiantly proclaiming that he would fight on until the heap had vanished. (Interview with Andrew J. Gallagher; *Labor Clarion*, Dec. 18, 1903.)

it was in a much more secure position to meet an organized employer attack than it had been in 1901, when it was younger and untried.

For San Francisco labor the years 1902–1903 were among the most successful in its history before the 1930's. Despite organizing failures in some industries, the loss of a few significant strikes, and the death or arrested growth of a number of infant organizations, unionism on the whole moved forward over an extended front. It was a period when youthful exuberance ran high within labor ranks: new unions sprang into existence, leading union officials took their places among the best-known figures in San Francisco, the mayor was elected and reëlected under the banner of the Union Labor Party, and unionists derived great satisfaction from the portrayal of San Francisco as the nation's stronghold of labor power.

Yet the 1902–1903 period marked the culmination of the union resurgence that had begun to move with accelerating speed in 1899. Though the growth of unionism was still vigorous through most of the period, its pace had slackened considerably since 1901. And by 1904 the organizational advance was virtually at an end. Workers not caught up in the contagious union expansion of 1899–1903 proved difficult to organize in the less favorable years ahead. In this respect local and national labor developments were in close conformity; throughout the country union growth was giving way by 1904 to a relatively static condition that prevailed for some years. San Francisco unionism was exceptional in the extent to which it had pushed forward in the period since 1899, but it was not exempt from the loss of impetus affecting the American labor movement. Nor was it immune to the open-shop spirit now pervading the nation. The revival of antiunion militance had spread from the East to San Francisco by the beginning of 1904, and in the months ahead the local union movement shifted from the offensive to the defensive, intent upon holding the ground it had won rather than striving to make additional gains.

Chapter IV | *A New Open-Shop*
Offensive
1904–1905

IN THE YEARS 1904–1905 the center of the labor relations stage was held by the San Francisco Citizens' Alliance, the local protagonist of the nationwide open-shop movement. The emergence of a new, militantly antiunion organization posed these questions at the beginning of 1904: Was unionism well enough entrenched to beat back an employer offensive? Could the business community, after the experience of 1901, be rallied behind a determined battle for the open shop? Over the months ahead, a series of clashes in various industries would demonstrate whether or not the alliance would make any more progress toward suppressing unionism than had its predecessor, the Employers' Association. By contrast with the 1901 open-shop drive, however, that launched by the alliance brought only scattered and relatively small-scale engagements, and never reached a climax of violent conflict involving thousands of workers.

The economic setting in which the Citizens' Alliance challenged the local labor movement was, on the whole, a neutral one. Though business activity and employment were moderately healthy during most of 1904–1905, the rapid economic expansion that had nourished the turn-of-the-century organizational boom was lacking. Both prices and wages were generally stable, and economic conditions were neither favorable for the presentation of new union demands nor yet conducive to employer attempts to encroach upon the previous advances of workers.

The Citizens' Alliance crusade against unionism had several features of particular interest. It attracted attention far beyond San Francisco, for officials of the National Association of Manufacturers and other open-shop organizations hoped to see labor's Western stronghold overthrown. Instead of relying upon local leadership, the San Francisco Citizens' Alliance used imported professional antiunion organizers. For the first time, publicity campaigns and other promotional techniques were systematically and extensively utilized to stimulate open-shop fervor within the business community and the public at large. Moreover, the injunction was first brought into widespread use in San Francisco, as alliance lawyers resorted time and again to the courts for assistance in curbing union picketing and boycotting. Finally, the alliance pushed its battle against labor into the political arena, where it strove to wrest the city administration from the hands of the Union Labor Party. The San Francisco municipal election of 1905, consequently, was marked by a class conflict that helped create unaccustomed unity in labor ranks. The outcome of the 1905 election and its repercussions were, in fact, perhaps the most significant developments in local labor history for which the alliance appears to have been largely responsible.

The Citizens' Alliance

As the year 1904 opened, San Francisco union leadership took official notice of the Citizens' Alliance; the *Labor Clarion* informed its readers, as fully as possible, about the policies and intentions of the new organization. Labor leaders could only speculate about the potential power of the alliance, but they warned unions to build up their treasuries and to avoid making "radical demands." [1] Anticipating the possibility that small conflicts would spread into a general engagement, as in 1901, Labor Council spokesmen called upon unionists to abandon "the idea entertained by many men that a strike of the union . . . should be followed at once by sympathetic strikes of every organization . . . in any way associated." The *Labor Clarion* advised unions to prepare to deal more frequently with strong and perhaps hostile employer groups, rather than with isolated employers, and "to accept it as a settled fact that the immediate future will bring us face to face with the Organized Employer—he is here, and he has come to stay." [2]

Although the Citizens' Alliance maintained an air of mystery about its strength and plans, it did not seek the anonymity and secrecy of the Employers' Association of 1901. Its executive secretary, Herbert George, had been brought to San Francisco at a substantial salary by businessmen impressed by his reputation as a leader of the Citizens' Alliance movement in Colorado.[3] The importation of a professional organizer of antiunion campaigns aroused the anger of San Francisco labor, particularly because George was identified with the Colorado mineowners then engaged in a battle of extermination against the Western Federation of Miners. San Francisco unionists, who were strongly sympathetic to the miners, were infuriated by George's pronouncements implying that he was bringing to San Francisco labor relations the enlightenment achieved in Colorado.

Arriving in California in the winter of 1903–04, George helped local businessmen establish branches of the Citizens' Alliance in Los Angeles, Stockton, and other cities. The Los Angeles branch of the alliance was claimed to be the largest in the nation, relative to the size of the city. Headed by Harrison Gray Otis, publisher of the *Los Angeles Times* and California's most prominent antagonist of organized labor, it worked closely with the Merchants' and Manufacturers' Association to maintain the open shop in Los Angeles. During 1904 branches of the alliance were active in California cities from Bakersfield in the south to Fort Bragg in the north. In the Bay Area the Citizens' Alliance of Oakland was reported to have 3,000 members by early spring, and vigorous branches appeared in San Jose and Palo Alto. San Francisco's alliance, the largest in the state, claimed 16,000 members by the fall of 1904. If the membership had consisted entirely of employers, it would have been a formidable force. But as an organization that portrayed itself as working chiefly for the public, rather than for employers alone, the alliance sought members among all groups except workers affiliated with labor unions. Some business firms, labor leaders charged, put pressure upon their employees, especially white-collar workers, to join the alliance. To mobilize businessmen, the Chamber of Commerce circularized its membership, recommending the alliance as worthy of the support of all "desiring industrial peace and harmony."[4] Many of those formerly active in the Employers' Association of 1901 worked with particular enthusiasm to promote this revival of an open-shop movement. Although its membership claims were almost certainly exaggerated, the alliance developed substantial strength in San Francisco and attracted large-scale financial support.

During 1904 George built up a small full-time staff and was able to boast late in the year that the Citizens' Alliance possessed a "corps" of five lawyers and its own "secret Service." [5] His lieutenant was W. E. Alexander, an associate from his Colorado battles with unions. For legal work George relied largely on two local lawyers, James Emery and Bush Finnell. In the late spring George began publication of a small periodical, the *Citizens' Alliance News*. In addition, the alliance enjoyed favorable publicity in the *San Francisco Evening Post*. During most of 1904 the *Post* was a forthright spokesman for the alliance, fulminating against organized labor and calling for support of the new crusade to rid the city of union power.

In seeming caricature, the Citizens' Alliance took on some of the outward trappings of its opponent, organized labor. Each member was issued a "union card" which was needed to gain admittance to closely guarded meetings, held in a conspiratorial atmosphere deemed characteristic of union meetings. The alliance posted pickets before firms under union boycott to urge the public to patronize those who resisted labor domination. It hired sandwich men to walk the streets with placards proclaiming that "The People Demand the Open Shop." It placed its own "union label," closely resembling the label of the Allied Printing Trades Council, on circulars and other printed matter. As a counterforce to the California State Federation of Labor, Herbert George organized the State Federation of Citizens' Alliances and announced that its first annual convention would be held early in 1905, on the same date and in the same city as that of the labor federation. As a more practical measure, the alliance, recognizing the efficacy of labor's boycott weapon, occasionally issued only slightly veiled warnings that uncoöperative business firms might be boycotted by the alliance's 16,000 members. [6]

On paper, the Citizens' Alliance was a strongly centralized organization of impressive power. Its constitution vested control in a nine-man executive committee and provided for expulsion of any member who settled "a difference or strike involving a question of general interest to the Alliance without first obtaining the approval and consent of the Executive Committee." [7] To encourage resistance to unions it provided that two-thirds of the members could vote to compensate employers for losses incurred in strikes or other labor difficulties. Given sufficient membership among San Francisco employers and the ability to maintain discipline over that membership, the alliance could have established a labor relations policy for all local industry. Subsequent developments showed, however, that comparatively few employers, even alliance members, were willing to relinquish control over their labor policies to the alliance's executive committee.

The Stablemen's Strike

Despite its elaborate preparations, the alliance took no significant action against unions in the early months of 1904. It spent its time building up patronage for such prominent opponents of unionism as Mathias Johnson, the restaurateur, and Morris Siminoff, the cloak manufacturer. But it made no direct attack on unionism, and in April Walter Macarthur wrote: "Whatever the Citizens' Alliance may be in other places, in San Francisco it is nothing more nor less than a great big bluff . . . it has no existence except in the florid press announcements of its promoters." [8]

Within a few days, however, came the first open-shop drive inspired by the alliance. On April 15 members of the Stable and Carriage Owners' Association posted the following notice:

> To Whom it May Concern: From this date, this stable will be run as an "Open Shop." . . . We will not recognize the Business Agent or "Walking Delegate" of any labor union. . . . Approved by the Executive Committee, Citizens' Alliance of San Francisco. [9]

Since early in the year the association had balked at renewing its annual agreement with the Stablemen's Union, although Labor Council officers had persuaded the union to drop demands for a wage increase and accept continuation of its scale of $2.50 for a twelve-hour day. [10] Now the association, under the leadership of the Citizens' Alliance, issued a direct challenge to the union.

The resulting strike to reëstablish union recognition brought out 300 to 400 stablemen at more than 40 stables. The Stable and

Carriage Owners' Association, each of whose members was reported to be under a $2,000 bond forfeitable upon desertion, held firm in the face of mass picketing, sporadic incidents of violence, and secondary boycotts. About seventy-five members of the Horseshoers' Union struck in a refusal to work upon horses from open-shop stables. But their support of the striking stablemen soon weakened; by mid-May they were back at work, under pledges to the Master Horseshoers' Association to shoe all horses, regardless of ownership. The Hackmen's Union gave more determined assistance to the strikers. Early in May, 1904, its members, about half of whom were employed by firms of the Stable and Carriage Owners' Association, began to boycott several of the struck stables. The association immediately locked out about 200 hackmen and hired strikebreakers.[11]

The men hired to fill the positions of union hackmen found themselves exposed to intimidation and violence. Some of them were harassed by rock- and brick-throwing crowds of union sympathizers. A few were lured to isolated addresses on faked calls to pick up passengers, and were there assaulted by unionists. The stablemen, meanwhile, chose several employers upon whom to concentrate their picketing. As many as fifty or more pickets were at times massed around selected individual stables. In late June a picketing stableman was killed by shots fired by a frightened strikebreaker.[12]

The Citizens' Alliance furnished stable owners with both white and Negro strikebreakers and hired armed guards to protect them from pickets. The alliance recruited in part through the employment agency of Murray & Ready, who circularized employers with warnings that "the heavy engagements are yet to come . . ." and advertised its services in bellicose terms:

Listen to the following questions we put to some we engage. Young man, if we engage you as a watchman or special police, and we put two guns in your hip pocket, two in your hand and fill every chamber with lead, will you allow the mob to destroy the Company's property until every chamber is empty? If he quivers an eyelash we do not hire him. . . .[13]

Despite this colorful portrait of ambidextrous gunmen, the guards at open-shop stables were actually armed with sawed-off shotguns, a tactic chosen by the Citizens' Alliance to counter the propensity of strike-sympathizing policemen to arrest strikebreakers on charges of carrying concealed weapons.[14]

By early summer labor leaders had become seriously disturbed by the alliance's battle against the stablemen and the hackmen. Unionists, exhorted to raise more than $1,000 per week to support the strikers, were warned that defeat would "mark the beginning of a general onslaught on Labor Unionism" in San Francisco. Although labor was aroused to the importance of this initial encounter, the alliance emerged the victor. At the end of August, 1904, after almost four months of struggle, the Hackmen's Union accepted defeat. Through the mediation of Mayor Schmitz, its leaders met with representatives of the Stable and Carriage Owners' Association and agreed to send the hackmen back to work under open-shop conditions, in return for verbal assurances of no discrimination against union members. The association, which had refused to meet with a joint committee representing the Hackmen's and Stablemen's unions, thus split its opponents' ranks. The *Coast Seamen's Journal*, denouncing the surrender of the hackmen as "abject and disgraceful," questioned the integrity of the "so-called 'labor leaders'" responsible for it—Schmitz and Michael W. Coffey, president of the Hackmen's Union and a close political associate of Schmitz. Several days after the agreement was reached the Hackmen's Union, at a turbulent meeting, considered resumption of the strike, but was persuaded by Coffey, Mike Casey, and other conservative labor leaders to vote against such action.[15]

Upon the defection of the hackmen, the strike of the Stablemen's Union dwindled rapidly into impotence. The stable owners continued to refuse negotiations with the union, although they did reëmploy most of its members. By late autumn the defeated union was attempting to rebuild its depleted membership and restore its broken morale, while employers were reducing stablemen's wages to $2 for a twelve-hour day.[16]

The "Injunction Mill"

A significant development in the stablemen's conflict was the use of drastic injunctions against picketing. In the spring of 1903 the political power of organized labor had stimulated a liberal California state legislature to pass a statute narrowly limiting the authority of courts to issue injunctions in labor disputes. The statute, labor jubilantly claimed, afforded virtually complete protection to picketing and boycott activities. For more than a year employers did, in fact, make few attempts to win injunctions against such union tactics.[17]

In 1904, however, this apparent immunity ended for San Francisco unions. Prodded by the Citizens' Alliance, employers began for the first time to rely heavily upon the injunction, which had long proved a valuable antiunion weapon in Eastern cities. What unionists soon came to describe as the "injunction mill" began to grind early in August, when a Superior Court decision banned all picketing before the Nevada Stables and held the 1903 anti-injunction law unconstitutional. The decision, greeted exultantly by open-shop forces, was reprinted in full in the journal of the National Association of Manufacturers as a favorable omen of the downfall of union power in San Francisco.[18]

Later in 1904, and in 1905, a flow of decisions granted injunctions against picketing stablemen, culinary workers, bakers, and members of other unions. San Francisco unions financed appeals, as test cases, from two 1904 court orders forbidding picketing by the Stablemen's Union, only to be disappointed, after several years, by California Supreme Court decisions upholding the lower courts and in effect ruling that even peaceful picketing was unlawful.[19] But not all San Francisco firms involved in labor disputes in 1904–1905 resorted to injunctions, and not all court orders forbidding picketing were carefully observed by the unions enjoined. Nevertheless, the issuance of injunctions seriously hampered the power of strikers to bring economic pressure to bear upon employers, and was a potent factor contributing to the alliance's opening victory over the Stablemen's Union.

Other Alliance Battles of 1904

In announcing the capitulation of the Hackmen's Union at the end of August, 1904, the San Francisco Evening Post proclaimed that the " 'open shop' in San Francisco . . . has won a great victory —and more are to follow. . . . The work of the Citizens' Alliance has just begun." The new organization, it confidently announced, would first curb the power of unions, and then "purge the municipal government" of Union Labor Party domination.[20] But the alliance's initial battle against the stablemen and the hackmen proved to be its chief triumph in San Francisco, though during 1904 it participated successfully in other union-employer conflicts. In the late spring it intervened in a strike of almost 100 members of the Leather Workers' Union against four harness and saddlery firms that had cut wages. It furnished armed guards and stiffened the resistance of the weaker firms sufficiently to prevent a split in employer ranks. The strike dragged on for a year, with financial aid from Labor Council unions, before ending in defeat. For several months in mid-1904 the alliance supported a group of small hardware manufacturing shops in resisting a strike of more than eighty sheet metal workers to establish the conditions prevailing in other shops of the local industry. The strike failed to shut down the employers' operations and was called off in late September after negotiations that resulted in minor concessions. At the end of June the alliance encouraged the Carriage Manufacturers' Association to refuse to renew its expiring union-shop contract with the carriage workers' unions, and to announce a shift to the open shop. The expected strike did not materialize, however. The unions voted in mid-July to continue working without a formal contract so long as employers made no attempt to cut wages or lengthen hours.[21]

In the fall and winter of 1904 the contests of the Citizens' Alliance were almost exclusively with unions of the provision and culinary trades. Attorneys for the San Francisco organization assisted the Citizens' Alliance of Oakland to obtain injunctions against picketing by culinary workers involved in minor clashes with open-shop restaurants. In the attempt to avoid injunctions, East Bay culinary workers had their pickets pose as newspaper vendors, selling labor papers whose headlines proclaimed the picketed firm's unfairness to labor. Citizens' Alliance spokesmen issued repeated statements in late 1904 that the Restaurant Keepers' Association of Oakland would soon launch a determined battle for the open shop, but no major conflict came until mid-1905, when almost 200 culinary workers struck about twenty East Bay restaurants to enforce union-shop conditions. The restaurants remained open throughout the strike, and the majority successfully resisted the union efforts. In San Francisco, late in 1904, the Citizens' Alliance furnished guards and won injunctions for several bakeries and restaurants that had broken off relations with their respective unions. It also organized a Poultry Dealers' Association, which soon posted open-shop notices, increased weekly working hours, and provoked a strike of more than sixty members of the Poultry and Game Dressers' Union—the "chicken-pickers" scoffed at by P. H. McCarthy and defended by the *Labor Clarion* as following "an humble occupation . . . that has been the object of sneers and jibes . . . from men who have little to boast of." The strike of the "chicken-pickers" proved ineffective. In a longer but likewise unsuccessful contest in September, a small group of sheep butchers struck against slaughterhouses refusing to sign contracts providing the union shop and regulations upon output. An attempt to boycott the unlabeled products of the struck firms foundered in futile appeals to unionists to stop eating lamb and mutton. Coöperating with the Citizens' Alliance, the slaughtering firms, in October, 1904, broke off contractual relations with the beef butchers and soon destroyed union strength in the local meat-packing industry.[22]

In the fall of 1904 the alliance stimulated an open-shop campaign among San Francisco wholesale and retail meat dealers. This campaign was preceded by a struggle in the meat retailing industry across the Bay. In March an employers' association of East Bay meat markets had responded to demands for wage increases with an industry-wide lockout of the approximately 150 members of the Butchers' Union. Wavering employers were held firm by threats that their supplies would be withheld by meat wholesalers. Within a few months the open shop had been firmly established in Alameda County meat markets. Despite financial aid from San Francisco butchers and other workers, union membership dwindled among the demoralized East Bay butchers. By the end of the year the chief employer of those still adhering to the union was the California Cooperative Meat Company, a labor-owned organization established in June with funds subscribed by San Francisco and East Bay unions. Generously financed, this company circumvented attempts to block its access to meat supplies and eventually developed a considerable volume of sales. The company's first manager was John L. Davie, one of Oakland's leading political figures, who later attributed the company's success in winning the patronage of workingmen's saloons to such "less delicate" tactics as the wrecking by unionists of saloon free lunch counters found displaying "scab meat." Operating continuously from 1904 until its liquidation in the 1920's, the California Coöperative Meat Company was a rare example of successful survival among union coöperative ventures. The Butchers' Union in the East Bay survived the 1904 lockout, but in badly weakened condition.[23]

This East Bay example was before the San Francisco butchers when, on October 2, 1904, an open-shop challenge came from the Butchers' Board of Trade. Assured of the coöperation of wholesalers, the board commanded all retail meat markets to remove union cards and to post signs reading: "This is an open shop. By order of the San Francisco Butchers' Board of Trade, endorsed by the Citizens' Alliance." [24] This order, backed by the board's power to withdraw supplies, was obeyed by several hundred meat markets. The Butchers' Union, which claimed more than 500 members and had possessed sufficient strength to sign a large number of markets to union-shop agreements, was nevertheless persuaded by Olaf Tveitmoe and others to take no action unless employers infringed directly upon union conditions. Union members consequently worked through 1904 and 1905 under open-shop signs in retail markets. Thus the union avoided the risk of a crushing defeat, but the long period of tacit acceptance of unchallenged employer control reduced its membership and weakened its morale.[25]

The organizations of meat wholesalers and retailers continued to police the industry thoroughly for signs of rebellion against the open shop. Early in 1905 meat market employees were forbidden to wear union buttons, a device used by certain markets to attract labor patronage. Throughout the year virtually no San Francisco meat market exhibited a union card. The continued dominance of the open shop was acknowledged late in 1905, when an employers' association threat of an industry-wide lockout quickly brought a plea from the Butchers' Union that it had not, as charged, instructed its members to refuse to work in markets employing nonunion men.[26]

Industrial Peace

Although the Citizens' Alliance touched off open-shop campaigns that weakened unions of stablemen, butchers, and other workers in 1904, its activities did not raise industrial conflict to a high level. San Francisco labor disputes in 1904 involved appreciably fewer workers and lost fewer man-days than in either of the two previous years. In 1905 the number of workers idled and the number of man-days lost through strikes fell sharply below the 1904 level.[27] The Citizens' Alliance claimed, with some justification, that it had forced unions to be cautious.

Other factors, however, were more significant in reducing the incidence of industrial disputes. The local labor movement had entered a period of comparative stability after its turn-of-the-century resurgence. Available estimates indicate that San Francisco union membership continued to increase slowly in 1904–1905, but, by comparison with earlier years, very few new unions emerged among previously unorganized workers. Only occasionally did the San Francisco labor movement sponsor unorthodox organizations, as in the formation in 1904 of a short-lived federal Union of Chorus Girls and Assistants. The number of Labor Council affiliates hovered around 130 through 1904–1905, failing to increase. The majority of local unions, moreover, were inclined to rest on the gains they had achieved earlier. The rising prices that had previously helped stimulate union expansion, demands, and strikes had been succeeded by a generally stable price level. The national economy experienced a mild recession in 1904, and there was sufficient unemployment in the Bay Area to elicit union protests when the employer-financed California Promotion Committee sought to increase the inflow of workers from the East.[28] Under such circumstances union demands were comparatively infrequent, and few situations threatened open conflict.

San Francisco labor leaders encouraged unions, in this relatively slack period, to take a conservative approach toward employers. P. H. McCarthy and Olaf Tveitmoe maintained the Building Trades Council's policy, announced in 1903, of insisting that its affiliates await a renewal of boom conditions before pressing demands for wage increases. Mike Casey managed to allay the restlessness of the Teamsters' Union membership, and postponed efforts to improve the union's contract with the Draymen's Association. The leaders of the Sailors' Union renewed contracts without change in 1904, and, despite the employers' demands for adverse revisions, did the same in 1905. Labor Council officers worked assiduously to persuade federal unions of production workers in sugar, paint, and other manufacturing plants to abandon wage demands, and aided these and other weak unions to settle grievances and renew agreements with little or no change in 1904–1905.[29]

Crisis on the United Railroads

As in 1903, the greatest tension in San Francisco industrial relations in 1904 was produced by the threat of a conflict between the Carmen's Union and the United Railroads, whose contract was due to expire on May 1. The yearly struggle began in April when the union again demanded a union shop and curtailment of the hiring of trainees at wages below the union scale. It asked only a modest wage increase, but held firm to its insistence upon a union-shop contract despite the disapproval of San Francisco labor leaders. As May 1 approached, the United Railroads placed newspaper advertisements and distributed thousands of circulars setting forth its counterproposals to the union demands. W. D. Mahon, the union's national president, came to San Francisco and negotiated a tentative agreement with the company only to have it voted down by the local membership on April 25.[30] On the same day the open-shop employment agency of Murray & Ready announced in newspaper advertisements that "within a short time this city will be plunged into the greatest labor trouble in the history of this or any other city." [31]

As the United Railroads began to import strikebreakers and house them in its carbarns, Mayor Schmitz intervened as mediator. On April 30, through Schmitz's persuasion, the union voted a three-day extension of its strike deadline. On the night of May 3 the union met again, and Schmitz made a strong personal appeal for acceptance of terms proposed to him by the United Railroads. After a long and excited session the union voted in the early morning hours to accept the company's offer of a contract retaining the ten-hour day and raising wages slightly to a range of $2.50 to $2.75 per day.[32] Through Schmitz's intervention the carmen thus gave up their chief demand, the union shop. Circumstances lent weight to Schmitz's counsel of peace. The stable owners' battle for the open shop was now well under way, arousing caution among unionists anxious to avoid the spreading of conflict.

The carmen were aware, moreover, that several hundred professional strikebreakers were on hand, prepared for immediate action. James Farley, head of one of the nation's leading strikebreaking organizations, who brought more than 300 trained and armed men from the East to San Francisco, later said that his firm's formula for success was to "make the malcontents know that the cars are going to be run, and that anybody who gets in the way is going to be hurt. That's all there is in breaking a streetcar strike." [33] Facing such opposition, the Carmen's Union relieved a tense situation by accepting the proffered contract.

Those workers who did strike in 1904–1905 found that the period was not propitious for union victory, whether or not employers were supported by the Citizens' Alliance. A major exception was the strike in mid-1904 of the strongly entrenched Brewery Workers' Union. After an industry-wide walkout of only two days, the union's more than 1,000 Bay Area members won a compromise wage increase of $1 per week. Other unions met stiffer employer resistance. In the spring of 1904 East Bay machinists walked out of the Santa Fe Railroad shops at Point Richmond, as part of a system-wide strike for recognition called by the national union. The Santa Fe quickly won injunctions against picketing, brought in replacements, and kept its shops functioning. As in later railroad shop conflicts, the Machinists' Union did not officially declare the strike ended until long after it had clearly failed. For several years it continued to call upon California unionists to boycott the open-shop Santa Fe in their trips to and from the East. In San Francisco a much briefer strike was called in June, 1904, against the Southern Pacific Railroad by the young Interior Freight Handlers' and Warehousemen's Union. About 300 workers earning $2.25 for a ten-hour day struck for a nine-hour day at higher wages. The Southern Pacific hired strikebreakers and housed them in its yards under the protection of armed guards. The Teamsters' Union, to the disappointment of the strikers, refused to boycott cargo from "scab" freight handlers. After several weeks the strike was called off with the Southern Pacific amicably announcing its willingness to reinstate union freight handlers at their previous wages. In mid-1905, also, an employer successfully resisted the powerful Teamsters' Union. Alleging failure to maintain union conditions, teamsters in both San Francisco and the East Bay struck the Bekins Van & Storage Company, one of the largest moving firms in the West. But Bekins possessed the size and financial strength to hold out against union pressure, and for the next ten years it successfully resisted unionization.[34]

Several factory workers' strikes failed in 1904. In March, despite protests by Labor Council leaders, the Can Makers' Union called out more than 1,000 employees of the American Can Company in a strike for higher wages. The walkout ended within two weeks when the Labor Council's executive committee persuaded the union to withdraw its demands and send its members back to work under conditions established earlier in the year. Late in April about eighty workers struck at the G. M. Kutz shoe factory, protesting a change in work methods. After two weeks the organized San Francisco shoe manufacturers ordered a lockout at six factories employing almost 600 workers, until such time as the Kutz strikers returned to their jobs. Collis P. Lovely, a vice-president of the national union, hurried to San Francisco, placed pressure upon the Kutz workers to end their strike, and brought the lockout to a close late in May. Although Kutz agreed to arbitrate the disputed issues, the company's workers resented the order to return. Later in 1904 the small Cap Makers' Union called out almost fifty workers at two firms that had defied union rules by reinstituting piecework. Early in 1905 the union, badly weakened, admitted defeat.[35] For the remainder of 1905, partly as a result of the Labor Council's admonitions, virtually all San Francisco factory workers' unions avoided pushing demands to the point of a strike.

Continued Bargaining Relationships

As the Citizens' Alliance open-shop campaign commenced in the spring of 1904, the employment agency of Murray & Ready published thousands of copies of a manifesto proclaiming that

> The Pin-Head McCarthy's [*sic*] . . . who abound in this city are so swollen with their sense of power that they fail to discern the signs of the times. . . . Time was when unionism . . . was accepted with a sort of good natured toleration by the people of this city, but that time is past forever. . . .[36]

Despite this optimistic prediction, however, the Citizens' Alliance was able to breach only a few of the established collective bargaining relationships. Moreover, most of the relationships thus broken off were in industries with a background of recurrent tension or conflict between employers and unions over the issue of union recognition. The organizations of stable owners, restaurant proprietors, carriage manufacturers, and wholesale and retail meat dealers, which had offered strong resistance to unionization in 1901 and later, were clearly predisposed to respond to the alliance's call for throwing off union bonds. Other groups of employers might also have declared for the open shop in 1904–1905, if confronted with sweeping demands and strikes by their workers. Such provocations were few, however. Accordingly, the majority of union-employer relationships remained apparently unaffected by the presence of the Citizens' Alliance.

During 1904–1905 teamsters, milkdrivers, sailors, and members of most of the other established unions worked under agreements renewed with little or no change. A few negotiations gained unions improved terms or more firmly established bargaining relationships. The Laundry Workers' Union won a wage increase, thus continuing its unusual success as an organization of semiskilled women workers. In 1904, despite attempts by the Citizens' Alliance to instigate an open-shop campaign in the baking industry, the Bakers' Union won from the Master Bakers' Association a renewed contract giving higher wages and reducing hours from sixty to fifty-five per week. In contrast to its experience with the Santa Fe, the Machinists' Union peacefully reached an understanding with the Southern Pacific Railroad in 1904, providing for recognition of union shop committees and union apprenticeship rules in the company's shops in the Bay Area and elsewhere in northern California. The Gas Workers' Union negotiated a higher wage scale in 1904, bringing the minimum daily rate to $2.50. In 1905 the Pacific District Council of Electrical Workers signed the California Gas & Electric Company to one of the most comprehensive early contracts formally drawn up in the nation's light and power industry. The contract specified wages for members of all IBEW locals employed by the company, but did not include a union-shop clause. The unions of electrical workers and gas workers had moved toward industrial unionism through an understanding late in 1904 that each would adhere to agreements reached by the other with Bay Area utility companies.[37]

However, this avowed intention of establishing a joint bargaining unit was not effectively carried out in later contract negotiations.

Decline of the Citizens' Alliance

In mid-November, 1904, the annual convention of the American Federation of Labor met for the first time in San Francisco. The selection of the city indicated both the more closely coördinated, national character of the labor movement after the 1890's, and the AFL's acknowledgment that San Francisco was a prized stronghold. The convention found a vigorous local union movement, little shaken by the activities of the Citizens' Alliance. Although the alliance had proved more dangerous than some labor spokesmen had predicted, it had failed to gain sufficient support for a widespread, mass offensive against local union power. Organized labor in San Francisco, well entrenched by 1904, had met no assault from the Citizens' Alliance comparable to the ordeal through which the Employers' Association had put it in 1901.

Spokesmen of the alliance continued to complain that the "merchants of San Francisco are exceedingly cowardly. . . . Were it not for the few who are willing to bear the burdens of the many, San Francisco would now be as it has been for many years—the laughing stock of the industrial centers of the world." [38] Herbert George and other alliance leaders nevertheless exuded optimism, setting forth grandiose plans to bring in another 10,000 members by mid-1905 and to establish a large employment agency to provide a ready supply of nonunion labor. To house its "secret service," its employment agency, and other staff facilities, the alliance planned to erect its own ten-story building—to be built, in defiance of P. H. McCarthy and the Building Trades Council, under open-shop conditions. [39] The future, as portrayed by alliance leaders, indeed promised breath-taking expansion. In December, the alliance's chief legal counsel, James Emery, was invited East to address the convention of the Citizens' Industrial Association of America. In a jovial, buoyant speech, Emery painted a glowing picture of the past accomplishments and the confident expectations of the alliance in San Francisco. "Do not think that we are a barbarous city . . . but we have some barbarians," he told his audience, describing to them the struggle to impose law and order on San Francisco's approximately 185 unions, ". . . the most differentiated unions there that the sunlight of the Almighty ever shone upon." [40] Shortly thereafter the Citizens' Industrial Association retained Emery as general counsel. He transferred his activities to the East, where he eventually attained prominence as one of the chief legal advisers and lobbyists of the National Association of Manufacturers.

In San Francisco the Citizens' Alliance was destined for less success than that achieved by Emery in his personal career. Toward the end of 1904, as in the previous winter, there were rumors that the alliance would launch an unparalleled battle for the open shop in January, with a general lockout of union members by San Francisco employers. As before, the rumors proved unreliable. They were touched off in part by advertisements placed in Eastern papers in the fall of 1904, calling for thousands of men willing to come to California to take jobs under the "Open Shop Plan." The rumors were further stimulated by Herbert Ready, of the Murray & Ready employment agency, who announced, after a tour of Eastern cities, that his "trusted agents in every city . . ." had recruited a backlog of 35,000 open-shop workers ready to pour into San Francisco in response to a call from the Citizens' Alliance.[41] The call, however, did not come. San Francisco employers were no more eager in 1905 than in 1904 to follow the alliance into a general encounter with organized labor.

By early 1905 there were indications that enthusiasm for the alliance and its programs was dwindling. The cost of supporting a campaign for the open shop had been revealed by the struggle with the Stablemen's Union, in which the alliance had hired 200 armed guards and had spent more than $50,000 in order to cripple one relatively vulnerable union of unskilled workers. Herbert George, moreover, had not proved the inspiring leader hoped for by the employers who had brought him to San Francisco. He and his associate, W. E. Alexander, displayed a marked capacity, through their self-important and at times arrogant pronouncements, for antagonizing not only union labor but also influential businessmen, civic and religious leaders, city officials, and journalists.[42] Their bravado and exaggerated promises failed to win the respect and confidence of local employers.

At the beginning of January, 1905, George presided in Sacramento over the first annual convention of the State Federation of Citizens' Alliances, a meeting that had been heralded with much fanfare as a counterdemonstration to the State Federation of Labor's concurrent convention there. The gathering disclosed an embarrassing apathy among the alliance's claimed 30,000 members in California. It drew less than fifty representatives of alliance branches in San Francisco, Oakland, and a dozen smaller northern California cities, and was quickly adjourned with the face-saving announcement that a "regular" convention would be held later.[43] By early 1905, moreover, the Citizens' Alliance had lost the backing of its chief publicity organ, the *San Francisco Evening Post,* which had recently expressed opposition to a "fight to the finish" and had insisted that there must never again be a repetition of the 1901 conflict. Citing Mike Casey as a conservative, responsible union leader, the *Post* advised: "If anybody believes that . . . a strike does not cause as much suffering as is generally supposed, let him ask Michael Casey. . . . Mr. Casey will tell anybody who asks him what the meaning of a big strike is to women and to little children. . . ." [44] A few weeks later, the *Post* dropped all editorial support of the alliance and virtually ceased to report its activities.

Open-Shop Struggle in the Restaurant Industry

The alliance's chief accomplishment in 1905 was the disruption of the rather frail bargaining relationship established between culinary unions and restaurant owners in 1902–1903. When the culinary unions asked the Restaurant Keepers' Association for renewal without change of their master contract expiring January 1, 1905, they learned that the association had been superseded by the Amalgamated Restaurant and Hotel Keepers' Association. This new organization had been promoted by the Citizens' Alliance in an effort to create a stronger, more broadly based body of employers which would end the practice of signing agreements with unions. Its membership, predominantly of unionized restaurants, included also hotels in which the culinary unions had as yet failed to develop strength. For effective action and maintenance of discipline, power was centralized in the hands of the association's executive committee.[45] Charges were soon raised that the Citizens' Alliance was threatening to withhold supplies and bank credit in order to force firms to break off contractual relationships with the culinary unions and join the new association. Hints of such pressure appeared in circulars sent by Herbert George to restaurant and hotel proprietors early in 1905. Describing the association as "simply an auxiliary of the Citizens' Alliance," George protested that "above all things, I aim to avoid using the flour, meat, poultry, oyster, and milk interests (which we have organized . . .) to coerce anybody." But, he warned,

We realize that many are hanging back believing they can get something for nothing. . . . It is not our intention to let any man enjoy such privilege. The membership is secret, and everyone must join and do his share. That is what the Citizens' Alliance is for. It is not fighting unions as much as it is fighting that class of people in its own ranks who refuse to do what they know is the right thing. . . .[46]

Despite the threat of sanctions against noncoöperative firms, the new association apparently failed to build a strong membership among the employers of culinary workers. There was little evidence of economic retaliation against restaurants that later continued their union agreements.

Early in 1905, the new open-shop employers' association refused to enter negotiations with the culinary unions, although it did offer verbal assurances that existing conditions would be continued. The unions therefore postponed a direct clash, and embarked upon a patient campaign to sign individual restaurants to renewed agreements. The Citizens' Alliance, aware of the danger of desertions from the employers' association, issued appeals to "forget that there are big and little restaurants and accept the fact that everyone in your line of business has the Cooks & Waiters' Union to deal with." [47] But by early summer the culinary workers, claiming substantial success in their campaign, shifted to more forceful tactics against restaurants holding out for the open shop. In June the unions' Joint Executive Board proclaimed strikes at six downtown restaurants, selecting two of them as targets for immediate picketing. The two restaurants sued for injunctions forbidding the use of pickets. The conflict quickly spread to other major downtown establishments. By early July almost twenty restaurants had been granted injunctions. In mid-August the culinary unions reported that approximately thirty restaurants and saloons had won restraining orders.[48]

From this point the situation stabilized itself into a quiet struggle that continued into the following year. By early fall the culinary workers reported renewed agreements with about 250 cafés and restaurants, most of them quite small. Later on the unions claimed to have won over a few firms that had initially invoked the injunction process, but admittedly they had little success in inducing desertions from the hard core of leading restaurants committed to the open shop. After a Superior Court ruling in August, which banned even peaceful picketing, the unions generally observed the injunctions and pursued their conflict with the restaurants into early 1906 through a boycott campaign.[49]

Attacks on the Building Trades

The Citizens' Alliance made ineffective efforts in 1905, chiefly through legal action, to loosen the control of the Building Trades Council over the San Francisco construction industry. It sponsored an abortive attempt to form an open-shop builders' association and harassed building trades unions by bringing several injunction suits on behalf of small nonunion contractors. Championing the cause of a worker expelled from union membership and thereby virtually barred from employment in the San Francisco building industry, alliance lawyers filed a heavy damage suit against the union for deprivation of earnings. The suit failed, however, to win a court decision holding labor organizations liable for economic loss suffered by members as a result of expulsion—a decision that would have opened the way for devastating legal action against a number of unions. The alliance also gave support to the prolonged but ineffectual suit for $100,000 damages brought by the Union Lumber Company against the Building Trades Council and the San Francisco Planing Mill Owners' Association, alleging a conspiracy to boycott the firm's lumber as "unfair" and to intimidate contractors into refusing to handle it.[50]

Although alliance activity was only a minor irritant to San Francisco building tradesmen in 1904–1905, several branches of the alliance elsewhere in northern California aroused more vigorous open-shop sentiment among building trades employers. The Alameda County Building Trades Council contended in this period with several "unfair" planing mills and a large number of nonunion contractors, many of whom joined an open-shop contractors' association organized by the Oakland Citizens' Alliance. Building trades unions also came into serious conflict with alliance-supported employers in Palo Alto and Sacramento in 1904 and experienced minor difficulties in 1905 with Citizens' Alliances in several northern California cities.[51]

The Open-Shop Fiasco in the Printing Trades

In the summer of 1905 the prestige of the Citizens' Alliance was badly shaken by an embarrassing defeat in its one major encounter with a group of solidly established, veteran unionists—the printing tradesmen. This clash, the largest-scale labor dispute of 1905 in San Francisco, ended in a debacle for the participating employers and foreshadowed the demise of the alliance as a significant force in local labor relations. Moreover, as one of the chief episodes in the printers' nationwide struggle to establish the eight-hour day, it had repercussions beyond San Francisco.

On January 1, 1905, in accordance with the agreement reached two years earlier, the final step in the reduction in working hours brought the eight-hour day to the book and job printing industry of San Francisco, making this the nation's first major city in which the printing tradesmen achieved this goal. But employers soon protested that the shorter working hours crippled their ability to meet Eastern competition, and in May they demanded a return to the nine-hour day. Early in June they issued an ultimatum naming July 1 as the date for reinstitution of the nine-hour schedule, and warning that all workers who resisted would be locked out. By now, leaders of the Citizens' Alliance were trying to rally all commercial printing firms behind the impending battle for a longer workday.[52]

As July approached, the printing tradesmen became convinced that the attack on the eight-hour day was being urged not only by the local alliance, but also by the United Typothetae of America, the national association of book and job printing employers. For months the United Typothetae had been on notice from the International Typographical Union that, beginning January 1, 1906, the union would enforce the eight-hour day for its members throughout the nation. The employers were thus preparing for a widespread defensive fight in the coming year, but apparently felt that a limited offensive in advance of the ITU's chosen date of action would be a sound tactic. To wipe out in 1905 the eight-hour day won by the San Francisco book and job printing trades-men would deal a demoralizing blow to the ITU. Accordingly, John MacIntyre, national secretary of the United Typothetae, arrived in San Francisco late in June to help local employers fight this crucial battle.[53]

Notwithstanding the efforts of the alliance and the Typothetae, only 16 of the city's more than 100 unionized printing firms posted notices proclaiming a return to the nine-hour day. This small group, however, probably contained a majority of the larger plants. Some employers placed advertisements in the *Labor Clarion* to assure unionists of their continued adherence to the eight-hour day.[54] San Francisco newspaper publishers, who had long accepted the eight-hour day for their own printing tradesmen, were united in condemning this attack against it. By July 5 more than 400 printers, pressmen, press feeders, and apprentices were on strike against the nine-hour firms, under circumstances aus-picious for union victory. They were skilled workers, difficult to replace. They were assured generous strike benefits from well-stocked union treasuries. And they faced a minority group of em-ployers who were in the difficult position of fighting to lengthen working hours, an overwhelmingly unpopular cause.

The unequal contest was soon decided. Rumors that the Citi-zens' Alliance would force other firms into the conflict by cutting off their paper supplies proved false. Some strikebreakers were brought into the city to work under the protection of armed guards furnished by the alliance, but they fell far short of supply-ing the replacements needed. On July 10 the first firm defected from the employers' ranks and resumed operations on the eight-hour basis. The remaining firms proposed that the Pressmen's and Press Feeders' unions desert the Typographical Union and return to work under a separate settlement continuing the eight-hour day for pressroom workers. On July 21 the two unions voted down this offer, denouncing it as a "cold-blooded proposition" conceived by MacIntyre, of the United Typothetae. On July 22 the employer front caved in when the firm of H. S. Crocker, largest in the local industry, signed a two-year agreement with all unions, maintain-ing the eight-hour day and the union shop. Other employers hastily followed suit. Only two firms continued to operate nine-hour plants, utilizing strikebreakers and injunctions, and enlisting Citizens' Alliance legal counsel in a vain attack against the San Francisco city charter requirement that all printing contracts awarded by the city must be performed under the eight-hour day. By the end of the year, however, these firms also surrendered, and the union victory was complete.[55]

The eight-hour issue had thus been settled in San Francisco when the International Typographical Union launched its drive in January, 1906, to establish the eight-hour day nationally. The United Typothetae, defeated in San Francisco, organized more effective resistance in a number of other cities. By contrast with San Francisco pressmen, the large majority of pressmen's locals elsewhere did not participate in the 1906 typographers' struggle, but continued to work under unexpired contracts. Advocates of industrial unionism protested for months against the almost suicidal absence of coördination which led union pressmen to remain at work beside the strikebreakers who had replaced union printers.[56] The ITU, however, proved strong enough to win unaided a virtually nationwide victory for the eight-hour day.

The 1905 Election

With its reputation damaged by participation in the printing industry fiasco, the Citizens' Alliance moved toward another embarrassing defeat in 1905. Since the spring Herbert George had been agitating against the Union Labor Party in circulars announcing that the alliance's preëminent remaining task was "the election of a Mayor who will be a Mayor for all the people. . . ."[57] He called for a city government that would use the police to keep "law and order," complaining that "I have been practically compelled to maintain a police force of my own in order to protect the 17,000 members of the Citizens' Alliance of San Francisco."[58] By summer, George's vociferous campaigning enabled Union Labor Party politicians to portray the coming city election as a crucial struggle between labor and its deadly enemy, the alliance. Citing the need for labor unity against the alliance, P. H. McCarthy for the first time threw the Building Trades Council's support to the ULP—the party in which McCarthy had apparently at last decided that his own political future lay. Union leaders employed the convenient specter of the alliance to spur workers to register and vote. The defunct Employers' Association "was a very lively ghost during the campaign," as unionists were exhorted to remember that it had allegedly received assistance from an employer-controlled city government in its 1901 battle against labor, and were warned that another such battle would undoubtedly be launched if alliance forces won the election. The 1905 Labor Day parade took on special significance as a massive demonstration of labor's power.[59]

Alliance support was far from welcome to many who hoped to rid the city of the Ruef-Schmitz regime. Anxious misgivings were repeatedly voiced: "The forces earnestly at work for good government cannot succeed unless they make this incubus get off their back." [60] "If a man whom the unions believe to be a Citizens' Alliance candidate is nominated . . . every mother's son of a unionist will cast his ballot for the present mayor." [61] Determined to prevent Schmitz from winning reëlection, Democrats and Republicans combined in 1905 to support a "Fusion" ticket headed by their joint nominee for mayor, John Partridge. Although Partridge and the other Fusion candidates had the backing of the business community, they were not antilabor and strove to shake off their unjustified label as tools of the alliance. Partridge made speech after speech to groups of workingmen, assuring them that he was neither a member of, nor influenced by, the alliance.[62]

But hatred of the alliance had been skillfully exploited. On election day the ULP won a sweeping victory, of dimensions far beyond the expectations of its political boss, Abe Ruef. It reëlected Schmitz as mayor, captured the Board of Supervisors' entire eighteen seats, and won absolute control of the city government.[63] This control would soon prove embarrassing to the local labor movement, but for the moment the city's workers celebrated their victory as a smashing blow against the Citizens' Alliance and as proof that union power in San Francisco was invincible. In the aftermath of labor's victory, the *Coast Seamen's Journal* reported that Herbert George was planning an early departure from the scene of his failures; he "came to San Francisco as a great, though self-styled, 'Union Buster of Colorado' . . . he never busted anything in San Francisco save his own reputation as a buster." [64] And although George was in San Francisco as late as mid-1907, still heading the alliance,[65] the 1905 campaign was the last episode in which he played a prominent role. The Citizens' Alliance of San Francisco continued to exist for a number of years, but, like George, it faded into comparative obscurity after the election of 1905.

Accomplishments of the Citizens' Alliance

In summary, the alliance's campaign of 1904–1905 must be evaluated as a failure. Although it increased the resistance to unionism in some industries, struck crippling blows at several of the weaker unions, taught San Francisco employers to use the injunction, and shook union complacency, its impact on the local collective bargaining structure was limited. After two years of open-shop agitation, organized labor appeared as firmly established in the economy as before. Most union-employer relationships remained stable. And on the political front the alliance had helped to give labor its greatest ostensible triumph. The election of 1905 brought the most complete control over the city administration ever achieved by men who were, at least nominally, union members and officers.

By the early months of 1906 it was evident, in fact, that even the alliance's initial successes had not been decisive. Unions that had been severely shaken by encounters with the alliance were reviving in strength and aggressiveness. The Butchers' Union was making gradual progress in a membership rebuilding campaign.[66] The Hackmen's Union had reasserted its power to hold up funeral processions until nonunion drivers were removed, provoking again the complaint that "it is beginning to seem as if a corpse may not be buried . . . if it be a non-union corpse." [67]

In the spring of 1906 the culinary unions made heavy inroads into the ranks of restaurants that had resisted them since early 1905 under the stimulation of the alliance. For the first time these unions used not only men but also women pickets, from the Waitresses' Union; this tactic proved valuable in arousing public sympathy for the union cause. Culinary pickets also displayed sensitivity to the public's reactions by shifting to the more subdued technique of "silent picketing." Instead of shouting at passers-by, pickets stood quietly, holding signs proclaiming restaurants as unfair. Local courts were less willing than formerly to grant injunctions against peaceful picketing, especially of this quiet nature. Faced with the threat of renewed picketing, and weary of the long battle, many restaurants settled their labor disputes. By mid-April, 1906, the culinary unions reported agreements with twelve of the approximately twenty-five restaurants that for almost a year had operated under the shelter of antipicketing injunctions. In the East Bay, the comparatively small union of culinary workers also maintained its struggle against the open shop. When the Citizens' Alliance and a restaurant owners' association exerted pressure on wholesale butchers to cut off the sale of meat to unionized Oakland restaurants, a score of these firms were induced to buy from the labor-owned California Cooperative Meat Company, and to continue displaying the culinary union house card.[68]

Even the organization most damaged by the alliance, the Stablemen's Union, was ready for renewed battle early in 1906. After months of organizing activity, it presented the Stable and Carriage Owners' Association with demands for a signed contract reëstablishing the union shop and a $2.50 wage for a twelve-hour day, the terms prevailing before the union's defeat in 1904. Its demands rejected, the union struck late in February against approximately twenty-five stables. The weakened Citizens' Alliance gave only limited assistance to the stable owners, whereas the Stablemen's Union had acquired valuable outside support. Although the Hackmen's Union kept its members at work at struck stables, the Horseshoers' Union refused to work on horses from "unfair" stables and staged a sympathy strike which shut down most of the horseshoeing shops for several days. The Master Horseshoers' Association, reversing its 1904 policy, coöperated with the union by announcing that no work would be accepted from stables failing to pay the $2.50 union scale. In addition, Mike Casey induced the Draymen's Association to endorse the stablemen's wage demands. The draymen were more easily persuaded because they disliked uncontrolled price competition, and they had learned from the stablemen's 1904 defeat, which was followed by a round of wage- and price-cutting in public stables, that the absence of a strong union could increase competition. By mid-

1905 the Stable and Carriage Owners' Association had become sufficiently alarmed to attempt to stabilize prices by calling for strict observance of a $2 minimum daily wage.[69]

Pressure from the Draymen's Association and the master horse-shoers helped to bring the Stable and Carriage Owners' Association into a series of conferences with the Stablemen's Union. The association was soon persuaded to restore the $2.50 wage, but negotiations broke down when it refused to accept the union shop. Although the stablemen made individual settlements with a few firms, almost 200 members of the union were still on strike in April.[70] This struggle was thus still in progress when, on April 18, 1906, earthquake and fire disrupted the life of San Francisco and drastically changed the local labor relations environment.

| Chapter V | Labor Relations after the San Francisco Earthquake 1906–1907 |

THE DISASTROUS FIRES touched off by the San Francisco earthquake of April 18, 1906, laid waste approximately four square miles of the city, demolished almost 30,000 buildings, and destroyed an estimated $350 to $500 million in property.[1] The central business district was left in ruins. Office buildings, stores, and factories were wiped out, and with them the jobs of many San Francisco workers. "South of the Slot," in the working-class district south of Market Street, the fires left thousands without shelter. A flood of homeless, jobless San Franciscans poured into emergency relief camps, and into Oakland and other neighboring cities. With union headquarters destroyed and union memberships widely scattered, the local labor movement became temporarily disorganized.

Labor leaders, however, promptly set out to restore a functioning body of unions. Finding stopgap publishing facilities, the San Francisco labor newspapers soon reappeared. They gave the addresses of union officials as temporary union headquarters, and urged all members to report. Delegates were gathered to attend meetings of central councils, which pledged labor's full and unselfish coöperation in the mammoth task of rebuilding the city.

Initial Labor Harmony

Many observers hoped that the catastrophe would inaugurate an era of harmonious industrial relations in which business and labor would work wholeheartedly, and with singleness of purpose, to restore the city. At the outset a spirit of selfless dedication was indeed evident. In the first chaotic week after the disaster, the Building Trades Council proclaimed that it would tolerate no attempts to increase wages during the crisis. Moreover, in order to speed reconstruction, its unions would waive jurisdictional rules and remove restrictions on the entry of new workers into the building industry. Likewise, the Labor Council announced its opposition for the duration of the emergency both to wage increases and to the jealous guarding of jurisdictional lines.[2] The disaster of April 18 had fallen upon employers and wage earners alike, and for a brief period their past differences seemed to be transcended by a mutual determination to coöperate in raising a new San Francisco from the ruins surrounding them.

The atmosphere of good feeling and coöperation, however, proved to be transitory. Suspicions and recriminations soon marred the façade of union-employer harmony. The heavy destruction of houses and apartment buildings had produced a housing shortage which was promptly reflected in rising rents. The disruption of the local economy and the temporarily limited supplies of commodities in strong demand raised the prices of building materials, furniture, clothing, and other items. Simultaneously, upward pressures on wages appeared, stemming first from the immediate need for skilled building tradesmen. In an attempt to attract bricklayers to San Francisco, contractors soon announced an increase from $6 to $7 per day in the wage rate of this key craft.[3] Other building tradesmen were quick to realize their enhanced bargaining power and to begin pressing for abandonment of the Building Trades Council's policy of wage stabilization.

By contrast, many workers initially faced a brief threat of deterioration in wages and conditions. Within a few weeks of the earthquake the Labor Council shifted to the defensive, calling for resistance to attempted inroads upon prevailing wages and hours. Labor spokesmen accused employers of selfishly raising prices while at the same time taking advantage of the large pool of unemployed to force lower wages upon such vulnerable groups as retail clerks, culinary workers, and common laborers. In May union leaders protested against a proposal that common laborers hired by the city on reconstruction projects be required to work nine hours a day at the standard wage of $2.50, instead of the eight hours specified by the city's charter. Some private employers, it was charged, had already cut the wages of unskilled laborers to $1.75 per day.[4]

By midsummer, however, the rebuilding of San Francisco and the restoration of its economic life were under way at remarkable speed, re-creating conditions reminiscent of its early boom-town years. The heavy demand for workers, combined with the stimulus of the rising cost of living, brought on a wave of wage demands and wage increases. The initial avowals of union leaders that wages would be held stable gave way to protestations that the greed of landlords and merchants had forced labor to protect itself against rising rents and prices. Accusations came rapidly: "The lying down of the employer lion with the labor lamb, that we heard so much of two months ago, is a pipe dream. The labor union men are out for all they can get." [5] The general rise of wages was offered as additional evidence of the rapacity of San Francisco labor, and reports were widely publicized that the unions had unmercifully exploited the rebuilding of their stricken community.

The Seamen's Strike of 1906

The first major labor dispute after the April disaster took place on a familiar union-employer battleground, the water front. The maritime industry was particularly sensitive to sudden, pronounced changes in labor relations, such as those caused by the earthquake. The 1906 conflict, however, had been brewing since well before the disaster. The employers' righteous portrayal of themselves as fighting in the public interest against unions that had selfishly ignored the necessity of preventing wage and price increases during the crisis was misleading. The members of the Sailors' Union had worked under agreements since 1902 without an increase in wages, and early in 1906 they voted down their leaders' cautious recommendation that contracts again be renewed without change. Along with its fellow unions of marine firemen and marine cooks and stewards, the Sailors' Union asked steam schooner operators for a $5 wage increase. Before the ensuing negotiations were interrupted by the earthquake, the sailors had announced May 1 as the deadline for enforcement of the wage increase. Their contract had expired several months earlier.[6]

Although canceling this ultimatum after the earthquake struck the city, the three offshore unions had by mid-May renewed their insistence upon wage increases for steam schooner crewmen. The pressing need for lumber, building materials, and other supplies was bringing an increased flow of shipping into the San Francisco harbor. Freight rates were rising, the demand for seamen was high, and circumstances were favorable to wage demands.[7]

The steam schooner owners, however, notified the maritime unions in late May that they had been instructed by the United Shipping and Transportation Association, whose authority they acknowledged, to deny wage increases. The USTA, the unions soon learned, was headed by R. P. Schwerin, president of the nonunion Pacific Mail Steamship Company and a member of the executive committee of the Citizens' Alliance. The association was an outgrowth of alliance efforts to stimulate organization among employers. Like other similar associations, it aimed to bring together into one centrally directed body firms from the various branches of a given industry. Its articles of agreement specified as its ultimate goal "that the *open shop principle* may sooner or later prevail . . . ," and set forth its intention to remedy the complaint that "Stevedores, Steamship Companies and Shippers of San Francisco have not pulled together as they should in times of strike troubles." Accordingly, the USTA combined a number of major steamship companies in the offshore trade, most of which had never formally recognized the maritime unions, with the Master Stevedores' Association of San Francisco. Its sphere of control soon embraced the steam schooners in coastwise shipping, but the organization failed to win the coöperation of the Shipowners' Association of the Pacific Coast, representing coastwise sailing vessels.[8]

The wage demands of the offshore unions gave the USTA its first opportunity to test the effectiveness of an alliance between employers of seamen and of longshoremen. At the beginning of June the seamen struck to enforce higher wage scales on steam schooners. The USTA, after publicly announcing that it could tolerate no wage concessions that would add to the cost of rebuilding San Francisco, launched a counterattack upon a vulnerable flank of its opponents. On June 6, its member firms locked out a large number of the longshoremen employed on San Francisco docks and threatened to extend the lockout to the entire water front.[9]

Leaders of the Sailors' Union charged that this blow at the longshoremen was designed to provoke a general encounter between the unions of the City Front Federation and all shipowners. A paralysis of San Francisco shipping by strikes and lockouts would involve firms that so far had refused to join the USTA, and would place painful pressure upon members of the City Front Federation who were not prepared for an exhausting conflict like that of 1901. Many longshoremen had been impoverished by the loss of their homes and possessions in the fire. Moreover, the longshoremen's unions lacked the financial resources and, in the view of many Sailors' Union officials, the disciplined morale required to make them reliable allies in a severe test. On June 19, therefore, in order to counteract any justification the USTA might offer for implementing the threatened port-wide lockout of longshoremen and other City Front Federation members, the three offshore unions withdrew from the federation and thereby ostensibly absolved the remaining member unions from any obligation to support the strike.[10] "The seamen's unions are prepared to make the fight alone, if need be," the Sailors' Union proclaimed. "In fact, they prefer to do so. . . . Seamen need . . . no sympathetic strikes and no sympathetic encumbrances of any kind." [11] The general water-front lockout did not materialize, and the longshoremen continued to work on the docks as neutrals, handling cargo from union-manned and "scab" vessels alike.

The course of the struggle indicated that the USTA was determined to end the practice of recognizing and entering into formal agreements with the offshore unions. With prices and wages rising in San Francisco in mid-1906, and with a heavy demand for shipping at profitable freight rates, the incentive to resist a $5 monthly wage increase was hardly sufficient to account for the stubbornness with which the association fought this long and costly battle. It is noteworthy that in the midst of their combat with the seamen the shipowners acceded quickly to demands of the longshoremen for a wage increase of 10 cents an hour, considerably more on a monthly basis than the $5 asked by the striking sailors. The USTA tried to persuade the Shipowners' Association of the Pacific Coast to order a lockout of union seamen on coastal sailing vessels, and to induce shippers to cut off cargoes from steam schooners meeting the union demands. But its efforts were largely unsuccessful. By September the SAPC had granted the $5 increase, and a growing number of steam schooners had resumed operations with union crews at the union wage scale. At heavy expense the USTA imported nonunion seamen from such widely separated points as the Great Lakes and Hawaii. Strikers soon persuaded or intimidated many of them into desertion. In August, Mayor Schmitz rejected a USTA plea for additional police protection, replying that there was no sign "that you have sincerely desired a reasonable and fair adjustment," and that the city would not incur added expenses to provide bodyguards for nonunion seamen. Violence was mild in comparison with that of several subsequent water-front strikes in San Francisco, but it brought death to one member of the Sailors' Union; he was shot by armed guards who fired on the union's picket launch as it patrolled the harbor. The strikers denounced the incident as an unprovoked murder. An impressive gathering of San Francisco unionists demonstrated their sympathy for the seamen's cause by marching in the victim's funeral procession.[12]

The conflict ended, after five months, in union victory. In July the USTA had announced that its members "do not propose to arbitrate with Mr. Furuseth, or recognize him in any manner." [13] Nevertheless, at the end of October, Furuseth and other leaders negotiated with the shipowners a joint settlement for the three maritime unions. The $5 monthly wage increase was granted by the coastwise steam schooner operators, and wage concessions were also won from several steamship companies in the offshore trade. The only major concern in coastwise shipping which refused to negotiate a settlement was the Hammond Lumber Company, which, along with the American-Hawaiian Steamship Company and other firms in the offshore trade, for years successfully resisted union recognition. The steam schooners' organization merged into the Shipowners' Association of the Pacific Coast, and the USTA, like other employers' associations inspired by the Citizens' Alliance in 1904–1906, soon disappeared from the scene.[14]

Disunity among Maritime Workers

Although the 1906 seamen's strike ended in union victory, its disruption of the City Front Federation boded ill for the long-run future of unionism in the maritime industry. On this occasion the offshore workers were able to dispense with the active assistance of the longshoremen, but in later years conditions were not always so favorable for a singlehanded battle against shipowners. The 1906 strike brought to a head the underlying disharmony among the maritime workers. Since 1904 the Sailors' Union had been engaged in a jurisdictional squabble with the International Longshoremen's Association. In the Bay Area an uneasy peace had been maintained only through the acceptance by all the longshoremen's locals of a Sailors' Union ultimatum that they disaffiliate from the ILA.[15] During the 1906 strike Andrew Furuseth charged that the West Coast longshoremen had seized this opportunity to infringe on the sailors' jurisdiction by working inside the ship's rail. The longshoremen's behavior, according to Furuseth, had at last taught the sailors a needed lesson: "The seamen on this Coast have reached a full realization of the necessity of an organization of, by, and for themselves." [16]

Actually, Furuseth exaggerated the seamen's grievances. Some longshoremen had supported the strike. In San Francisco the Lumber Longshoremen's Union had refused to unload strikebreaker-manned lumber schooners, thus provoking the USTA into threatening "to abandon our trade in the lumber business of San Francisco." This decision may have been influenced, as employers alleged, by assaults upon longshoremen by striking sailors. In San Pedro, however, the longshoremen, according to Furuseth's own report, had voluntarily "refused to receive cargo from scab seamen," and had suffered a retaliatory port-wide lockout that severely damaged their organization.[17] But, whatever the extent of the longshoremen's loyalty or betrayal in the 1906 strike, the episode helped strengthen Furuseth's determination to keep the Sailors' Union clear of alliances with shoreside workers.

Renewed Conflict with the United Railroads

The other major San Francisco labor dispute of 1906 involved the street railways. The United Railroads characteristically attempted to hold out against the general trend toward higher wages which was well in progress by midyear. Developments across the Bay earlier in the year furnished the background for the San Francisco conflict. Months of organizing activity had raised the membership of the Carmen's Union in the East Bay to about 600, and by March it felt strong enough to demand, and threaten to strike for, formal recognition and a wage increase from the Oakland Consolidated Traction Company. Public tension grew as the company began to import strikebreakers and to fit up its carbarns with beds, food, guns, ammunition, and protective boarding. Meanwhile, however, the company entered negotiations with union spokesmen headed by W. D. Mahon, president of the national union, who had rushed to Oakland from the East. On April 3 Mahon negotiated a contract giving full union recognition, a prescribed grievance procedure, and several minor concessions in return for the carmen's agreement to waive wage demands for the remainder of the year. The East Bay union voted acceptance, the company paid off its strikebreakers, and the two parties settled permanently into an amicable bargaining relationship.[18]

But the United Railroads dispute did not end so peaceably. When disaster struck San Francisco on April 18, 1906, the carmen were working under a contract that did not expire until May, 1907. By mid-July rising prices and rising wages for other workers induced about 200 electrical linemen and stationary firemen to strike against the United Railroads for wage increases and the eight-hour day. On July 30 another strike for higher wages and the eight-hour day was called by the new Street Railway Construction Workers' Union, whose approximately 700 members were employed in repairing the company's tracks. The carmen did not long refrain from entering the conflict. Contending that the "extraordinary situation" resulting from the earthquake had nullified their obligation to wait until their contract expired before seeking improved conditions, they demanded the eight-hour day and a $3 daily wage. The Carmen's Union was informed that no decision could be reached on the demands of any of the unions concerned until Patrick Calhoun, the company's president, arrived from the East. Calhoun was well overdue when, on August 26, the carmen struck in violation of their contract.[19]

Calhoun soon reached San Francisco in the vanguard of a large number of strikebreakers. He denounced the Carmen's Union for its breach of contract and flatly refused to meet with any union representatives until the employees had returned to work. In a conciliatory letter, however, he offered to arbitrate the wage and hour issues once the strikes had been called off. This offer was accepted on September 5 by the union leaders, who did not relish an encounter with Calhoun's strikebreakers. After some difficulty, the members of the four striking unions were persuaded to go back to work.[20]

Formal arbitration hearings soon began before a tripartite board headed by the chief justice of the California Supreme Court. The arbitration award, handed down on February 28, 1907, gave substantial wage increases to all four unions, and the eight-hour day to all except the Carmen's Union. Doubtful that it could reschedule streetcar service so as to place the carmen on eight-hour shifts, the board left unchanged their ten-hour day. Notwithstanding their improved wage scale, the carmen bitterly denounced the long and expensive "arbitration farce" for its "rank injustice" in not shortening their working day.[21]

Effect of the Earthquake on Organized Labor

The maritime and street railway strikes of 1906 were part of the movement toward higher wage levels which spread rapidly among San Francisco workers from midsummer on. Most employers did not try to check this movement. The Building Trades Council attempted at first to enforce its orders forbidding wage demands, but the urgent need for skilled building tradesmen weakened P. H. McCarthy's control over his membership. In July the Plumbers' Union defied the council by striking for an increase from $5 to $6 per day. McCarthy denounced the strike and attempted to gather for the Master Plumbers' Association an adequate supply of "union $5 men." But his efforts to break the strike were unavailing, as one plumbing contractor after another accepted the higher wage scale in order to avoid an unprofitable work stoppage in a period of booming construction. McCarthy soon realized the council's inability to hold the wage line, and beat a face-saving retreat by announcing that rising prices now necessitated higher wages. By early fall virtually every building trades union had raised its wage scale, with increases averaging from 15 to 20 per cent.[22]

The example of the building tradesmen was contagious. Spurred by rising prices and by the determination to maintain their customary rankings within the interunion wage structure, a large number of unions achieved higher wages in the summer and fall of 1906. Some employers took the initiative in raising wages; others acceded with little resistance to union demands. Metal tradesmen, printing tradesmen, teamsters, culinary and provision trades workers, factory workers, and other groups peacefully established improved conditions, thanks partly to the revival in economic activity. William Randolph Hearst ordered a $1 per day increase for all printing tradesmen employed by his *San Francisco Examiner*, and other newspapers quickly followed his lead. The Waiters' Union enforced a new minimum scale of $2 per ten-hour day, and the culinary workers reported that virtually all antipicketing injunctions outstanding against them before the April disaster were dismissed. The Butchers' Union, still weak in early 1906 from its encounters with the Citizens' Alliance, grew rapidly in midyear and reported no serious difficulty in persuading almost 300 retail meat markets to accept an increased wage scale. The Stablemen's Union, struggling before the earthquake to reëstablish its $2.50 daily wage, now won general acceptance of a $3 scale. This previously isolated federal union strengthened its bargaining power in 1906 by acquiring a charter as a teamsters' local. Despite an increasing membership, it was unable to persuade the Stable and Carriage Owners' Association to grant it formal recognition.[23]

Although not all union and nonunion workers shared in the general wage rise, the state Bureau of Labor Statistics estimated that minimum San Francisco union scales typically advanced about 20 per cent within the year following the disaster. As usual in boom periods, the Labor Council leadership congratulated itself for its public service in restraining young and "radical" unions from impetuous action to win unwarranted gains. Labor Council unions generally won increases of 25 to 50 cents in daily wages. Building trades unions, many of which probably did not fully exploit their very favorable bargaining positions, raised their rates by 50 cents or $1.00 per day. In a number of the building trades, however, the demand for skilled workers temporarily pushed wage rates well above the minimum union scales. Although with diminished force, the upward pressure on wages spread to the East Bay, where unions of building tradesmen, printing tradesmen, metal tradesmen, teamsters, and other workers followed the lead of San Francisco unionists in establishing higher scales. As in San Francisco, the wage increases were usually 25 to 50 cents or more per day, representing large percentage increments over previous levels.[24]

The 1906 disaster also touched off an upward spurt in San Francisco union membership, which had risen comparatively little since 1903. The net increase, however, was almost entirely accounted for by the building trades unions. Through 1905 and early 1906, estimated union membership in the city hovered around 55,000. Labor Council affiliates reported approximately 40,000 members at the beginning of 1906, of whom more than 10,000 were in the coast-wide unions of sailors, marine firemen, and fishermen, and in other offshore unions with headquarters in San Francisco. The Building Trades Council unions reported almost 15,000 members. A year later, in early 1907, total Labor Council membership had held steady, but membership in the Building Trades Council had grown to almost 30,000 because of the many "earthquake mechanics" pouring in to help rebuild the city.[25]

There was also a significant increase in union membership in the East Bay in 1906, both in the building trades and in other occupations. The increase was great enough to narrow the differential in unionization between San Francisco and the East Bay. After the earthquake many San Francisco firms temporarily transferred their operations to the East Bay, and not all of them returned when the crisis was ended. The normally rapid growth rate of the metropolitan Oakland area, stimulated further by the influx of population and firms from San Francisco, made 1906 a year of flourishing business and construction activity. The unions of the Alameda County Building Trades Council reported a doubling of their numbers between early 1906 and early 1907, bringing the council's membership to a total of more than 9,000. The remaining East Bay unions, exclusive of the railroad unions, reported an increase during the year from less than 3,500 to more than 5,000 members.[26] Growth was especially rapid among culinary workers, laundry workers, milkdrivers, and lumber longshoremen.

Organizational Losses among Manufacturing Workers

Though total San Francisco union membership increased in 1906, not all unions emerged satisfactorily from the disruption caused by the earthquake. A lasting result of the disaster was the damage it did to noncraft unionism in manufacturing plants. The unions of unskilled manufacturing production workers, which normally experienced a high turnover in membership, and whose position was far from secure, were especially handicapped in regrouping widely scattered members and reorganizing their jurisdictions. The devastation in many San Francisco manufacturing industries left large numbers of factory workers unable for months to find employment in their customary occupations. Many of them drifted into other lines of work, or left San Francisco. Some unions, severely crippled by membership losses, were unable to reëstablish collective bargaining relationships when production at last resumed.

Unionism was particularly damaged in the clothing manufacturing industries, which always faced heavy outside competition. San Francisco firms had difficulty in recapturing markets lost while their plants were out of operation. The Garment Workers' Union, which reported almost 1,000 members before the disaster, had only half its former membership in the years after 1906. Some overall and work-clothing factories were not rebuilt, and others reopened as nonunion firms; five years after the disaster the union label was in use by only two San Francisco manufacturers. The ILGWU Cloakmakers' Union did not revive after the 1906 disaster and soon lapsed into dormancy. The Capmakers' Union dissolved, was rechartered in 1907, but afterward played no significant role in this declining local industry. The San Francisco glove manufacturing industry, wiped out by the fire, was not reëstablished. The Glove Makers' Union, which at its peak had boasted 400 members, was reduced in the years after 1906 to a handful of workers in the few small shops that resumed production.[27]

A number of unions in other occupations also found difficulty in reasserting control over their jurisdictions. The Retail Delivery Drivers' Union required years to restore its membership to the predisaster level, and was unable to win recognition from department stores or other large establishments. The Machine Hands' Union, a weak organization of unskilled metal trades workers, retained only a nucleus of members after the earthquake.[28] The large and formerly aggressive Can Makers' Union was not revived among the production workers of the American Can Company. And few of the factory workers' unions that survived the chaotic months of 1906 displayed in later years their former vigor.

Union-Employer Antagonism

Peace generally prevailed on the San Francisco labor front during the months of booming construction and rising wages in 1906, but underlying tensions between employer and labor groups were evident. Although the Citizens' Alliance survived the disaster only as an emasculated, feeble organization, labor continued to watch suspiciously for signs of renewed open-shop drives. Some employers attempted to arouse a movement against the building trades unions, denouncing their power in setting the terms upon which the city was being rebuilt. They charged P. H. McCarthy with arbitrarily restricting the use of concrete as a substitute for brick, thereby protecting the employment of highly paid bricklayers at the expense of increased construction costs. When building tradesmen refused to install window glass manufactured in open-shop Los Angeles, McCarthy was denounced for his dictum, "We will not allow any goods from that scab town to be sold here." [29] In the early fall the Downtown Property Owners' Association, meeting to protest the greatly increased wages of building tradesmen, heard Patrick Calhoun of the United Railroads speak on the "right of a man to work." Calhoun, amid rumors that powerful business interests were mobilizing to combat union power, had just made an ominous prophecy: "I am not heading this movement which is proposed to remedy these conditions, but, if I were, I could restore them to a normal basis in ninety days." [30] A group of building trades employers organized the short-lived Greater San Francisco Construction Association, with the slightly veiled aim of bringing a large supply of nonunion workers into the city. James Emery, the onetime Citizens' Alliance lawyer who was now national secretary of the Citizens' Industrial Association, returned from the East to inspirit the new organization. "If you don't hang together," Emery exhorted its inaugural meeting, "you will hang separately. . . . The other cities of the United States will term your city an outcast: either cowards or contemptible." [31]

These stirrings of resistance to union power led to no overt clashes between labor and employers, but they heightened union apprehension concerning employer hostility. In October a group of businessmen organized a citizens' mass meeting for the avowed purpose of considering action against the disturbing increase in crime and violence following the April disaster. The meeting called for the formation of a new committee of safety, six of whose proposed 100 members would represent organized labor. But union leaders refused to participate, on the ground that the movement was being promoted by "the Citizens' Alliance element" with the ulterior purpose of crushing unions by means of a "latter-day Vigilance Committee." [32]

Exposure of the Union Labor Party Administration

In the fall of 1906, with conditions in San Francisco still unsettled, a long-delayed storm broke over the city administration. Almost from the beginning of Eugene Schmitz's term as mayor, Schmitz and Abe Ruef had been charged with corruption. It was well known that Ruef had won for the Union Labor Party the political support of the city's saloon and brothel-keeping element. Many union leaders feared that this unsavory alliance would damage the reputation of local labor. A later observer, pointing out that "a nucleus of actual bona fide working men" made the ULP a confusing "medley of the honest and the corrupt," said that,

> As conceived by Ruef, the Union Labor Party was an instrument by which labor might have the police, and the politicians might have the town. Hence the incomprehensibility of the Union Labor Party from the beginning . . . a very disjointed monster, shaking a solemn official head in the offices of the Labor Councils, and flirting a bedraggled tail in the purlieus of the tenderloin.[33]

It was the ULP's ties with the tenderloin which first led to the exposures, confessions, and indictments of the party's office-holders in 1906–1907. Fremont Older, editor of the *San Francisco Bulletin*, and Rudolph Spreckels, one of the city's wealthiest residents, had dedicated themselves in the winter of 1905–06 to a campaign to rid the local government of Ruef, Schmitz, and their dubious associates. Spreckels, a liberal and idealistic reformer, was primarily interested in uncovering the ultimate source of corruption—the business interests that Spreckels believed were engaged in wholesale bribery of public officials. Soon after the April disaster a group of investigators, financed by Spreckels and directed by private detective William J. Burns, set quietly to work. By autumn their efforts had unearthed sufficient evidence to lead the grand jury, on November 16, to indict Abe Ruef and Eugene Schmitz on charges of extortion. Testimony showed that Ruef and Schmitz had split between them a $5,000 bribe, nominally in the form of legal fees paid to Ruef by the "French Restaurant Keepers' Association of San Francisco." The "French restaurant" was a popular local tenderloin institution which featured private dining rooms discreetly available as places of assignation. Essential to the operation of such establishments was the possession of a liquor license, and it had been made evident early in 1905 that the good will of Abe Ruef might be a *sine qua non* for renewal of expiring licenses. Accordingly, the French Restaurant Keepers' Association was formed, and Ruef was retained as its legal counsel. Schmitz was a silent lay partner in Ruef's remunerative practice for this generous client.[34]

Schmitz was indicted for extortion while he was in Europe, relaxing after the strain and responsibility of the April disaster. He returned to San Francisco and continued, though under indictment, to serve as mayor. Meanwhile, investigators were directing their attention toward the city's Board of Supervisors. Until 1905 the Union Labor Party had never dominated this powerful board, and Ruef and Schmitz had thus been unable to exploit certain profitable opportunities to grant special privileges. This restriction was at last removed in November, 1905, when the ULP elected all eighteen supervisors. Ten of them were San Francisco union leaders. The group included Michael Coffey, president of the Hackmen's Union and long considered a self-seeking "labor politician"; the presidents of the Iron Trades Council and the District Council of Carpenters; and officials of the unions of bakery drivers, shoeworkers, printing pressmen, and electrical workers.[35] Almost to a man, the new supervisors were eager to share in the rumored spoils of office. Late in 1905 Abe Ruef protested to Schmitz that these avaricious newcomers might expose the administration through a disorderly rush to reap their anticipated profits: "I can't stand for all these labor union bums you have gathered around you. . . . They would eat the paint off a house." [36]

Investigation of the Board of Supervisors produced the revelations that completed the process of discrediting the Ruef-Schmitz regime. Several of the new supervisors, by late 1906, were carelessly giving indications of sharp improvement in their personal finances. Among them was Thomas Lonergan, president of the Bakery Drivers' Union, who announced plans for taking his family on a tour abroad, to revisit his native Ireland. The tour never materialized. Early in 1907 William J. Burns's detectives trapped Lonergan and Edward Walsh, a fellow supervisor and an officer of the Shoe Workers' Union, into accepting bribes from *agents provocateurs*. On March 7 Lonergan was confronted with the evidence of his bribe-taking and promised immunity from prosecution in return for information about the dishonest transactions of ULP officeholders. He accepted the offer, and his confession gave the investigators an opening wedge with which to pry confessions from fifteen other ULP supervisors guilty of accepting graft. All were induced to confess by written guarantees of immunity, as the essential aim of the investigation was to send to prison the corporation executives and others responsible for bribing city officials. On March 18, 1907, the sixteen grafting supervisors, including the ten labor leaders elected to office in 1905, were brought before the grand jury to unfold their tale of corruption.[37]

The testimony of these supervisors and Abe Ruef's later confessions revealed that certain corporations, chiefly public utilities, had made heavy cash payments in return for valuable favors from the municipal government. Prominent among the guilty corporations were the Pacific Gas & Electric Company, the Pacific Telephone & Telegraph Company, and the United Railroads. Their dealings with ULP politicians will illustrate the revelations of the graft investigation.

In the fall of 1905 a merger of the principal power and light companies in the Bay Area and its environs had created the Pacific Gas & Electric Company, thereafter one of California's largest and most influential corporations. According to Ruef, immediately after the Union Labor Party's overwhelming 1905 victory Frank Drum, one of PG&E's leading stockholders, hired him as an attorney for the company at a retainer of $1,000 per month. Early in 1906, as the new Board of Supervisors began hearings on the setting of gas rates, Drum allegedly paid Ruef an additional $20,000 fee for "legal" services. Of this $20,000, Ruef claimed, he kept $3,000 and distributed the remainder among Mayor Schmitz and the supervisors.[38]

ULP officeholders had been even more lavishly treated by the telephone industry. The Pacific States Telephone & Telegraph Company, transformed by a merger early in 1907 into the Pacific Telephone & Telegraph Company, allegedly paid more than $50,000 to eleven supervisors in February, 1906, to keep them from granting a franchise to a competing firm, the Home Telephone Company. But, as Ruef later confessed, the Home Telephone Company paid him a legal fee of $125,000, of which he turned over $60,000 to thirteen supervisors who voted to grant Home the desired franchise.[39] Unfortunately for PT&T, it had underestimated the price at which the supervisors could be bought.

One of the first corporations to recognize the value of Ruef's good will had been the United Railroads. Beginning in 1902 Tirey L. Ford, the company's chief counsel, had paid Ruef a monthly retainer. The retainer was raised to $1,000 a month after the 1905 election sharply increased Ruef's power to assist his "clients." Early in 1906, Ruef later alleged, Ford offered him $200,000 to "buy" the supervisors' permission for the United Railroads to convert its street railway system to the less costly overhead trolley operations. The issue was politically controversial, for many citizens, including labor leaders, opposed the overhead trolleys as unsightly and dangerous. However, Ruef did not fail his client. On May 21, 1906, the board authorized the company to rebuild its damaged lines entirely as an overhead trolley system. The Labor Council, motivated partly by chronic hostility toward the United Railroads, promptly denounced the action. The Union Labor Party supervisors who voted for the overhead trolleys received $85,000, and Ruef and Schmitz shared the remainder of the $200,000. Allegedly responsible for authorizing and handling the payoff were Patrick Calhoun, president of the company, and Thornwell Mullally, his chief assistant.[40]

Much of this account of large-scale bribery came from its chief beneficiary, Abe Ruef. In order to use Ruef as a damning witness against the men who had hired him, the prosecution promised to dismiss all charges against him except the original one of extortion from the "French restaurants." Ruef agreed to coöperate, pleaded guilty to the extortion charge on May 15, 1907, and testified at length before the grand jury. By the end of May the confessions of Ruef, reinforcing those of the supervisors, had created a public uproar in San Francisco, and had brought from the grand jury a long list of indictments for bribery of public officials. Among those placed under indictment were Patrick Calhoun, Tirey Ford, and Thornwell Mullally of the United Railroads; Frank Drum and two other executives of PG&E; two officials of PT&T, including Louis Glass, its executive vice-president; and four representatives of other business firms that had made payments to ULP officeholders.[41]

In May of 1907, as Ruef testified and as the grand jury handed down its indictments, San Francisco was experiencing one of the most disturbed periods of its history. The disgrace of the ULP administration had temporarily deprived the city of official leadership at a time when it had still not fully recovered from the chaos produced by the earthquake. And, moreover, San Francisco was suffering its most violent industrial conflict since 1901, the climax to months of unsettled labor relations ushered in by the 1906 disaster.

Labor Strife in 1907

Because of rising prices and a tight labor market, San Francisco unions had enforced wage increases with comparative ease after the earthquake. Their success stimulated requests for additional gains in 1907, chiefly for the eight-hour day. The first significant dispute, however, concerned wages. In January the Electrical Workers' Union struck for an increase from $5 to $6 in its daily wage rate. Because the union had already advanced its scale by $1 in 1906, the Building Trades Council condemned the strike. After the earthquake the council's effort to hold the line against wage increases had collapsed, but now the central body was again the controlling power in the building trades. To break the strike, P. H. McCarthy created a dual union affiliated only to the council, and with its help drove from the building industry those who stuck with the rebellious union, Local 6 of the International Brotherhood of Electrical Workers. IBEW Local 6 was disorganized for months before international officers intervened, early in 1908, to effect its reinstatement in the Building Trades Council.[42]

The major strike wave of 1907 began in the spring. On April 1, after unsuccessful negotiations, laundry workers' unions in San Francisco, Oakland, and San Jose struck for wage increases and the eight-hour day.[43] Including sympathy strikers from the Laundry Drivers' Union in San Francisco, this conflict brought out more than 1,500 union members, predominantly women. There was little violence. By late April San Francisco laundries employing several hundred workers had acceded to union demands, but most Bay Area laundries were still resisting the strike in May, when other industrial strife increased.

On May 1 the Bay Area metal trades unions began their first general strike since 1901. Months earlier, the militant San Francisco and Oakland unions of machinists had stimulated the Iron Trades Council to launch a drive for the eight-hour day. Early in 1907 the council served notice on employers that as of May 1 the eight-hour day would be enforced. This announcement aroused the opposition of the California Metal Trades Association, a new organization comprising many San Francisco and several leading East Bay firms. The CMTA, from 1907 on, would be the most important agency influencing the labor policies of Bay Area metal trades employers. Though its members had given no formal recognition to unions, the CMTA entered into lengthy discussions with the Iron Trades Council in an attempt to avert a serious conflict over the eight-hour issue. Pleading the rigors of outside competition, it offered a 5 per cent wage increase and adoption of the eight-hour day whenever it should be established in 50 per cent of metal trades plants in the East. The council rejected this offer, dismissing the threat of Eastern competition as a bugaboo perennially raised by Bay Area manufacturers. When no agreement was reached by the May 1 deadline, the council called out more than 4,000 men in a strike that idled several more thousands of less skilled, nonunion workers and virtually shut down the Bay Area metal trades industry.[44]

Two days later, on May 3, approximately 500 women and girls of the Telephone Operators' Union went on strike. This union had received an AFL federal charter only three weeks before. It faced a powerful antagonist in Henry T. Scott, president of the Pacific Telephone & Telegraph Company, who had earlier, as manager of the Union Iron Works, acquired a reputation of unbending hostility to unionism. When PT&T discharged a number of union members, and flatly refused to negotiate over union demands for recognition and wage increases, the operators voted to strike.[45] The strike violated cherished precepts of San Francisco's conservative union leadership. It was called without preparation, and by an inexperienced union without financial resources. Nevertheless, the local labor movement displayed unusual sympathy for the cause of these poorly paid women workers.

Mortal Combat on the United Railroads

Immediately after the metal trades and telephone strikes came a much more serious conflict. The Carmen's Union, dissatisfied with the recent arbitration award which maintained the ten-hour day and raised daily wages to a maximum of $3.30, rejected a proposal from Patrick Calhoun, president of the United Railroads, to renew their agreement, due to expire on May 1, without change. Once again the union demanded the eight-hour day at a $3 wage. After discussions with Calhoun, however, union leaders offered to withdraw the eight-hour demand if the company would adopt a scale recently won by the East Bay streetcar men, providing a maximum wage of $4 for a ten-hour day. Because Calhoun had so far bargained amicably, union representatives expected to achieve a satisfactory compromise. But as the expiration date approached, Calhoun's resistance stiffened, and he refused to make either wage or hour concessions. President Richard Cornelius of the Carmen's Union, Mike Casey, Father Peter Yorke, and others with influence in the labor movement considered a strike unwise at this time. Calhoun's uncompromising stand, however, left them no hope of dissuading the aroused carmen from taking action. On May 4 more than 1,500 members of the Carmen's Union voted overwhelmingly to strike for the eight-hour day.[46]

The strike began on May 5, 1907. It was the most violent

streetcar strike ever seen in San Francisco, or probably in any other American city. Upon its commencement Calhoun proclaimed his unalterable decision never again to deal with the Carmen's Union, which, he said, was controlled by "radicals" whose continual demands and strikes had become insufferable.[47] Five of the six years from 1902 to 1907 had witnessed strikes, or narrowly averted strikes, by the streetcar men. The union had struck in 1906 in violation of its contract and was again on strike less than a year later, and Calhoun publicly washed his hands of the organization.

Calhoun knew that a battle of extermination against the Carmen's Union would draw enthusiastic support from businessmen who had long resented union power in San Francisco. Calhoun needed such support. On May 3, two days before the strike began, the grand jury questioned him about the $200,000 paid out by the United Railroads in bribes to members of the Union Labor Party administration. Pleading his constitutional right against self-incrimination, under the Fifth Amendment, Calhoun refused to discuss the subject. Late in May he was indicted for bribery.[48] From then on, in the eyes of a large part of the business community, Calhoun filled a dual heroic role. He was the outstanding target of the graft investigators who had determined to send to prison some of the city's leading corporation executives, and he was waging a courageous battle against a strong union.

Calhoun was well prepared for the battle. Through James Farley, whose national strikebreaking agency specialized in street railway disputes, he had arranged to import a supply of men hardened in previous clashes with striking unions. Farley's strikebreakers were well-trained carmen, receiving premium wages which many of them generously supplemented from the fares of passengers.[49] They carried weapons and were quite prepared to use them.

On May 6, hundreds of strikers, sympathizers, and onlookers surrounded the United Railroads carbarns, where barbed-wire barricades were being erected to protect the strikebreakers housed inside. The company made no serious attempt to operate its cars, and police managed to keep the crowd in hand. The next day a similar crowd gathered, but this time half a dozen cars, manned with armed guards, were run out of the barns. This touched off a savage battle; the infuriated mob hurled rocks and bricks at the cars, and the guards began a running gun fight with men firing revolvers from nearby vacant lots. From inside the barns, strike-breakers and private detectives hired by Calhoun opened fire on the crowd. Before the gunfire ceased, two men had been shot to death, and more than twenty wounded. The dead and seriously wounded included not only strikers but one policeman and several teen-age boys who had adventurously joined the crowd. One United Railroads detective was wounded by shots fired from the mob. Calling the day "Bloody Tuesday," unionists joined with the San Francisco chief of police in denouncing the shootings as a wanton massacre by imported gunmen.[50]

The violence on May 7 aroused fears of a spreading, uncontrollable battle between unions and employers. That night Labor Council officers called an emergency meeting. With approximately 10,000 streetcar men, metal tradesmen, laundry workers, and telephone operators on strike, they feared that hatred of the United Railroads might lead to a general strike. To head this off, the council appointed a committee consisting of Mike Casey, Andrew Furuseth, Walter Macarthur, Andrew J. Gallagher, and other influential union leaders.[51] The committee first dissuaded the Electrical Linemen's Union from carrying out a planned sympathy strike against the United Railroads. On May 8 it met with representatives of the Civic League and the Church Federation. The meeting drew up a proclamation appealing for the maintenance of order and industrial peace, and formed the Joint Conciliation Committee to combat "the sentiment of 'fight to a finish' . . . shared equally by the agitators in the ranks of labor and of capital." [52] The peace appeal was printed on hand-bills and distributed among the crowds in downtown streets and near the carbarns. Members of the Joint Conciliation Committee also pleaded with individual unions and employers to avoid further labor conflict.[53]

The fears of widespread industrial strife between unions and employers were exaggerated, but in May, 1907, the danger of such strife was at its highest level since 1901. Among both unions and employers, voices called loudly for an immediate general encounter. A group of unionists, most of them militant Socialists, distributed circulars urging workers to "Tie Up the Town." A few Labor Council delegates led by Selig Schulberg, a Socialist official of the Waiters' Union, demanded a general strike.[54] On the other side, advocates of the open shop exhorted businessmen to launch a battle for the overthrow of unionism. The *Argonaut* demanded the creation of a vigilance committee and pleaded with employers for united action: "We want no sloppy compromise of our differences." San Francisco labor, the *Argonaut* insisted, was "living in a house of glass which one firm blow would shatter." Only "one large employer, . . . one man with the courage to do this thing . . . ," was needed to rally the business community and "bring about the revolution."[55] James Emery, national secretary of the Citizens' Industrial Association, was in San Francisco in May and offered coöperation to local employers. The National Association of Manufacturers, meeting in annual convention in May, wired Patrick Calhoun an enthusiastic resolution of support for the battle for "fair American conditions" in San Francisco. National open-shop periodicals spoke of plans for an imminent general lockout by employers. The NAM, according to reports, had offered to raise several million dollars to support a campaign to destroy labor's power in San Francisco.[56]

Although these rumors kept San Franciscans apprehensive for several weeks, the conflict did not spread. Serious incidents of violence continued to mark the United Railroads strike, but clashes on the scale of the May 7 fighting did not recur. Agitation for a general strike faded away. Employers did not respond to the plea for an open-shop "fight to the finish," and by June the *Argonaut* was railing in frustration at the apathetic "jellyfish of our capitalistic and mercantile community."[57]

Settlement in the Metal Trades

The first progress toward restoration of industrial peace came in the metal trades. From the outset of the metal trades strike, at the beginning of May, a committee of prominent citizens representing the Civic League had been working steadily to mediate a settlement. The California Metal Trades Association continued to negotiate with the Iron Trades Council; its members did not attempt to use strikebreakers, and the strike remained quiet and nonviolent. President Joseph Valentine of the national Molders' Union, formerly a San Franciscan, soon arrived to lead the union negotiators. By the end of May Valentine and James Kerr, chief negotiator for the CMTA, had reached a compromise agreement which awarded the eight-hour day but specified that it be instituted by gradual reductions between December 1, 1908, and June 1, 1910. The agreement, though silent on the union shop and other forms of union security, firmly established a formal contractual relationship between the CMTA and the Iron Trades Council.[58] Brief and simply worded, it was one of the most significant agreements in Bay Area labor relations history. Not only did it contribute greatly toward relieving the tension created by the industrial conflict of 1907, but it inaugurated a new era of acknowledged union recognition and industry-wide bargaining in the Bay Area metal trades industry. Moreover, it was the first eight-hour victory won by metal tradesmen in any major American community.

Yet the agreement disappointed many unionists in the Iron Trades Council. It postponed for three years the full attainment of the eight-hour day, and for eighteen months the first reduction in working hours. Furthermore, the contract included firms that had already granted the eight-hour day. According to union spokesmen, more than one-third of the metal tradesmen therefore had to relinquish the immediate enforcement of the eight-hour day. The San Francisco Machinists' Union was especially disgruntled over the settlement. Metal trades plants remained closed for more than ten days in June before the machinists reluctantly ratified the agreement.[59]

The metal trades pact helped to smooth the way to settlement of the two-months-old laundry workers' strike for the eight-hour day. The Joint Conciliation Committee set up by the Labor Council, the Civic League, and the Church Federation persuaded the union and the employers to accept a contract closely patterned upon the metal trades compromise. On June 11, 1907, a three-year agreement was signed, giving the San Francisco Laundry Workers' Union an immediate reduction to a fifty-one-hour week, and successive annual one-hour reductions to bring the forty-eight-hour week on June 1, 1910.[60] By contrast, the laundry workers' strike in Oakland and San Jose failed, leaving the East Bay union badly disrupted. By early June the Oakland laundries had resumed operations under the open shop.[61] The

1907 strike again pointed up the fact that unionism among relatively unskilled Bay Area workers outside San Francisco tended to be weak and vulnerable.*

Strike Failures in 1907

The remaining major San Francisco strikes of 1907 ended finally in union defeat. Henry T. Scott, president of the Pacific Telephone & Telegraph Company, consistently refused to deal with the striking telephone operators. The union carried its case to the public, arguing that a company that had paid out more than $80,000 in bribes to city officials could easily afford to increase the wages of its employees. Early in June approximately 200 members of the Electrical Linemen's Union struck in sympathy against PT&T.[62] The Labor Council endorsed the sympathy strike, but Frank McNulty, president of the International Brotherhood of Electrical Workers, denounced it as in violation of an agreement between the company and the IBEW's Pacific District Council. Though national officers of the IBEW had apparently reached some form of understanding with the company, the San Francisco union insisted that "it was not party to the agreement if, in fact, such an agreement actually existed." Upon its refusal to call off the strike, McNulty revoked the union's charter and formed a new IBEW linemen's local to furnish PT&T with strike replacements.[63]

The strike ended abruptly in the first week of August, 1907,

* In San Francisco the veteran Laundry Workers' Union continued to enjoy a secure bargaining relationship. One of the major factors supporting this relationship was the union's active coöperation with employers in attempts to control competition. During the 1907 strike laundry owners had vainly insisted that they could grant the eight-hour day only if the union forced the same schedule upon the unorganized Oriental and French laundries. After the settlement, employers and unions increased their efforts to combat Japanese laundries, the chief threat from within the unorganized sector of the industry. In 1908 the Laundry Workers' and Laundry Drivers' unions combined with employers to establish and finance the Anti-Jap Laundry League, which for years campaigned intensively against Oriental competition. (Lillian R. Matthews, *Women in Trade Unions in San Francisco* [Berkeley: University of California Press, 1913], p. 35; Robert M. Robinson, "A History of the Teamsters in the San Francisco Bay Area, 1850–1950" [unpublished Ph.D. dissertation, University of California, Berkeley, 1951], p. 137.)

when representatives of the Labor Council and the Building Trades Council informed the Telephone Operators' Union that the company had promised to increase wages and to rehire strikers without discrimination. Claiming victory, the union voted to return to work, despite announcements by PT&T officials that no agreement had been made and that all employees would be required to apply as individuals for reinstatement. The electrical linemen halted their sympathy strike and later in the year made their peace with the IBEW. Organization among the linemen, however, was severely shaken by the inconclusive telephone strike, the attendant intraunion conflict, and the failure of a linemen's sympathy strike against the United Railroads. For the Telephone Operators' Union the strike's aftermath was fatal. Months after the operators had made individual applications for reinstatement, most of them were still waiting to be rehired. PT&T effectively purged the more active unionists from its force of telephone girls, and the operators' union finally disappeared.[64]

Another group of communications workers met defeat in mid-1907 in a strike against stanchly open-shop national corporations. Late in June approximately 150 members of the Commercial Telegraphers' Union struck Bay Area offices of Western Union and Postal Telegraph, demanding union recognition and improved conditions. Fearing that a nationwide strike crippling telegraph service might result, President Theodore Roosevelt instructed the federal commissioner of labor, Charles P. Neill, to intervene as mediator in the Bay Area dispute. Neill won from Western Union a written promise to hear grievances raised by any of its Bay Area employees, but only as individuals. He also elicited statements from both companies that all strikers would be rehired, with the exception of a small group of alleged troublemakers. In mid-July the Bay Area operators, after hearing personal appeals from Neill and from the national officers of the CTU, reluctantly voted to end their strike. They returned to work in a mood of resentment against their national union leaders because of the forced settlement. A number of strike leaders were not rehired.[65]

Only a brief truce resulted from this settlement. Union telegraphers in the Bay Area, and elsewhere in the nation, continued to complain of systematic harassment. In August a walk-out of Western Union operators in Chicago started the nationwide strike feared by federal authorities. Bay Area telegraphers joined in the strike, despite Neill's protests at their scrapping of the "agreement" he had mediated in July.[66] Although this was the most widespread union battle yet launched against the telegraph companies, it ended in defeat. It failed, both in the Bay Area and nationally, to establish collective bargaining.

Defeat of the Streetcar Strike

Meanwhile, throughout the summer and early fall of 1907, the United Railroads strike continued on its violent course. The bloody encounter on May 7 had demonstrated the company's determination to operate its cars. In succeeding weeks, as the United Railroads tried to restore normal operations, strikers and their sympathizers responded with boycotts and guerrilla warfare. Unions imposed heavy fines on members seen on streetcars. In addition, the very real danger of physical harm frightened many cautious citizens away from the cars. Manned by strikebreakers openly wearing revolvers, the moving cars frequently were targets for bricks and rocks, and occasionally for bullets. There were minor riots when hostile crowds smashed car windows and attacked strikebreakers. Attempted sabotage, combined with the nervousness and apprehension of the strikebreakers, greatly increased the accident hazard. Trees were cut down across car tracks in outlying districts; strikers were accused of greasing the rails on steep hillside sections of track. The United Railroads' accident rate had always been high in precipitously hilly San Francisco, but now it rose to an appalling level.[67]

The San Francisco labor movement, heeding Father Peter Yorke's plea that Patrick Calhoun must not be permitted to "burst [*sic*] a Union that had every Union behind it in a Union town," [68] conducted a strong, unified campaign in support of the striking carmen. For the first time the Building Trades Council gave unstinted aid to a striking union affiliated with the Labor Council. Early in June the two councils set up the General Campaign Strike Committee under the direction of Olaf Tveitmoe. This committee levied weekly strike assessments upon every union member in the city. By late August the building trades unions had contributed more than $100,000, a sum far larger than that raised by the Labor Council.[69]

The Building Trades Council's unprecedented role as chief financial backer of the strike was almost certainly a result of P. H. McCarthy's political ambitions. Late in May, Mayor Eugene Schmitz went on trial for extortion from the "French restaurants," with Abe Ruef serving as chief witness for the prosecution. On June 13 Schmitz was found guilty. The trial judge, expressing regret that the law provided no severer punishment, sentenced him to the maximum penalty of five years' imprisonment.[70] With the titular head of the Union Labor Party out of the way, McCarthy determined to become the party's candidate for mayor in the approaching November election. As such he could hardly afford to ignore the United Railroads strike. It gave him an auspicious opportunity to bid for labor votes by organizing well-publicized support for a cause that had deeply aroused the local labor movement.

The streetcar men, despite strong backing from fellow unionists, faced an immovable opponent. Calhoun's uncompromising stand greatly increased his prestige among business leaders, who linked his battle against the union with his battle against the graft investigators. As the United Railroads strike continued, the furor over the graft investigation mounted. In August, 1907, Louis Glass, vice-president of the Pacific Telephone & Telegraph Company, was convicted of bribery. The first of the indicted business executives to stand trial, he received a five-year sentence.[71] Then followed the trial, in September, of Tirey Ford, legal counsel for the United Railroads.

The trials of businessmen charged with bribery helped to create factional dissension that weakened the labor movement's support of the Carmen's Union. McCarthy, campaigning as Union Labor Party candidate for mayor, ran on a platform calling for prosecution not only of the men who had proffered bribes, but also of the supervisors who, upon promises of immunity, had confessed their acceptance of the bribes. Whatever McCarthy's intentions —and there was widespread suspicion concerning them—the graft investigators were convinced that he wanted to prevent them from convicting the business executives they deemed fundamentally responsible for the corruption.[72] The guilty supervisors, if their guarantees of immunity were withdrawn, would certainly refuse to testify for the prosecution.

Mike Casey, Andrew Furuseth, Andrew J. Gallagher, and other Labor Council leaders advocated continuance of the graft investigation. So also did Richard Cornelius, head of the striking Carmen's Union. They now publicly gave their support to McCarthy's opponent, Dr. Edward Taylor, who headed a ticket of candidates pledged to vigorous prosecution of the indicted businessmen through reliance on the testimony of the supervisors. As the summer ended, serious dissension over the coming election broke out between Labor Council and Building Trades Council representatives on the General Campaign Strike Committee. Despite the huge sum raised by the building tradesmen for the Carmen's Union, Cornelius and other influential labor leaders were openly working against McCarthy's election. Olaf Tveitmoe announced late in August that the Building Trades Council would soon end its contributions to the carmen,[73] on the ground that the Labor Council had failed to raise its share of strike assessments. It was clear, however, that political factionalism was bringing to an end the brief unity achieved by the two councils in support of the strike.

The Carmen's Union, in any event, was fighting a losing battle, for the United Railroads made steady progress toward restoration of normal service. In July the *Argonaut* announced that "the street car strike is looking around for a place to fall." By early August Calhoun had recruited enough permanent replacements to allow most of the professional strikebreakers to return to the East. The company reported almost 1,300 new employees at work, in addition to the approximately 200 in its employ at the outset of the strike. Richard Cornelius acknowledged that the transportation service set up by the General Campaign Strike Committee to serve those boycotting the streetcars was incurring a monthly deficit of $5,000 because of insufficient patronage.[74]

The last major act of violence in the strike occurred on Labor Day, as thousands of workers paraded in downtown San Francisco. A streetcar approaching the line of march of the Building Trades Council was attacked by unionists, and in the ensuing melee a young building tradesman was shot to death, one strikebreaker was seriously wounded, and half a dozen men were injured. The funeral for the riot victim was attended by McCarthy and hundreds of union members. On their way back from the funeral, some of the mourners broke the windows of a streetcar and injured two strikebreakers before police restored order. But the strike was nearing its end. On September 12 the General Campaign Strike Committee lifted the boycott against the United Railroads in order, it claimed, to expose the company's inability to maintain service with its new employees. Its action, however, was a tacit acknowledgment of Calhoun's victory over the Carmen's Union.[75]

The strike was not officially called off until March, 1908. Before it ended it had taken more lives than any single strike in San Francisco history. Among the dead were strikers and their sympathizers, strikebreakers, policemen, and streetcar passengers. At least 6 men had been shot to death, and more than 250 had been injured. Most of the injured were strikebreakers hit by flying rocks and bricks. Streetcar accidents during the strike resulted in a staggering number of casualties; more than 25 people had been killed and approximately 900 had been injured.[76] The strike more than justified the forebodings of those who had long dreaded a conflict on the San Francisco street railways.

This devastating union defeat had cost the labor movement more than $300,000 in strike donations. Labor spokesmen used it as an object lesson to deter overaggressive unions from rushing into disaster over the protests of their conservative officials. Father Peter Yorke blamed "the Labor Leaders . . . with their wretched politics . . ." for the defeat because they had neglected the strike while battling one another in the 1907 election campaign. A Socialist faction in the labor movement denounced Mike Casey for permitting members of the Teamsters' Union to haul supplies to the carbarns housing the strikebreakers.[77] The carmen's defeat, however, was chiefly attributable to Patrick Calhoun's determined resistance, and to the United Railroads' financial ability to sustain the costs involved. Moreover, the exposure and removal from office in mid-1907 of the Union Labor Party administration deprived the strikers of police support.

At the beginning of the conflict Richard Cornelius had attacked Calhoun as a "Tin God on Wheels" who "won't treat with the

union forever and ever and therefore, there can be no union. . . .
He has wiped us off the face of the earth." [78] And that is exactly
what Calhoun did. The demoralized Carmen's Union turned in
its charter late in 1908,[79] and Calhoun had destroyed one of the
largest, best-financed, and most militant unions in San Francisco.
He had convincingly demonstrated the power of a resolute employer, and had so completely stifled the Carmen's Union that
the United Railroads enjoyed twenty-five years of freedom from
strong labor opposition.

The 1907 Election

In November, 1907, San Francisco voters went to the polls to
elect a new city government. The overriding issue was the graft
investigation. It brought together an incongruous set of elements
in support of P. H. McCarthy, whose platform was, people suspected, designed to block prosecution of the men exposed by
the investigation. Among McCarthy's adherents were the saloon-
keeping, brothel-keeping, and other tenderloin interests; thousands of union members whose loyalty to the Union Labor Party
had remained firm despite the revelations of corruption; Patrick
Calhoun and other businessmen who opposed both the graft investigation and San Francisco unions; and Father Peter Yorke,
ardent champion of the city's labor movement. Father Yorke managed simultaneously to denounce Calhoun as a vicious union
smasher and Calhoun's enemies—the graft investigators—as conspirators intent upon blackening the reputation of organized labor
and wresting control of the local government from the workers.
Opposing McCarthy were the most influential leaders of Labor
Council unions, a few rebellious building trades leaders banded
together in the "Building Trades Good Government Club," and
other citizens anxious to see the graft prosecutions continue. On
election day McCarthy's opponents proved more numerous than
his supporters. Dr. Edward Taylor, interim mayor since the conviction of Schmitz, and William H. Langdon, incumbent district
attorney, were returned to office under pledges to continue the
prosecutions.[80] The repudiation of McCarthy ended the six-year
regime of labor government in San Francisco. But labor's influence in local politics was not ended, nor was its controversy
over the activities of ambitious "labor politicians."

End of a Period of Upheaval

The years 1906 and 1907 were unsettled ones for both San Francisco and San Francisco labor relations. The earthquake of April, 1906, temporarily disorganized the local economy and set in motion a chain of developments that brought price inflation, labor unrest, and aggressive union action. The feverish process of rebuilding the city increased the tensions between unions and employers, and ultimately caused the extensive industrial conflict of 1907. The number of workers on strike rose briefly to the highest level since 1901, a level that was not surpassed, or even approached, until the agitated years of World War I.

Significantly, however, San Francisco unions and employers weathered the turmoil without becoming involved in a general strike. Calhoun's uncompromising stand for the open shop, and his role as the symbol of defiance to the graft investigators, won the admiration of the business community; but employers showed no great eagerness to emulate his example of union destruction. Though the defeat of the carmen was the outstanding labor event of 1907, the peaceful settlement of the metal trades strike was more indicative of the prevailing temper of San Francisco employers, and more revealing of the future course of labor relations in the city. Under circumstances that might easily have created a militant open-shop spirit, employers in an industry noted for its past labor battles entered into their first master contract with the metal trades unions. They chose collective bargaining rather than continued strife.

The collective bargaining structure in San Francisco remained essentially intact at the close of the 1906–1907 period, despite the strains placed upon it. Most unions regrouped their forces rapidly after the earthquake, and soon reëstablished their previous relationships with employers. Yet San Francisco labor, on net balance, did lose ground. Organizational footholds were wiped out or reduced to insignificance among some groups of manufacturing production workers. Unionism was destroyed among street railway workers, and the United Railroads was established as an open-shop citadel. The City Front Federation was revealed as unable to maintain unity between offshore and onshore workers. And the revelations of corruption within the Union Labor Party dethroned a city administration composed chiefly of union leaders.

The end of 1907 was a significant transition point in San Francisco labor history. From the beginning of the turn-of-the-century upsurge in union membership, most of the years through 1907 had been marked by turbulence in industrial relations. Following the union growth wave of 1899–1903, the labor scene had become more settled in 1904–1905, despite the disturbing presence of the Citizens' Alliance. But the movement toward equilibrium had been suddenly interrupted by the 1906 earthquake. Now, with the conflicts of 1907 over and the economy entering into a period of slack business activity, stability was again being established. For almost a decade after 1907, local labor relations were more placid and less eventful than in the years since 1899.

Chapter VI	*Depression and*
	Revival
	1908–1910

IN JUNE, 1907, Walter Macarthur, editor of the *Coast Seamen's Journal*, applauded the laundry and metal trades unions for their wisdom in settling their strikes for the eight-hour day by entering into three-year contracts with their employers. Macarthur urged other unions to seek similar long-term contracts, warning that "San Francisco has reached the end of the boom conditions that have existed in that city during the past year. . . . The labor movement of San Francisco will be fortunate if it be able to hold the position it now occupies during the coming three years." [1] Macarthur's advice was well timed. The summer of 1907 brought a turning point in the nation's economic activity and ushered in the short, but steep, business decline of 1907–1908. This change produced a period of comparative quiescence in Bay Area industrial relations. Falling unemployment and downward pressure on wages forced organized labor to mark time. In contrast to the turmoil of the preceding two years, in 1908–1910 there were almost no labor conflicts serious enough to disturb a major sector of the local economy.

In the early part of the period the local labor movement was tested by its first economic depression of consequence since the mid-1890's, and it passed the test successfully. But the recovery to a normal level of business activity did not lead to a new spurt of union growth. Organized labor had reached a position of relative stability, from which it was not dislodged by the economic changes of 1908–1910. Yet there were developments of particular interest and importance in the metal trades, which maintained a peaceful collective bargaining relationship despite the strains of low-cost competition outside the Bay Area. The search for a solution to the problem of competition was largely responsible for a singular chapter in American labor history: the ambitious campaign by the unionists of one large metropolitan area to destroy the open shop in a rival city, 400 miles away. The Bay Area labor movement fought its one outstanding battle of this period not in its home territory, but in Los Angeles.

The Panic of 1907

The business downturn began mildly enough in the summer of 1907, but was soon accelerated by a financial panic that closed a number of leading banks in New York City and engendered a contagious rush for liquidity throughout the economy. Runs on banks by depositors, the frantic calling of loans, and the sudden stringency of credit caused a wave of bankruptcies and forced severe cutbacks in business activity. Production and employment fell sharply. The stage of acute financial crisis was over by the end of the year, but the economy required time to recover from the blow. The drop in production and employment was not arrested until the summer of 1908, and much of 1909 passed before economic activity in the nation again reached the level of mid-1907.[2]

Although it did not feel the full force of the financial panic, which was centered in the East, the Bay Area economy experienced a flurry of bank runs and a general tightening of credit. Work on a number of major construction projects was halted when builders suddenly found needed funds unavailable. Expansion gave way to retrenchment in other local industries. The depression came at an unfortunate time for San Francisco, as the city was still recovering from the 1906 earthquake. By the winter of 1907–1908, a variety of unions, especially those in the cyclically volatile metal trades, had become seriously disturbed over falling employment. Early in 1908, small groups of unemployed workers in both San Francisco and the East Bay were agitating for relief measures. Demand for labor continued slack throughout 1908,

202 | *Depression and Revival*

and even in the first half of 1909 Bay Area unions were concerned over unemployment.[3]

Labor on the Defensive

These adverse economic circumstances put labor on the defensive. The real question was whether employers would make a serious effort to curtail union influence. Certainly, as depression deepened in the winter of 1907–08, the local labor movement appeared vulnerable. The Union Labor Party had been ousted from control of the San Francisco government, and employers could expect Mayor Edward Taylor's new administration to afford them improved police protection in the event of industrial conflict. Patrick Calhoun had given them an instructive exhibition of union-breaking by a determined and well-financed employer. The *Argonaut* reported with satisfaction that "it is one of the blessings of a relatively dull time that labor unionism is more cautious in its aggressions than it was a while back," and pointedly hinted to employers that "there are fifty men in San Francisco—possibly twenty-five—who could by united action say authoritatively to organized labor what its rights are. . . ."[4]

San Francisco businessmen, however, showed no strong sentiment for an offensive against unions. They directed most of their energies toward surviving the depression, and few of them were able to finance a struggle to uproot entrenched unions. Employers, in fact, welcomed the respite from wage and hour demands, and were enjoying the period of comparative calm on the labor scene. And there was no effective inspiration or central direction for an open-shop drive. Patrick Calhoun, the hero of the antiunionists, was the logical person to lead employers in a campaign against labor. But Calhoun had come out from the East in order to protect his investment in the United Railroads, and was interested in San Francisco labor problems only when they affected the street railways. He was, in addition, preoccupied with his prolonged legal fight against conviction on the charge of bribing city officials.

The Citizens' Alliance of San Francisco, after months of dormancy following the 1906 disaster, showed signs of increasing activity in the winter of 1907–08, under renovated leadership. But it did not receive much financial support from employers, nor did its new officers acquire substantial prestige in the business community. Aside from the alliance, no organization addressed itself to the problem of creating a unified employer policy in regard to labor. Although some of the leaders of the San Francisco Chamber of Commerce later participated prominently in struggles for the open shop, the chamber in this period was small —it had less than a thousand members—and not directly concerned in the "labor question." [5] Yet organized labor was kept on the defensive through 1908 and 1909, as many individual firms and employers' associations attempted to reduce wages.

Employers had only limited success in reducing pay rates. The Teamsters' Union in the East Bay was persuaded to accept the demand of the Alameda County Draymen's Association for a cut from $3.50 to $3 a day in the minimum union scale. The powerful San Francisco Teamsters' Union, however, under the leadership of Mike Casey and John P. McLaughlin, rejected a demand for an identical wage reduction. Casey and McLaughlin countered with a proposal that the industry maintain stability of both prices and wages by calling a halt to price-cutting by individual drayage firms. Although an unaccustomed level of tension developed in this relationship when the Draymen's Association then refused to renew its annual contract with the union, a truce was quickly achieved in the form of a verbal agreement maintaining the existing wage scale subject to thirty days' notice of intended change by either party. As employment dropped abruptly in the San Francisco building trades in late 1907, contractors ceased to pay the premium rates that many skilled craftsmen had enjoyed during the 1906–1907 reconstruction boom.[6] But building tradesmen had little difficulty in retaining the substantial increases in basic union scales won after the 1906 disaster. No significant pressure for lower wages developed in the depressed Bay Area metal trades industry, where unemployment had increased union vulnerability. Most unionized firms continued to honor the terms of the three-year agreement made by the California Metal Trades Association in mid-1907.

Wage rates in the printing trades were not affected by the depression. One of the rare unions to win improved conditions in 1908 was the San Francisco Typographical Union, whose members employed on newspapers were awarded a $2 weekly wage increase by the arbitration board set up by the national union and the American Newspaper Publishers' Association. When a large San Francisco printing firm, the Schmidt Label & Lithograph Company, failed to maintain a strict union shop, it was struck in mid-1908 by its pressmen and press feeders. Neither boycotts, picketing, nor intimidation of strikebreakers could bring the company to terms, and it remained for years an open-shop citadel within the local printing trades.[7]

Several unions of skilled workers encountered vigorous employer efforts to lower operating costs during the post-1907 depression. In mid-1908 upholsterers rejected insistent demands for wage cuts by the several unionized San Francisco furniture and bedding manufacturing firms. A conflict threatened briefly before the employers abandoned their demands. When freight rates declined, the Steam-Schooner Managers' Association, in February, 1908, demanded a reduction in the number of licensed engineers normally employed aboard each schooner in the coastwise lumber trade. The Marine Engineers' Beneficial Association opposed this as a scheme to increase individual work loads. The controversy was settled through a compromise agreement late in March, but only after a strike by the MEBA had idled more than seventy-five coastal schooners. In the winter of 1908–09 the Merchant Tailors' Protective Association in Alameda County gave the Tailors' Union brief notice of a sharp reduction in the piece-rate scale provided by agreement between the two parties. The union's refusal to accept the reduction brought on a lockout, in February, 1909, by members of the association. The large dry-cleaning and tailoring establishment of Marshall Steel replaced its union workers and resumed operations under the open shop. Other firms ended their lockouts within a month, having failed to break down union resistance. In this conflict the East Bay tailors received significant financial aid from their national union.[8]

Setbacks for Less Skilled Workers

Although most skilled tradesmen maintained wages and conditions at predepression levels in 1908–1909, wage cuts were imposed upon some organizations of relatively unskilled workers, which were less able to withstand employer pressure than well-established craft unions. The San Francisco Stablemen's Union continued to have difficulty in gaining control of its jurisdiction. It offered little resistance when the open-shop Stable and Carriage Owners' Association lowered wages below the $3 daily rate achieved after the 1906 earthquake. Unions of retail delivery drivers, cemetery employees, milkers, culinary workers, and other less skilled groups reported themselves harassed by wage reductions and widespread disregard of union conditions. In the East Bay the well-organized streetcar men maintained their pay scale of 30 to 42 cents per hour, claimed to be the highest in the nation. The scale of the San Francisco carmen, however, was lowered by the United Railroads to a minimum of 25 cents per hour.[9]

Several unions struck against pay cuts. A small union of glass factory workers, most of whom were women, challenged wage reductions imposed in 1908 by the Illinois-Pacific Glass Company and another leading manufacturer. The strikers resisted for more than three months before returning to work with their union still largely intact. Approximately 250 members of the Carriage and Wagon Workers' Union struck in mid-1908 against firms that refused to renew annual agreements at the existing wage scale. The strike ended within two months, after Labor Council leaders induced employers to maintain wages unchanged until further notice. Nevertheless, Holmes & Company, one of the largest carriage manufacturers, soon flouted the agreement and began to operate as an open-shop firm. The Boxmakers' Union staved off an attempted wage reduction early in 1908, but the following year wooden box manufacturers cut wages from $3 to $2.50 per day. When the union struck, the leading firms declared for the open shop, sued for injunctions against picketing, and enlisted the aid of the Citizens' Alliance in importing strikebreakers. The strike became San Francisco's longest labor dispute of 1908–1909. The boxmakers received generous donations from a number of unions, but this strike, like other strikes of the period, suffered from labor's inability to provide adequate financial backing. The strain of supporting the strike against the United Railroads had left San Francisco unions too poor to make further sacrifices in a period of depression and unemployment. But the Boxmakers' Union paraded on Labor Day, 1909, with placards proclaiming

"Out for Six Months, Good for Six Months More." Although the strike continued through the rest of the year, the union failed to force concessions from the major open-shop firms.[10]

In the declining Bay Area shoe manufacturing industry, hard pressed by Eastern competition, it was inevitable that employers would attempt to reduce their operating costs after the panic of 1907. The Shoeworkers' Union was one of the few in San Francisco which had failed for years substantially to improve working conditions. In the winter of 1908–09, the union's opposition to wage reductions led the shoe factories to abandon use of the union label. On June 2, 1909, after the union rejected the demand of Buckingham & Hecht for arbitration of the wage issue, and the firm refused to continue the current wage scale, its approximately 125 workers struck. Two other shoe manufacturers locked out their employees and joined Buckingham & Hecht in demanding reduced wages. The shoeworkers received financial aid from their national union, despite the latter's reluctance to support militant action by its affiliated locals. Early in July the union negotiated a wage agreement with the two firms that had locked out their employees, and a week later Buckingham & Hecht reached a similar agreement. The Shoeworkers' Union claimed to have won satisfactory wage settlements, but all three firms refused to resume use of the union label.[11]

Early in 1910 business revival brought new conflict in the shoe manufacturing industry. The firm of Cahn & Nickelsburg, which had moved to Oakland, had successfully imposed wage cuts during the depression. Demanding restoration of their previous wage level, and alleging that union members had been discharged, approximately eighty workers struck this firm in April, 1910. The strike dragged on unsuccessfully through the year. The national union stopped financial assistance after a few months, and disunity among Bay Area shoeworkers contributed significantly to the strike's failure. The Shoe Cutters' Union in San Francisco, a separate local of skilled craftsmen, continued to work on "hot" shoes sent from the struck factory in Oakland despite protests from the strikers and the San Francisco Labor Council. For this act of disloyalty the Cutters' Union was expelled from the Labor Council late in 1910. By then, however, the Oakland strike had met defeat.[12]

Conflict in the East Bay Building Trades

Bay Area unionism suffered its outstanding setback of the 1907–1910 period in the East Bay building industry, where the post-1907 depression proved especially damaging to union vitality. The East Bay building trades unions, though gaining many new members during the 1906–1907 building boom, suffered severe losses in both membership and morale when construction activity and employment sharply declined. Many employers were able to hire workers, union as well as nonunion, at less than union wage scales. The lumber companies located along the East Bay water front induced their organized teamsters and lumber handlers to make wage concessions. Early in 1908 the large Pacific Mill & Lumber Company cut wages and broke off relations with the Oakland Millmen's Union. Backed by the Citizens' Alliance, the firm became the leading champion of the open shop in the East Bay building industry. It successfully resisted a prolonged, concentrated union campaign of boycotts and picketing.[13] Early in 1909 a strike by the Plasterers' Union met defeat when plastering contractors found an adequate supply of nonunion workers and deserters from the strikers' ranks. Their inability to enforce union conditions in 1908 led members of the Alameda County District Council of Carpenters to demand reduction of the union scale of $5 per day to a realistic level, and permission for union carpenters to accept employment with "unfair" contractors. Early the next year Alameda County carpenters voted to lower the union scale to $4 per day.[14]

The deterioration of union strength in the East Bay construction industry highlighted the contrast between the secure power achieved by the San Francisco Building Trades Council and the frequent struggles of other Bay Area building tradesmen to maintain organization. The Alameda County Building Trades Council lacked not only strong leadership but also coöperation among its affiliated unions. East Bay workers in some of the specialized building crafts were virtually unorganized because certain San Francisco unions claimed exclusive jurisdiction on both sides of the Bay. In comparison with San Francisco, it was much more difficult and expensive for union business agents in the East Bay to police construction activity. Construction was spread over a larger geographical area, and was confined more to the erection of scattered individual houses and cottages. Small contractors who chiefly built homes could most easily avoid surveillance by building trade unions.[15] According to Olaf Tveitmoe, the post-1907 depression brought "a continuous skirmish and guerrilla warfare . . . throughout the suburbs of Oakland and the hills of Alameda County" in the effort to curb small nonunion contractors.[16] As an additional disturbing factor, the Citizens' Alliance maintained sufficient influence among East Bay building trades employers to develop a degree of open-shop sentiment which aroused serious concern among the unions.[17]

By 1909 unemployment and desertion had reduced Alameda County Building Trades Council membership to approximately one-half of its 1907 peak strength. The council's leaders reported that "the general membership seemed to lose confidence in the Council, the affiliated unions and themselves. . . ."[18] The situation was so serious that San Francisco leaders launched a major effort early in 1909 to reinvigorate the demoralized building tradesmen across the Bay. Upon the orders of P. H. McCarthy and Olaf Tveitmoe, more than fifty officers of San Francisco Building Trades Council unions devoted a large portion of their time to organizing East Bay workers. Initiation fees were temporarily reduced, and deserters were promised "forgiveness" if they would return to the fold.[19]

The organizing effort was concentrated on the carpenters, the largest individual craft. The State Building Trades Council and the United Brotherhood of Carpenters supplied funds to send full-time organizers into Alameda County under the direction of Anton Johannsen, a militant veteran of carpenters' labor disputes in Chicago. Johannsen was an energetic and articulate unionist who frankly argued that labor must at times use violence to combat open-shop employers. He made some progress in rehabilitating the East Bay carpenters' unions. In the spring of 1909 the carpenters voted to renew their efforts to enforce the $5 daily union scale, but it was not until late in 1910 that union leaders could claim to have won over a majority of contractors.[20] In 1910 several other organizations won full or partial restoration of wage cuts imposed during the depression, and the morale of Alameda

County Building Trades Council unions was portrayed as much improved.

The Alameda County organizing campaign was, however, hardly a success. Failing to attract new members in substantial numbers, it left building trades union membership by the end of 1910 at approximately 4,000, far below the number enrolled at the height of the 1906–1907 boom.[21] The meager results of this well-financed campaign testified to the difficulty of extending to other parts of the Bay Area the strength and spirit of the San Francisco labor movement.

Maintenance of Labor's Status Quo

The years immediately following 1907 brought little significant change in the relationships of Bay Area unions and employers or in the extent of collective bargaining. With the exception of the building trades, union membership was apparently well maintained through the post-1907 depression. In San Francisco, Building Trades Council membership dropped to 15,000 to 18,000 before stabilizing. Olaf Tveitmoe noted, however, that the decline was almost entirely due to the departure of the "floating membership" attracted by the 1906–1907 rebuilding of San Francisco. Membership among "the fixed home guard" had suffered little loss. The total number of workers in San Francisco unions in 1909–1910 was estimated at 55,000 to 60,000, of which approximately 40,000 were members of unions outside the building trades. These estimates indicate that in 1910 the San Francisco labor movement, both in size and in relative strength of the Building Trades Council and the Labor Council, was very much the same as it had been at the time of the earthquake. Though holding its own, it had not made substantial, lasting membership gains for some years. In the East Bay, also, there was evidence that union strength in 1910 was at about the same level as in 1906. Exclusive of railroad operating employees, estimated East Bay union membership in 1910 was approximately 8,000 to 10,000, split almost evenly between building trades unions and other unions.[22]

Labor's ability to maintain its strength in San Francisco through the post-1907 depression was partly due to the conservative leadership of the Labor Council, which tried to make the council an effective force in coördinating and guiding the policies of its affiliates. Late in 1907 Andrew J. Gallagher was elected secretary of the council, and during his long tenure made substantial progress in building up the influence of the central body. Having observed the council's failure to raise its share of support for the 1907 streetcar strike, Gallagher firmly insisted that future financial obligations must be met. When necessary, he exacted payment of strike assessments from delinquent unions by threats of expulsion from the council. Along with other leaders, Gallagher also strove to prevent the calling of strikes without council sanction. A cooling-off period was imposed upon impetuous unions by notifications that the council would support only strikes that it had authorized.[23]

Moreover, in this period the council developed the practice of advance consultations among leaders of unions whose members would be affected by a threatened strike. This was an important innovation, for such consultations revealed how much coöperation and support each union would give to the strike effort. They also served, on occasion, to persuade a union to modify or withdraw extreme demands, when it became apparent that other unions would not coöperate. In this period, as earlier, Labor Council leaders viewed strikes as risky ventures which placed financial strain upon the labor movement and threatened widespread conflict through sympathy strikes and lockouts. Council officers adhered to their policy of averting strikes whenever possible, though industrial unionists, Socialists, and radicals called for a more militant leadership. Despite these critics, control of the central body remained in the hands of the conservative majority.[24]

Sporadic Organizing Efforts

Conditions in the post-1907 depression were not conducive to aggressive attempts at union expansion. During 1908, in fact, organizing activity was almost at a standstill, though Richard Cornelius, head of the shattered Carmen's Union, did attempt to organize the new workers hired by the United Railroads to replace the 1907 strikers. But he was handicapped by the Labor Council's decision that it could not, in the current depression, help him financially. Cornelius moved cautiously, assuring the carmen that names of union members would be kept secret, and that the union would not involve them in a rash strike. Patrick Calhoun, however, was determined that unionism should not gain a foothold among his employees. The United Railroads discharged a number of workers identified as union members, and the organizing drive soon foundered. In the spring of 1909 Cornelius renewed his efforts, with assistance from his national union, but again met defeat.[25]

Late in 1909 the Labor Council appointed John O. Walsh, president of the Iron Trades Council, as organizer. As economic conditions improved in 1909–1910, Walsh worked energetically to further the growth of unions. But he lacked sufficient funds and personnel for a thorough organizing campaign. The Alameda County Central Labor Council, with its limited resources, made even less effort to win new recruits for unionism. Walsh gave part of his time to East Bay workers who requested assistance, and attempts were launched, though with little success, to rehabilitate the unions of butchers and laundry workers. These two unions survived primarily because of employment offered by one meat firm and one laundry which were coöperatively owned or subsidized by the labor movement. More satisfactory organizing progress was made in 1909–1910 among East Bay teamsters; a new Bakery Drivers' Union was chartered, and the Milkdrivers' Union won agreements covering most of the milk dealers in Alameda County.[26]

In San Francisco, business revival in 1909–1910 brought the formation of several new unions and facilitated membership drives by existing organizations. Unions of culinary workers, tailors, jewelry workers, and stablemen reported growth during 1910. The small Grocery Clerks' Union, upon the recommendation of the Labor Council, shifted from its traditional concentration on early closing to a wider program of a minimum wage scale and maximum working hours. It won agreements providing a minimum wage of $15 for a sixty-seven-hour week from a few groceries. But the difficulty of organizing small groups of clerks in widely scattered stores kept union membership low through the 1908–1910 period. The difficulty was aggravated by sporadic jurisdictional conflicts with the Retail Delivery Drivers' Union.[27]

Organization was revived in 1910 among workers in the San Francisco ladies' garment manufacturing industry, whose veteran ILGWU Cloakmakers' Union had been virtually wiped out by the disruption of the 1906 earthquake and the ensuing 1907–1908 depression. The union was reorganized with a nucleus of about fifty members, late in 1910, and again tackled the difficult task of ending piecework and standardizing labor conditions in a highly competitive industry. Unions were also reëstablished, in 1909–1910, among workers in the few glove and cap manufacturing shops that had resumed operations after the 1906 disaster. Strong unionism did not again develop, however, in these small industries. Efforts were also made to organize unskilled workers. Unions of janitors and elevator operators attempted, with little success, to recruit employees of downtown office buildings and department stores. A new AFL federal union tried briefly to organize ship cleaners and scalers, who were largely of Latin nationality origins and among the lowest-paid workers in the city. San Francisco's several cracker factories became thoroughly unionized in 1909–1910, when the bakers chartered the Cracker Packers' Union. The new union took in the approximately 200 women and girls, most of them Italian, employed in the cracker-baking industry, and established a collective bargaining relationship with employers.[28] Like the organizations of bindery women and waitresses, it was dependent for survival upon close ties with strong unions of male workers employed in the same industry.

The impact of technological change was reflected in the formation of several new Bay Area unions in 1909–1910. Small but aggressive unions of motion picture projectionists became active on both sides of the Bay. They derived added strength from alliances with organizations of musicians, stagehands, and theater janitors. Minor disputes developed as the projectionists pressed demands for strict union-shop conditions, but comparatively few employers were willing to subject their nickelodeons and movie theaters to boycotts and picketing in order to resist unionization. Increasing use of the automobile led to the establishment in San Francisco of the Chauffeurs' Union, chartered in 1909. It made rapid progress in organizing drivers of taxicab and rental limousines. Fighting a hopeless rear-guard battle, the Hackmen's Union attempted to exclude autos from funeral processions, warning undertaking firms in 1910 that no horse-drawn carriages would be furnished for any funeral in which an auto appeared. The Labor Council's threat of expulsion forced the Hackmen's Union to abandon its effort to preserve a monopoly of its traditional jurisdiction. The doomed organization dwindled away, and the last of its members transferred into the Chauffeurs' Union in 1915.[29]

Racial Barriers

The extension of organization among San Francisco workers in 1910 drew attention to the long-standing issue of racial discrimination. Early in the year, upon complaints from several San Francisco Negroes, the Labor Council recommended that all affiliated unions admit qualified Negro workers.[30] The resolution carried by a very slim majority, however, and council leaders made only a nominal attempt to encourage the organization of Negroes.

The traditional policy of rigid exclusion of Orientals was reaffirmed early in 1910, when the council asked its unions to withdraw their members from any establishment employing Chinese or Japanese. This policy met opposition from culinary union leaders, some of whom were advocates of industrial unionism. The Bartenders' Union rejected council requests for a strike against all saloons employing Chinese help, proposing instead, along with the Cooks' Union, that Orientals be admitted to union membership on the plea that a campaign to force restaurants, hotels, and saloons to hire white employees exclusively was not feasible.[31] But the culinary unions represented a minority viewpoint toward Oriental workers. Racial antagonism was still at a high level in 1908–1910, though now directed chiefly against the Japanese. Unions gave substantial aid to the Asiatic Exclusion League, an organization formed in 1905 to protest the entry of Japanese and Koreans into California industry. Under the direction of Olaf Tveitmoe, the league was active for some years.[32]

Racial hatred was also exploited by the Anti-Jap Laundry League, established by white steam laundry owners and the unions of laundry workers and drivers. The league effectively illustrated collaboration between organized workers and organized employers against competition from nonunion firms. It placed pickets before Japanese laundries, hired "secret service men" to trace deliveries, and appealed to customers to cease patronizing the Japanese. Boycotts organized by the league forced Japanese laundries to buy their supplies outside San Francisco, and the league boasted that it could administer political defeat to city officials who favored the granting to Japanese of licenses to operate steam laundries. It was, in fact, credited with marked success in curbing the patronage of Japanese laundries in San Francisco. For purposes of comparison, league supporters pointed to the open-shop laundry industry of the East Bay, where no organized effort was made to harass Japanese competitors. A branch of the league existed briefly in the East Bay, but the absence of strong organizations among both laundry owners and their employees kept it from functioning effectively.[33]

The Promotion of Home Industry

As in the San Francisco laundry industry, several other groups of employers showed unusual interest in 1908–1910 in enlisting union coöperation for the solution of economic difficulties. One of the most interesting developments was the attempt to arouse enthusiasm for the promotion of "home industry." The destruction in 1906 of much of San Francisco's manufacturing capacity, followed by the 1907–1908 depression, had increased the concern of local manufacturers over their ability to meet Eastern competition.

Employers in the metal trades were particularly anxious to stimulate local manufacturing. In mid-1908 the California Metal Trades Association launched a well-publicized campaign to popularize the civic duty of patronizing home industry,[34] soliciting the support of both the metal trades unions and the local labor movement generally. By its 1907 contract with the metal trades unions, the CMTA had in effect rejected the policy of fighting competitors by cutting wages and lengthening working hours. Now it was turning to the alternative of developing harmonious union-management relations. Instead of decrying strong unionism as stifling the Bay Area metal trades, CMTA spokesmen described their industry as one that had outgrown past labor difficulties. H. F. Davis, the association's executive secretary, defended the industry's acceptance of collective bargaining by arguing that an effort to "stem the tide of the trades-union movement on this Coast" would be "as foolish as it is absurd." [35] Past experience had shown the costliness and inefficiency of attempting to maintain production with ill-trained strikebreakers. Davis espoused the idea of "organization to counteract organization," and enthusiastically recommended industry-wide bargaining between unions and strong employer associations.

CMTA representatives also defended Bay Area labor relations against attacks by the National Association of Manufacturers, the open-shop National Metal Trades Association, and other employer sources. They denied accusations that local employers were "knuckling down" to labor, and that their own 1907 agreement promising the eight-hour day evidenced a "lack of wisdom and nerve." [36] Prominent among the critics with whom the CMTA took issue was Charles Schwab, the industrial magnate who controlled Bethlehem Steel. Schwab occasionally visited San Francisco to inspect the Union Iron Works and the Hunters Point drydock, large Bethlehem properties. In 1908 he said in a Rotary Club speech: "We will not build a single ship on San Francisco Bay until conditions here have entirely changed. The members of the San Francisco labor unions do not perform an honest day's work. . . . I lost three million dollars in this city in one year because of the attitude of union labor. . . ." [37] In reply to such charges CMTA officials praised Bay Area metal tradesmen as unexcelled craftsmen and denied that union members restricted output. They pointed out that factors other than shorter hours and higher wages, such as the distance from sources of raw materials and freight-rate differentials, gave Eastern manufacturers a competitive advantage.[38]

The CMTA's overtures to labor in its campaign to strengthen local industry met an encouraging response from union leaders, and stimulated other employers to invite labor's coöperation in similar promotional efforts. Officers of the Labor Council and of various individual unions conferred with representatives of such industries as book and job printing, shoe manufacturing and retailing, custom tailoring, and work-clothing manufacturing on the problems of increasing sales and employment in the local economy. Labor leaders backed the CMTA's efforts to win naval shipbuilding contracts for Bay Area shipyards, endorsed a proposed

"Home Industry Week," and solicited the support of individual business firms for the home industry campaigns. In 1910 the Home Industry League was organized under the direction of an economic consultant hired by the CMTA to develop a program for expanding the market for local metal trades products. The league's board of directors included a delegate from the Labor Council, although the council qualified its support by affirming that San Francisco unionists were obligated to patronize union-label products, wherever manufactured.[39]

This joint union-employer campaign to promote home industry had, however, a limited impact upon the Bay Area economy. Perhaps its most concrete accomplishment was the decision of the Iron Trades Council in 1910 to lower the wage scales of boilermakers and other craftsmen employed in shipbuilding, in the hope of increasing the Bay Area's slim share of this nationally depressed industry.[40] But the campaign did indicate that a variety of employers had adopted a conciliatory policy toward entrenched unionism.

Employer Apathy toward the Open Shop

During this period advocates of the open shop continued to feel frustration whenever they contemplated San Francisco. In mid-1909 James W. Van Cleave and James Emery, representing the National Association of Manufacturers, toured the West Coast to persuade employers' associations to give stronger resistance to organized labor. In San Francisco, Van Cleave announced hopefully that "I may be of assistance in concentrating the anti-union forces into a more efficient body."[41] But he and Emery left the city in dissatisfaction. Their report to the 1910 NAM convention expressed their gratification that NAM principles were supported by the employers of Los Angeles, Portland, and Seattle. Significantly, the name of San Francisco was omitted.[42]

The Citizens' Alliance of San Francisco likewise failed to develop a strong following among employers. The alliance maintained a small staff, published a monthly circular, and established employment offices in San Francisco and Oakland to recruit workers for open-shop firms. These activities were on a limited scale, however, and gave no serious concern to the local labor movement. The alliance was unable to regain the influence it had enjoyed before the 1906 earthquake among retail meat dealers and restaurant owners. The Butchers' Union maintained union conditions with little difficulty in most San Francisco meat markets. The well-organized culinary workers maintained generally peaceful relations with employers after 1906, although restaurants resisting unionization occasionally enlisted the aid of the Citizens' Alliance in suits to enjoin picketing.[43] In the East Bay, during 1908–1910, the alliance helped to weaken the building trades; but in San Francisco the only conspicuous open-shop victory in which the alliance participated was the 1909 defeat of the Boxmakers' Union.

The employers financing the alliance continued to seek, without success, the leader required for the task of combating organized labor in San Francisco. In 1908 they imported a former British army officer and "dashing Boer war hero," Captain "Jack" McKinery, to serve as the alliance's executive director. McKinery proved an even less fortunate choice than Herbert George, the Coloradan originally brought in to head the alliance. Welcomed into the Union League Club, the popular war hero entered upon an active and expensive social life. In July, 1909, only two months after he had optimistically predicted at the NAM's annual convention that he would cure San Francisco's reputation as a "plague spot," [44] McKinery abruptly resigned. His resignation was explained by statements that "McKinery's fighting spirit, the spirit that had won glory for him . . . in South Africa, had led him into minor labor disputes in which the Alliance did not care to engage." [45] But the captain's departure from San Francisco shortly thereafter revealed that he had left behind him bad debts running to several thousand dollars. He turned up later, safely beyond his creditors' reach, in London.[46] The Citizens' Alliance recruited new leadership and continued to function for a few more years. After 1912, however, it faded into almost complete obscurity.

Resurgence of the Union Labor Party

The defeat of the Union Labor Party in 1907 had evoked considerable concern that the new city administration, under Mayor Taylor, would be hostile to the labor movement. In fact, Taylor's administration maintained a tone of fairness and impartiality.

During 1908–1909 San Francisco suffered no major disturbance of the prevailing industrial peace, and city officials did not come under severe pressure to abandon their neutrality in labor disputes. The preëminent political issue from late 1906 through 1909 was the conduct of the graft prosecutions by the district attorney, William Langdon, and his assistants, Francis Heney and Hiram Johnson. The public grew increasingly weary of a seemingly interminable series of inconclusive trials. By early 1908 only three men had been convicted on charges of giving or receiving illegal payments: Eugene Schmitz, the former mayor; Michael Coffey of the Hackmen's Union, formerly a supervisor; and Louis Glass, vice-president of the Pacific Telephone & Telegraph Company.[47]

Before starting these trials, the prosecutors had induced Abe Ruef to plead guilty to extortion under promise of immunity from further prosecution should he testify against his colleagues in corruption. Ruef's coöperation with the prosecution, however, ended after some months in mutual suspicion and recriminations and in the withdrawal of immunity. Without their key witness, the prosecutors failed, in three extended trials in 1907–1908, to convict Tirey L. Ford, charged with bribery on behalf of the United Railroads. They received another setback early in 1908 when the California Supreme Court, in a much-criticized decision, reversed the conviction of Eugene Schmitz on legal technicalities. The prosecutors won partial revenge later in the year when Abe Ruef was convicted on a charge of bribery and given a fourteen-year sentence. In January, 1909, Patrick Calhoun of the United Railroads was put on trial for bribery. This trial was the longest of all. After six months the jury, whose selection had necessitated the examination of more than 2,000 prospective jurors, reported itself unable to agree upon a verdict.[48] With the 1909 city election approaching, the outcome of Calhoun's trial gave political hopefuls an opportunity to bid for votes by exploiting public disillusionment with the graft prosecutions.

The 1909 Election

In 1909, as in 1907, P. H. McCarthy was the Union Labor Party's nominee for mayor. Once again he ran on a platform designed to attract those hostile or lukewarm toward continuation of the prosecutions. The post-1907 depression, although nationwide, had been seized upon as a basis for charges that the trials and their noisome publicity had demoralized San Francisco business and frightened away potential investors. The city could only suffer from being "advertised as a sort of criminal community where there is a perpetual prosecution." Adopting this ready-made line, McCarthy, in his campaign speeches, linked the prosecutions to the "stagnation of business in our city in the last two years." [49] He promised a "business-like" administration that would not harass business; a "tolerant" one that would make pleasure-loving San Francisco the "Paris of America." [50] Reading between the lines, businessmen resentful of the graft exposures, and tenderloin proprietors intent upon avoiding restrictive regulation, had little difficulty in recognizing McCarthy as their man.

McCarthy's platform contained no hint of class-consciousness, and little else to identify him as a "labor" candidate. He was bitterly attacked during the 1909 campaign by Selig Schulberg, culinary union leader, and other vociferous spokesmen of the Bay Area's small Socialist Party. Schulberg charged McCarthy with sending strong-arm men to break up street meetings addressed by Socialist candidates, and denounced him as a spurious representative of San Francisco workers. But Schulberg and his fellow Socialists were only a small minority of the city's unionists. In 1909, for the first time, no influential union leaders opposed the Union Labor Party ticket. Mike Casey and John P. McLaughlin, who in 1907 had urged Teamsters' Union members to vote against McCarthy, were among his most active supporters in 1909.[51] Few leaders of Labor Council unions voiced objections to the ULP nominee. They had accepted the standards of practical politics, and McCarthy appropriately embodied those standards.

Seeking a unified labor vote, ULP campaigners tried to ease the long-existent frictions between the Labor Council and the Building Trades Council. McCarthy and his associates displayed unwonted sympathy for the problems of union members outside the building trades; they raised funds for the shoeworkers and other unionists on strike in mid-1909. *Organized Labor*, the journal of the Building Trades Council, gave the strikers generous publicity. On Labor Day the council abandoned its traditional exclusiveness, and McCarthy, as grand marshal of the parade, marched at the head of thousands of unionists in an impressive demonstration of the new solidarity of San Francisco workers.[52]

The Building Trades Council declared the 1909 election day a holiday throughout the San Francisco construction industry. Apparently unconcerned about the propriety of its action, it also spent $2,500 to hire poll watchers on behalf of McCarthy. The election outcome was an emphatic victory for the Union Labor Party, a remarkable feat for a party whose corrupt leadership had been exposed only two years earlier. The voting patterns indicated a heavy shift of normally Republican voters to McCarthy. With Democratic campaigners calling for Calhoun's retrial and for continuation of the graft prosecutions, business executives and others opposed to the prosecutions abandoned the Republican ticket in order to prevent a Democratic victory.[53]

Most of the other ULP nominees, many of whom were not unionists, were swept into office with McCarthy. As sheriff the party elected Tom Finn of the Stablemen's Union, who was to be a powerful figure in local politics for many years. It won eleven of the eighteen seats on the Board of Supervisors, electing, among others, John P. McLaughlin of the Teamsters' Union; John Walsh, president of the Iron Trades Council; and John Kelly, president of the Labor Council. The ULP victory brought many other union leaders into the city administration through appointment to boards and commissions, including Mike Casey, who was reappointed chairman of the strategic Board of Public Works, and Frank C. MacDonald, a rising building trades leader named to the Civil Service Commission.[54] Like the unionists elected in 1909, McCarthy's appointees reflected the predominantly Irish-Catholic flavor of the politically successful segment of San Francisco labor leadership.

The 1909 election placed in office not only a mayor but also a district attorney who could be relied upon to bring the long series of graft prosecutions to an end. Charles Fickert, the new district attorney, had been sponsored as a candidate by a group of businessmen seeking to kill the prosecutions. Running on the Republican ticket, he received also the endorsement of the Union Labor Party. Fickert, years later, was to climax his career as district attorney with a viciously corrupt prosecution of a group of innocent labor radicals. He began his career, appropriately, with an attempt to block the prosecution of men who were almost certainly guilty of bribery. Virtually his first official action in early 1910 was to request dismissal of the indictment against Patrick Calhoun. Two Superior Court judges in San Francisco rebuffed this effort, but in 1911 Fickert's appeal to a higher state court brought dismissal of all indictments outstanding against Calhoun and other business executives. The California Supreme Court, moreover, overturned on technical grounds the convictions of Louis Glass of the Pacific Telephone & Telegraph Company, and Michael Coffey of the Hackmen's Union.[55] Neither was tried again. Of all those whose corrupt practices had been exposed, only Abe Ruef eventually went to prison. The graft investigation, launched so ardently in 1906, thus ended in disillusionment for its once-hopeful supporters.

In addition to halting the graft prosecutions, the 1909 election finally ended the isolationist policy of Building Trades Council leaders toward the rest of the labor movement. Mayor McCarthy realized that a solid labor vote would help him retain his present office, and perhaps further his ambition to move on toward higher political goals. Early in 1910 he lifted his long-standing ban against the affiliation of building trades unions with local labor councils. Throughout California building tradesmen were now free to ally themselves more closely with other unionists. On April 1, 1910, for the first time in years, official delegates from the Building Trades Council sat in a meeting of the San Francisco Labor Council. Olaf Tveitmoe and others lauded this *rapprochement*, and called for wiping the slate clean of remembrances of past differences.[56] During 1910–1911 most of the city's building trades unions became Labor Council affiliates, and from 1910 on the Building Trades Council accepted the unifying custom of a joint Labor Day parade. No open breach again developed between the two councils.

Increased Union Activity in 1910

San Francisco unions made very few demands in the years immediately following the 1907 panic, but by 1910 business revival led a number of organizations to renew their efforts to win concessions from employers. Early in the year several building trades unions pressed for wage increases, and the Laborers' Union and a few others that had not yet won the eight-hour day sought shorter hours. Among them was the Building Material Teamsters' Union, many of whose members still worked more than eleven hours a day. Mayor McCarthy, anxious to have his term of office characterized by industrial peace, refused to sanction these demands, regarding them as threats to stable union-employer relations, and as economically unjustifiable in the still-continuing depression in the construction industry. Almost all the demands were withdrawn.[57]

Outside the building trades, wage increases were peacefully negotiated by a small number of unions in various industries. The Bookbinders' Union signed a three-year agreement raising wages $1.50 a week to a new journeymen's scale of $22.50. Blacksmiths employed in Bay Area and other West Coast shops of the Southern Pacific Railroad negotiated an increase of approximately 25 cents a day. Unions of tailors and beer bottlers also bargained successfully for higher wages.[58]

In 1910 the Upholsterers' Union, which had thoroughly organized the skilled journeymen of its jurisdiction, asked members of the Furniture and Carpet Trades Association to raise wages by 50 cents a day. The association resisted, claiming that the union practiced output restriction and that an increase in labor costs would cripple the ability of its members to compete with Los Angeles and Portland firms. In mid-September the union called out approximately 200 workers on strike. The association recruited strikebreakers and allegedly attempted to have supplies cut off from firms that met the upholsterers' demands. The Labor Council, in turn, threatened to boycott retailers who continued to buy products from the struck firms. Late in October both parties accepted Mayor McCarthy as impartial arbitrator, though the strike was not called off until the association had discharged its strikebreakers. In November McCarthy awarded the union the 50-cent daily increase, which raised the minimum scale to $4 for the eight-hour day. He won praise from employers, however, by ruling that the Upholsterers' Union must abolish its practice of limiting output.[59]

Several other labor disputes occurred in 1910. The emergence of the cafeteria posed a minor challenge to the culinary unions, who met opposition to their attempts to organize the workers in this new type of establishment. In both San Francisco and the East Bay, prolonged campaigns of boycotts and picketing were carried on against nonunion cafeterias. Strikes by the small, weak union of ship scalers failed to enforce demands upon San Francisco water-front employers. These minor disputes along the docks, however, added to the toll of strike casualties; while on picket duty, the union's president was shot to death and another striker wounded. Late in 1910 the new Chauffeurs' Union called its first strike. Demanding a union shop and abolition of the practice of charging drivers for gasoline, more than 100 chauffeurs struck the leading San Francisco taxicab companies. W. E. Travis, head of the Taxicab Company of California, largest in the city, rallied employers in resistance to the strike. Armed guards hired to ride taxis with nonunion drivers occasionally clashed with rock-throwing strikers. The strike was soon called off. The companies eliminated the charge for gasoline, but did not establish the union shop. During the years following 1910 the Chauffeurs' Union maintained agreements with the Undertakers' and Auto Owners' Association, embracing almost every San Francisco funeral establishment, to exclude rental autos driven by nonunion chauffeurs from funeral processions. As late as 1915, however, the union had still failed to win recognition from the city's largest taxicab firms.[60]

Friction in the Building Trades

In mid-1910 a dispute over working hours in the building industry aroused the first significant employer resistance to union control since 1900. The hod carriers, who were required to work half an hour beyond the customary eight-hour day in order to prepare mortar for the bricklayers and plasterers, struck late in July after employers had rejected the union's demand for the eight-hour day. The strike, which involved about 800 hod carriers, forced contractors to shut down construction jobs employing 4,000 to 5,000 men. Within a few days the employers organized the Affiliated Association of Contractors which, with the backing of leading supply firms, threatened to make the hod carriers' strike an excuse for launching a general open-shop battle in the construction industry.[61] The *Argonaut* urged such a campaign, proclaiming that "surely a time must come when the property-owners and businessmen of San Francisco will rise in their might. . . ."[62]

Mayor McCarthy, who had originally opposed the hod carriers' demands, now moved quickly to crush incipient employer revolt. The Board of Public Works, headed by Mike Casey, harassed contractors by ordering immediate removal of building materials stacked on streets or sidewalks. It also threatened to revoke the spur-track privileges of the Cowell Cement Company and other supply firms. The moment of crisis soon passed. No open-shop campaign developed, and the hod carriers' strike was brought to a halt within ten days after it had begun. A settlement negotiated by the Building Trades Council gave the union a fifteen-minute reduction in the working day. But even this compromise was hailed as an employer victory and as an encouraging demonstration of effective resistance to the powerful building trades organizations. For some years the Affiliated Association of Contractors, reorganized in 1911 as the Building Trades Employers' Association,[63] continued its efforts to counterbalance union power by unifying employers in the construction industry.

The Eight-Hour Issue in the Metal Trades

The relative peace in local labor relations in 1910 was threatened for months by the prospect of serious conflict in the metal trades. The eight-hour day was to become effective in plants of the California Metal Trades Association on June 1, 1910, when the 1907 contract was due to expire. From the beginning of the year the question of contract renewal and maintenance of the eight-hour day dominated local labor discussions. Metal trades employers across the nation, seeing the Bay Area precedent as a threat to themselves, were exerting pressure upon the CMTA for a reversal of its decision to institute the shorter workday. And some members of the CMTA, now resentful of the competitively unfavorable differential in working hours, also demanded a return to former conditions. Accordingly the CMTA notified the Iron Trades Council in the spring of 1910 that Bay Area firms would not renew the eight-hour agreement so long as their Pacific Coast competitors worked their employees nine or ten hours a day.[64]

As tension over the eight-hour issue developed in 1910, the San Francisco Commonwealth Club was attempting to find a solution to the problem of local union-employer antagonisms. The club had been established in 1903 largely on the initiative of Harris Weinstock, a wealthy department store merchant whose liberal mind embraced a broad range of interests. Conceived as a forum for honest discussions of current issues from various points of view, it included not only men outstanding in the city's business and professional life, but also several labor leaders. Their inclusion was indicative both of the recognition they had already achieved in the city, and of their tendency to seek social contacts within influential circles beyond the ranks of organized labor.

Harris Weinstock, first president of the Commonwealth Club, had a strong and sympathetic interest in the labor movement. Appropriately, San Francisco labor relations were the topic of the club's first major symposium, in 1903.[65] In 1909 Weinstock aroused the club's interest in a plan to establish permanent arbitration machinery for the peaceful resolution of labor disputes. By the spring of 1910 the club had held several meetings to discuss this and other proposals for improving local industrial relations. It invited representatives of unions and of major employer interests to speak at these meetings. The discussions emphasized the question of San Francisco's ability to attract investment and compete effectively as a manufacturing center. The eight-hour issue in the metal trades loomed particularly large in the debate provoked by this question. Joseph J. Tynan, representing Bethlehem Steel locally as head of its Union Iron Works, warned the club that unless the eight-hour agreement were abandoned, "it would be only a matter of time when the iron, steel and allied industries, in and about the bay cities, would rank as relics of the past." [66] Charles A. Murdock, a leading printing trades employer, gave the club a contrasting point of view. He argued that well-paid, satisfied union workers achieved greater output in eight hours than discontented workers did in nine. Though admitting that "some printing goes East, no doubt, for there are those who know no law but cheapness . . . ," he proclaimed: ". . . but if the price of keeping it here is poorly paid operatives, I say 'let it go.' Let San Francisco stand for men at any cost, and for money when it can be made by honorable means and the decent treatment of all engaged in the process." [67]

The Commonwealth Club discussions brought no immediate resolution of the eight-hour issue, but they afforded a public airing of this and other labor questions. At the conclusion of the meetings, the club voted approval of the principle of collective bargaining, and called for the extension of industry-wide negotiations between employers' associations and unions. A club survey had revealed that San Francisco's leading employers recognized the practical benefits of forming associations "as a source of strength in dealing with unions; also in regulating prices." [68] A committee of the club, headed by Harris Weinstock, therefore urged employers not only to organize individual industry associations but also to federate them into a central body analogous to the San Francisco Labor Council. Weinstock also tried to win general acceptance for his arbitration plan. He proposed a large permanent panel, composed equally of employer and union representatives, from which arbitrators would be drawn to judge the issues in each labor dispute arising in the city. In March the Labor Council voted to endorse this plan, stipulating only that it preferred the employer representatives on the panel to be Commonwealth Club members. [69] In the following months the continued threat of conflict in the metal trades gave urgency to Weinstock's plea for establishing arbitration machinery.

The 1910 Struggle in Los Angeles

The impasse over the eight-hour day in the Bay Area metal trades, meanwhile, helped bring on developments in Los Angeles which were in marked contrast to the calm discussions before the Commonwealth Club. Early in the year P. H. McCarthy, Olaf Tveitmoe, Andrew J. Gallagher, and other San Francisco labor leaders had met with Los Angeles unionists to consider a major drive to break the domination of the open shop in the southern city. The decision to undertake this campaign in 1910 received an added stimulus from the insistence of Bay Area metal trades employers that they could not accept the eight-hour day so long as Pacific Coast competitors enjoyed the advantage of longer working hours. By early spring the national metal trades unions and their San Francisco locals had placed ten skilled organizers in Los Angeles. In May the State Building Trades Council sent organizer Anton Johannsen to stimulate revival of the Los Angeles building trades unions. Working quietly to avoid alarming the powerful open-shop Merchants' and Manufacturers' Association, the organizers made rapid progress in strengthening union membership and morale.[70]

In mid-May the metal tradesmen abandoned the secretiveness veiling their organizing campaign and formally served demands upon employers for a contract providing immediate establishment of the eight-hour day. The Los Angeles metal trades employers' association contemptuously rejected the demands and ignored union proposals for negotiations. Accordingly, on June 1, 1910, the metal trades unions launched the greatest strike Los Angeles had ever witnessed, bringing out approximately 1,500 workers.[71]

On that June date, as scheduled, the eight-hour day became effective in the Bay Area metal trades industry. Representatives of the Iron Trades Council had persuaded the California Metal Trades Association to accept the shorter workday temporarily while negotiations toward a permanent settlement continued. This arrangement gave the metal trades unions time to pursue their campaign to force the eight-hour day upon outside competitors.[72]

In the first week of June the conflict spread into the Pacific Northwest. Demanding the eight-hour day, machinists' unions struck in Portland and the Puget Sound district against plants of the open-shop United Metal Trades Association of the Pacific Coast. With battles in progress to the north and the south, Bay Area union leaders decided to call upon their memberships for the greatest financial effort they had ever made, and to concentrate the effort on Los Angeles. Early in June the central labor councils of San Francisco and Alameda County and the State Building Trades Council voted assessments of 25 cents per week per member, to continue indefinitely while the Los Angeles struggle went on. The General Campaign Strike Committee, headed by Olaf Tveitmoe and Andrew J. Gallagher, was appointed to direct the drive for funds. The committee exerted strict discipline to enforce payment of the assessments, and Gallagher was soon traveling from San Francisco to Los Angeles each week to deliver approximately $6,000 in collections from Bay Area union members. Although strike benefits were paid to several different groups of Los Angeles workers, most of the funds went to metal trades strikers.[73]

The fight for the eight-hour day in the Los Angeles metal trades ran on through the summer and early fall, at heavy cost to the Bay Area labor movement. The Los Angeles Merchants' and Manufacturers' Association gave employers a degree of centralized leadership and financial assistance which unions had never encountered in their conflicts with San Francisco employers. In July, through their influence over the city government, Los Angeles business interests won passage of an antipicketing ordinance which afforded police a legal basis for arresting large numbers of strikers. Union leaders instructed those arrested to clog court calendars by demanding jury trials, and the General Campaign Strike Committee brought down four lawyers from San Francisco to defend these cases. Bail charges and legal fees increased the financial strain upon organized labor. More than $80,000 had been spent by the committee by the end of September, with no end to the costly conflict yet in sight. But San Francisco union leaders still hoped for victory. Hired informants within the ranks of Los Angeles employers—generously paid by the committee—reported that the Merchants' and Manufacturers' Association had nearly exhausted its power to raise further contributions in support of the metal trades firms.[74] At this critical point, however, a shocking act of violence appalled the Los Angeles community and seriously prejudiced the labor cause.

The Los Angeles Times *Explosion*

In the summer of 1910 the Bay Area had observed that men practiced in the use of explosives were available for service in labor disputes. Late on the night of August 20, a charge of dynamite partially destroyed the planing mill of the Pacific Coast Mill & Lumber Company, in Oakland. For several years this open-shop firm had been the leading opponent of the embattled Alameda County building trades unions. When funds promised to the General Campaign Strike Committee by the building tradesmen were withheld, San Francisco Labor Council leaders suspected that the money had been used to finance such sabotage as the explosion on August 20.[75]

Six weeks later, shortly before dawn on October 1, 1910, a dynamite blast started a fire that destroyed the plant of the *Los Angeles Times* and brought death to twenty employees.[76] The *Times* was the journalistic voice of Harrison Gray Otis, arch-advocate of the open shop, and bitterly hated by unionists throughout California. The destruction of his newspaper was immediately linked by public opinion to organized labor. The dynamiting inevitably rallied employers more closely behind the leadership of Otis and the Merchants' and Manufacturers' Association, and aroused greater sympathy among Los Angeles citizens for the fight to maintain the city as a stronghold of the open shop. The Bay Area–financed campaign to unionize Los Angeles continued. But now, with the belief in labor's collective guilt for the *Times* atrocity widespread, it met a pronounced stiffening of employer resistance.

Settlement in the Bay Area Metal Trades

In San Francisco, meanwhile, progress had been made toward implementing Harris Weinstock's plan for the use of mediation and arbitration to avert industrial conflict. After a series of joint meetings, union leaders and interested employers formally established the San Francisco Industrial Conciliation Board late in September, 1910. The board offered its services to all parties involved in labor disputes and soon won for itself the critical assignment of settling the eight-hour issue in the Bay Area metal trades.[77] With the strikes for the shorter workday making little progress in Los Angeles and the Pacific Northwest, it had become evident that achievement of a new agreement in the Bay Area industry could no longer wait upon resolution of the eight-hour question elsewhere on the coast.

The California Metal Trades Association, though determined not to yield directly to union pressure for continuation of the eight-hour day, was anxious to avoid a strike that would be long and bitterly fought. The Conciliation Board offered a face-saving way out of this impasse. The CMTA and the Iron Trades Council therefore agreed to present their cases to the board, and on October 13, 1910, hearings began before a selected six-man committee. Harris Weinstock headed the committee's three employer members, and Mike Casey, Andrew J. Gallagher, and Walter Macarthur represented labor. The committee set for itself the difficult standard of reaching a unanimous decision. It met this standard; on November 10 it handed down recommendations fully supported by all six members. Announcing its strong hopes for the permanent establishment of the eight-hour day, the committee proposed that the eight-hour schedule temporarily remain in effect until November 1, 1911, at which time negotiations would be reopened on the question of equalizing working hours in the Bay Area metal trades with those prevailing in other Pacific Coast cities. As a concession to employers, the committee recommended that the Iron Trades Council enter into a three-year contract freezing wages at their current levels until the beginning of 1914.[78]

This compromise was accepted by the CMTA and the Iron Trades Council, although only after some weeks of debate among their respective memberships. The CMTA was especially reluctant to accept the agreement, and exacted from the board in December a clarification of its proposal as calling for a return to longer working hours, should the eight-hour day not be established elsewhere on the coast by the end of 1911. Finally, in January, 1911, the two parties signed another three-year contract, embodying the terms laid down by the board.[79] The settlement was an important demonstration of the ability of local unions and employers to reach agreement through collective bargaining and mediation.

Aftermath of the Times Bombing and the Eight-Hour Dispute

In sharp contrast to the Bay Area settlement, the battle for the eight-hour day continued beyond 1910 in both Los Angeles and the Pacific Northwest. In Seattle the machinists eventually won the eight-hour day from a number of smaller firms, but the strike generally failed there, as in other Pacific Northwest cities, against members of the open-shop United Metal Trades Association. Throughout 1911 the General Campaign Strike Committee continued to pour into Los Angeles a steady stream of funds from Bay Area unionists. By June, 1911, one year after the committee's formation, it had sent approximately $250,000. But the metal trades strike, the chief effort supported by these funds, was making little progress. In September, 1911, the committee warned Los Angeles unions that the assessments could not be long continued.[80] By then, events stemming from the *Los Angeles Times* explosion were moving to a conclusion that shattered any remaining hopes of union victory.

"We know that Los Angeles, in spite of its name, is a wicked city," Olaf Tveitmoe had proclaimed in mid-1910, as he hailed the departure of "missionaries" from San Francisco to bring unionism to the workers in the south.[81] Early in 1911 it was discovered that among the "missionaries" were two accomplished dynamiters. William J. Burns, the private detective who had exposed the Union Labor Party corruption in San Francisco, had been called in to track down those responsible for the *Times* explosion. Burns soon gathered information convincing him that the crime was the work of men who had participated in the nationwide dynamiting campaign directed against structures built by member firms of the open-shop National Erectors' Association. A long series of bomb explosions had caused millions of dollars in damage since 1906, when the employers' association had broken off relations with the International Association of Bridge and Structural Iron Workers. In April, 1911, in Detroit, Burns's agents arrested Ortie McManigal and James B. McNamara, expert dynamiters in the pay of the structural iron workers' union. Burns had traced the paths of the two men in 1910 to California, where they had left behind ample clues linking them to the bomb destruction in Los Angeles.[82]

Confronted with the damning evidence against him, McManigal made a full confession, describing in detail the dynamiting operations he and McNamara had undertaken on the orders of officers of the International Association of Bridge and Structural Iron Workers. The chief director of the sabotage campaign was John J. McNamara, secretary-treasurer of the international union and older brother of James McNamara. In the summer of 1910 John McNamara had sent his brother to San Francisco. There he received instructions for the bombing of the *Los Angeles Times*. According to McManigal, James McNamara alone had planted the bomb in Los Angeles; but the planning and the preparations for the bombing had been carried out in San Francisco with the help of Olaf Tveitmoe, second-in-command in the Building Trades Council; Eugene A. Clancy, a leading official of the council and business agent of the local union of structural iron workers; David Caplan, a Russian refugee of anarchist persuasion; and Matt Schmidt, a militant union carpenter. Schmidt was a close friend of Anton Johannsen, the organizer assigned by the State Building Trades Council to lead its 1910–1911 Los Angeles campaign. The two had been fellow members of a carpenters' union in Chicago, where Schmidt had acquired experience in assaulting strikebreakers.[83]

McManigal's confession and other evidence brought criminal indictments, on various charges, against all these men. The first and most spectacular prosecution was that of John and James McNamara for the murder of the *Times* bombing victims. From April through November, 1911, unions throughout the United States responded generously to the appeal issued by Samuel Gompers and the AFL Executive Council for contributions to the McNamaras' legal defense. Convinced that the two brothers were the innocent targets of an antilabor frame-up, the AFL leaders launched the greatest financial campaign organized labor has ever officially undertaken on behalf of American union men standing trial for a capital crime. But on December 1, 1911, on the advice of their counsel, Clarence Darrow, the McNamaras suddenly pleaded guilty in a Los Angeles court, James to the charge of murder, and his brother John to the charge of conspiracy in the dynamiting activities.[84]

The abrupt ending to the McNamara trial stunned thousands of unionists who had contributed to the defense, confirmed charges that labor was responsible for the *Times* bombing, and demoralized the campaign against the open shop in Los Angeles. Clarence Darrow insisted, then and later, that the evidence against the McNamaras was so overwhelming as to leave him no choice but to recommend a plea of guilty, if the two brothers' lives were not to be forfeited. Only in return for their admission of guilt did the prosecution agree to forego the death penalty.[85] The McNamaras, if Darrow's account is to be accepted, thus saved themselves from execution—but at heavy cost to the reputation of the American labor movement. Guilty though they were, had they elected to hold fast to their pose of innocence and stand their chances of conviction, they would at least have left much of the public in doubt concerning labor's role in the Los Angeles atrocity, and would have spared the AFL the embarrassment of having two men whom it had portrayed as labor heroes suddenly reveal themselves as criminal dynamiters.

Within a year another widely publicized prosecution gave further support to those wishing to fasten the stigma of violence upon the labor movement. In the fall of 1912 trial began in the federal court in Indianapolis against forty union members. The defendants, most of them officers of the International Association of Bridge and Structural Iron Workers, were charged with illegal interstate transportation of dynamite.[86] Among the men standing trial were Olaf Tveitmoe and Eugene A. Clancy of the San Francisco Building Trades Council. Their associate, Anton Johannsen, had been indicted on the same charge, but the indictment was eventually dropped.

In December, 1912, the trial ended in the conviction of thirty-eight of the forty defendants, including Tveitmoe and Clancy. Both men received six-year sentences. Awaiting the outcome of their appeals, they returned to San Francisco and met a hero's welcome. A hearty crowd of unionists, accompanied by a brass band, was on hand to cheer them as they arrived from the East and to accompany them in an exuberant parade up San Francisco's Market Street. In a conspicuous gesture of defiance, the State Building Trades Council made their reëlection to office the first order of business at its next convention. Clancy's tenure of office was cut short by his entry into prison after the failure of his appeal, but Tveitmoe was more fortunate. A higher federal court set aside his conviction on grounds of insufficient evidence.[87] He thus continued to serve as P. H. McCarthy's chief lieutenant in the Building Trades Council.

The final act in the drama of the *Los Angeles Times* bombing began in 1915 with the arrest of Matt Schmidt and David Caplan, who had disappeared immediately after the 1910 crime. During 1915–1916 they received separate trials in Los Angeles on charges of complicity in the *Times* explosion. Olaf Tveitmoe and other San Francisco unionists gave the two men loyal support, raising a large sum on their behalf and sending lawyers to Los Angeles to participate in their defense.[88] Both Schmidt and Caplan were convicted, however, and belatedly joined the McNamara brothers in San Quentin prison.

The Eight-Hour Issue and the Metal Trades

In September, 1911, representatives of the California Metal Trades Association and the Iron Trades Council met in San Francisco to reopen negotiations on the eight-hour issue. Since the struggle for the shorter workday in Los Angeles and the Pacific Northwest was clearly failing, the CMTA called upon the Iron Trades Council to honor the implicit agreement to adjust working hours after November, 1911, so as to alleviate the competitive handicaps of Bay Area employers.[89]

The council, however, had no intention of relinquishing the eight-hour day. As negotiations reached a stalemate, rumors of conflict in the metal trades began to circulate. Allegedly, the CMTA was being urged to belligerence by two huge corporations noted for the extermination of unionism in their plants in the East—Bethlehem Steel, owner of the Union Iron Works; and United States Steel, which had taken over the Risdon Iron Works. The Industrial Conciliation Board was again utilized to avert a serious clash. In November, 1911, the eight-hour issue was submitted to it for further hearings and recommendations. In 1912, after months of deliberation, the board proposed a five-year contract maintaining the eight-hour day and the current wages of all crafts but machinists, whose daily rate of pay was to be increased from $3.50 to $4.00 by the end of 1914. The board's proposal was not accepted, but the long period of waiting for, and then considering, its recommendations helped to cool emotions on both sides. The shorter workday was tacitly accepted by the CMTA as a *fait accompli,* and the Bay Area metal trades industry continued to operate under the terms of the three-year agreement reached early in 1911.[90]

In Los Angeles, in February, 1912, the metal trades strike for the eight-hour day was finally called off. The McNamara confessions, followed by the termination of financial support from the General Campaign Strike Committee, had made continuation of the fight hopeless. Labor representatives received verbal assurances that strikers would be rehired without discrimination as job openings appeared, but the long conflict had all but destroyed unionism in the Los Angeles metal trades.[91] The General Campaign Strike Committee, which had ended its assessments on

January 1, 1912, published in April a detailed account of the more than $330,000 it had spent in Los Angeles since June, 1910. Most of the money had come from union members in the Bay Area. Olaf Tveitmoe and Andrew J. Gallagher gave their report an unintentionally ironic title: "California Labor's Greatest Victory." [92]

Quiet Years on the Labor Scene

Although Bay Area union leaders were largely responsible for the industrial strife—and perhaps, in part, for the violence—that shook Los Angeles in 1910, union-employer relationships in the Bay Area itself generated little open conflict in the 1908–1910 period. Indeed, the ability of the local labor movement to pour so much money into Los Angeles was a reflection of the quietude at home. Perhaps the chief characteristic of this period was the marked absence of major strikes.

During 1908–1910 organized labor scored some noteworthy achievements. Unions maintained their strength through a moderately severe depression; the Union Labor Party recovered from defeat to recapture the office of mayor in San Francisco, thereby demonstrating that the graft prosecutions had done little, if any, lasting damage to the reputation of local labor leadership; labor peace and the eight-hour day were preserved in the metal trades; a *rapprochement* was at last reached between the Building Trades Council and the Labor Council in San Francisco; and labor found itself welcome as an essential partner in the tentative efforts to build up home industry. On the other side of the ledger, it was becoming clear by the end of 1910 that local labor's major effort of the period—the battle against the open shop in Los Angeles— was doomed to costly defeat. It was not a defeat, however, that would have direct repercussions upon the strength of unionism in the Bay Area.

At the close of 1910, local unions and employers were still enjoying stable labor relations. The years immediately ahead were neither so quiet nor so free of conflict as the 1908–1910 period of economic depression and recovery. But no marked change in the Bay Area collective bargaining environment was reached until the mid-point of the coming decade.

Chapter VII | *Years of Stability*

1911–1915

THROUGH THE FIRST HALF of the period 1910 to 1920, labor relations in the Bay Area did not deviate markedly from the comparative quiet and stability prevailing at the close of the previous decade. Organized labor was indeed more active than during the post-1907 depression, but by the end of 1915 collective bargaining had been extended little beyond its boundaries of 1910. The scattered organizing efforts undertaken in these years led to only a few solidly rooted new contractual relationships between unions and employers. This was essentially a static period for Bay Area unionism.

Similarly, Bay Area employers showed little inclination to break ties already established with unions. In the East Bay unionism was neither sufficiently strong nor widespread to provoke campaigns against organized labor. Many San Francisco employers remained resentful of union power, and were by no means reconciled to the city's status as the most prominent stronghold of the American labor movement. Even without the Citizens' Alliance, the spirit of the open shop was still alive. Yet circumstances were not favorable for the stimulation of an enthusiastic antiunion campaign. Though still hopeful of curbing labor power, influential San Francisco businessmen opposed to unionism realized that they must bide their time.

The economic environment was largely responsible for the even tenor of local industrial relations. The stability of the price level influenced both workers and employers to accept the *status quo*. Without the spur of a rising cost of living, unorganized workers were less motivated to band together, and unions were less disposed to press wage demands that would arouse employers' resistance. A few unions did gain higher rates, but for most Bay Area workers wages remained at the 1910 level. In addition, no downturn in business activity had sufficient deflationary impact to cause employers to reduce wages. The national economy, however, did experience recessions both in 1911 and in 1913–1914 —the first very mild, the second moderately severe. These recessions were felt in the Bay Area and helped prevent a degree of tightness in the local labor market which would have strengthened the bargaining position of workers and encouraged them to make demands.

The comparatively slack pace of economic growth during 1911–1915, by California standards, lessened the potentialities for aggressive union action and eruption of labor conflicts. Even after business recovery from the 1907–1908 depression, organized labor displayed more concern over recurrent unemployment than it had in the period from 1897 to 1907. The turn of the century had greatly expanded the California economy, but the rate of expansion fell off after 1907. In the Bay Area, as in all California, population grew comparatively less rapidly in the post-1907 period. The 1910 San Francisco population of about 415,000 represented an increase of somewhat more than 20 per cent over the 1900 level, but most of this gain had been achieved by the time of the 1906 earthquake. By 1920 the population of the city had again increased by slightly more than 20 per cent, to almost 510,000. Population growth in the major East Bay cities was proportionately more rapid after 1907. Nevertheless, the pace set in the 1900–1910 decade was not maintained. The combined population of Oakland, Berkeley, and Alameda more than doubled in that decade, reaching approximately 215,000 by 1910. In the following ten years, it grew to just above 300,000, an increase of 40 per cent.

The Panama-Pacific Exposition

In San Francisco the stability of industrial relations in 1911–1915 was reinforced by an event whose influence spanned the same five-year period. Early in 1911 Congress selected San Francisco as the site for the Panama-Pacific Exposition, celebrating the scheduled completion of the Panama Canal in 1915. The Exposition assured the San Francisco economy of a welcome stimulus. In addition to drawing thousands of tourists to the city, it would bring millions of dollars in construction contracts. It was expected that 5,000 to 7,000 building tradesmen would be employed at the fairgrounds in the peak construction period.[1]

Both employers and union leaders were anxious to counteract any harmful effects that might stem from San Francisco's reputation as a labor-dominated and strife-ridden community. They hoped to prevent labor disputes during construction of the Exposition buildings, and, indeed, to avert any industrial conflict that might prejudice exhibitors or visitors against coming to the city. Especially in 1915, the year of the Exposition, this consideration exerted a modifying influence upon unions that might otherwise have pressed their demands more forcefully. And it helped to deter employer groups who espoused open-shop principles from attempting to launch major campaigns to reduce union power.

The issue of labor's power in San Francisco was inevitably raised by outside organizations interested in the Panama-Pacific Exposition. Late in 1910 the United Metal Trades Association, representing open-shop employers in the Pacific Northwest, had threatened to oppose the San Francisco bid for the Exposition unless assured that construction would not be under closed-shop conditions. In the 1911 session of the California legislature, spokesmen for Los Angeles employers attempted to amend the bill providing for the issuance of Exposition bonds by attaching a clause specifically requiring open-shop construction.[2] The attempt failed, but the business leaders directing the Exposition remained under heavy pressure from both Pacific Coast and national employer groups to exempt this project of nationwide interest from closed-shop rules.

In order to allay protest and display a spirit of coöperation in this civic enterprise, San Francisco labor leaders made a number of concessions to the Exposition management. In mid-1912 the Building Trades Council and the Labor Council sent a joint letter to Charles C. Moore, president of the Panama-Pacific Exposition

Company, pledging that no union would demand higher wages or shorter hours for members employed in the construction of the Exposition; that union workers would handle all building materials, whether produced under "fair" or "unfair" conditions; that the building trades unions would waive their usual restrictions and accept as members all men at work upon the Exposition; that no rules limiting output would be enforced; that exhibitors would be allowed to bring in their own employees to set up exhibits; and that no objection would be offered to the hiring of nonunion men whenever local unions failed to furnish sufficient qualified workers.[3]

These pledges represented a definite relaxation of normal union controls in the San Francisco building industry. Moore welcomed them as "constructive," and in effect tacitly acknowledged the terms as reasonable, but he did not actually enter a formal contract binding the Exposition management to observe the terms. Officials of the National Association of Manufacturers, nevertheless, readily believed a report that Moore had made a *sub rosa* agreement providing exclusively closed-shop conditions. In the ensuing controversy, the NAM sent its executive secretary to San Francisco to investigate the alleged agreement. He failed to receive satisfaction, and after his return to the East wrote Moore a series of letters insisting upon a plain statement of "the cold facts" and demanding a signed statement from every union in San Francisco, promising that all union rules would be waived in connection with transporting and installing exhibits. Otherwise, he hinted, NAM members might refuse to participate as exhibitors.[4]

The argument was not ended until the summer of 1913, when David M. Parry and John Kirby, the most prominent leaders of the NAM, visited San Francisco. The Exposition management satisfied them that it was awarding all contracts to the lowest bidders, without discrimination against open-shop firms. Nonetheless, unionized San Francisco contractors did, in fact, perform almost all the construction work at the Exposition site, though substantial quantities of building materials were supplied by nonunion firms.[5]

Although local business organizations showed little real interest in this issue, San Francisco unionists were somewhat uneasy about a possible attack against organized labor. In January, 1911, William Gerstle, president of both the Citizens' Alliance and the Chamber of Commerce, warned the latter that San Francisco must abandon hopes of becoming a great manufacturing center unless its employers made a courageous stand for the open shop.[6] Gerstle's speech, plus rumors that local banks would cut off credit to business firms failing to join in an antiunion campaign, drew a verbal counterattack from labor leaders. Olaf Tveitmoe said: ". . . if they want a fight we will give it to them. . . . If they withhold credit from union contractors and union supporters . . . we will have a line of union depositors that will break every bank in San Francisco."[7] Labor Council officers announced that they would organize any Negroes imported to serve as strike-breakers and open-shop workers.[8] And Paul Scharrenberg, secretary of the State Federation of Labor, predicted: "If Mr. Gerstle, of the Chamber of Commerce, ever sees the nonunion shop in San Francisco, he will see it after a fight. All of the forces of organized labor will face that fight in one solid line."[9]

Labor's fears of an open-shop campaign in 1911 were largely groundless, but union leaders kept a vigilant watch on unfriendly employer groups. In April William Gerstle and other leaders of the Citizens' Alliance participated in a meeting at Portland which created the Federation of Employers' Associations of the Pacific Coast, an organization dedicated to "freedom of individual contract in the matter of employment" and prevention of interference with "the right to work." The federation was a logical step toward the coast-wide coördination of open-shop policies, and its formation gave rise to the usual reports of an imminent onslaught against labor. Although groups of California employers openly hostile to unions joined the federation, it was relatively inactive and exerted only nominal influence on labor relations in West Coast cities. A move of greater potential significance to San Francisco labor came later in 1911, when the Merchants' Exchange, the Merchants' Association, and the Downtown Association merged into the Chamber of Commerce. The merger increased the chamber's membership to more than 3,000,[10] enlarged its responsibilities, and made it the undisputed leader of the business community. During 1911–1915, however, the chamber maintained it had no official interest in "the relations of employer and employee except . . . the maintenance of law and order." [11]

Legislative and Political Developments

During 1911–1915, conflict between organized labor and organized employers was transferred, in part, to the legislative front. The election of Governor Hiram Johnson, in November, 1910, gave California an administration exceptionally favorable to social reform, and brought a flood of legislative proposals designed to improve the economic position of workers. Johnson was the candidate of the "Progressive" Republicans, who represented in California the liberal movement within the Republican Party led nationally by such men as Theodore Roosevelt and Robert M. La Follette.[12] A San Francisco lawyer who had won recognition as a prosecutor of the officeholders and corporation executives involved in the graft scandals, Johnson campaigned on a platform stressing his determination to destroy the long-standing influence of certain corporate interests, preëminently the Southern Pacific Railroad, over the state authorities. His victory signified a definite shift toward a government more responsive to the popular will and made Johnson the first of a number of California Republican governors whose reputation for progressivism won them strong bipartisan and labor support.

In 1910, as in his later campaigns, Johnson received the almost solid backing of Bay Area labor leaders. He had performed legal work for the teamsters and other San Francisco unions, and was in sympathy with their generally conservative officials. But although Johnson was more favorably disposed to labor than most of his associates in the Progressive movement, who supported many reforms desired by unions but feared an increase in labor's political or economic power, he was never primarily a spokesman for union interests. He did not become closely involved with the labor movement and was detached enough to write an associate in 1911 of his suspicions that the union leaders able to wield the most political influence on his behalf in San Francisco were "wholly corrupt." [13]

In the 1911 session of the state legislature, following upon Johnson's election, lobbying activities in regard to labor legislation increased in intensity. The San Francisco Labor Council named John I. Nolan of the Molders' Union as its salaried legislative representative for the session.[14] Other labor officials traveled frequently to Sacramento to persuade individual legislators and to testify at committee hearings on proposed bills. From this time on, the California labor movement never failed to have one or more representatives assigned to full-time duty at the biennial sessions of the state legislature.

From the standpoint of organized labor, the 1911 session was a landmark of legislative achievement. An unprecedented number of the bills urged on behalf of workers were enacted, some of them over strenuous opposition from employer representatives. Labor's most important victories came in the passage of a workmen's compensation act and a law limiting the working hours of women to eight per day. The women's eight-hour law had met energetic resistance from employers, especially those in the hotel business, in food-processing companies, and in retail stores. Almost all San Francisco newspapers, heavily dependent upon retail merchants for advertising revenues, had called for the bill's defeat. Only a few employers, including Harris Weinstock and the heads of two large San Francisco department stores, Hale Brothers and the White House, favored the eight-hour law. After the bill passed, the Chamber of Commerce, the Women's Garment Association, and other groups of employers appealed unsuccessfully to Governor Johnson to veto it.[15] The eight-hour law excluded from coverage one of the largest categories of women workers— those employed in fruit and vegetable canneries. Their exclusion reflected not only the strong political influence of agricultural and food-processing interests, but also labor's willingness to accept a compromise bill.

Two important items of labor legislation failed to win passage in 1911. A bill curbing the use of injunctions in labor disputes passed the state senate, but died in the lower house. The failure of this bill, which was drafted along the lines of a model anti-injunction act proposed by the AFL, was the session's outstanding disappointment to labor. As a partial offset, union influence prevented passage of a bill that would have forbidden strikes against utilities and other public service corporations until after a thorough investigation by a government board.[16] This bill had been proposed by Harris Weinstock, who cherished the hope that arbitration and mediation could eventually eliminate serious industrial conflicts. Then as later, however, organized labor was suspicious of any legislation that might open the way to compulsory arbitration of disputes.*

During Governor Hiram Johnson's tenure of office there were other tests of strength between organized labor and employers over legislative proposals. Bills enacted by the 1913 legislature greatly strengthened the 1911 workmen's compensation act and required employers to announce the existence of a labor dispute in all advertisements for replacements for strikers. The improved workmen's compensation law was introduced by Senator Albert Boynton, later a key figure in San Francisco labor relations. After the law's passage he served without fee as counsel for the State Federation of Labor in a test case of its constitutionality. Labor's anti-injunction bill met a second defeat in the 1913 legislature and again failed to pass in 1915. Labor suffered another loss in the 1914 general election, when a referendum vote rejected a proposed eight-hour law covering all California workers. Open-shop employer organizations in Los Angeles, Oakland, and San Francisco had campaigned strongly against the measure and against another defeated proposal, a minimum wage law for women and minors. The minimum wage law, however, had received only scattered support from organized labor. In San Francisco, the Labor Council and the women's union of garment workers opposed it on the grounds that it would frustrate union efforts to raise wages to a level above the legally prescribed minimum.[17]

The Election of 1911

Although the year 1911 brought major gains for workers through state legislation, it marked the decline of the Union Labor Party in San Francisco. Mayor P. H. McCarthy ran for reëlection in

---

* Weinstock's optimistic plan for industrial peace in San Francisco was also frustrated. The Industrial Conciliation Board he had created in 1910 survived as an *ad hoc* organization for a few years, and on several occasions helped maintain the truce in the metal trades industry. But it was never called upon for service in other significant local labor disputes.

1911 against a formidable opponent, James Rolph. Rolph was a genial banker and shipowner whose buoyant personality won him the affectionate sobriquet, "Sunny Jim." He was sponsored by the Municipal Conference, a political group composed primarily of Republican businessmen. But Rolph was quite devoid of open-shop sentiment. McCarthy, nevertheless, ran on a platform emphasizing the industrial peace that had prevailed during his term of office, and warning of an antilabor offensive should "the workers" lose control of the city government. Samuel Gompers, touring California on behalf of the McNamara brothers, came to San Francisco as the principal Labor Day speaker. He pleaded for a solid labor vote in support of McCarthy. Just before the primary election Gompers returned to address a final, strong appeal to a large McCarthy rally.[18]

Despite this unusual intervention by the AFL president in a local political contest, Rolph mustered strong labor support. During the water-front strike of 1906 he had resigned from the Shipowners' Association in protest against its policy toward the maritime unions. In 1911, therefore, he had the backing of men like Andrew Furuseth and Walter Macarthur, who had never accepted McCarthy. "The fact is," Macarthur argued, "there is no labor issue in the local campaign. The defeat of Mr. McCarthy . . . will be brought about in part by the votes of thousands of union men who resent his attempt to 'put the whip on 'em,' as he expressed it." The results of the 1911 election bore out Macarthur's prediction, for Rolph won by a huge majority.[19] In January, 1912, "Sunny Jim" entered upon a remarkably popular nineteen-year reign over San Francisco which ended only with his election as governor in 1930.

The election of 1911 marked the close of an era in San Francisco municipal politics. It brought a final end to the Union Labor Party's control of the office of mayor—a control which the party had held for eight of the previous ten years. After 1911, the ULP never reëstablished itself as a formidable political machine. Measured by success in winning the city's highest office, the political power of the San Francisco union movement reached its greatest height in the first decade of the century. To date, P. H. McCarthy still stands as the last union leader to have served as mayor of San Francisco.

Labor Leaders in Politics

Far from being destroyed, however, the political influence of San Francisco labor remained strong after 1911, despite the defeat of the Union Labor Party. True, only two ULP candidates won significant offices in 1911: Andrew J. Gallagher was elected to the Board of Supervisors, and Charles M. Fickert was reëlected as district attorney.* But union influence in the city administration was also represented by Edward L. Nolan and Daniel C. Murphy, labor leaders who had supported Rolph and were elected to the Board of Supervisors. Moreover, Rolph awarded appointive offices to others among his union supporters; most notable was Tim Reardon, a metal trades leader who was long an important figure in the municipal government.[20]

After its defeat in 1911, the ULP ceased to be a formal political party. It became instead, and has remained to the present day, a body of delegates from various unions meeting in election years to endorse friendly candidates. ULP endorsements and the labor vote have been urgently sought by many political aspirants, and at all times since 1911 men with union membership or with close ties to labor have held office on the Board of Supervisors, on appointive commissions, or on the San Francisco bench.

San Francisco labor leaders also acquired influential positions beyond the sphere of municipal politics. Over the years union officers have frequently been elected to the state legislature. In 1912 John I. Nolan, secretary of the Labor Council, was elected to Congress as a candidate on the Progressive Republican ticket. From that time to the present, one of the San Francisco congressional seats has usually been held by a man prominent in the local labor movement. Hiram Johnson's election in 1910 brought appointive state offices to a number of his union adherents. John P. McLaughlin, of the Teamsters' Union, was named commissioner of the Bureau of Labor Statistics and was given a greatly

* Fickert, anomalously, had been endorsed by union leaders controlling the ULP in preference to James Maguire, a former congressman who had given long and valuable service to labor causes. The *San Francisco Daily News*, which had replaced Hearst's *Examiner* as labor's chief journalistic champion, refused to stomach Fickert's candidacy. It denounced him as "known beyond the question of a doubt to be backed by the United Railroads, a thieving, bribing, labor-hating corporation." (Dec. 6, 1911.)

enlarged budget which allowed the bureau for the first time to approach adequate fulfillment of its duties. The *Labor Clarion* lost its eloquent and liberal editor, Will J. French, through his appointment to the new Industrial Accident Commission.[21]

The success of union leaders in becoming governmental office-holders could be viewed as an encouraging indication of labor's continuing influence in the sphere of politics. But it could also be looked upon less favorably. There was, in fact, much concern over the persistent tendency of many San Francisco labor leaders to seek elective office or patronage appointments. In 1911 Andrew Furuseth protested that political ambition was draining local unions of too much of their best leadership material. Frank Roney, aging pioneer of the San Francisco labor movement of the 1880's, warned in 1912 that "labor politicians" were a greater disruptive threat to unionism than such extremist groups as the Industrial Workers of the World.[22] And from Socialists and other labor radicals flowed the usual stream of criticism against alleged "labor skates" interested only in exploiting their leadership positions for personal economic and political gain.

Whether the political activity of union officials was healthy or harmful for unionism is a question for subjective evaluation. But it is likely that the internal unity and dynamic quality of the San Francisco labor movement were weakened by the extramural ambitions of its leaders. It is true that many of those who became influential lawyers, legislators, judges, and city officials often gave needed assistance to labor causes. They promoted labor legislation, impeded the political moves of organizations hostile to unionism, and at times used their contacts and prestige with employers to aid unions in critical negotiations. But the San Francisco labor movement may have paid for these services by the loss of effective leaders whom it could ill spare, or by the dissipation of the energies of those who continued in union office while holding paid political positions.*

* The losses were perhaps inevitable. The insecurity and economic unattractiveness of most careers in union service before the late 1930's made many ambitious labor officials receptive to other opportunities. By comparison with the present, salary differentials gave greater incentive to exchange union for political office. At best, few union business agents during 1911–1915 earned much more than $1,500 a year. Members of the San Francisco Board

Moreover, political office-holding heightened the factional dissension always present to some extent among unions. Rival political ambitions furthered personal animosities. Rank-and-file
union members were more easily persuaded to suspect the good
faith and working-class identification of leaders with high-salaried
political positions. Suspicion and conflict over the activities of
"labor politicians" were aggravated by the fact that almost all
San Francisco union leaders who attained political power between 1910 and the 1930's were Republicans, and therefore adherents of the party supported by most of the city's employers.
Throughout the nation organized labor tended to have closer
ties with the Democratic Party, whereas in California the state
and most local governments were under Republican control. The
practical route to political achievement was the Republican Party,
and most of the politically active San Francisco labor leaders
recognized this. So long as they supported such Republicans as
Hiram Johnson and James Rolph, they were comparatively immune to charges of compromising union interests. But more
widespread protest arose when they backed candidates of less
obvious good will toward labor's objectives.

Industrial Conflict in the East Bay in 1911

The San Francisco labor scene had been unusually peaceful during P. H. McCarthy's two years as mayor. Few unions had advanced demands likely to occasion serious conflict. Business activity was quiet, and by the end of 1911 San Francisco unions
were disturbed about unemployment. The number of jobless men
in the city always rose steeply each winter, as migratory agricultural laborers and other seasonal workers flowed in to await
the coming of spring before moving on to farms, lumber camps,
and construction projects. In the winter of 1911–12, however,
San Francisco unemployment was worse than usual; the Cali-

---

of Supervisors at that time received annual salaries of $2,400. Mike Casey,
as president of the Board of Public Works, was paid a salary of $4,000 in
1911, whereas most members of his Teamsters' Union earned less than
$1,000 in that year. (*Daily News*, July 18, 1911.) Even minor political ap-
pointments and jobs in city departments were sought after with sufficient
frequency by union officers to testify to the limited financial rewards available
within the labor movement.

fornia Bureau of Labor Statistics estimated the peak number of idle workers as high as 30,000. Early in 1912 the Labor Council and the Building Trades Council formed a joint committee which canvassed unemployment conditions among local unions and induced the Board of Supervisors to warn workers not to come to the city. The two councils financed the mailing of thousands of postcards which spread this warning to unions throughout the country.[23]

Unions were not, on the whole, more aggressive in the East Bay than in San Francisco during 1911. Nevertheless, for the first time since the 1894 Pullman strike, industrial disturbance in the East Bay rose to a level above that in San Francisco. Several disputes turned into sharp conflicts before being settled.

The Milkdrivers' Strike

The first East Bay dispute concerned the new Milkdrivers' Union, which had been accepted by the Alameda County Milk Dealers' Association until its leader, Alexander Dijeau, aroused the antipathy of employers. Dijeau's previous record did not inspire confidence. As head of the San Francisco milkdrivers, some years earlier, he had been a figure of constant suspicion and controversy. In 1905, after Mike Casey had protested against corruption in the International Brotherhood of Teamsters, the teamsters' convention had retaliated by electing Dijeau vice-president for the Pacific Coast, replacing Casey. But in January, 1906, Dijeau was expelled from the Milkdrivers' Union for accepting a bribe from an *agent provocateur* assigned to test his integrity. Dijeau's subsequent career, before he emerged across the Bay as leader of the milkdrivers, included minor patronage jobs under Union Labor Party administrations, and an office in the Stablemen's Union.[24]

In 1910 the Alameda County Milk Dealers' Association protested alleged contract violations by the drivers, and offered to enter a new agreement with "any union excluding your present business agent and president." Shortly thereafter, in January, 1911, Dijeau ordered the milkdrivers to strike for higher wages. More than 100 men walked out, but, the association claimed, about half of them returned to work within a few days. Oakland police arrested a number of strikers on charges which included attacking drivers and dumping their milk into the streets. One striker was shot and wounded in a clash between pickets and armed guards from the Thiel Detective Agency. A factional split within the union, however, doomed the strike. The Milk Dealers' Association appealed to the anti-Dijeau faction, offering them the same wages and conditions enjoyed by San Francisco milkdrivers. The strike was called off in mid-April. Dijeau returned to San Francisco where he later served as Labor Council delegate from the Musicians' Union. The strife-torn union of milkdrivers he had left behind reorganized in 1912, and for years thereafter maintained peaceful relations with employers under master contracts establishing parity with the conditions of drivers in San Francisco.[25]

The Sunset Lumber Strike

Shortly after the milkdrivers' strike began, a more serious conflict broke out in the East Bay lumber industry. Although unionism was insecure in local planing mills and lumber yards, a majority of lumber dealers had entered an agreement with the Alameda County Building Trades Council in 1910 to restore most of the wage cuts imposed during the post-1907 depression. But in February, 1911, the council ordered more than 100 workers to strike against the Sunset Lumber Company, charged with cutting wages below the agreed scale and systematically replacing union with nonunion men. Sunset was a subsidiary of the Charles Nelson Lumber Company, which employed more than 3,000 workers on the West Coast and was headed by James Tyson, a leader in Bay Area open-shop organizations. Like C. R. Johnson, head of the Union Lumber Company, Tyson had exterminated unionism in his northern California lumber mills. But in his Bay Area and coastal operations, he reluctantly dealt with strongly entrenched unions.[26]

Tyson put up strong resistance to the 1911 strike, one of the more violent conflicts in East Bay labor history. The Oakland Socialist weekly, *The World,* reported in March that "a familiar sight nowadays is a wagonload of scab lumber driven by a scab driver and protected by a strikebreaker with a great revolver strapped about him, glowering in truculent ferocity at all." [27] Pickets followed Sunset Lumber wagons in order to alert all building tradesmen to the arrival of "hot lumber," and Tyson later reported that more than 100 strikebreakers and armed guards had been attacked and that several of them had been hospitalized for months. In August, after two pickets had been shot and wounded, the Oakland city government intervened. It disarmed most of the private guards and furnished police escorts instead for lumber deliveries. This helped abate violence, although it brought union denunciation of the Oakland authorities, especially of Police Captain Walter J. Petersen.[28]

The Alameda County Building Trades Council was unable to break down Sunset Lumber's resistance. It failed also to unionize a number of other open-shop lumber firms, but brief strikes by building tradesmen forced several planing mills and lumber yards to cease handling Sunset lumber or hiring nonunion workers. Late in 1912, after almost two years of futile struggle, the council permitted union members to seek jobs with Sunset Lumber, in the hope of eventually organizing it. But in 1915 the firm was still open-shop, although its parent company, Charles Nelson, continued to operate a lumber yard in San Francisco under strict union-shop conditions. Finished lumber produced by Nelson's ten-hour planing mill in northern California was barred from the San Francisco market, but was distributed in the East Bay. Stimulated in part by the example of Sunset Lumber, a number of East Bay planing mills abandoned the use of the union stamp, though generally observing union hours and wage scales.[29]

The ability of these planing mills to jettison the union stamp was another reflection of the weakness of building trades unionism in the East Bay. In 1915 the membership of the Alameda County Building Trades Council was little larger than in 1908. The council could only voice the semiapologetic claim that, in the intervening years, "taking it altogether, our Council has held its own." [30]

Rebellion of the Cotton Mill Workers

In 1911 the California Cotton Mills, one of the largest plants in Oakland, employed 600 to 700 workers, most of them teen-age girls. A high proportion of these young employees were the children of Portuguese immigrants, some of whom also worked at the mill. Labor spokesmen had long accused the firm of em-

ploying boys and girls under the age of fourteen, then the minimum legal age for leaving school. Portuguese parents were alleged
to have signed false statements about the ages of their children,
in order to augment low family incomes. Under the mill's piece-
rate wage system, most of the adolescents earned from 65 cents to
$1.60 per nine-hour day. Although these earnings were not far be-
low average for teen-age workers, they were in marked contrast to
the $2.50 or higher daily wage that most Bay Area unions had
established for even their least skilled adult male members.[31]

Before California's eight-hour law for women and minors was
passed in 1911, the owners of the California Cotton Mills had persuaded many of their women workers to sign petitions protesting
that the law would threaten their jobs. Competing with Southern
textile mills which hired women and children at extremely low
wages, the company pleaded its inability to sustain increased
labor costs. Passage of the law indirectly precipitated a strike
among the mill's employees, who were not unionized.[32]

Early in May more than 500 workers, in an apparently spontaneous walkout, struck against the mill. Mrs. Hannah Nolan, an
experienced San Francisco organizer who promptly championed
the strikers, said that the company had sparked the uprising by
cutting wage rates to compensate for the shift from the nine- to
the eight-hour day. To raise funds, Mrs. Nolan brought groups of
the youngest strikers before the Bay Area's central labor councils,
where they received a warm response. The dispute was given
wide publicity as a strike of "little children," thereby provoking
the company into a defensive announcement that it currently
employed no workers under fourteen and would in the future
hire none under sixteen. But although it stirred the sympathies
of Bay Area labor, the strike was only a demonstration of protest
by unorganized workers. After several weeks an informal settlement returned the strikers to the mill. An embryonic union formed
during the conflict did not survive, and the California Cotton
Mills resisted unionization for many years.[33]

The C and H Sugar Strike

In the summer of 1911 another large East Bay manufacturing
plant was disturbed by a strike. At Crockett, in Contra Costa
County, the Bay Area's only significant union of warehousemen

was established at the C and H Sugar Company. But the hundreds of production workers, many of whom were Italian immigrants, were not organized. Early in 1907 State Federation of Labor organizers had formed a small union among them, despite the language difficulties. Almost a score of the new union's members were promptly discharged.[34] "Under ordinary circumstances," the federation later reported, "the method of procedure would have been to force the issue. . . ."[35] But in mid-1907 labor strife in San Francisco left no funds available to finance precarious ventures elsewhere. Deciding that a strike without financial backing at C and H Sugar would be "criminal," the federation temporarily shelved its organizing campaign.[36]

By 1911 the production workers were still unorganized, to the detriment of the Crockett Warehousemen's Union when it struck for higher wages in June. The strike brought out about 150 warehousemen, but left the great majority of employees at work in the refinery. C and H Sugar imported enough strikebreakers, many of them of Italian and Spanish origins, to maintain its operations, and housed them in a well-guarded hotel. But there were some casualties. Two strikebreakers were drowned in the Bay, one of whom, it was reported, had leaped into the water to escape a group of strikers. Early in August there was a fight at the Crockett railroad station, when a train carrying strikebreakers was met by union warehousemen. Wild shots fired by a strikebreaker killed one bystander and wounded two other men. No further episodes of serious violence occurred, however, as the strike faded into defeat. A state-wide union boycott was proclaimed against C and H products, but the company remained firmly open-shop after its victory over the warehousemen.[37]

The System Federation Strike

Another major East Bay strike, part of a conflict that involved workers in San Francisco and elsewhere, began in the fall of 1911. It was particularly significant in stressing, to an unusual degree, the issue of craft versus industrial unionism. Strongly supported by Socialists and other advocates of industrial unionism, the conflict revealed the preference of employers for dealing with a labor movement organized along conventional craft lines.

In June, 1911, unions of machinists and other skilled metal

tradesmen organized a system federation embracing repair-shop craftsmen employed by the Southern Pacific Railroad and other Western lines of the railroad empire created by E. H. Harriman. The new federation was headed by E. L. Reguin, a San Francisco machinist and ardent Socialist. It was a major step toward interunion coördination, for its purpose was to win from the Harriman lines a system-wide contract which would replace the separate contracts, with separate expiration dates, negotiated by individual crafts. The officers of the Harriman lines were determined to block this movement toward an all-inclusive bargaining unit, although they had for some years bargained peacefully with individual metal trades unions. Railroad executives feared that the movement among the shop craftsmen might open the way for an eventual nationwide federation with the power to call a strike crippling every railroad in the country. In their view the shop federation embodied the same disturbing philosophy of industrial unionism which had been exemplified in the 1890's by Eugene Debs's American Railway Union.[38]

In September, 1911, Julius Kruttschnitt, general manager of the Harriman lines, met in San Francisco with representatives of the shop crafts. The unionists demanded recognition of the System Federation, a union shop, apprenticeship regulations, the eight-hour day, wage increases, and the right of unions to review cases of members discharged from their jobs. Kruttschnitt objected to all these demands, and in particular to recognition of the federation, which, he stated, would muster "the whole body of workers behind a demand by any one craft, encouraging unreasonable requests."[39] He informed the union representatives that the Harriman lines would accept a strike rather than deal with the System Federation. The Southern Pacific posted notices in Bay Area shops warning that men going on strike would forfeit pension rights and that no striker over thirty-five would be rehired.[40]

On September 30 the System Federation strike for recognition by the Harriman lines began. Union leaders claimed that 35,000 workers in shops west of New Orleans answered the strike call. Although this estimate was exaggerated, the walkout was on a grand scale. In the Southern Pacific's northern California shops, the strike involved more than 1,000 workers in Sacramento, more than 800 in Oakland, about 300 in San Francisco, and almost 100 in San Jose. In the Bay Area the center of conflict was Oakland, where mass picket lines were thrown up around the barricaded shops in which large numbers of imported strikebreakers were housed. For a time women members of strikers' families served as pickets. The strike soon turned into an endurance contest, punctuated by incidents of violence. According to union spokesmen, more than 200 strikers were arrested in Oakland in connection with picketing and clashes with Southern Pacific employees. In April, 1912, more than six months after the conflict had begun, an Oakland unionist was fatally injured in a picket-line battle among strikers, strikebreakers, and armed guards.[41]

Oakland Socialists, who were always opposed to separation of workers by craft lines, were extremely interested in the federation's fight for a form of modified industrial unionism. They denounced the railroad brotherhoods for failing to strike in sympathy with the shopmen, and called for one big industrial union of all railroad employees. Early in 1912, E. L. Reguin, Socialist leader of the System Federation, issued an appeal for a nationwide shopmen's strike. If victory could be won for the System Federation, he pleaded, it would stimulate the formation of such federations in other industries and thereby greatly increase labor's unity and power.[42]

But Reguin's appeal for a sympathy strike brought no results. By mid-1912 the Harriman lines had recruited enough competent metal tradesmen to keep the repair shops operating, and the strike had lost all force. Soon thereafter the System Federation was abandoned, and a notable attempt to establish interunion solidarity in collective bargaining was ended. Some individual unions continued the struggle in the form of a boycott against the Harriman lines, and as late as 1915 the International Association of Machinists was still refusing to end the conflict that began in 1911.[43]

Limited Growth of Collective Bargaining

The loss of the strikes against the Sunset Lumber Company, the California Cotton Mills, the C and H Sugar Company, and the Southern Pacific Railroad helps to explain the reluctance of Bay Area labor leaders to engage in open conflicts with large and resolute employers. The cotton mill and sugar refinery disputes

also illustrate the failure of organized labor to broaden significantly its beachhead in local manufacturing industries. The Bay
Area labor movement, though in generally healthy condition, did
not grow vigorously during 1911–1915, in large part because it did
not penetrate more deeply into the ranks of factory production
workers and other less skilled groups. By 1915 San Francisco
union membership had not risen much above its 1906–1907 level.
Estimates from labor sources—presumably somewhat inflated—
placed the total number of unionists in the city at about 60,000
in 1915.[44] This would indicate a membership growth of at most
5,000 since the 1908–1910 period of relative stagnation.

During 1911–1915 most established collective bargaining relationships in San Francisco were maintained with little change. A
tendency toward longer-term contracts, of two to four years' duration, was a stabilizing factor in a few industries. Such unions as
those of the teamsters, milkdrivers, bakery workers, butchers,
brewery workers, laundry workers, newspaper printing tradesmen, and metal tradesmen negotiated regularly with employers.
Although tensions occasionally developed, disputes were usually
soon brought under control. In mid-1911 the Teamsters' Union
demanded a decrease in working hours from eleven to ten per
day—the first demand it had made in more than four years.[45]
"Year after year their officials have persuaded them to wait," the
Daily News reported, "to save up their funds, and to perfect every
detail of their organization. . . ."[46] Although the Draymen's Association at first rejected the demand, it soon negotiated a five-
year agreement that reduced the workday to ten hours and kept
wages at the previous scale of $2 to $4.50 per day.[47]

In the 1911–1915 period there were scattered attempts to organize various groups of San Francisco workers. The Grocery
Clerks' Union made its first definite progress in 1911–1912, growing to a membership of more than 200 and establishing a $15
minimum weekly wage and Sunday closing in many small stores.
The new Office Employees' Union received an AFL federal
charter in 1911, a development hailed as "one of the epoch making
events" in California labor history. Optimists proclaimed that it
would enroll hundreds of white-collar workers and become one
of the largest unions in the state. Instead, it became a small organization of city government employees. An AFL federal union

of elevator operators joined the Labor Council in 1911, and late in 1914 reported almost 300 members. But it was not widely successful in raising wages or in winning recognition from major hotels, department stores, and office buildings. Unionism made slow progress among other groups of building service employees. Although active, the Janitors' Union did not extend its membership far beyond its area of strength in certain theaters and fraternal halls. A proposal to organize hotel chambermaids never went beyond the planning stage. The Jewelry Workers' Union, organized in 1911, aroused immediate opposition from the Retail Jewelers' Association and from jewelry manufacturing shops. Several small firms recognized it, but were allegedly forced to break off the relationship through threats of withdrawal of supplies. The ineffective union soon lapsed into obscurity.[48]

Since organizing was viewed as primarily the responsibility of individual local unions and their respective internationals, the Labor Council did not attempt to launch major campaigns to spread unionism throughout San Francisco. In 1912, however, it joined with the State Federation of Labor in supporting E. H. Misner as a full-time organizer for a few months in areas of the local economy with prospects of potential unionization. Misner devoted most of his time to a newly chartered federal union of flour, feed, and grain warehousemen. He held mass meetings for these workers and temporarily lowered the union's initiation fee to 50 cents to encourage their joining. Late in 1912 the union petitioned the AFL for jurisdiction over all warehousemen in San Francisco.[49] This ambitious request, however, was premature. The union, failing to entrench itself solidly in any branch of local warehousing, soon became dormant.

In 1913–1914 the Joint Council of Teamsters formed a new union for drivers employed by dry-cleaning establishments, and the Journeymen Tailors' Union attempted to organize the inside workers of the same firms. Like earlier efforts to unionize the local dry-cleaning industry, these organizing campaigns were not successful. A small but expanding group of workers received attention from the Machinists' Union in this period. As use of automobiles steadily increased, the union developed a nucleus of membership among journeymen garage mechanics. The Butchers' Union was also active in 1913–1915. It negotiated increased wages from the Retail Butchers' Association, and organized a separate local of skilled butchers in San Francisco's slaughtering and meat-packing industry. The new union won recognition and wage increases from a number of firms.[50]

The Garment Workers

Organizing efforts among San Francisco clothing workers led to two of the more significant strikes of the 1911–1915 period. During these years the Journeymen Tailors' Union expanded its membership over a broadened jurisdiction. In 1911–1912 it won from some tailoring firms agreements abolishing the practice of contracting out piecework to individual tailors who worked long and irregular hours in their own homes. This move to centralize all work in the employers' shops was welcomed by the Merchant Tailors' Association, which wanted to stabilize competition by standardizing hours and piece-rate wages. But the union encountered less coöperative employers when it opened a campaign in mid-1912 to organize men and women employed as tailors, alteration hands, and pressers in department stores, and in November it struck against the city's leading stores for wage increases for all workers claimed to be under its jurisdiction.[51]

"The plague of the pickets is once more with us . . . ," the *Argonaut* wearily reported as the department store strike developed. "Greasy vagabonds with their monotonous yelp of 'Unfair to organized labor.'"[52] Soon pickets also appeared before several smaller clothing stores that had accepted union demands, but they were pickets hired by the Citizens' Alliance. They marked the alliance's last conspicuous intervention in a San Francisco labor conflict. To an editor sympathetic to unions the pickets appeared as "hard-faced plug-uglies . . . parading Market Street wearing 'Citizens' Alliance' badges and denouncing firms that had entered into agreements with their workmen as 'unfair'. . . ." The alliance, he declared, "has writ itself down an ass by its latest spectacular performance, and . . . has become the laughing stock of the community."[53]

In this final appearance on the San Francisco labor scene, the Citizens' Alliance failed to rally employers to an uncompromising stand against the striking union. Although the Retail Clothiers' Association, representing large department stores, proclaimed its

adherence to open-shop principles and helped to boycott unionized clothing firms, its leaders met with Labor Council officers
and soon offered to increase wages. The Tailors' Union insisted,
however, upon a union-shop contract, and it was not until
January, 1913, that the Labor Council could persuade it to forego
this demand and end its strike. The union finally entered into an
agreement providing for increased wages and for reëmployment of
the strikers. Most of the firms in the Retail Clothiers' Association
accepted these terms, but the agreement did not establish an
acknowledged bargaining relationship between the union and
San Francisco department stores. The union soon complained that
certain employers were not living up to the agreement. And for
the remainder of the 1911–1915 period it had difficulty in maintaining effective organization among the store tailors and alteration hands.[54]

In mid-1913 another group of garment workers went on strike.
The ILGWU Cloakmakers' Union, which had become inactive
after the 1906 earthquake, was reorganized in 1911 and began
once more the struggle to achieve control over its jurisdiction. As
in the past, disputes flared up easily between workers and employers in the ladies' cloak and suit manufacturing industry. On
several occasions in 1911–1913 the union was admonished for
striking against individual employers without seeking Labor
Council sanction or giving council leaders an opportunity to
negotiate a peaceful settlement.[55]

In August, 1913, the union again ordered a strike "without the
formality of seeking advice." It called out approximately 300
workers in 17 shops, demanding wage increases and closed-shop
conditions. The employers' association offered a compromise wage
increase, which Labor Council officers urged the union to accept.
When the cloakmakers refused, the council nevertheless voted to
pay them strike benefits. To raise additional financial aid, the
union's leaders appeared with Socialist speakers at mass meetings
and came before Bay Area women's groups to plead the cause of
the girl strikers who had rebelled against wages as low as $6 per
week. In mid-October an unusual meeting was sponsored by a
local women's organization. Leaders of the union and of the employers' association appeared on the same platform to make a
public presentation of their respective cases.[56]

But neither this open-forum discussion nor the mediation efforts of a prominent San Francisco rabbi brought a settlement. On October 30, 1913, a woman leader announced the union's capitulation: "We have been literally starved into submission. . . . We could not stand it any longer." [57] Like several other Bay Area labor conflicts involving young women workers, the strike had aroused widespread sympathy. By early 1914 the combined effects of its defeat and the depressed business conditions of 1913–1914 had disrupted the union. The rash leadership which had "plunged the cloak-makers of this city over the brink to their destruction . . ." [58] served as a prime example of folly for Labor Council spokesmen warning unions against imprudent policies. Unionism was not dead in the ladies' garment industry, however. Late in 1915, after another reorganization, the Cloakmakers' Union rejoined the council and began to rebuild its strength. [59]

The United Railroads

Throughout the 1911–1915 period one company was conspicuous for its resistance to repeated organizing efforts. Early in 1912 the United Railroads discharged a score of men, shortly after union organizers working secretly among its employees had reported themselves under observation by private detectives. Later that year a new carmen's union became active in San Francisco. Its members were employed under a union contract with the Municipal Railways, a city-owned line that went into operation at the end of 1912. The United Railroads, with the coöperation of P. H. McCarthy during his term as mayor, had fought a stubborn, but losing, battle to prevent the city from entering this field. The carmen of the new Municipal Railways automatically received the minimum wage of $3 for an eight-hour day, as prescribed by charter for workers hired directly by the city. The United Railroads paid only $2.50 for a ten-hour day, [60] a wage and hour schedule virtually identical with that prevailing in 1902.

In 1913 hopes of organizing the United Railroads were revived, when Patrick Calhoun resigned as president. Calhoun left behind him a worthless personal note, carried on the company books at a nominal value of $1, in return for more than $1,000,000 he had informally borrowed from the company and then lost in a disastrous speculation. [61] His successor was Jesse Lilienthal, a wealthy

San Franciscan universally respected as a philanthropist and civic leader. Andrew Gallagher, representing the Labor Council, optimistically wrote Lilienthal to request a conference on the subject of unionizing the company. He received only a polite reply stating that "the owners of the property . . . do not regard the matter as open to discussion." [62]

Soon after taking charge of the United Railroads, Lilienthal increased wages by about 8 per cent and initiated the payment of death benefits to families of deceased employees. But he steadfastly refused to countenance unionization. Early in 1915 organizers from the Oakland carmen's union and from the national organization formed a new local among United Railroads workers. On April 4 the company, announcing that it had kept the organizers under surveillance and had identified the officers of the new union, discharged approximately thirty employees. Protesting against such summary dismissals, Labor Council delegates voted a blanket endorsement "for any action the Council may deem necessary." No action came, however. Within a few weeks council leaders announced that in order to avoid a disturbance during the Panama-Pacific Exposition the new union would forego a strike which, they claimed, would have brought out a minimum of 1,000 streetcar men.[63] Despite its boast of such impressive strength, the union had nevertheless disappeared by the end of 1915.

In December of that year Lilienthal made a speech to a convention of street railway executives. "I have always believed in labor unions," he said. "It is an indefensible position to maintain that employees should not be allowed to organize. . . ." [64] But, he stated, any union of United Railroads workers would inevitably demand parity with Municipal Railways employees, which his company could simply not afford.

Slow Union Expansion in the East Bay

In the East Bay as in San Francisco, during 1911–1915, there was no large-scale increase in the number of workers covered by collective bargaining agreements. From the beginning of the 1907–1908 depression until the end of 1915, in fact, organized labor appears to have made less progress in the East Bay than in San Francisco, despite a faster growth rate of both population and

labor force. The Alameda County Building Trades Council succeeded only with difficulty in maintaining the over-all level of
organization achieved earlier. And few unions outside the building trades made important gains. By contrast with San Francisco,
organizing activity in the East Bay seldom touched such noncraft
groups as janitors, elevator operators, kitchen helpers, ship scalers,
and office workers.

Among the relatively few organizing efforts in the East Bay
were campaigns to unionize Latin bakery workers, department
store clerks, laundry workers, and butchers.[65] Late in 1910 a San
Francisco woman organizer was voted funds from the Labor
Council to rebuild the barely surviving East Bay union of laundry
workers. Appealing to employers to coöperate with one another
and with the union in fighting Oriental competition, she managed
to develop amicable bargaining relationships with a few firms.
Most East Bay laundries, however, remained nonunion.[66] In the
winter of 1912–13 representatives from San Francisco and from
the international union launched a major campaign to rehabilitate
the Oakland Butchers' Union, after almost ten years of impotence.
Early in 1913 the butchers struck for union conditions at a number of large retail meat markets. The conflict was settled in June
after lengthy negotiations in which San Francisco union officials
played a prominent part. The East Bay butchers acclaimed the
settlement as a victory, assuring acceptance of union wages and
hours by most local meat retailers. Early in 1914 a wage increase
and reduction of the workweek to sixty-one hours gave East Bay
butchers terms of employment approximating those in San Francisco. Collective bargaining was at last firmly established in this
industry on both sides of the Bay.[67]

The revival of the Butchers' Union was an unusual example of
unionization of a largely unorganized group of workers. More
often, the area of union-employer relationships in the East Bay
was enlarged only through piecemeal gains by better-established
unions. Such organizations as those of metal tradesmen, culinary
workers, and teamsters had moderate success in extending union
conditions to small firms. Late in 1910 the Joint Council of Teamsters for Alameda and Contra Costa counties was formed by
secession from the San Francisco Council of Teamsters. The new
organization reflected the desire of East Bay unionists for a local

labor movement with status equal to that in San Francisco.* The impulse toward independence appeared also in the founding, in 1910, of the *Tri-City Labor Review,* a weekly labor newspaper for Alameda County, and in the frequent protests voiced by the Alameda County Building Trades Council against its continued subjection to unpopular policies ordered by San Francisco leaders.[68]

Organized labor in the East Bay, however, fell far short of the San Francisco union movement in numbers, strength, and prestige. This disparity was apparent in the contrast in labor influence within local politics on opposite sides of the Bay. With union support, Socialist leader J. Stitt Wilson was elected mayor of Berkeley in 1911, though he remained in that office for only a brief term. Several union leaders, principally Republicans from the Building Trades Council, held minor positions in the administrations of Frank Mott, mayor of Oakland from 1905 to 1915. They were not in favor, however, with the many Alameda County Central Labor Council officers and other union leaders who joined the Socialists in denouncing Mott as a "reactionary" representative of business interests. In 1915 John L. Davie, former manager of the union-owned California Cooperative Meat Company, was elected mayor on a "reform" ticket largely supported by labor.[69] Mayor Davie was sympathetic to unionism, but labor representatives won few significant appointive or elective offices during the many years he headed the Oakland city government. In brief, the East Bay labor movement was less of a steppingstone to political success than the San Francisco movement.

Unionization of Manufacturing Production Workers

The problem of unionizing unskilled and semiskilled manufacturing workers emphasized the long-debated question of the adequacy of craft unionism to build a labor movement embracing all categories of wage earners. By 1915 unionism had spread to only a small proportion of factory production workers in San

---

* This desire for recognition had its counterpart among East Bay businessmen. The Oakland Chamber of Commerce ardently campaigned throughout 1911–1915 to portray the city as a "great business center in her own right," no longer a minor satellite of San Francisco. (Edgar J. Hinkel, ed., *Oakland, 1852–1938* [Oakland Public Library, 1939], pp. 154–163.)

Francisco and the East Bay. This occupational group was a major area for potential union expansion, yet few organizing efforts were directed toward it. Difficult though it was to unionize these less skilled workers, the structural form and the policies of the AFL contributed to the failure of unionism to entrench itself thoroughly among them.

The AFL international unions showed little inclination to claim jurisdiction over manufacturing workers, with the exception of skilled craftsmen. Outside the international unions, only limited funds and personnel for organizing activity were made available by the AFL or by state federations and city labor councils. Many groups of factory workers, partly on their own initiative and partly through assistance from local union officials, were formed into federal unions directly chartered by the AFL. Such organizational development, however, was haphazard, as systematic campaigns to unionize less skilled workers were rare. Moreover, the odds against attainment of strong bargaining power and long-continued existence by federal unions were high. Usually small and isolated, they lacked professional leadership, financial support at times of crisis, and the tradition and *esprit de corps* provided by affiliation with a large international union.

A number of federal unions had been chartered in San Francisco in the early 1900's, as part of labor's turn-of-the-century upsurge. Relatively few still survived by 1915. The more rapid rate of job turnover among less skilled workers, especially in industries employing a high proportion of young women, handicapped efforts to build organizational stability. Lack of the size and the financial strength required to maintain full-time union officers was another handicap. Membership losses, apathy, ineffective leadership, strike defeats, the chaos after the 1906 earthquake, and the 1907–1908 depression eventually caused the disappearance of most of their organizations. The years 1909–1915 were not conducive to revival or new growth of unionism in local manufacturing. Wages and prices were stable. The excitement of the rapidly expanding labor movement of the early 1900's had largely died away. With their own unions well entrenched, labor leaders lacked enthusiasm for organizing factory workers and other less skilled groups, or for raising funds for that purpose. Existing unions, moreover, provided unorganized workers with few stimulating examples of aggressive efforts to win improved conditions during these years. The economic environment and the comparative quiescence of the union movement gave non-union workers no compelling incentives to rebel against the *status quo*. That established unions kept up their membership and morale through long periods of little change in wages or other conditions was in itself an achievement. The Sugar Workers' Union, for example, a federal union formed early in the 1900's, was still active in 1915 despite repeated failures to raise its minimum wage above the low level of $2.50 for a ten- or eleven-hour day.[70]

In East Bay manufacturing industries, unionism had gained less of an initial foothold than in San Francisco, and had failed to expand substantially as new plants and factories were established. The most prominent union enclave in manufacturing was among the skilled craftsmen of the metal trades. The union conditions established by the Iron Trades Council's contract with the California Metal Trades Association were generally enforced throughout both San Francisco and Alameda County. Although metal trades firms were most often cited by businessmen who complained that unions were driving employers from San Francisco to the East Bay,[71] the Oakland area did not have a large supply of lower-priced, nonunion skilled labor in this industry. An executive of the Atlas Gas Engine Company explained that his firm had moved to Oakland because "San Francisco was so overrun with agitators and walking delegates . . . ," but "at the present time it does not appear to be in a better condition on this side." [72]

By 1915 rapid industrial growth in Contra Costa County had concentrated manufacturing workers in a number of large plants. The county was still lightly populated. Richmond, the largest town, had less than 15,000 residents, although it had expanded approximately threefold between 1906 and 1915. Located in Richmond and elsewhere in the county, however, were such large establishments as Standard of California, Union, Associated, and Shell oil refineries; a branch plant of the Pullman Car Company; the Western Pipe & Steel Company; the C and H Sugar Refinery; the Columbia Steel Company; and the Cowell Cement Company. Unions of molders, machinists, carpenters, and other skilled craftsmen had a substantial number of members employed in these plants.[73] But noncraft workers, comprising the great majority of employees, remained virtually untouched by unionization.

Most of the Contra Costa County firms refused to enter into collective bargaining relationships. The Pullman Company defied the building trades unions by constructing its plant in 1910 under open-shop conditions. It then withstood efforts by metal trades unions to organize both its skilled and unskilled workers. Union boilermakers fought a long series of battles during 1911–1915, with only limited success, to enforce observance of their wage and hour scale in the erection of storage tanks by oil refineries. Columbia Steel was black-listed by Bay Area metal trades organizations in 1913, when it resisted a strike for union conditions by molders and patternmakers. Organized labor maintained a long boycott against products of the Western Pipe & Steel Company. Headed by J. W. Mason, a prominent member of the National Association of Manufacturers, this firm had moved from San Francisco to Richmond avowedly to escape union regulations. Mason, in company with James Tyson and other executives of such open-shop firms as the Charles Nelson Lumber Company and the California Cotton Mills, was a leader in the Merchants' and Manufacturers' Association of Central California, composed chiefly of East Bay employers. In 1913 the association financed a campaign in Richmond for an antipicketing ordinance modeled upon that in Los Angeles. The campaign failed, as did a similar effort in Berkeley; but in 1915 the association won passage of such an ordinance in the industrial town of Martinez.[74]

Industrial Unionism

The problem of organizing factory workers was related to the long struggle within the labor movement between the advocates of craft and industrial unionism. A significant aspect of the period 1911–1915 in the Bay Area was the vigorous debate on the question of organizational structure. Members of the Industrial Workers of the World, the syndicalist organization founded in 1905 and dedicated to the ideal of "one big union," became more active on the Pacific Coast. Socialists increased their attacks on the "American Separation of Labor" fostered by the AFL's traditional craft unionism. Other unionists, of less class-conscious persuasion, also supported proposals for unions that would embrace all workers, skilled and unskilled, of a given industry.

Enthusiasm for industrial unionism would have been stronger among Bay Area workers had the local branches of the Socialist Party achieved greater success in attracting union leaders. But the "business unionist" type continued to prevail among those holding major union offices. Despite ardent efforts, Socialists and their sympathizers failed to play dominant roles within the Bay Area labor movement or to win control of the San Francisco Labor Council and other central bodies. They did represent, however, a minority of definite influence. Socialists held the leadership of some Bay Area unions, led strong factions within others, and were usually well represented among delegates to and minor officers of central labor councils.

Despite their opposition to the AFL philosophy of business unionism, Socialists were not subject to widespread hostility or intolerance by more conventional unionists. Socialist speakers were often welcomed at labor meetings. The *Labor Clarion*, especially in 1909–1914, published many articles by Socialist members of local unions, and provided an open forum for debate on such topics as the acceptability of private enterprise, or the relative merits of craft and industrial unionism. Socialist candidates for political office frequently received endorsements from individual unions, particularly in the East Bay. In mid-1912 the Alameda County Central Labor Council worked closely with the Socialist Party in Oakland in a special election to recall Mayor Frank Mott. The election, which failed to unseat Mott, was a protest against Oakland police action in breaking up peaceful meetings held by Socialists and Industrial Workers of the World. Later in 1912, endorsement by the Alameda County Building Trades Council and by individual unions helped J. Stitt Wilson, the Socialist mayor of Berkeley, to poll approximately 40 per cent of the vote in an unsuccessful race against the incumbent congressman, Joseph R. Knowland.[75]

The influence of the Industrial Workers of the World upon the Bay Area labor movement was less than that of the Socialists. From 1910 to 1915, the IWW often won a substantial following among migratory agricultural laborers and seasonal workers in logging and construction camps in Western states. But urban workers, rooted more securely by steady jobs and family life, did not respond readily to the militant class-consciousness and the visionary romanticism of the IWW. Leaders and members of AFL unions rarely accorded to IWW doctrines the serious consideration that many unionists showed toward Socialism. The IWW goal of a classless society, to be created by a revolutionary syndicalist labor movement, was generally rejected as a hopeless and dangerous dream.

Through 1915, however, the bitter hostility toward the IWW that later suffused AFL union leadership was not yet in appreciable evidence in California. The IWW was not strong enough to present a serious threat to conventional trade unionism, and was usually scoffed at as the "I Won't Work's" or the "Idle Wonder Workers." And sympathy was quickly aroused among AFL unionists for IWW members subjected to police and vigilante violence in various California and Pacific Northwest communities. In 1912 the brutality practiced upon the men active in the San Diego "free speech fight," the most famous IWW demonstration in California, aroused union protests. The San Francisco Labor Council sponsored a mass meeting to denounce the suppression of IWW street speakers, and distributed thousands of copies of a report by Paul Scharrenberg and Olaf Tveitmoe attacking the police actions they had observed in San Diego.[76]

The IWW was continuously active in the Bay Area from 1909 on, but its impact upon the labor movement was slight. The IWW locals in San Francisco and Oakland together claimed little more than 200 members by 1911, many of them probably transients. IWW organizers often held inspirational meetings in their Bay Area headquarters, and attracted small crowds by open-air speeches on downtown street corners. The street speakers were especially active in Oakland during 1911–1912, where they encountered sporadic police harassment in the form of beatings and arrests. In more cosmopolitan San Francisco, the police were less disposed to suppress the IWW unorthodoxy, but a minor "free speech fight" did occur in mid-1911, when Italian speakers trying to organize French and Italian bakers into an IWW union were arrested. After about a dozen arrests, the police dropped the matter. IWW spokesmen claimed that approximately 100 Italian bakers had joined the union before its demise.[77]

The 1913 Shoeworkers' Strike

The influence of the IWW was evident in a 1913 shoeworkers' strike, an episode of particular interest in that it marked the first appearance in a local labor dispute of two militant unionists who were to be prominent figures in San Francisco labor history. Late in 1912 the shoe manufacturing firm of G. M. Kutz became the Frank & Hyman Shoe Company. The new owners shut down the plant for several weeks and then, in January, 1913, recalled employees to work at sharply reduced wage rates. Some of the more active members of the Shoeworkers' Union were not asked to return. A strike broke out immediately for restoration of the wage cut and rehiring of the entire work force. About seventy-five workers, almost half of them women, walked out. Frank & Hyman brought in a small group of skilled men from St. Louis, housed them under armed guard in the plant, and hired inexperienced men and women locally to help them maintain production. The San Francisco IWW local, some of whose members were leaders in the Shoeworkers' Union, helped to organize picketing by workers who sang the ballads of Joe Hill, the IWW song writer, as they paraded before the struck firm. Strikers, IWW members, and sympathizing women workers from nearby union laundries swelled the picket line into a continuous chain at closing time, when employees emerged under guard to return to their homes.[78]

The strike brought together for the first time two men whose names would soon be known to unionists in many parts of the world, Warren K. Billings and Thomas J. Mooney. Billings was a foot-loose nineteen-year-old union shoeworker who had just arrived in San Francisco from the East with a half-formed plan to join Pancho Villa's revolutionary army in Mexico. Becoming acquainted with leaders of the IWW and the Shoeworkers' Union, the young man was soon persuaded that he might find adventure closer at hand. Accordingly, he took a job as an ostensible "scab" with Frank & Hyman, from which vantage point he kept his new associates informed of developments within the strike-bound plant.[79]

Meanwhile, Mooney, a member of the Molders' Union, was active among the pickets outside the plant. As the owner of a motorcycle, his job was to follow the automobiles carrying women employees to and from the firm and exhort the women to join their fellow workers on the picket line. Mooney, then not quite thirty years of age, was a belligerent and energetic man who was beginning to annoy San Francisco union leaders by his aggressive advocacy of industrial unionism, a radical overhauling of American labor leadership, and an uncompromising class struggle. Never a doctrinal purist, at one time he had simultaneously held membership in the AFL Molders' Union, the IWW, and the Socialist Party. In 1908 he had demonstrated his effectiveness as a speaker and a fund raiser while traveling through the country with the "Red Special," the campaign train of Eugene Debs, Socialist candidate for president.[80]

Taking up residence in San Francisco in 1909, Mooney professed himself "amazed at the extreme conservatism of the local labor leaders," and at their anxiety "to appear 'respectable.' " [81] He offered an alternative brand of leadership. In 1911 he helped establish a left-wing Socialist weekly, *Revolt—The Voice of the Militant Worker*. During its brief life *Revolt* devoted much of its space to charges that San Francisco union officials were following class collaborationist policies, especially as embodied in the Union Labor Party and in P. H. McCarthy's bid for reëlection as mayor on a platform that stressed his maintenance of industrial peace.[82] In Mooney's eyes, the San Francisco labor movement was in desperate need of redemption from conservative craft unionists and "labor politicians."

Late in 1912, Mooney was elected by the San Francisco Molders' Union as its delegate to the international's convention. His election represented a personal triumph over the union's conservative leaders, headed by Congressman-elect John I. Nolan. But it was to prove the high-water mark in Mooney's career in the labor movement. At the 1912 convention he took the initiative in fighting for "a militant industrial union" that would enlist not only skilled molders but all foundry workers. Although this attempt failed, it gained widespread notice and brought Mooney enthusiastic encomiums from William Z. Foster, the left-wing Socialist who later became the leader of the American Communist Party.[83] Soon after his return from the 1912 molders' convention, Mooney volunteered to help the shoeworkers in their strike against Frank & Hyman.

The strike continued for almost four months. During its course a number of pickets were arrested, some hundreds of dollars worth of shoes were destroyed by sabotage, and a San Francisco judge strolling by the plant was slightly wounded when fired upon mistakenly by a strikebreaker. Tom Mooney's activity in the strike ceased abruptly in March, 1913, when he broke his leg in a motorcycle accident. A month later Warren Billings was forcibly ejected from the plant by a suspicious foreman. He received a minor flesh wound when his revolver discharged as he was fighting with the foreman.* The strike finally ended in May with a negotiated settlement. The former wage scale was restored, and apparently all workers were promised reinstatement. Labor Council leaders, who had raised substantial support for the strikers despite their IWW connections, hailed the settlement as an outstanding victory.[84]

Movements toward Broader Union Groups

Although the extreme position taken by the Industrial Workers of the World attracted few adherents, many Bay Area workers displayed increasing interest in industrial unionism or in plans to achieve greater unity and coöperation among related unions. The tendency to look beyond craft unionism for more effective aggregations of union strength was one of the most noteworthy features of the local labor scene during the period 1911–1915. Concern over union structure and interunion solidarity was especially evidenced by labor organizations with Socialist or militantly class-conscious leaders, such as the unions of culinary workers, bakers, brewery workers, machinists, tailors, ladies' garment workers, shoeworkers, and longshoremen, and some locals of carpenters. Among these, the culinary workers, the longshoremen, and the machinists stood out as the Bay Area's leading advocates of broader organizations.

The culinary unions of San Francisco constituted the chief force within their international pressing for abandonment of traditional craft unionism. Hugo Ernst, a Socialist leader of the Waiters'

* Ironically enough, the *Labor Clarion*, unaware of Billings' deceptive role in the strike, seized upon this incident as reported in the newspapers. The *Clarion* described Billings as a classic example of the depraved, gun-wielding "scab." (April 25, 1913.)

Union, was the most influential of the men generally sympathetic to Socialism and industrial unionism who controlled the culinary workers' Joint Executive Board. This group constantly irritated the international's leaders by calling on them to organize not only skilled cooks and waiters, but also waitresses, bus boys, dishwashers, and general kitchen helpers. Ernst and his associates insisted, moreover, on a new approach to the task of breaking down the resistance of the hotel industry to the culinary unions. They proposed that organizing drives include chambermaids, bell-boys, and other workers on hotel staffs. The international, however, refused to allot the necessary funds or organizers for campaigns to broaden the membership base among restaurant and hotel employees. San Francisco thus continued to be conspicuous as a city where unionism was solidly entrenched among all categories of restaurant workers; but in its hotels, although the cooks' and waiters' unions enlarged their footholds during 1911–1915, no significant progress was made toward industry-wide unionization.[85]

In mid-1912 there was a demonstration of the type of solidarity called for by industrial unionists. The San Francisco Bakers' Union, without the approval of its international or of the Labor Council, struck to have the union label placed on all loaves of bread. Bakery drivers struck in support, and stationary firemen walked off their jobs in several bakeries. Culinary workers threatened a general strike against employers who required them to handle "hot" bread, and a few restaurant workers were in fact called out in a show of unity with the bakers. Although the strike spread sufficiently to suggest the potential force of unions allied in a common cause, it did not become a major conflict. It ended after a month in a face-saving settlement providing that bakeries would use the label only if their customers demanded it.[86]

Later in 1912 the unions of culinary workers, bakers, butchers, and several other categories of workers established the Provision Trades Council.[87] A previous council, formed a decade earlier, had gradually died from the loss of interest and the pursuit of independent policies by its affiliates. Industrial unionists hoped that the new organization would establish a unified command and would assume the authority to negotiate master contracts with employers, where feasible. Like its predecessor, however, the

Provision Trades Council never achieved significance in the local collective bargaining structure. It eventually dissolved, after an uneventful existence.

From about 1912 on, Bay Area members of the International Longshoremen's Association displayed deep interest in broader industrial organizations. Their leaders professed serious concern over the influence of the IWW within their unions. Whatever the extent of IWW infiltration, longshoremen were the Bay Area's most forthright proponents of the "one-big-union" concept. In 1913 the San Francisco Longshoremen's Union supported for a time a plan to establish, by secession from the ILA, a separate Pacific Coast association of longshoremen, organized along industrial union lines. Early in 1914 it urged that teamsters, sailors, marine firemen, and other workers connected with maritime transportation merge with the longshoremen into a single, industry-wide union. The teamsters and the sailors gave a cold response to this proposal; but later in 1914 the Waterfront Workers' Federation was established in San Francisco, chiefly through the initiative of longshoremen who planned to make it the first step toward a federation that would embrace all marine transportation workers on the Pacific Coast.[88]

This new organization, a reincarnation of the City Front Federation of 1901, had both the Teamsters' Union and the Sailors' Union among its affiliates. The Sailors' Union had joined over the opposition of Andrew Furuseth, who had come more and more to believe that seamen were a unique class of workers who could trust only their own, exclusive organizations to protect their interests. Irreconcilably antagonistic toward the ILA after years of jurisdictional fighting, Furuseth constantly warned offshore workers against committing themselves in any way to coöperate with or support the longshoremen. He argued that they would destroy the Sailors' Union should its members refuse to handle cargo from nonunion longshoremen in the event of an ILA strike. Furuseth was not only troubled about his union's *rapprochement* with the longshoremen; he had also become alarmed at signs of IWW influence within the Sailors' Union at such ports as San Pedro and Seattle.[89]

In addition to fostering closer ties with other transportation unions, ILA leaders reached out among Bay Area workers for a wider membership base for their own organizations. In 1912 an ILA local of lumber clerks employed by East Bay water-front lumber firms had no difficulty in gaining permission from leaders of the State Building Trades Council to organize shipping clerks, packers, and warehousemen in Alameda County. Efforts to unionize these workers went little beyond the initial statement of intention, but the impulse to extend ILA influence continued to manifest itself. During 1912–1914 the ILA locals on both sides of the Bay merged gradually into one large union, with its headquarters and most of its members in San Francisco. This union, claiming more than 3,500 members in late 1915, described itself as the largest union local west of Chicago. By then it was moving into the fringes of an industry offering a potential for large additional membership gains, as it had begun to organize workers in the warehouses bordering the San Francisco water front.[90]

While ILA members in the Bay Area were combining forces into a single large local, which was attempting to expand its jurisdiction among transportation and distribution workers, leaders of the Pacific Coast District of the ILA were seeking effective coast-wide coöperation among the unions of all ports. As in the past, however, they found it difficult to coördinate longshoremen from San Diego to Vancouver into a disciplined unit. In 1914 a proposal to introduce a coast-wide uniform wage for longshoremen was carried by only a thin margin in a referendum vote of the district's membership. The Bay Area longshoremen, enjoying the high wage of 50 cents an hour, voted against the plan to raise hourly rates in all ports to parity with their own. Throughout the district sentiment for a uniform wage was not sufficiently strong to support a coast-wide strike for its enforcement, which some longshoremen advocated.[91]

In 1915, however, district leaders were largely successful in inducing affiliated ILA locals to refuse to handle cargo being shipped to or from Vancouver during a strike of longshoremen at that port. John Kean, San Francisco union leader and president of the district organization, argued that the ILA must incur the risk that the boycott might turn a local conflict into a major battle with employers along the entire Pacific Coast. Otherwise, he indicated, employers might adopt the strategy of defeating the longshoremen piecemeal, in isolated contests in individual ports.[92]

By 1915 ILA leaders were acutely aware of the need for coast-wide unity, but the low breaking point of the unity attained was soon to be demonstrated.

The machinists' unions of the Bay Area also displayed sympathy toward industrial unionism. Their leaders were frequently Socialists who gave them a more class-conscious orientation than was typical of the Bay Area labor movement. Control of the San Francisco machinists' local, with approximately 1,500 members, alternated between traditional craft unionists and self-styled "industrial unionists," many of whom were Socialists. Machinists throughout the country were also interested in broader organizational forms. Late in 1914 a referendum vote of the International Association of Machinists showed a majority in favor of merging all metal trades crafts into a large industrial organization.[93] The IAM urged its fellow metal trades unions to vote on such a merger, but found them apathetic. In many cities, however, metal tradesmen had in essence achieved a major goal of industrial unionism by forming central councils possessing the authority to determine industry-wide union policy. One of the most important of these bodies was the long-established Iron Trades Council of the San Francisco and East Bay unions. Though subject to recurrent internal stress, the council held its affiliates together in a single bargaining unit and maintained their united front at times of crisis.

The Building Trades Council

It is ironic that in the building industry, the chief stronghold of old and aristocratic craft unions, the central council developed by P. H. McCarthy should be in part an industrial form of organization. The control of the Building Trades Council over its affiliates eliminated not only jurisdictional conflict, but also much of the craft autonomy characteristic of building tradesmen elsewhere. McCarthy had no ideological sympathy for industrial unionism, yet he created an organization prepared to act as an industry-wide unit upon his command. And Olaf Tveitmoe, his chief lieutenant, had a strong interest in the establishment of unions of wider scope. He called for a series of mergers in the building trades to reduce the number of separate unions and the incidence of jurisdictional bickering. Moreover, he repeatedly endorsed the industrial union movement.[94] Addressing the delegates to the State Building Trades Council convention in 1914, Tveitmoe argued that the council "is an industrial organization. . . . Why, then, do we shudder over mere words?" [95]

The Building Trades Council's policy-making power was in keeping with the principles of industrial unionism, but the industrial unionist's championship of the less skilled worker was not characteristic of McCarthy's reign over the council. Although a 1910 amendment to the San Francisco charter established a minimum wage of $3 for an eight-hour day for all workers employed directly by the city, five years later private contractors were still paying most members of the Laborers' Union in the building trades $2.50 per eight- to nine-hour day. Despite the restiveness of these workers, the council repeatedly refused to sanction their demands for a higher minimum wage. Early in 1913 the Alameda County Building Trades Council announced an increase to $3 in the scale of its affiliated Laborers' Union. East Bay contractors thereupon complained to McCarthy, and the council was forced to withdraw its support of the proposed increase. In 1915, when the Alameda County Council renewed its effort for the $3 wage, the State Building Trades Council officers intervened again to back up the contractors' insistence that the East Bay laborers' scale must be held down to the $2.50 minimum maintained in San Francisco.[96]

Unionism for Migratory Workers

One major group of unskilled workers received unusual attention from organized labor during the 1910–1915 period. A pioneer AFL effort was launched late in 1909 to organize the thousands of migratory workers in California. Paul Scharrenberg, a young and progressive Sailors' Union officer who had become secretary of the State Federation of Labor in 1909, planned this undertaking in company with Olaf Tveitmoe, Andrew Furuseth, and several other San Francisco labor leaders. They had a dual purpose: to aid heretofore neglected men, and to forestall the increasingly active IWW. The immediate practical aim, however, was to unionize casual laborers who constituted a ready source of strikebreakers. Directed by the State Federation, the organizing drive was carried on throughout 1910–1915, although its momentum fell off toward the end of the period. AFL federal unions were chartered in Oakland, San Francisco, Richmond, San Jose, Sacramento, Fresno, and a few other cities. Their headquarters served as gathering places and, to some extent, as employment offices for laborers who stopped in these cities between jobs on farms or in railroad, lumber, and construction camps. To prevent these unions from becoming exclusive organizations seeking only to control job opportunities for present members, initiation fees were held to $1 and memberships were made transferable without cost among the various locals.[97]

By 1914 organizers reported that about 5,000 men had been enrolled by the federal unions of the United Laborers of America, as this group of California organizations was ambitiously entitled.[98] But, Scharrenberg pointed out in 1913, "thousands have disappeared after joining." [99] Yet he was optimistic about the long-run success of the campaign. Along with Tveitmoe and Furuseth, he had long urged the AFL to launch a similar nation-wide drive. As the years passed, however, California labor leaders became increasingly disillusioned over the possibilities of unionizing casual unskilled laborers. Despite their efforts, the United Laborers' unions never established collective bargaining relationships on any significant scale, and never exerted real influence upon the wages or working conditions of their members.[100]

Attempts by both AFL and IWW organizers to establish unions among California cannery workers made even less progress. Most of the cannery workers were women, working up to twelve hours a day at the seasonal peak for piece-rate wages of $6 to $13 per week. Many of the employees in Bay Area canneries were Italian immigrants impeded by the language barrier from responding to union organizers. The task of organizing seasonal, female, and foreign-born workers proved sufficiently formidable to bring from Paul Scharrenberg in 1914 a discouraged admission that all past AFL efforts among cannery workers indicated their unionization to be almost impossible.[101]

Criticism of Craft Unionism

The problems of organizing unskilled workers, of achieving unity of action by all unions within an industry, and of resolving the issue of craft versus industrial unionism drew the attention of labor leaders not only in the Bay Area but throughout the nation.

The AFL annual conventions, especially from 1912 on, were marked by intense debate on these questions. At each convention there were attempts to win passage of resolutions calling for such policy changes as reorganization of the American Federation of Labor on an industrial union basis, institution of simultaneous contract expiration dates for all unions within a given industry, and reduction of union initiation fees to a modest level. But because traditional craft unionists controlled the AFL, these resolutions invariably met defeat. Large minorities of delegates, however, usually supported them. The principles of industrial unionism found strong backing among the large international unions of mine workers, brewery workers, and machinists. And a substantial gain was recorded for the industrial union movement when, in 1913, the AFL's Metal Trades Department voted that local metal trades unions had to act as a unit in initiating and settling strikes.[102] This decision would prevent union workers from remaining at their jobs in a firm under strike by a fellow union.

The need for mutual support and industry-wide coördination of policy among related unions was emphasized by three outstanding Bay Area strikes in the 1911–1915 period. These episodes showed how the lack of coöperation among all groups of organized workers employed by an establishment under strike undermined union strength. The three conflicts involved the *San Francisco Examiner,* the book and job printing industry, and the Pacific Gas & Electric Company.

The Printing Pressmen versus Hearst

In the spring of 1912 a dispute over working rules led to a strike by printing pressmen employed on the Chicago newspapers of William Randolph Hearst. The strike against Hearst, who was no longer an outstanding friend of labor, became intensely bitter. In 1907 George L. Berry, formerly a militant leader of the San Francisco pressmen, had been elected president of the International Printing Pressmen's Union.* In May, 1912, shortly after the Chicago dispute began, Berry ordered a sympathy strike of the

---

* Berry was in the early stages of a long career that made him one of the most prominent men in the American labor movement and included, in his later years, such episodes as a brief period of service in the United States Senate and a conviction on charges of income tax evasion. (Press clippings on George L. Berry, in library of *San Francisco Chronicle.*)

pressmen employed by Hearst's *San Francisco Examiner.* Members of the other printing trades employed by the *Examiner* refused to become involved, however, and stayed on their jobs.[103]

As it became evident that Hearst was not weakening either in Chicago or in San Francisco, strong sentiment built up for a strike by all unionists employed on the *Examiner.* The Machinists' Union appealed for such a walkout, offering to withdraw its few members at the newspaper plant if other unions would follow suit. The Labor Council boycotted the *Examiner* and called for strike action, placing pressure primarily upon the printers, the largest and most powerful group of workers within the industry. In August, 1912, the Labor Council voted almost unanimously to petition the International Typographical Union to order a strike against the *Examiner.*[104]

But the printers would not countenance a sympathy strike against an employer during the life of a collective bargaining agreement. No action came, and the pressmen's strike went down to defeat early in 1913, amidst the strikers' embittered reproaches of other printing tradesmen for their lack of support. The *Examiner* continued under Labor Council boycott for some years, operating an open-shop pressroom while otherwise maintaining union conditions throughout its mechanical department.[105]

Strike Failure in the Book and Job Printing Industry

In mid-1913 a strike, on a much larger scale, but with features very similar to those of the *Examiner* dispute, began in San Francisco. Late in 1912 a three-year closed-shop contract expired between the Press Feeders' Union and the Franklin Printing Trades Association, representing most of the major book and job printing employers. The association proposed a new three-year contract, to assure industrial peace through the Panama-Pacific Exposition of 1915, but insisted that it include a clause forbidding the union to participate in a sympathetic strike. Labor Council officers and George L. Berry were drawn into the ensuing negotiations, which lasted for more than six months. In June, 1913, with the parties still deadlocked on the sympathetic strike issue, the Press Feeders' Union abruptly gave the employers' association ten days' notice of an intended wage increase. When the demand was rejected, the union struck. The skilled pressmen walked out in sympathy with the press feeders, bringing the total number of strikers to almost 300. Printers, bookbinders, and bindery women, however, continued at work. The Franklin Printing Trades Association imported nonunion pressmen, hired unskilled workers locally to replace the press feeders, and settled down to resist the strike.[106]

The association's members, who had posted bonds to guarantee their adherence to a common front, held together well in the strike. Excellent financial support enabled the strikers to maintain their battle throughout a year marked by heavy picketing of the struck firms and numerous assaults on nonunion workers. Although it caused no deaths, the continued violence produced many minor injuries and aroused the Chamber of Commerce to protest the failure of Mayor Rolph's new administration to suppress strike disorders. But the violence had little effect on the outcome of the strike, which remained essentially a struggle fought in isolation by the pressmen and feeders. The Allied Printing Trades Council withdrew its label from the resisting firms, and provided generous financial donations for the strikers. When the San Francisco printers, however, proposed to take a strike vote, their international leaders forbade it. Union printers stayed at their jobs, giving IWW leaders the opportunity to point to the self-destructive divisiveness of craft unionism. But the printers, who had been so indifferent to the 1912 *Examiner* strike, were now sufficiently disturbed to demand that the International Typographical Union take immediate steps to bring all printing trades unions into an alliance able to prevent repetitions of the embarrassing situation in San Francisco. Delegates from San Francisco pressed for such action at the 1913 convention of the ITU and helped stimulate the ITU's leaders to work during 1914 and later for closer coöperation among the unions of the printing industry.[107]

In June, 1914, the pressmen's and press feeders' strike was finally called off, after the Franklin Printing Trades Association signed an agreement promising only to reëmploy strikers without discrimination, as job openings occurred. The association had won a sweeping victory. The few strikers for whom positions were immediately available returned under open-shop conditions, at the wages prevailing before the dispute. Opponents of unionism acclaimed the outcome as the most encouraging blow delivered to organized labor in San Francisco since Patrick Calhoun's destruction of the Carmen's Union in 1907.[108]

Unlike the United Railroads, however, the printing trades firms did not follow up their victory by stamping out any revival of union strength. Constant pressure from leaders of the Typographical Union and the Labor Council, who warned of a possible strike by all printing industry unions, induced the Franklin Printing Trades Association to meet with the pressmen in conference in 1915. These talks did not lead to any formal agreement. But, as strikers were gradually reinstated and as unionism spread among nonunion workers hired during the strike, employers were eventually persuaded to reinstate union-shop conditions for their pressmen and press feeders.[109]

The Light and Power Council Strike

Another Bay Area labor conflict clearly demonstrated the demoralizing results of disharmony among related unions within an industry. In the winter of 1912–13 a group of unions with members employed by the Pacific Gas & Electric Company formed the Light and Power Council of California to act as their joint collective bargaining agent.[110] Creation of the council marked the culmination of a decade of sporadic efforts, chiefly by electrical linemen and gas workers, to weld public utility employees into some form of industrial organization which would give them a united front in dealing with employers.

Attainment of such a united front had been handicapped by a schism within the International Brotherhood of Electrical Workers. In 1908 the international had split into two warring sects, headed respectively by F. J. McNulty and J. J. Reid. After a venomous battle, the McNulty faction won the sanction of the American Federation of Labor. When unions of the Reid faction refused to acknowledge McNulty's authority, the AFL proscribed them as outlaws and ordered their expulsion from all AFL central bodies. This order aroused resentment in the Bay Area, where virtually all electrical workers outside the building trades were Reid adherents. The Alameda County Central Labor Council refused to expel the Reid IBEW local, and in retaliation had its charter revoked by the AFL in August, 1912. Two months later the San Francisco Labor Council bowed, under strong protest, to the expulsion decree. It ordered the disaffiliation of its Reid local, but assured the departing union of the council's loyal support in any future labor disputes.[111]

Formation of the Light and Power Council of California soon led to a labor dispute involving Reid faction electrical workers. When the council, early in 1913, demanded recognition and a single contract covering all affiliates, the Pacific Gas & Electric Company's general manager, John A. Britton, refused to deal with the new organization. He insisted on continuation of the practice of separate negotiation by individual unions. Nevertheless, when threatened with a strike, he recognized the council and reached agreement with its leaders on the demands of all unions except the electrical linemen and the stationary firemen. To Britton's surprise, he found the council fully prepared to order a strike of its entire membership on behalf of these two unions. His last-minute arbitration offer was rejected on May 6, 1913, and on the following day a strike began against PG&E installations throughout northern California. More than 1,700 men, a substantial majority of the company's union workers, walked off their jobs. In the Bay Area the strike call was honored by every union in the council—electrical linemen, stationary firemen, machinists, boilermakers, and East Bay gas workers. Certain unions, however, had refused to join the council, in part because they rejected any association with the Reid faction of the IBEW. Steam engineers and plumbers remained at work on both sides of the Bay, as did the members of the San Francisco Gas Workers' Union.[112]

The presence of Reid faction IBEW locals within the council complicated matters for the PG&E strikers. After the conflict began, Britton announced that he would have no further dealings with the council, but would negotiate a separate settlement with each individual union. He was soon approached by L. C. Grasser, a vice-president of the McNulty faction IBEW. In mid-May, after brief discussions, PG&E and the McNulty union signed a three-year contract providing wage rates below those demanded by the striking electrical linemen of the Reid faction. To furnish the strike replacements called for by the contract, Grasser enlisted the aid of the San Francisco Building Trades Council. The council placed some members of its electrical workers' union, a McNulty local, in jobs with PG&E.[113]

This hastily signed contract, undercutting the position of the strikers, injected rancor into the conflict. Of the important central bodies on both sides of the Bay, only the San Francisco Building Trades Council supported the bargain reached between Britton and Grasser. The Labor Council repudiated "this most ignoble agreement" and, by a vote of more than five to one, black-listed PG&E as unfair to labor. Mike Casey, fearing a renewal of the old feud between the Labor and Building Trades councils, had opposed this action, pleading instead that Labor Council officers and McCarthy compromise their differences in regard to the McNulty intervention in the strike. But feeling ran too high for compromise. Over Casey's protest, Labor Council president Andrew J. Gallagher called on all union men still employed by PG&E to join in the strike, insisting that no council affiliate had the right to keep its members at work for firms officially declared unfair.[114]

Repeated Labor Council appeals for strike action were rejected by the unions that had maintained their peace with PG&E. Disunity and factionalism within the labor movement continued to attend the strike. On June 15 a mass meeting of almost 2,000 unionists at the San Francisco Civic Auditorium heard violent speeches denouncing the McNulty agreement and McCarthy's support of it. The speakers ranged from the conservative Gallagher to Selig Schulberg, the militant Socialist culinary worker. "The business of organized labor in this crisis," Schulberg proclaimed, "is to whip P. H. McCarthy—as well as the PG&E Company." [115] Schulberg charged that McCarthy's political ambitions had led him to curry favor with PG&E, politically one of the most powerful corporations in the state. This accusation was soon taken up by a large carpenters' local that had long opposed McCarthy's leadership.[116]

In July, in the midst of the furor, McCarthy and a representative of the Labor Council traveled East to argue their respective cases before the AFL Executive Council. The council ruled in favor of McCarthy and the McNulty agreement with PG&E. The

Labor Council's emissary reported that the AFL's leaders refused to endorse the strike and were determined to destroy the Reid faction "at any price." In November, 1913, at the AFL convention, Bay Area delegates headed by Paul Scharrenberg made a final plea for support of the PG&E strikers; but the convention instead passed resolutions forbidding AFL unions to assist Reid adherents and endorsing the McNulty-PG&E contract.[117] "I shall always be proud," Scharrenberg stated afterward, "of my association with the men of that fighting minority . . . opposed to the furnishing of strikebreakers to any employer, under any pretext." [118]

The Light and Power Council strike against PG&E was carried on from May, 1913, to January, 1914. It was the leading Bay Area industrial dispute of 1913 and was later judged by a historian of public utility labor relations to have been the outstanding strike in the American light and power industry before the 1930's. It produced a great deal of minor violence, especially in Oakland, but also in San Francisco, Sacramento, and elsewhere in northern California. John A. Britton reported almost 400 assaults on PG&E employees during the conflict. There was sporadic fighting among pickets, strikebreakers, and armed guards. Sabotage and lack of strike replacements caused occasional power failures, chiefly in the early months of the conflict. The striking electrical workers traced PG&E lines in outlying areas, and several dynamite explosions occurred in attempts to disrupt transmission of current.[119] But after the summer of 1913, as PG&E showed itself able to maintain service, the violence began to subside.

The strike had clearly failed by the end of November, 1913, when Samuel Gompers, other members of the AFL Executive Council, and F. J. McNulty came to San Francisco to seek a *rapprochement* with the Western leaders of the Reid faction. After a week of conferences a peace treaty was signed providing for the reaffiliation of the Pacific District Council of Electrical Workers and its constituent unions with the IBEW, as headed by McNulty and recognized by the AFL. With this destructive internal battle settled, the electrical workers and other unions in the Light and Power Council attempted individually to enter into negotiations with PG&E. Before departing for the East, Gompers met with Britton to request an early and amicable settlement of the dispute. Britton, however, declined to treat with the striking unions. Within a few weeks the council surrendered unconditionally, voting in January, 1914, to call off its strike.[120]

The Light and Power Council never reattained significance during its subsequent brief life. But PG&E, despite its complete victory, did not adopt an open-shop policy. Like the member firms of the Franklin Printing Trades Association, it eventually resumed collective bargaining.

Mooney and Billings: A Reputation as Dynamiters

The PG&E strike was a major episode in the quest of the Bay Area labor movement for interunion unity. It was also a significant chapter in the careers of two of San Francisco's least cautious and conservative union members. Rebounding from their mishaps in the shoeworkers' strike against Frank & Hyman, earlier in the year, Tom Mooney and Warren Billings enthusiastically joined in the battle against PG&E. They worked with leaders of the striking electrical linemen who were interested in disrupting the transmission of PG&E power. In September, 1913, Billings boarded a train for Sacramento, carrying a suitcase filled with dynamite entrusted to him by Edgar Hurley, an officer of the Oakland linemen's union who was later elected a state senator. Unfortunately for Billings, the arrival of the dynamite was expected by Martin Swanson, a Pinkerton detective hired by PG&E to protect its property against sabotage. Shortly after reaching Sacramento, Billings was arrested by Swanson and local police officers. Tom Mooney, in town to meet Billings, narrowly escaped apprehension. Billings was tried on a charge of transporting dynamite in a public conveyance, promptly convicted, and sentenced to a two-year prison term.[121]

Tom Mooney, in his turn, soon found himself the defendant in a criminal case. In December, 1913, Mooney and two striking electrical workers were arrested in Contra Costa County on a charge of illegal possession of explosives. In April, 1914, Mooney went on trial, with an attorney for PG&E acting as special prosecutor. The San Francisco Labor Council endorsed Mooney's appeal for funds, and affiliated unions donated some hundreds of dollars to his defense. Despite their distaste for Mooney's personality and tactics, Andrew J. Gallagher and several other union leaders visited Contra Costa County to exert their influence on his behalf. In June, after two previous trials had ended in hung juries, Mooney won an acquittal. A final effort by PG&E failed to bring him to trial in Sacramento on a charge of having conspired with Warren Billings to transport dynamite.[122]

Back in San Francisco Mooney ran into Michael Roche, a lawyer and Molders' Union officer who had served as assistant to District Attorney Charles Fickert. "Tom," Roche warned him prophetically, "some day they are going to lock you in jail, and throw away the key." [123]

The Depression Winter of 1913–14

During the second half of 1913 there was a substantial amount of industrial conflict in San Francisco. For a time Labor Council unions contributed more than $1,000 per week to support the strikes of the pressmen, the PG&E workers, and the ILGWU cloakmakers. At the same time the nationwide recession in economic activity, which had begun earlier in the year, deepened. The decline in business and employment stiffened employer resistance to union pressure and contributed in part to the defeat of these three strikes. By the end of 1913 unemployment in local industry and an unusually large seasonal influx of casual laborers had aroused serious concern. It was estimated that the number of unemployed reached a peak of from 20,000 to 35,000 or more during the winter. From December, 1913, into the spring of 1914, large throngs of men frequently gathered in open-air meetings on lots south of Market Street. Under the influence of excited orators, some of whom were believed to be IWW organizers, the unemployed engaged in agitation mildly reminiscent of the mob demonstrations led by Dennis Kearney in the depression of the 1870's. Demanding food and work, more than 1,000 men paraded on New Year's Day, 1914, before the San Francisco home of Governor Hiram Johnson.[124] Other parades and mass meetings in succeeding weeks brought occasional scuffles with police and arrests of leaders of the unemployed. Though these episodes did not seriously threaten the maintenance of order, they were a disturbing reminder of the potentially explosive resentment of men unable to find work.

In the Bay Area, as in the nation, business remained generally depressed through 1914, but the number of unemployed in San Francisco shrank as the coming of spring drew casual workers back to agriculture, lumbering, and other jobs. The winter's unrest ended in the spring when a self-styled "army" of jobless men left the city. Charles T. Kelley, a local leader of the unemployed, conceived a grandiose plan to reënact the famous march on Washington by followers of Jacob Coxey in the depression of the 1890's. On March 3, with the tacit blessing of the city government, "General" Kelley's army of 1,500 to 2,000 men marched to the San Francisco Ferry Building, and crossed over to Oakland. Anxious local authorities hastily passed this unwelcome legion on through Richmond and Benicia to Sacramento, where it arrived on the evening of March 6. There it camped while Kelley demanded that Governor Johnson furnish the army with transportation east, toward its distant goal. The march on Washington, however, ended abruptly on March 9, when several hundred police and deputized Sacramento residents attacked Kelley's followers with pick handles and fire hoses. Dozens of men were injured, some severely, as the army was driven in disorder across the Sacramento River and into neighboring Yolo County. As Kelley began serving a six months' sentence in the Sacramento County jail, his army dissolved into scattered groups of wandering unemployed.[125]

Employer Protest in the Building Industry

After the strikes of 1913 and the demonstrations among the unemployed in the winter of 1913–14, the local labor scene became more calm. The nationwide economic slump continued through 1914, weakening union impulses to strive for new gains. During this quiet year the most significant San Francisco labor dispute came in the building trades, where certain employers had been making sporadic efforts since 1910 to regain control over their industry.

The Building Trades Employers' Association which emerged from the 1910 hod carriers' dispute had exerted a definite influence upon labor relations on several occasions. In 1912, when the Building Trades Council notified the master housesmiths that the eight-hour day was to be established for structural and ornamental iron workers, the association persuaded P. H. McCarthy to oppose the move because competing firms elsewhere maintained the nine-hour day. The iron workers struck against the housesmiths' shops despite McCarthy's withdrawal of the council's endorsement, but they soon returned to work when the council threatened to form a new union to furnish strike replacements.[126]

In 1913 the Building Trades Employers' Association supported the protests of master roofers against alleged limitations of output by their union workers. Pressure from the association induced the Building Trades Council to sign a stipulation that the Composition Roofers' Union would neither restrict output nor challenge the authority of roofing contractors to specify methods of job performance. In September, 1913, the association presented its stiffest challenge to the council. When hoisting engineers struck on unusually short notice for overtime pay for certain work, the association demanded that the Building Trades Council order them back to their jobs pending a settlement by negotiation, or face a lockout of building tradesmen throughout San Francisco and Oakland. Reports that supply firms were backing the ultimatum and would withhold building materials from contractors who failed to obey a lockout order created tension, but McCarthy soon bowed to the threat of force. The strike was called off, and McCarthy then gave the customary ninety days' notice of the proposed introduction of overtime rates. In December the issue was resolved through a compromise agreement signed by the association and the council.[127]

In the spring of 1914 occurred the most explosive episode in the series of encounters between the employers' central organization and the Building Trades Council. In 1911 the District Council of Painters and the Master Painters' Association had signed a contract providing that union painters in San Francisco, Alameda, San Mateo, and Marin counties would work only for members of the association. This agreement was strongly opposed by other employer organizations, especially by that of the general contractors. In 1912 the master painters withdrew from the Building Trades Employers' Association when it insisted upon the right of general contractors and other employers to hire journeymen painters directly. A year later the Building Trades Council ordered the District Council of Painters to drop its exclusive agreement and to cease "continually harassing" painting contractors by attempts to force them into the Master Painters' Association.[128]

Soon after the forced termination of their collusive agreement, master painters and union painters fell into a dispute. Early in 1914 the District Council of Painters demanded an increase from $4.50 to $5 in the daily wage in order to achieve parity with carpenters' wages. The demand was rejected, and on April 15 painters struck throughout the Bay Area. More than 2,000 men were reported to have walked off their jobs. Within a few days the master painters reaffiliated with the Building Trades Employers' Association, appealing for assistance. The association, not reluctant to intervene, served notice upon the Building Trades Council that a general lockout would begin on May 12 in San Francisco and Oakland, unless the painters returned to work.[129]

The lockout threat evoked from council leaders both loud protests and statements dismissing the association as too weak to cause them concern. The association embraced almost a dozen employer groups, but it had failed to win the affiliation of firms in plumbing, electrical work, plastering, masonry, and several other contracting lines. These specialty contractors announced that neither they nor their suppliers would coöperate in a lockout, and that the association's ultimatum was "a bluff, pure and simple." Before the strength of the association could be tested, however, several leading businessmen stepped in as mediators to avert a potentially serious conflict. Among them were Herbert Fleishhacker and I. W. Hellman, Jr., two of the city's most prominent bankers. On May 12, the lockout deadline date, representatives of the association and the council were brought together by the mediators. After several hours of conference, they were persuaded to sign an agreement ending the strike and submitting the wage issue to arbitration. A month later an arbitration board awarded the painters the $5 wage, to become effective January 1, 1915.[130]

Dominance of the Building Trades Council

The ability of the Building Trades Employers' Association to force the Building Trades Council to negotiate with it at critical moments in 1912–1914 was a significant indication that employers in the building industry were not so completely under union domination as they were popularly portrayed to be. Nevertheless, the association failed to unite employers into an organization coequal to the council. Nor was it able to establish a master bargaining relationship with McCarthy's tightly centralized organization. Still holding most of the power in the industry, the council could brush aside efforts to tie it to conventional collective bargaining contracts of specified duration.

In the late summer of 1914, when the United States Commission on Industrial Relations appointed by President Wilson came to San Francisco for hearings, Grant Fee, head of the Building Trades Employers' Association, appeared before it. Fee gave the federal commissioners, among whom was Harris Weinstock, a discouraged account of employer weakness in the building industry despite four years of activity by his association. He gave a detailed description of employer grievances, including tight union apprenticeship restrictions, refusal to admit to union membership qualified journeymen who had moved to San Francisco, exaction of union membership dues from foremen and employing contractors, the ½ of 1 per cent "tax" recently levied by the Bricklayers' Union upon the cost of all brick work erected in the city, alleged output limitations, and the refusal of the Building Trades Council to enter collective bargaining contracts. Fee also complained about a rule of the District Council of Carpenters which fined workers found guilty of "pace setting," and about the continued restriction of output by the Composition Roofers' Union in violation of the promise given in 1913. He described the dissolution in 1912 of a small contracting firm, under union pressure. Objecting to a partner in the firm who had formerly worked for the United States Steel Corporation, the structural iron workers' local had warned the company that "if you want to contract in this town, you had better get rid of him." The partner soon left San Francisco.[131]

Like many of the city's contractors, Fee was himself a former union member and by no means intolerant of labor organizations. Far from advocating an open-shop policy, he avowed with apparent sincerity that his association was entirely willing to deal with the building trades unions. But he expressed hopes for an eventual balance of power between well-organized employers and workers in the industry.

The Building Trades Employers' Association gave voice to the resentments of those who professed to deplore the entrenched power of P. H. McCarthy and his Building Trades Council. Yet a large proportion, if not a majority, of employers almost certainly considered the *status quo* to be reasonably satisfactory. Most of the important organizations of specialty contractors refused to affiliate with the association. Collusive and restrictive arrangements between specialty contractors and unions in such lines as plumbing, plastering, and masonry were additional evidence of employer equanimity. Despite union entry barriers, skilled labor was not in short supply. Contractors were not harassed, as they often were in New York and Chicago, by the exaction of "strike insurance" payoffs to union leaders.[132]

As indicated previously, the council's discipline over its affiliates prevented jurisdictional squabbles from penalizing employers through frequent work stoppages. McCarthy continued to exert his personal influence on the side of peace and stability. Time and again he opposed aggressive action by individual unions. At periods of tension he was, in fact, more likely to uphold an employer's contentions that a union's demands were excessive or ill-timed than to encourage the union to press its demands. So long as McCarthy retained firm control of the council's affiliates, employers would not be provoked into a major drive to eliminate union power in their industry. And his position remained unshaken. In 1914 he easily quelled an effort by insurgent unions to democratize building trades leadership through referendum votes on council policies. In 1915 the continued respect for McCarthy's authority was concretely manifested when a committee representing the General Contractors' Association, several other employer groups, and "organized labor of San Francisco," gave him a large automobile.[133]

Open-Shop Organizations

Although labor peace prevailed in the Bay Area in 1914, there were indications that certain employers were preparing a new open-shop campaign. Organized support for the open shop had never died away, but for years it had failed to arouse serious concern among San Francisco unionists. In 1912 the Citizens' Alliance had tried to arouse employers by warning that business firms throughout the Pacific Northwest would boycott San Francisco unless union control in the building trades was broken, so that nonunion finished lumber from the Northwest could enter the city.[134] This call for action met little response, and by mid-1913 the Citizens' Alliance had become virtually dormant.

In the spring of 1914, however, a new organization sought to rally employers. A group of influential businessmen established the Merchants' and Manufacturers' Association of San Francisco, which soon absorbed by merger both the Citizens' Alliance and a similar M and M Association in the East Bay. Many of the leaders of the new central body had been prominently associated for years with open-shop crusades—James Tyson, C. R. Johnson, Wallace M. Alexander, Frederick Koster, Frank C. Drew, William H. George, and J. W. Mason. Among the companies represented in the M and M's leadership were the Southern Pacific and Santa Fe railroads, Cowell Cement, Paraffin Paint, Union Lithograph, Owl Drug, Atlas Gas Engine, PG&E, and the Emporium.[135]

The association's membership was comparatively small, but it included powerful firms and individuals. It failed, however, to enlist the strategic group of employing draymen. Teamsters' Union leaders claimed in 1914 that members of the Draymen's Association, "who were so severely bitten in the trouble of 1901, when so many false promises were held out to them as to the paying of expenses," had informed the M and M that "they might consider about joining" if a large certified check were first placed on deposit to cover "all their losses in the future." [136]

The Merchants' and Manufacturers' Association maintained an employment office for nonunion workers, publicized charges that high labor costs were stunting San Francisco's economic growth, campaigned against state legislation supported by labor, and appealed for close coöperation among employers' groups throughout the country. It became a leading affiliate of the Federation of Employer Associations of the Pacific Coast, which embraced open-shop organizations in Stockton, Portland, Seattle, Spokane, and other cities. J. W. Mason and Frederick Koster were elected as vice-president and treasurer of the federation, respectively, and San Francisco was chosen as the site for two coast-wide confer-ences on labor policy during 1914–1915. No major open-shop drive developed in San Francisco, however, despite this employer activity. As Koster later described it, many businessmen were restlessly chafing under restraints imposed by their desire to avoid any outbreak of labor conflict at least until after the close of the Panama-Pacific Exposition of 1915. But the "necessity . . . to carry that enterprise to success forced upon many of the conflicting elements the obligation of laying aside their differences." Although Koster and his associates were satisfied that they had made progress in strengthening such organizations as the Chamber of Commerce and in arousing a greater sense of solidarity among employers, they reluctantly accepted an industrial peace built "largely on the basis of compromise." [137] The city's "more responsible" labor leaders, Koster acknowledged, had helped maintain this peace. Aggressive union actions that might have afforded employers an excuse for an open-shop campaign were rare.

Labor War in Stockton

In mid-1914, as calm continued to prevail in Bay Area labor relations, the nearby city of Stockton became a battleground for California's most bitter union-employer encounter since the 1910–1911 upheaval in Los Angeles. In Stockton, a city of about 30,000 population situated approximately fifty miles inland from the Bay, a militantly open-shop Merchants', Manufacturers' and Employers' Association had been formed in 1913. In December its executive secretary had presented to Oakland businessmen its plans to cut down union power, and had called upon Bay Area employers to coöperate in a widespread offensive against organized labor in northern California. Trouble began shortly thereafter. In the spring of 1914 restaurant and retail store owners in Stockton refused to renew agreements with culinary workers and clerks. When the unions responded with boycotts and picketing, the employers' association notified building tradesmen, the core of union strength in Stockton, that they must not support the boycotts, and must end the practice of discharging union members for patronizing black-listed stores and restaurants. Local building trades union officers, joined by several San Francisco labor leaders, were unable to persuade the association to withdraw its demand. Early in July the association's member firms posted notices declaring for the open shop. The association claimed that its approximately 400 members employed more than 90 per cent of the workers in the city.[138]

The open-shop declaration led to a series of strikes and lock-outs, as individual Stockton firms attempted to employ nonunion workers or otherwise ignored union conditions. The center of conflict was the construction industry. Anton Johannsen, veteran organizer of the State Building Trades Council, soon arrived to lead the embattled unionists. Allegedly proclaiming that "he would show Stockton what a real labor war was," Johannsen massed both men and women on picket lines at construction sites. Minor outbreaks of violence soon began. Stockton employers charged labor officials with having imported strong-arm union men for picket duty, and freely admitted that the association had brought in strikebreakers, private detectives, and armed guards. The State Federation of Labor and the State Building Trades Council sent more than $50,000 to Stockton, most of it raised through assessments on San Francisco union members. Olaf Tveitmoe, Mike Casey, John P. McLaughlin, and other San Francisco labor leaders assumed the task of determining union strategy and negotiating for a peace settlement. Less officially, Tom Mooney intervened in the Stockton affray by furthering the prosecution of an association detective arrested in the possession of dynamite. The detective eventually won an aquittal, although the evidence strongly indicated that he had participated in a plot to bring about the arrest of Tveitmoe and Johannsen by "discovering" dynamite secretly planted in their suitcases.[139]

It was repeatedly said that members of the Merchants' and Manufacturers' Association of San Francisco were channeling funds into the contest. Conclusive evidence of such financial assistance was not offered, but unquestionably the M and M was intensely interested in the outcome of the struggle. James Tyson and other prominent leaders of the association attended meetings of Stockton employers both before and after the outbreak of conflict, thus creating apprehension that the smaller city had been chosen as a testing ground for a future open-shop battle in San Francisco.[140] Labor Council secretary John O'Connell, nevertheless, assured a 1914 Labor Day crowd that local employers would doubtless "view with alarm and disgust the starting of a similar fight in this city."[141] And in September, Paul Scharrenberg appealed to a Commonweath Club meeting for business acceptance of conservative AFL unionism. Citing "the work done by unions in cooling hotheads and repressing extremists," he argued that employers in Stockton must either deal with "sanely organized labor" or "be forced to defend themselves against . . . men . . . who will be satisfied with nothing but revolution." [142]

Despite the fears aroused, the battle for the open shop did not spread beyond Stockton. There it continued for almost six months before the exhausted combatants called a halt. One week before Christmas, 1914, representatives of the MM&E and of the Stockton unions signed a truce agreement negotiated with the aid of Mike Casey and other San Francisco labor leaders. Wage and hour scales remained unchanged, picketing and boycotts were ended, and the association lifted its ban on the employment of union workers. Labor spokesmen acclaimed the apparent stalemate as a great victory and contended, plausibly enough, that the inconclusive outcome had cooled the enthusiasm of other California employers for open-shop campaigns. Yet the MM&E, notwithstanding its failure to destroy union influence in Stockton, gained more from the encounter than its opponents. The peace settlement did not provide for the reëstablishment of broken collective bargaining relationships, nor guarantee the rehiring of all workers idled by strikes and lockouts. Union leaders admitted, late in 1915, that organized labor in Stockton still remained shaken from its 1914 ordeal and was having difficulty in enforcing union conditions upon hostile employers.[143]

1915—Final Year of Industrial Peace

On January 1, 1915, the *Labor Clarion* cautioned every union to "husband its resources during the next year. Then if the disgruntled employers who are planning a fight after the close of the Exposition start anything labor will be amply prepared." Similar forebodings were occasionally voiced later in the year. Union leaders remained uneasily aware of the presence of the Merchants' and Manufacturers' Association and of its hostility toward a strong labor movement. Though not seriously alarmed, they gave due attention to reports describing the association as growing in membership and in financial resources. In the spring the editor of a business journal proclaimed that the association's struggle against "our 'peace at any price' people . . . has advanced the cause of the open shop educationally until the city stands almost ready to embrace it. . . . And it will do more." [144] Meanwhile, the Chamber of Commerce continued to gain in strength and influence,[145] though it had not yet displayed any official interest in labor relations.

The year 1915 was characterized by labor peace amidst business revival. The outbreak of World War I in August, 1914, reversed the downward economic trend by bringing American manufacturers an increasing flow of orders from the Allied nations. The demand for labor, especially for skilled metal tradesmen, grew rapidly in industries producing munitions, machinery, and other war material. Although the impact of the war was felt earlier and more strongly in the heavy manufacturing industries of the East, Pacific Coast industry also expanded output and employment during 1915. In particular, the previously depressed shipbuilding industry was revitalized by the growing demand for freighters, tankers, and warships. By mid-1915 local shipbuilding plants were in the early stages of the boom that made them the area's greatest source of industrial employment in the war years.[146]

The Panama-Pacific Exposition opened in February, 1915, and ran until early December. It drew thousands of visitors to San Francisco during a year of unusually peaceful labor relations. On Labor Day a large crowd of unionists gathered at the Exposition grounds for their annual celebration. There they heard representatives of the Labor Council and the Exposition Company exchange speeches of mutual congratulation on the good will maintained in carrying out this civic enterprise. M. H. de Young, publisher of the *Chronicle* and vice-president of the Exposition Company, presented the Labor Council and the Building Trades Council with bronze plaques in a gesture which clearly recognized their important role in the community.[147]

The Municipal Election and the AFL Convention

At the close of 1915 two familiar issues—the power of labor in local politics, and the controversy over craft versus industrial unionism—again became prominent. In the fall political campaign, members of the Merchants' and Manufacturers' Association, along with many other businessmen, gave heavy support to the "Municipal Conference" ticket, whose platform demanded a city government that would encourage the investment of funds in San Francisco. Labor spokesmen, of course, denounced the conference as a front for open-shop forces.[148]

The businessmen's ticket failed to achieve victory in the election of 1915. A majority of those elected to the Board of Supervisors had, in fact, been endorsed by the Union Labor Party, and a number of them were union members. The union vote and inadequate support by business for its own candidates, M and M leaders later complained, had once again placed in office enough "subservient" officials to give labor effective control of the city government. Included among the "subservient" officials, in the view of most open-shop adherents, was Mayor James Rolph. Elected originally with business support, Rolph had soon disillusioned many of his original backers by demonstrating his sympathy for the local labor movement. He easily won reëlection in 1915, gathering thousands of union votes despite the candidacy of Andrew J. Gallagher, running for mayor with the endorsement of the Union Labor Party.[149]

In the same November election week, the 1915 convention of the AFL met in San Francisco. The delegates were warmly welcomed by Mayor Rolph and by C. C. Moore, president of the Panama-Pacific Exposition Company. The convention engaged in heated debate over resolutions calling for the imposition of simultaneous contract expiration dates upon all unions active in the same industry, and the restructuring of the labor movement along industrial union lines. But, as in the past, the resolutions were voted down.[150] The delegates departed from San Francisco, in the closing weeks of this peaceful Exposition year, having reaffirmed the dominant position of craft unionism. The AFL thus remained strongly committed to its traditional policies as it moved into the wartime boom era of great expansion and opportunity for labor.

1911–1915: A Quiet Prelude

The period 1911–1915 was characterized by relative stability both in the local economy and on the local labor scene. Viewed in its historical context, however, it was a prelude to unsettled conditions in Bay Area labor relations. The increasing tempo of business activity in 1915 pointed to major changes in the economic environment, to rising prices and growing labor unrest. The 1914 battle in Stockton and the increased interest in open-shop organizations on the part of prominent San Francisco employers—particularly those with influence in the greatly strengthened Chamber of Commerce—foreshadowed the approach of large-scale industrial conflict. The municipal election of 1915, with its open effort by organized businessmen to eliminate labor sympathizers from office, was a prologue to the more serious political challenge that faced San Francisco labor in 1916.

Union developments during 1911–1915 also brought into focus trends and issues that were of marked significance in the coming years. The troublesome problem of interunion unity and coördination, as exemplified in a number of strikes, continued to arouse concern in the war and immediate postwar periods, when labor solidarity proved wanting in certain critical episodes. The dispute over craft versus industrial unionism, and the proper approach to organization of the unskilled, acquired new meaning in the war years 1917–1918, as unionism once again began to make appreciable gains among less skilled noncraft workers. During the war years, also, internal factionalism in the local labor movement, seen clearly but in relatively moderate degree in 1911–1915, swelled greatly both in scope and in intensity, with open controversy over the personalities and policies of Bay Area union leaders rising to unprecedented heights by the end of the war. The attacks in the prewar period on orthodox craft unionists and conservative "labor politicians" by Socialists, IWW's, and such class-conscious militants as Tom Mooney provided a foretaste of the bitter dissensions to follow. And the prosecutions of Tom Mooney and Warren Billings in connection with dynamiting activities in this period were omens of dramatic events which later catapulted these two men into highly controversial roles as martyrs of the San Francisco labor movement.

Thus, in a number of ways, the developments of 1911–1915 served as introductions to the troubled period ahead. But the close of 1915, like the close of 1907, marked an important transition in Bay Area labor history. It ended a long period of eight years in which comparative equilibrium had been maintained in union-employer relations. No major shocks had upset the equilibrium, nor had heavy strains been placed upon it. Not until the early 1920's would equilibrium be reëstablished, after a long interim of turmoil and of pronounced shifts in the balance of power between organized labor and organized employers.

| Chapter VIII | *Wartime Ferment* |
| | *1916–1918* |

BY THE SPRING of 1916 the effects of the wartime boom were clearly evident in the Bay Area economy. The cost of living had begun to move upward at an accelerating pace. Goaded by rising prices and encouraged by the increasing demand for labor, many Bay Area workers were beginning to push vigorously for improved conditions. The period 1916–1918 thus began in a setting of price inflation and restlessness within the local labor force. These three years were a period of upheaval such as Bay Area industrial relations had not experienced since the turn of the century. A new wave of union growth greatly extended the boundaries of collective bargaining and significantly increased the aggressiveness of labor unions.

With economic activity on the upswing and labor once again on the march, the level of industrial conflict rose sharply. Both in the United States as a whole and in California the number of recorded strikes doubled in 1916 as compared to 1915.[1] In San Francisco the termination of labor calm was, characteristically, marked by conflict on the water front, with the usual disturbing repercussions on the labor life of San Francisco. For the struggle on the docks created a provocatory incident that unleashed a new open-shop campaign in the city.

In the East Bay the 1916–1918 period began less dramatically than in San Francisco, but the war impact there was more pronounced in terms of union growth and reinvigoration of union spirit. During 1917–1918 developments in the East Bay figured more prominently on the Bay Area labor scene than ever before. As in San Francisco, the Oakland-Alameda water front drew particular attention, though not with respect to union-employer struggles in the maritime industry. Shipbuilding now became the most conspicuous center of wartime labor ferment, and the shipyards along the East Bay shore fostered an especially militant surge of new unionism.

Though 1916 marked the transition to an era of labor turbulence, America's formal entry into the war, early in 1917, was an additional stimulus to Bay Area labor activity. In one respect, it is true, American involvement alleviated union-employer tension by postponing for the duration of the war the possibility of another struggle over the issue of the open shop. But it also greatly increased economic activity and price inflation. As industrial conflict rose in 1917, governmental encouragement of collective bargaining and governmental intervention to avert labor disputes were introduced into the unsettled situation created by booming wartime production. Federal authorities, with the coöperation of unions and employers, had appreciable success in holding down the level of labor strife through 1918. But the factors responsible for greatly increased strain in the relationships of unions and employers were still present at the end of the war, making it evident that the disturbed years of 1916–1918 would not be followed by a new period of quiet on the labor front.

1916: Rising Wages

In early 1916 the clamor of union wage demands had not yet become general throughout the local economy, but labor had begun to stir in a number of important industries. Late in April the Pacific Coast unions of sailors, marine firemen, and marine cooks and stewards asked wage increases of $5 per month in joint bargaining for renewed contracts. Enjoying war-born prosperity, shipowners quickly granted these demands, the first gains won by offshore workers since 1906. A large wage increase was also easily negotiated in May by the licensed officers' union of marine engineers.[2]

The San Francisco Building Trades Council, in the spring of 1916, finally endorsed the demand of the Laborers' Union for a

$3 daily minimum wage. In the Bay Area shipyards, the rapidly expanding Boilermakers' Union negotiated higher rates for many journeymen and helpers. In May it intervened to persuade Bethlehem Steel's Union Iron Works to make wage concessions to almost 200 low-paid, unskilled, nonunion workers who had spontaneously walked out on strike.[3]

Demands for shorter hours also began to appear. In April, 1916, the Structural Iron Workers' Union gave Bay Area iron and steel fabricating shops ninety days' notice of its intention to institute the eight-hour day. In San Francisco restaurants, the Miscellaneous Culinary Employees' Union began on May 1 to enforce a reduction from twelve to ten hours in the workday of its large membership of dishwashers and kitchen helpers. And, later in the month, this union joined with those of cooks and waiters in formulating an ambitious proposal for the immediate establishment of the eight-hour day for all culinary workers.[4]

Despite demands for improved wages and conditions, San Francisco remained free from serious labor clashes until the summer. The chief strike in the spring occurred when less than 200 auto mechanics demanded an increased wage of $4.50 per day from San Francisco repair shops and new car dealers. The mechanics, members of the Machinists' Union, struck on May 1 at about a dozen establishments, claiming that most of the employers had by then agreed to the higher scale. Within a few weeks the strike settled down into a long campaign of boycotts, picketing, and occasional sabotage directed against six or seven firms, principally the larger auto agencies. One of the key participants in this conflict was Warren Billings, who had been released from prison a year earlier after serving fourteen months for transporting dynamite during the PG&E strike. As in the 1913 shoeworkers' strike, Billings again acted as a union intelligence agent. Holding a job with a struck firm, he fed inside information to Machinists' Union leaders. His contact among these leaders was Edward D. Nolan, a one-time member of the IWW and a militant associate of both Billings and Tom Mooney. Like his two friends, Nolan espoused the principles of industrial unionism and was prominent in the vocal minority of class-conscious workers who attacked San Francisco's conservative labor leadership.[5]

The 1916 Water-Front Strike

The date of June 1, 1916, marked the effective beginning in the Bay Area of the period of turbulent labor relations brought on by World War I. On that day approximately 10,000 longshoremen walked out in the first unified coast-wide strike ever undertaken by these water-front workers in all major Pacific ports. Almost 4,000 struck on Bay Area docks. The strike was ordered by officers of the Pacific Coast District of the International Longshoremen's Association when employers rejected demands for increased hourly rates of 55 cents for straight time and $1 for overtime after nine hours a day. Simultaneously, about 600 members of the Bay and River Steamboatmen's Union struck on boats operating between the Bay Area and Sacramento, after failing in negotiations to win a $5 monthly wage increase and a reduction in their exceptionally long working hours.[6]

The longshoremen's strike paralyzed Bay Area shipping. It could hardly fail to provoke San Francisco employers, for the city's chief economic activity was the shipping, receiving, and distributing of goods. Aggravating the normal resentment of the business community, moreover, was the fact that the strike was called in violation of a formal agreement. In December, 1915, locals of the Pacific Coast District of the ILA had signed contracts with the Waterfront Employers' Union of San Francisco, and with employers in other ports, specifying terms of employment and stipulating that sixty days' notice must be given of any intended change in these terms. But the longshoremen struck after giving less than a month's notice of a new wage scale. Their action drew immediate protest from Secretary of Labor William B. Wilson, himself a former union leader. "The statement that you are not proposing to change the agreement but to cancel it deceives no one," he wired Pacific Coast ILA leaders on June 3. "The average workingman has little to lose other than his honor and integrity," Wilson argued, as he appealed for a prompt end to this unjustifiable strike before it might damage the reputation of all organized labor in the eyes of the public.[7]

Like every crucial San Francisco water-front conflict, the 1916 strike brought to the fore the problem of interunion solidarity— a problem never permanently resolved. On this occasion the longshoremen's disregard of their contract afforded the other key affiliates of the Waterfront Workers' Federation a convenient explanation for standing aside from the struggle. With or without an excuse, officers of the Sailors' Union would have forbidden a sympathy strike, but now they had a good reason for turning down the membership's request for action. Mike Casey and John P. McLaughlin likewise refused to allow the Teamsters' Union to strike in support of an organization that had dishonored its contract. It is highly questionable that they would have been willing in any event to risk serious damage to their union by aiding the longshoremen, though eventually they did assist the steamboat hands by instructing teamsters to refuse to handle cargo to or from boats manned by strikebreakers.[8] This smaller strike, however, was not likely to arouse widespread or dangerous employer reaction.

During the first week of June employers began to bring both white and Negro strikebreakers into the Bay Area. But before any violence occurred, a truce sent most of the longshoremen back to their jobs. On June 9, with the aid of a federal mediator and officers of the Waterfront Workers' Federation, the Bay Area local of the ILA and the Waterfront Employers' Union reached an interim agreement that work be resumed under the higher wage scale demanded by the strikers, while negotiations continue toward a final settlement of the wage issue. The agreement left longshoremen on strike only against Bay Area water-front lumber yards. In San Francisco these firms were banded together in the Retail Lumber Dealers' Association, whose leaders were determined to administer a defeat to the ILA.[9]

The truce of June 9 did not lead to a permanent, negotiated peace. Tension continued high as the water-front lumber yards uncompromisingly battled the longshoremen, and as some firms of the Waterfront Employers' Union retained their strikebreakers despite ILA protests. Recurrent incidents of violence soon precipitated a new crisis. On June 17 an ILA member was shot to death in Oakland, in a fight between strikers and armed guards protecting strikebreakers being transported to the Sunset Lumber Company, the open-shop firm headed by James Tyson. The next day a union picket was shot and killed by a strikebreaker on a San Francisco dock, reportedly without provocation. With two longshoremen dead, ILA officers notified the Waterfront Employers' Union that the strike would be resumed unless armed strike-breakers and guards were removed from the piers. On June 21 WEU representatives met with union leaders and rejected this ultimatum. On June 22 the longshoremen struck once again in the Bay Area.[10]

A New Open-Shop Challenge

The fresh outbreak of water-front conflict led to the first inter-vention in a labor dispute by the San Francisco Chamber of Com-merce, which had for so long held aloof from industrial relations problems. As the new walkout began on the docks, the chamber's Board of Directors passed a resolution which threw down an unmistakable challenge not only to the longshoremen but to the entire local labor movement:

> The Chamber of Commerce favors the open shop and insists upon the right to employ union men or non-union in whole or in part, as the parties involved may elect. Under no circumstances should the employ-ment of union men exclusively be enforced by duress or coercion. . . . Therefore, the Chamber . . . pledges its entire organization and the resources it represents to the maintenance of these principles . . . and will oppose any attempt on the part of any interest . . . to throttle the commercial freedom of San Francisco.[11]

The chamber's forceful new president, Frederick J. Koster, and his associates had for years resented the strength of organized labor in their city. Now the crippling of vital port activities gave them an extraordinary opportunity to arouse the business com-munity to take a stand against aggressive unionism. With the issuance of the chamber's open-shop declaration, the 1916 water-front strike threatened to take on the ominous aspect of the City Front Federation's battle with the Employers' Association of 1901.

The Waterfront Employers' Union, however, was not prepared for such a battle. On June 26 it formally disavowed any intention of undertaking an open-shop campaign against the longshoremen. Moreover, it offered to increase hourly wages to 55 cents for straight time and 82.5 cents for overtime, and to discharge all strikebreakers upon final settlement of the dispute. But during the negotiations on this offer, additional nonunion men were put to work on the docks. Although the level of violence was lower than in the 1901 conflict, frequent attacks on strikebreakers helped the Chamber of Commerce to publicize its call for action against the "intolerable situation on the waterfront." On July 5 a large delegation from the chamber, including Koster, asked Mayor Rolph for authority to hire at least 500 special policemen to protect the movement of goods. Rolph flatly refused to sanction the establishment of such a private army and instead ordered the city police to search for concealed weapons on all strikebreakers coming off the docks. Koster thereupon invited employers throughout the city to attend a special Chamber of Commerce meeting on Monday, July 10.[12]

Hundreds of businessmen crowded into one of the most dramatic meetings in San Francisco labor history. Koster set the mood of the occasion by warning that anyone "who is not in the frame of mind where he will be prepared to do his full duty . . . would best quietly and promptly leave." The time had come, Koster said, to stamp out "that disease permeating this community, of which the waterfront situation is at present the most outstanding manifestation." The task of rebuilding the city after the 1906 earthquake and the subsequent civic enterprise of the Panama-Pacific Exposition had "kept us all occupied to such an extent that this industrial and political disease made great inroads." The Chamber of Commerce had no wish to destroy unions, and "no law-abiding union man" need fear its intentions; but it was determined to free San Francisco from "its reputation . . . of being a class-ruled city." An end must be put to the shameful attitudes of businessmen who demanded that "their goods be moved or that their buildings be completed, urging their own selfish immediate interests as against their own ultimate, and their community's interest." Instead, San Francisco employers must "back up to the limit intelligent and constructive leadership," and give it the necessary financial resources. The most immediate goal was to open the water front to an unimpeded flow of goods.[13]

Among the other speakers were executives of shipping firms, the Bank of California, the Southern Pacific Railroad, and California's largest canning corporation. Captain Robert Dollar, the aging but fiery shipowner, impulsively provided labor leaders with a belligerent statement they would cite for years against him. To restore "peace and quiet" on the water front, Dollar proposed that henceforth "when they compel us to send one ambulance to the receiving hospital, we send two of theirs." As the climax of the meeting, those assembled voted full authority to a committee of five men, headed by Koster, to raise funds and take immediate action against the water-front tie-up and any other "intolerable" harassments of local business. In proper vigilante tradition, Koster and his four associates entitled themselves the Law and Order Committee. Within a week the committee had raised pledges of more than half a million dollars from the city's employers.[14]

Despite the ambiguity of its professed intentions, the Law and Order Committee unquestionably represented the most significant move in years to mobilize local antiunion sentiment. For a few tense days San Francisco appeared likely to undergo another destructive water-front battle over the issue of the open shop. On July 13 the Waterfront Employers' Union announced that it would let the committee handle its affairs. Instead, however, it offered the longshoremen a new compromise: the return to work of all strikers under union conditions and at wages prevailing before the June 1 walkout, with further negotiations to determine new rates effective as of August 1. Although these terms were less favorable than those originally offered by the WEU, the longshoremen accepted them on July 17 after a hasty membership vote which might well have been influenced by the fear of an open-shop campaign. By July 20 only the lumber yards were still under strike along the Bay Area water front. Backed by the Law and Order Committee, the Retail Lumber Dealers' Association had declared for the open shop. Although the Steamboat Owners' Association was also adhering to the open shop, the Bay and River Steamboatmen's Union had called off its strike after the Law and Order Committee promised that its members would be rehired without discrimination.[15]

The Waterfront Employers' Union, by contrast, had declined the opportunity to attempt to establish open-shop conditions on the docks. The longshoremen returned to work with their union intact and still party to a collective bargaining relationship. Their strike, however, was a fiasco. Called in violation of contract, it prejudiced ILA leaders in the eyes of more conservative unionists and appreciably strengthened the case of employers who advocated a drive to cut down labor power. After several weeks of violence and two deaths, the strike had ended without having achieved any immediate gains. And, most important, it had provided the occasion for powerful business interests to launch a righteous crusade for the open shop in San Francisco.

The separate settlement in the Bay Area, moreover, produced a fatal breach in the principle of coast-wide unity of action by longshoremen. In San Pedro and the Pacific Northwest ports, ILA members remained on strike in a mood of strong resentment toward those who had deserted them. In these other ports the longshoremen's efforts eventually failed, thus demonstrating the difficulty of making effective a Pacific maritime industry strike not simultaneously affecting shipping in all harbors. The ill feeling aroused by the 1916 episode led to a formal split in Pacific Coast longshoremen's ranks; the Bay Area union seceded from the ILA and took on independent status.[16]

Renewed Fight against the United Railroads

In the same tense week of July 10–17 which brought the creation of the Law and Order Committee and settlement of the longshoremen's strike, a brief labor disturbance flared on the United Railroads. In February, 1916, the Labor Council had set up a special committee to plan a renewed campaign to organize this open-shop stronghold. Nothing came of the committee's deliberations. Meanwhile, however, another effort was under way. Tom Mooney, in the winter of 1915, had persuaded President W. D. Mahon of the Amalgamated Association of Street Railway Employees to give him credentials as an organizer. With the aid of his wife, Rena, Mooney worked through the spring of 1916 to arouse the streetcar men. Optimistically, the Mooneys sent letters to hundreds of these nonunion workers, pleading: "Slaves of the United Railroads. Awaken!" [17] By June 10 Mooney felt sufficiently confident to summon the carmen to attend an organizational mass meeting, to be held that evening. The same afternoon, the United Railroads management posted a notice in all carbarns:

This is to inform you that . . . Thomas J. Mooney . . . who was arrested and confined in jail as a dynamiter . . . is at present endeavoring to enroll some of our employees. . . . It is needless to advise you that the company is thoroughly familiar with his every move and takes this occasion to notify you that any man found to be affiliated with Mooney or any union, will be promptly discharged.[18]

The meeting was held as scheduled on the night of June 10. Several hours after it adjourned, small charges of dynamite damaged three PG&E transmission towers south of San Francisco. The explosions appeared to be an attempt to sabotage the power supply of the United Railroads.[19]

In the next few weeks Mooney tried without success to persuade Labor Council leaders to approve an early strike against the company. After months of organizing he was still unable to claim the existence of any significant union membership among the carmen. But he argued that the vast majority of them would respond to dramatic action by a few leaders.[20] On July 13, accordingly, Mooney and his wife distributed handbills outside the United Railroads carbarns announcing that a streetcar strike would begin the following evening. And at the afternoon rush hour on Friday, July 14, a handful of men walked off their cars on Market Street. A brief flurry of excitement ensued. Rena Mooney climbed aboard a blocked car, holding out a union button to the surprised motorman. She was seized by police, who moved in quickly to arrest half a dozen of those involved in the tie-up. On their idled cars operators waited quietly for traffic to be cleared. The strike did not spread. The cars were soon moving again, and another episode in the long series of efforts to unionize the United Railroads was over.[21] Tom Mooney, in the one major opportunity he would ever have to demonstrate his ability as a union organizer and strike leader, had met ignominious failure.

To the Labor Council leaders, with whom Mooney was distinctly *persona non grata,* his failure was not unwelcome. They publicly disclaimed the council's responsibility for the abortive strike. James Mullen, ultraconservative editor of the *Labor Clarion,* depicted Mooney as "steeped in the doctrines of that combination of mental defectives known as the Industrial Workers of the World . . ." and utterly bungling his campaign against the United Railroads. "The truth is," Mullen wrote, "these persons with IWW proclivities never produce anything but trouble. . . ."[22]

One of Mooney's acquaintances at this time was Israel Weinberg, owner of a jitney-taxicab and an officer of the recently formed Jitney Bus Operators' Union. Weinberg later testified that on July 17, three days after the streetcar strike misfire, he was approached by Martin Swanson, the private detective who had caught Warren Billings with a suitcase of dynamite during the 1913 PG&E strike. Swanson was now the head of the Public Utilities Protective Bureau, a detective agency supported chiefly by PG&E and the United Railroads. Swanson allegedly attempted to persuade Weinberg to give evidence linking Mooney to the dynamite explosions that had damaged PG&E towers a month earlier. A $5,000 reward offered by the United Railroads for evidence concerning this crime was held out to him as bait, Weinberg claimed. Swanson also urged Warren Billings, according to the latter's story, to collect the reward by testifying against Mooney.[23] If their charges of an attempted frame-up are true, Weinberg and Billings may have done Mooney a disservice by rejecting Swanson's overtures. Had they agreed to accuse him of the crime, he might have been safely in jail several days later, when the Preparedness Day Parade marched up Market Street.

The Preparedness Day Parade

During the week that began Monday, July 17, the labor relations scene remained unsettled in San Francisco. Auto mechanics and water-front lumber-yard workers were still on strike. On July 10 another dispute had come to a head when structural iron workers walked off their jobs at ten fabricating shops which refused to grant the eight-hour day.[24] The likelihood of a strike was mounting in the restaurant industry, to establish the eight-hour day demanded by the culinary unions. San Francisco's most serious labor conflict, however, was over, as the longshoremen had returned to work. By comparison with the previous week, calm prevailed in the city.

In this setting came the Preparedness Day Parade, on Saturday, July 22. Since it was first announced, the parade had provoked intense controversy. Sponsored by the Chamber of Commerce, it was seen by most Bay Area labor leaders as a militaristic demonstration by businessmen opposed to President Wilson's policy of keeping the United States out of the European war. Widespread antagonism existed among San Francisco's heavily Irish-Catholic, German, and Scandinavian body of unionists toward any group suspected of seeking American intervention on the side of Britain. Antiwar sentiment was even stronger among members of the IWW, the Socialist Party, and other class-conscious groups, who for months had been protesting that America's workers must not be dragged into this "capitalist" holocaust. The parade was also opposed by labor and left-wing organizations because of its inevitable identification with the open-shop stand just taken by the Chamber of Commerce, for the parade was to be led by Thornwell Mullally, who had been anathema to the local labor movement since 1907. Then, as Patrick Calhoun's chief assistant, he had helped smash the carmen's strike against the United Railroads.[25]

The parade thus became a symbol of cleavage between San Francisco's business leadership and organized labor. Central labor councils on both sides of the Bay voted resolutions attacking it. Paul Scharrenberg, Olaf Tveitmoe, Hugo Ernst, and a mixed group of both Socialist and conservative union leaders formed a committee which sent out circulars to union members, appealing: "Do not march. . . . Do not let your employers coerce you. . . ." On Thursday night, July 20, the committee drew a capacity crowd of more than 5,000 to a "peace demonstration" at Dreamland Rink to hear speeches denouncing the parade, militarism, the United Railroads, other public utility corporations, and Mullally.[26] And on Friday night, July 21, the Labor Council adopted a resolution just passed by the Building Trades Council:

Whereas . . . because united labor is opposed to the fostering of the war spirit by "preparedness parades," an attempt may be made by the enemies of labor to cause a violent disturbance during . . . the parade and charge that disturbance to labor. . . .

Therefore, be it resolved: That in order to forestall any possible frame-up of this character . . . we hereby caution all union men and women . . . to be especially careful and make no other protest than their silent non-participation. . . .[27]

On Saturday afternoon, July 22, 1916, at 1:30 P.M., the Preparedness Day Parade got under way. Its leaders claimed that more than 50,000 had turned out to join in the long procession that formed on the Embarcadero, San Francisco's water front, and moved impressively up Market Street. Thornwell Mullally, at the head of the parade, had marched more than a mile from the starting point when, a few minutes after 2 P.M., an explosion rocked the intersection of Market and Steuart streets, one block up from the Embarcadero. There, in the midst of a dense crowd of paraders and bystanders, a bomb had gone off. It left ten dead or dying and approximately forty wounded people scattered along the pavement.[28]

Shortly after the explosion, District Attorney Charles Fickert assigned Martin Swanson, the public utilities detective, to the bomb case as a special investigator for the city. By July 27 five people had been arrested: Tom Mooney; his wife, Rena; Warren Billings; Israel Weinberg, of the Jitney Bus Operators' Union; and Edward D. Nolan, left-wing leader of the Machinists' Union. On August 2 the San Francisco Grand Jury indicted each of the five prisoners for murder.[29]

The Law and Order Committee

In establishing the Law and Order Committee on July 10, Frederick J. Koster and his fellow leaders of the Chamber of Commerce had represented their drive against unionism as a civic campaign to free San Franciscans from intimidation and violence. The bombing of the Preparedness Day Parade, just twelve days later, offered them a magnificent opportunity to dramatize their campaign. "This outrage is another expression of the disease our Law and Order Committee has started out to combat," Koster proclaimed.[30] Posting a $5,000 reward for the detection of the murderers, the committee unhesitatingly implied that organized labor was responsible for the crime: "Recent disturbances on the waterfront were accompanied by violence. Intimidation was practiced on merchants and their employees. . . . The spirit of lawlessness in the community logically terminated in the damnable outrage on Saturday." [31]

On the night of July 26 the committee drew a tense crowd of 5,000 or more to a mass meeting at the Civic Auditorium—a meeting whose highly melodramatic tone was heightened by rumors that an attempt would be made to dynamite the building. As conservative newspapers were most careful to emphasize, neither Koster nor other speakers took advantage of the occasion to attack unionism or "stir class hatred." They confined themselves to denouncing the Preparedness Day atrocity, invoking the spirit of the vigilantes, and demanding the "redemption" of San Francisco from its lawlessness.[32] To labor leaders, however, the sponsorship and the character of the meeting were ample evidence that its unspoken aim was to stir up enthusiasm for the "redemption" of San Francisco employers from the grip of powerful unions.

The open-shop drive of the Law and Order Committee gained in intensity through the business community's reaction to the bombing. Frederick Koster denied time and again that the committee was pursuing any "general campaign against labor." "We are positively not opposed to collective bargaining," he insisted. The committee's program was not, in fact, comparable to that of such antilabor organizations as the Merchants' and Manufacturers' Association of Los Angeles. The committee, able to accept the existence of unions, displayed no intention of destroying the well-established union-employer relationships in San Francisco. Koster himself, as president of the California Barrel Company, had for years been on excellent terms with the Coopers' Union. In the late summer of 1916, amid labor denunciations of the Law and Order Committee, this union presented Koster with an engraved testimonial expressing appreciation of his fair treatment of his employees and his recent granting of the eight-hour day. And in December, 1916, Koster was reportedly the first employer in the city to sign a new agreement raising coopers' wages by 25 cents a day.[33]

The Law and Order Committee, nevertheless, presented a clear threat to the labor movement. Of its five members, only Koster had maintaind a long and amicable relationship with a unionized work force. Two members headed corporations conspicuous for their unyielding resistance to unionization: George M. Rolph, of the C and H Sugar Company; and C. R. Johnson, of the Union Lumber Company. Though not proposing to destroy unions, the committee was dedicated to weakening their political influence and economic power in San Francisco. It did not fulminate against collective bargaining, but it declared that the principle of the open shop could not be subject to compromise. Only those union-shop agreements made "not as a result of duress or coercion," as

Koster repeatedly explained, could be tolerated.[34] And almost any kind of union pressure might be defined as "duress or coercion." The committee intended to teach labor that "no strike has any hope of succeeding" unless called with "justification." [35] But it was obvious that few strikes would be regarded as justifiable. Against those that were not, the committee proposed to mobilize the resources of the entire business community.

By the fall of 1916 the Law and Order Committee had raised pledges of approximately $1 million from employers. More than half of this sum was eventually spent in combating individual strikes, in advocating legislative restrictions on union activities, and in promoting publicity campaigns to arouse the citizenry against alleged abuses of union power. Through newpaper advertising and elaborate brochures, the committee carried the employers' case to the public on a scale never before attempted in San Francisco. It was an expensive undertaking, but Koster was deeply convinced of the value of a forthright appeal to public opinion. As a member of the Citizens' Alliance, in 1904, he had resented the conspiratorial secrecy behind which the alliance carried on its affairs.[36] Now he prided himself on the openness of his Law and Order Committee. Despite the camouflage implicit in its name, the committee did prefer to publicize, rather than conceal, its intervention in union-employer relations.

The Culinary Workers' Strike

From the outset the Law and Order Committee was prepared for the eventuality of a general battle with organized labor. On July 19, 1916, it mailed to business firms throughout the city form copies of an unusual contract which proposed that each firm would cede to the committee, for three years, full power to make, continue, or cancel all contracts for drayage services. Recognizing the strategic role of transportation, the committee wanted to centralize in its own hands the authority "to control the teaming situation" should a widespread labor conflict involve the Teamsters' Union. Koster later reported that enough firms signed this contract to give the committee control over almost 90 per cent of the movement of goods in San Francisco, thus enabling it "to protect the drayage companies against defection of weaklings." [37]

Although the committee never had occasion to exercise this authority, it did intervene in several strikes. The one that received most attention was that of the culinary workers.

Since early July the culinary workers' Joint Executive Board had been negotiating with the Restaurant Men's Association over union demands for the eight-hour day for cooks, waiters, and miscellaneous employees, and a $2 weekly increase for cafeteria waitresses. The association offered the cooks and the waiters a workday of nine hours within thirteen, but refused any concessions to the two weaker unions. Hugo Ernst and other union leaders rejected this proposal, interpreting it as an attempt to split the unity of the culinary workers. They then reduced their demands to nine working hours within twelve for the three men's unions and a $1 increase for the waitresses. But further bargaining failed to narrow the gap between offer and demand.[38]

On August 1, with negotiations deadlocked, the Joint Executive Board ordered a strike at five restaurants. In so doing, it triggered a sweeping counterattack already prepared by the Restaurant Men's Association and the Law and Order Committee. The association had kept the committee closely informed on the progress of negotiations and had promised to make no concessions without its sanction. By mid-July association members had begun to sign an agreement providing for an industry-wide lockout, should the culinary unions strike against any restaurant. A large number of restaurant supply firms had promised the association full coöperation in the event of a labor conflict. As J. J. Eppinger, president of the association, explained:

> Our plan is to depend upon the influence of the seller upon the buyer; upon the weight of the man of large affairs upon the man of small affairs. In other words, to ask the merchants . . . affiliated with the Chamber of Commerce to bring . . . pressure . . . upon any of our signatories who show signs of weakening. . . .[39]

When the first restaurants were struck on August 1, the association called on all employers to lock out their union workers and declare for the open shop. Within two days more than 150 restaurants had responded, and a major struggle involving 3,000 to 4,000 workers was under way. The Law and Order Committee immediately came to the support of the restaurant owners, announcing that the culinary strike "affords a splendid example of just the conditions . . . that the Chamber of Commerce . . . is striving to remedy." The committee hired detectives and guards to protect the restaurants, set in motion a campaign for a city ordinance outlawing picketing, and worked with the Restaurant Men's Association to recruit both white and Negro strike-breakers.[40]

From the beginning of this lockout-strike the chances of union victory progressively faded. By contrast with the large funds at the disposal of the Law and Order Committee, the culinary unions had no significant resources for supporting hundreds of workers in a prolonged contest. From their international they received only limited aid. In mid-September Labor Council officers recommended that all unions assess their memberships to establish a defense fund against a possible general open-shop drive. Contributions were channeled to the culinary workers, but proved inadequate to finance regularly paid strike benefits. By then most of the waitresses were back at work under open-shop conditions, and a growing number of members of the other three unions were reapplying for jobs.[41]

Meanwhile the employers' ranks held firm. Union spokesmen claimed that more than 100 restaurants remained "fair," having defied orders to take down their union house cards and replace them with open-shop signs. But these were the smaller eating places which hired only a fraction of the industry's workers. Although organized employers placed severe pressure on these non-coöperative establishments, no drastic policy of withholding supplies appears to have been carried out. Almost all the larger firms adhered to the policy of the Restaurant Men's Association, which offered to take back workers without discrimination, but only under the open shop.[42]

Intervention by Mayor Rolph, early in August, failed to halt the conflict. Rolph, who feared that a struggle over the open-shop issue might spread through San Francisco industry, proposed establishment of a tripartite arbitration panel with authority to settle the culinary dispute and all others arising within the next twelve months. Although the Labor Council voted to accept this proposal, the Chamber of Commerce, confident of its strength, rejected it. "We will not consent to cloud the plain issue which this community is eager to face," Frederick Koster informed

Rolph. The chamber would not give arbitrators the power to compromise the principles of the open shop and the "free opportunity of labor." [43]

As usual, the culinary unions relied heavily upon picketing. Union tactics, according to the Chamber of Commerce, produced a series of "outrages"—chiefly picket-line scuffles and obscene or abusive language directed against customers and nonunion workers. Yet, in a detailed indictment of the culinary unions, the Law and Order Committee could cite only a few minor disturbances and the hurling of several stench bombs into restaurants. But although picketing was relatively peaceful, San Francisco courts issued the most copious stream of injunctions since the 1904–1905 union battles with the Citizens' Alliance. It was later reported that more than 200 restraining orders had been issued. Some forbade picketing entirely, others merely enjoined the use of threatening language and gestures. Several unionists were convicted for contempt of court, and given light fines or jail sentences. [44] The injunctions thus hampered picketing activity and further demoralized the strikers.

The 1916 Presidential Campaign

In mid-August, soon after the culinary strike began, there occurred an incident that may have had national political significance. Charles Evans Hughes, the Republican presidential candidate, arrived in San Francisco on the western swing of his 1916 campaign against President Wilson. During his visit, he was scheduled to speak at a banquet of the Commercial Club. Just before Hughes arrived, the club had voted to display an open-shop card in the dining room. Culinary union leaders, though not ordering a strike, publicly demanded to know Hughes's attitude in regard to the open-shop issue and the forthcoming banquet. Republican campaign managers reportedly elicited from the Waiters' Union a promise that its members would serve at the banquet, on condition that the open-shop card be removed. But when Hughes's managers were unable to persuade the club to grant this concession, the waiters walked out. The Republican candidate thus faced the choice of offending businessmen by canceling his speech, or of antagonizing labor by dining in an open-shop club. [45]

Hughes attended the banquet. In a glare of publicity he sat

in an open-shop dining room on August 19 and was served by strikebreakers. San Francisco's labor papers denounced the affair as a deliberate insult to all union workers. They described Hughes as being "wined and dined by the would-be-union-crushers" of the Commercial Club.[46] Whatever chances Hughes may have had of gaining San Francisco labor support, his ill-starred visit to the city had decidedly not improved them.

In November, 1916, Hughes lost to Woodrow Wilson in one of the most dramatic presidential elections in American history. Wilson's thin margin of victory was provided by California, where he defeated Hughes by only about 4,000 votes. In San Francisco, however, Wilson won by almost 15,000 votes.[47] The city's Democratic majority saved the state for Wilson, and left historians to speculate as to whether Charles Evans Hughes lost the presidency when he entered the Commercial Club of San Francisco on August 19, 1916.

The Antipicketing Ordinance

The 1916 election was a significant one for San Francisco labor, for it indicated that labor's political potency and public sympathy for the union cause had declined appreciably since the Union Labor Party's successes in the 1900–1910 decade. The Law and Order Committee had managed to place on the ballot both a proposed ordinance banning picketing and a proposed charter amendment that would make police court judges, who often sympathized with labor, appointive rather than elective officials. The charter amendment failed to carry at the November election. But the antipicketing ordinance had behind it a well-financed publicity campaign. The Law and Order Committee inserted a series of full-page newspaper advertisements which recited in detail the incidents of violence in the water-front and culinary strikes. Just before the election the committee put 400 telephone girls to work, calling every voter listed in the city telephone directory. On November 7, the antipicketing ordinance was passed by a vote of approximately 74,000 to 69,000.[48] Modeled on the ordinance in open-shop Los Angeles, it outlawed picketing without qualification and provided jail sentences of up to fifty days for violators. Its passage was the most serious political defeat administered to San Francisco labor since the turn of the century.

The new antipicketing ordinance gave the *coup de grâce* to the already doomed culinary workers' strike. Nothing materialized from union threats to institute a court case to test the constitutionality of the ordinance. Picketing dwindled rapidly, as Labor Council leaders recommended shortly after the election that all unions obey the ordinance. On December 15, 1916, the Labor Council called off the restaurant strike in admitted defeat.[49]

The failure of this long strike left the ranks of the culinary unions badly depleted. The unions of cooks and waiters had entered the conflict with a combined membership of almost 3,000; they emerged from it with about 1,200 members. Unionism in the restaurant industry was a hardy growth, however, and employers made no serious effort to uproot it. Members of the Restaurant Men's Association, "moved by a desire not to appear vindictive," soon took down their open-shop signs.[50] The association continued for some time to maintain a central hiring bureau set up during the strike. This bureau avoided the placement of "agitators," but it did not as a rule discriminate against union workers. And J. J. Eppinger, president of the association, displayed no open-shop sentiment in reviewing the strike early in 1917. "I have always felt that the work that we did last year was the poorest sort of work that an association of employers could do," Eppinger stated. He decried the fact that "the precarious condition of our industry did not permit that slight extra concession" which would have prevented the strike. "In the end," he predicted, "you will sit down at the table with labor. How much better that labor should come to the board as invited guests. . . ."[51]

Successes of the Law and Order Committee

The defeat of the restaurant strike and the passage of the antipicketing ordinance were the main antilabor achievements of the Law and Order Committee in 1916. Directly and indirectly, the committee achieved other successes. It launched a recruitment campaign which, between July and October, increased the membership of the Chamber of Commerce from approximately 2,500 to more than 6,000. By the end of 1916 the chamber claimed to be the largest in the United States. The open-shop proclamation by San Francisco business leaders had also aroused employers across the Bay. On June 29 the Oakland Chamber of Commerce followed closely behind its San Francisco counterpart by passing a resolution declaring for the open shop. A new employers' association of Alameda and Contra Costa counties soon launched a campaign to outlaw picketing. Through its efforts an Alameda County antipicketing ordinance was placed on the ballot in the spring election of 1917. It won passage by a slim margin, thus leaving unions on both sides of the Bay stripped—according to law, at least—of one of their most essential weapons.[52]

On a state-wide level, leaders of the Law and Order Committee and the San Francisco Chamber of Commerce sought to achieve employer goals in the area of labor legislation. In the fall of 1916 the chamber's legal counsel drafted a bill outlawing strikes against any public utility until after a thorough investigation of the disputed issues by a state board. The chamber also supported bills designed to outlaw the secondary boycott and to eliminate union apprenticeship restrictions. None of these bills passed the legislative session of 1917, but the chamber won an important defensive victory over organized labor. The AFL's model anti-injunction law, whose enactment California labor leaders had repeatedly sought, was finally passed by the 1917 legislature. But the chamber's counsel, Max J. Kuhl, representing employer organizations in San Francisco, Oakland, Los Angeles, Stockton, and smaller towns, persuaded Governor William D. Stephens to veto the bill. Not until the 1930's did California labor again persuade the legislature to restrict the use of injunctions.[53]

Open-Shop Victory over the Lumber Longshoremen

In June, 1916, the water-front lumber yards, unlike the stevedoring and shipping firms of the Waterfront Employers' Union, had decided to stand for the open shop and to refuse any concessions to their striking longshoremen. These yards thus remained under strike after the interim agreement in mid-July had returned longshoremen to work elsewhere along the docks. In the week following the July 22 bombing, however, the lumber longshoremen ended their walkout in a tacit admission of temporary defeat. For almost a month the water-front labor scene remained outwardly calm. On August 20 the Waterfront Employers' Union reached a final settlement with the dock workers. The WEU's new contract retained preferential hiring for union members and raised wages from 50 to 55 cents per hour, with time and a half for overtime.[54]

A few days after signing this agreement with the WEU, the Longshoremen's Union renewed its battle with the lumber yards. The more than thirty member firms of the Retail Lumber Dealers' Association had assured the Law and Order Committee that they would maintain the open shop. In mid-August the association organized the American Stevedore Company to furnish its affiliated firms with longshoremen hired without discrimination in favor of or against union members. On August 23 longshoremen at two of the city's leading lumber companies went on strike, refusing to work alongside nonunion men. The association responded with a proclamation of its open-shop policy. Within a few days the strike had spread to a number of other lumber firms, as several hundred longshoremen walked out in protest against the open shop.[55]

This second 1916 strike against the lumber yards was longer, but no more successful, than the first. The Law and Order Committee supported the Retail Lumber Dealers' Association, the American Stevedore Company recruited strikebreakers, and the struck firms successfully maintained operations. Late in November, after three months of futile struggle, the Longshoremen's Union called off the strike. Its members apparently met little or no discrimination in returning to the jobs available, but the outcome was an unqualified victory for the Law and Order Committee and the open shop.[56]

The Structural Iron Workers' Strike

The Law and Order Committee also supported an open-shop struggle by iron and steel fabricating shops. With the sanction of the Building Trades Council, the Structural Iron Workers' Union had set July 10, 1916, as the deadline date for employer acceptance of the eight-hour day. Though most shops acquiesced, ten leading firms agreed to stand together against the union's demand. These firms, which claimed to manufacture more than 90 per cent of the fabricated steel products made in San Francisco, posted bonds as guarantees of their pledges to deal with the union only through a committee representing the entire group. On July 10, accordingly, the ten shops refused to grant the eight-hour day and were shut down by a strike.[57]

By their show of defiance the fabricating firms gained the support of the Building Trades Employers' Association and the Law and Order Committee. Grant Fee, president of the association, presented the Building Trades Council with a demand that all structural iron workers return to their jobs under the nine-hour day by July 28. When this demand was rejected, the Law and Order Committee met with representatives of the association and the struck firms, and announced that operations would be resumed on an open-shop basis.[58] A strike for the eight-hour day was thus transformed into another test of strength over the open-shop issue in San Francisco.

The struggle continued for six months. Early in its course, however, the employer front split. In mid-August one of the ten shops reached a separate settlement with the union, agreeing to the eight-hour day. By early October three more shops had yielded. These four firms later claimed that they had joined the open-shop group because of warnings that credit and supplies would be cut off from recalcitrant employers, but "no such arrangements had been made . . . and firms that did not join the organization, but granted the eight-hour day immediately, had none of the troubles threatened." They also alleged that promises to provide an ample supply of strikebreakers were not made good. The defection of these firms led to years of litigation, for the other six employers brought suit against them for payment of almost $10,000 pledged as forfeitable bonds.[59]

The remaining six firms maintained their open-shop stand through the rest of 1916. The Law and Order Committee assisted them with a publicity campaign which appealed to each "loyal . . . patriotic San Franciscan" to condemn the "Unamerican" boycott proclaimed against their products by the Building Trades Council.[60] The committee also furnished guards, on occasion, to protect strikebreakers, and in November sent several armed men to the construction site of a city-owned hospital as an escort for nonunion workers employed by Dyer Brothers. This angered Mayor Rolph, who had previously charged the Chamber of Commerce with hypocritically dissembling an intention to destroy organized labor. "They would permit the unions to exist," he had stated at the 1916 Labor Day celebration, "if they would confine themselves to the function of benevolent societies." [61] Rolph now denounced the Law and Order Committee for stubbornly resisting reasonable employer concessions to unions. He ordered the police to arrest any armed guards found near the construction site and canceled the city's contract with Dyer Brothers for work on the hospital.[62] To employers, Rolph's action was additional evidence of official favoritism toward labor.

Despite the aid of the Law and Order Committee, the six firms finally gave up their battle against the structural iron workers. The stubbornness of the strikers and the failure to maintain employer unity had frustrated their effort to break free from a union relationship. In January, 1917, representatives of the Building Trades Employers' Association and the Building Trades Council settled the dispute, establishing the eight-hour day as of February 1 and reinstituting union-shop conditions.[63] The Law and Order Committee thus suffered one defeat in its encounters with unions in 1916, demonstrating that its intervention was not always a guarantee of employer victory. The negotiation of the fabricating shops' surrender was one of the last significant acts of the ill-starred Building Trades Employers' Association. It dissolved later in 1917, bringing to a close its seven-year history of unsuccessful strivings to redress the union-employer balance in the construction industry.[64]

The Mooney-Billings Case

During the second half of 1916 the prosecution was busy preparing its case against the five defendants charged with the murder of the July 22 Preparedness Day bombing victims. San Francisco was witnessing the first stages of the *cause célèbre* that would soon be known throughout much of the world as the Mooney-Billings case. Having hastily won indictments against Tom and Rena Mooney, Warren Billings, Israel Weinberg, and Ed Nolan, District Attorney Charles Fickert and the San Francisco police turned to the task of gathering evidence. No consideration was given to the possibility that the defendants might be innocent. Evidence casting doubt upon the prosecution's case was summarily rejected. And, in a barrage of inflammatory newspaper publicity, Fickert denounced the defendants as scheming radicals whose guilt was unquestionable.[65]

Mooney and Billings were obviously the most vulnerable to

attack. Billings' 1913 conviction for transporting dynamite and Mooney's later indictment on a similar charge provided Fickert with heavy ammunition for his pretrial publicity campaign. Early in 1916 Mooney had also been connected with a radical journal recently established in San Francisco by Alexander Berkman, a nationally known anarchist. Berkman had spent years in prison for his attempted assassination of H. C. Frick, the Pittsburgh steel magnate, during the bitter Homestead strike of 1892.[66] For his new journal he chose—in view of later developments—a peculiarly unfortunate name: *The Blast.* Mooney's association with Berkman helped surround him with a sinister aura of revolutionary extremism. Fickert capitalized upon this association by citing the pages of *The Blast* as proof of Mooney's penchant for violence. Scorning the AFL's policy of business unionism, *The Blast* featured such vaguely ominous statements as: "The workers have no more insidious enemy than the chicken-hearted labor leader who advises them to be patient and respectable. An ounce of direct action is worth more than tons of paid advice of labor politicians." [67]

Only the most confident of skilled advocates would have cared to take on the task of persuading an intelligent jury that either Mooney or Billings had any scruples against the use of violence and sabotage in industrial disputes. Yet nothing in the background or philosophy of the two men pointed to so senseless an act of indiscriminate murder as the Preparedness Day bombing. However visionary or irresponsible they may have appeared to conservative labor leaders, they were not fanatics. But they were convenient suspects who filled a set of imperative needs. An outraged and impatient public expected the crime to be quickly avenged. District Attorney Fickert required the defendants to be tried for murder, in order to display his diligence in office. Martin Swanson, the private detective for the United Railroads and PG&E, welcomed the opportunity to guarantee his employers against any future difficulty with men who had proven troublesome in the past. And Chamber of Commerce leaders wanted punishment meted out for a crime against the "law and order" the chamber had sworn to uphold.

In the ensuing months and years Frederick Koster repeatedly stated, with evident sincerity, that the Chamber of Commerce never attempted to exploit the Preparedness Day bombing for the purpose of arousing antiunion sentiment. Yet almost from the moment of the bomb blast, the chamber acquired a vested interest in this crime which it could not bring itself to relinquish. Having immediately interpreted the bombing as a manifestation of labor violence, San Francisco business leaders clung to this interpretation. Although not explicitly charging the labor movement with responsibility for the crime, they pointedly referred to the bombing in the same context as disorders in labor disputes.[68] The Law and Order Committee, District Attorney Fickert, and San Francisco union leaders all joined in proclaiming that Mooney and Billings were in no way representative of the local labor movement. Nevertheless, Mooney and his associates did symbolize the militant, often violent, unionism which the Law and Order Committee was publicizing in its campaign to place restrictions on all organized labor. The committee's intense interest in the case, and its dogmatic insistence upon the guilt of the defendants, could leave little doubt that it considered the prosecution to be significantly connected with its own effort to counteract the power of San Francisco labor.

Far from viewing the defendants as potential martyrs, San Francisco union leaders were anxious only to dissociate them from any identification with labor. A delegation headed by Andrew J. Gallagher and Mike Casey asked Fickert to promise that the prosecution would not be turned into a vehicle for antiunion propaganda. Fickert assured them that these were not "labor cases" and would not be treated as such. Satisfied, union leaders for months thereafter stubbornly resisted all suggestions that organized labor take a sympathetic interest in the defendants. The *Labor Clarion,* edited by James Mullen, pointedly ignored the impending murder trials except to comment briefly on the effort to raise funds for the defense.[69] To most union officials Mooney and his associates were simply a disruptive element of which the city's labor movement could well be purged. Mooney had always claimed that San Francisco workers were dominated by reactionary "labor politicians," and the men so designated had no intention now of coming to his assistance.

Outside San Francisco, however, interest in the defendants spread rapidly among labor and radical groups. The *Tri-City*

Labor Review, in the East Bay, attacked the prosecution and the San Francisco Chamber of Commerce in a series of articles. Leaders of the Alameda County Central Labor Council threw their support to the defense. William Spooner, the council's secretary, made an impassioned speech at the first large mass meeting held, at San Francisco's Dreamland Rink, in September. The council and some East Bay unions made small contributions to the defense fund. Larger amounts came from unions in the East. The heavy publicity campaigns and organized fund-raising which long characterized the Mooney-Billings case were well under way within a month after the indictments were handed down. The International Workers' Defense League, a unionist-radical organization with which both Tom Mooney and Ed Nolan had been connected, launched a nationwide drive to portray the defendants as the victims of a Chamber of Commerce conspiracy to defame organized labor. As excitement and anger mounted, contributions to the IWDL's defense fund rose; for a time they exceeded $10,000 a month.[70]

The Mooney-Billings case was one of the best-publicized episodes in American legal history. A voluminous flow of articles, pamphlets, books, and reports of official investigating commissions detailed a travesty of justice so gross and so indisputable that it profoundly disturbed a generation of observers concerned with the integrity of the judicial process. In retrospect the case still looms as a nightmarish example of surrender to prejudice and irrationality on the part of California courts, elected officials, and politically powerful business groups. The Sacco-Vanzetti case, in the 1920's, stirred thousands of Americans to deep sympathy for the defendants and anger at their execution. But the experience of Mooney and Billings provides a more thoroughly documented history of two men victimized by antiradical hatred and by the impregnable resistance to reason on the part of those with the power to give them just treatment.

Mooney and Billings were not the victims of an antilabor conspiracy. True, the defendants were arrested before any evidence had been gathered against them, and their case was immediately prejudiced by a torrent of unfavorable newspaper publicity. Witnesses were asked to identify them in face-to-face meetings, rather than in the customary police line-up.[71] Once this rather questionable identification had been made, the district attorney's office encouraged the witnesses to tell their stories with confidence and lavish detail. The coaching of certain witnesses, in order to make their testimony fit the needs of the prosecution, went so far as to approach subornation of perjury. But Fickert did not manufacture the testimony.

The case upon which the district attorney proceeded to trial was inherently so incredible that he could not possibly have fabricated it. The story his witnesses told had little logic, and the witnesses themselves were a dubious lot upon whom to depend for testimony in a murder trial where the penalty for guilt was hanging. The five principal witnesses, later described as "a weird procession composed of a prostitute, two syphilitics, a psychopathic liar, and a woman suffering from a spiritualistic hallucination," [72] identified the defendants as appearing individually or in varying combinations, at various places along Market Street and in the vicinity of the explosion, and at various times in the early afternoon of July 22. Although the accounts conflicted in significant details as they were told and retold in the trials of individual defendants, the prosecution's case was basically consistent. It pictured five or six conspirators—the Mooneys, Billings, Ed Nolan, Israel Weinberg, and, in most versions, a mysterious "Russian Jew" who was presumably to be identified eventually as Alexander Berkman—crowding into Weinberg's tiny jitney soon after 1:30 P.M., when the parade started up Market Street. With a suitcase containing the fatal bomb resting on its running board, the overloaded car traveled almost a mile down Market Street in full view of thousands of spectators, despite the presence of police to keep the street free of traffic. The jitney, moreover, was well known to Martin Swanson and other detectives who were presumably still keeping Mooney under surveillance. After working its way, without being seen, through much of the parade, the jitney arrived at the densely crowded corner of Steuart and Market. There it stopped briefly while Mooney, Billings, and the "Russian Jew" clambered out, deposited the lethal suitcase on the sidewalk, and got back into the cab. Weinberg then piloted his jitney away, presumably with remarkable dispatch, for the Mooneys were photographed at 1:58 P.M. as they casually watched the parade from the roof of their apartment house at 975 Market Street, more than a mile from the fatal corner. A few minutes later, at 2:06 P.M., the bomb exploded.[73]

Such was the prosecution's case. Judge Franklin Griffin, who presided over Mooney's trial, later made this apt comment: "We must have been slightly crazed by the hysteria of the time to have accepted for a moment the preposterous contention . . . that the alleged dynamiters . . . fully aware that they were being shadowed by private detectives, rode down a cleared street in the face of an oncoming parade. . . ."[74]

Warren Billings was the first of the defendants to be brought to trial, in September. Billings, according to his later account, had been occupied on the day of the bombing with a criminal venture of his own. Acting under instructions from Ed Nolan, he had spent July 22 squirting paint remover on brand-new automobiles parked on the streets and identified as sold by the auto agencies against which the Machinists' Union was then on strike. Billings thus possessed no strong alibi. But the prosecution's case appeared so flimsy and implausible that the International Workers' Defense League confidently announced late in the trial that it was "inconceivable that anything but acquittal can result." James Brennan, the assistant district attorney who handled the trial, was in fact so dubious of the state's witnesses that he could not persuade himself to seek the death penalty. Fearing that an irremediable injustice might be done if Billings were executed, he argued mildly to the jury that a conviction would force Billings to reveal what he knew about the crime.[75]

The jury's verdict of guilty, with a recommendation against the death penalty, was returned late in September. It clearly came as a shock both to Billings' sympathizers and to many disinterested observers. Even James Mullen, editor of the *Labor Clarion*, portrayed the conviction as unwarranted by the evidence and said the jury's action in finding Billings guilty of mass murder, yet recommending clemency, was "simply preposterous." Early in October the 1916 convention of the State Federation of Labor adopted a resolution criticizing the Billings verdict. The convention, though carefully disavowing that these were "labor cases," nevertheless recommended that all unions contribute to the legal defense of the accused, in order to assure them fair trials. Most San Francisco labor leaders, however, remained aloof. The executive committee of the Labor Council simply filed the federation's appeal for defense funds. And Mullen was soon editorializing that San Francisco unionists were "not the least interested or disturbed by the impending fate" of the defendants, in contrast to the gullibility of their "thousands upon thousands of innocent sympathizers" in the East.[76]

With Billings convicted and sentenced to life imprisonment, the trial of Tom Mooney began in January, 1917. Again the defense expected to win an acquittal. A number of witnesses testified that Mooney and his wife had spent July 22 in their apartment building at 975 Market Street. Snapshots taken as they watched the parade showed them on the roof of the building at 1:58 P.M. Unfortunately for Mooney, however, Fickert had found a new witness. After Billings' trial, an Oregon rancher named Frank Oxman came forward with a story of having been in San Francisco on July 22 and having observed the crime. Oxman, it was later proved, had visited San Francisco that day, but he had arrived well after the bomb explosion had occurred. His intervention was the most bizarre of the many strange features of the Mooney-Billings case. Apparently driven by a need to gratify pathologically exhibitionistic impulses, Oxman decided to cast himself in the role of star witness. He gave an impressive performance at the trial. Billed as "an honest cattleman," Oxman radiated homespun sincerity as he told his dramatic tale of having watched the arrival of Weinberg's jitney at Steuart and Market streets and the planting of the bomb-filled suitcase. His testimony, coming as a complete surprise to the defense, destroyed Mooney's chances of acquittal. The jury returned a verdict of guilty without a recommendation of clemency. Mooney was sentenced to be hanged, and his execution was set for May 17, 1917.[77]

Ironically, the same warped mentality that caused Oxman to seek the thrill of sending a man to death through perjured testimony also led him to a fantastic act which alone gave Mooney the chance to escape execution. Late in 1916, while waiting to testify against Mooney, Oxman had invited Edward Rigall, an acquaintance of his in the East, to come to San Francisco to serve as an "expert witness" in a forthcoming trial. His expenses would be paid by the state of California. The surprised Rigall accepted this odd invitation and came to San Francisco. For several weeks he shared in the hospitality that District Attorney Fickert lavished upon his prize witness, Oxman. Rigall, however, refused to testify that he had seen the defendants commit the crime, and was given a return ticket to the East. Some weeks after Mooney's conviction Rigall belatedly contacted the defense and turned over to them the letters and telegrams constituting written evidence of Oxman's efforts to persuade him to give perjured testimony.[78]

On April 12, 1917, Fremont Older, editor of the *San Francisco Bulletin,* published Rigall's documentary evidence impeaching Frank Oxman's testimony, beneath a banner headline: "Mooney Plot Exposed." The dramatic revelation brought a wave of reaction against the prosecution. Judge Franklin Griffin, who had sentenced Mooney to death, called for a new trial. The San Francisco labor movement at last rallied to the support of Mooney and his associates. Many union leaders remained indifferent to the ordeal of the defendants, but few were willing to stand out against the new flood of protest over the case. On April 27 the Labor Council passed a resolution charging that Mooney was the victim of a frame-up and demanding Fickert's removal from office. Fickert himself was stunned by the sudden discrediting of his star witness. Fremont Older and a defense lawyer met with the district attorney on April 18 and reported him badly shaken by the turn of events and quite willing to agree to a new trial for Mooney.[79]

Intervention of the Law and Order Committee

At this point the Law and Order Committee of the Chamber of Commerce stepped into the picture. The chamber's leaders had kept a close watch over the progress of the bomb cases. During Billings' trial Fickert had been seen in consultation with Frederick Koster, president of the chamber. Hugh Webster, executive secretary of the Law and Order Committee, had informed a reporter that the committee was wholeheartedly in support of the prosecution. Webster and Frank C. Drew, counsel for the chamber, had allegedly helped put Fickert in contact with Oxman.[80] From the outset the chamber's leaders were convinced that Mooney was guilty.

Yet the exposure of Oxman, which gave Koster and his associates the opportunity to speak out against a fraudulent conviction, brought no change in their position. When Fickert unexpectedly shifted his ground and began to attack the "anarchists" demanding a new trial for Mooney, Fremont Older and other supporters of Mooney charged that the district attorney had been influenced by Chamber of Commerce leaders.[81] And, as a federal investigator later concluded, there seemed to be "excellent grounds for believing that Fickert's sudden change of attitude was prompted by emissaries from some of the local corporate interests most bitterly opposed to union labor." [82] If Fickert did not receive behind-the-scenes encouragement from the chamber, he soon possessed its open support. On April 28, 1917, San Francisco's daily newspapers carried a huge advertisement printed in boldface and signed "Law & Order Committee, Chamber of Commerce, by Frederick J. Koster, Chairman." To all law-abiding citizens it proclaimed:

. . . those very forces that made the bomb outrage of Preparedness day possible have been taking FULL AND MEASURED AND UN-SCRUPULOUS ADVANTAGE of you to spread again their doctrine of anarchy, their intimidation of courts and of elected officials. . . .

Since District Attorney Fickert was now under attack by these sinister forces, "a committee of citizens" had met on April 25 at the offices of the Chamber of Commerce and had resolved that

. . . the Law & Order Committee . . . investigate what assistance may be needed by the District Attorney, and . . . offer to secure the services of such special counsel and such other services . . . as may be necessary . . . to the end that there may be no miscarriage of justice.[83]

With this high-sounding resolution the Law and Order Committee endorsed a thoroughly exposed effort to frustrate justice, and gave a solid basis to the claims of Mooney and Billings that they were the victims of antilabor sentiment. The Chamber of Commerce, with its impressive political influence, had determined that the convictions must stand. The guilt of Mooney and Billings became an article of faith to San Francisco businessmen. The opportunity to redress the legal wrong had passed. The conservative *Argonaut* clearly reflected this passage. On April 28, just before the Law and Order Committee intervened on the side of Fickert, the paper expressed deep concern that Mooney might have been fraudulently convicted. But a week later the *Argonaut* swung into line behind the committee, denouncing "the unsavory Older" and upholding the evidence against Mooney as "so positive, so overwhelming" that his guilt was beyond question.[84]

During the months after the exposure of Oxman, as Mooney's conviction was being appealed to the California Supreme Court, agitation over the case became more intense. Fremont Older, in the *Bulletin*, attacked Fickert almost daily. A committee of prominent San Francisco labor leaders, including the previously disinterested P. H. McCarthy, John O'Connell, and Congressman John I. Nolan, demanded a thorough probe of Fickert and Oxman. The case became a topic of heated discussion at meeting after meeting of the Labor Council. James Mullen gave only grudging support to Mooney and Billings in the *Labor Clarion*, but Paul Scharrenberg, in a series of editorials in the *Coast Seamen's Journal*, denounced "the million dollar 'law and order' committee" and its attempts "to keep the five defendants in jail and to keep Fickert . . . out of jail." [85] With other union leaders like Daniel C. Murphy, Hugo Ernst, and George Kidwell, Scharrenberg worked wholeheartedly to save Mooney from execution. Scharrenberg and Murphy, secretary and president respectively of the State Federation of Labor, appealed to workers throughout California:

> The charge that some of the defendants have gone outside of the rules of industrial warfare laid down by the AF of L should not operate to deprive them of their fundamental rights . . . they are languishing in jail today without the full sympathy of many honest trades-unionists. . . . We ask you to protest. . . . If you don't like Mooney . . . try and overcome your diffidence. . . .[86]

By midsummer a group of reformers and San Francisco union officers, sponsoring a movement to oust Fickert as district attorney, claimed to have gathered almost 15,000 signatures to petitions for a special recall election. "The people leading this fight against me," Fickert solemnly announced, "are anarchists . . . they fear prosecution. There were more than one hundred concerned in the Preparedness Day bomb explosions, and it is the anarchistic element which fears me. . . ." [87] In June Fickert sent Rena Mooney to trial. But the prosecution foundered without the services of Oxman, and Mrs. Mooney was acquitted late in July. In November the trial of Israel Weinberg likewise ended in acquittal. But Fickert, threatening retrials under new indictments, kept them in jail until well into 1918. Ed Nolan, the last of the five defendants, had been released on bail in April, 1917, after nine months of imprisonment. The discouraged district attorney never brought him to trial.[88]

The name of Tom Mooney, as the outcry against his death sentence grew in volume, became known not only nationally but internationally. Union and radical leaders in Britain, the Netherlands, Italy, and other European nations stirred their followers to anger over the case. The agitation abroad apparently began in Russia, when exiled radicals returned from San Francisco after the overthrow of the czar. By May, 1917, Russian crowds were demonstrating in front of the American Embassy in Petrograd, shouting the name of "Muni." President Woodrow Wilson was sufficiently disturbed to wire Governor William Stephens, asking him to stay Mooney's execution so as not to prejudice the effort to keep Russia in the war on the side of the Allies. A few months later, in September, 1917, Wilson appointed a federal commission to investigate the case.[89] Anxious to allay labor unrest during the crucial war years, the president thus acknowledged that Mooney's impending execution had become a nationwide issue.

Impact of the War

The wartime conditions that caused President Wilson to intervene in the Mooney case were also having a profound impact upon organized labor. Both nationally and in the Bay Area, unionism was on the march and fast gaining momentum. The powerful stimulus of the war interrupted the efforts of the Law and Order Committee to decrease union influence in San Francisco. In January, 1917, the committee distributed to businessmen's organizations across the nation a pamphlet describing the first six months of its crusade to redeem San Francisco from the abuses of an overpowerful labor movement. The pamphlet was entitled "Law and Order in San Francisco: A Beginning." The "beginning" so enthusiastically portrayed, however, was not destined to be followed up. The propitious environment created for organized labor by the war boom destroyed any possibility that the committee would lead an effective campaign for the open shop.

The committee, aided by the water-front strike and the Preparedness Day bombing, had aroused the businessmen of the city to a degree not seen since 1901. It had more than doubled the membership of the Chamber of Commerce and had brought that powerful organization for the first time squarely into the labor relations arena. It had won telling political successes over labor, had helped defeat most of the significant strikes of 1916, and had alarmed San Francisco union officials. By securing pledges of approximately $1 million, it had indicated the impressive resources that could be tapped for an open-shop drive by a leadership group that enjoyed the confidence of local employers. The committee, moreover, had achieved nationwide recognition among antiunion business groups. In May, 1917, the annual convention of the National Association of Manufacturers made Frederick Koster one of its featured speakers, and respectfully heard his account of the committee's work for "law and order," and its plans to have "responsible" citizens regain control of San Francisco's political and economic affairs.[90]

But by then the work of Koster and his committee was essentially ended. The committee maintained a nominal existence until early 1919, and intervened in a few wartime labor disputes. It continued to fight against any reëvaluation of the Mooney-Billings case and, according to Koster, helped governmental authorities to "ferret out IWW and other anarchistic elements" during the war.[91] However, the committee never again exerted a notable influence upon San Francisco industrial relations.

Wartime Inflation, Union Expansion, and Rising Wages

By the time the United States entered World War I, in April, 1917, wartime inflation was well under way. The general level of prices had been rising at an increasingly rapid pace. The wage rates of both organized and unorganized workers were increasing in the wake of prices, as business firms sought to allay unrest and retain their employees in a tightening labor market. The excitement of the wartime boom, the soaring cost of living, and the increasing demand for workers at higher and higher pay scales were stimulating the greatest expansion of organized labor since the turn of the century. From a membership of slightly more than 2 million in 1916, the AFL grew to approximately 3.2 million in 1919. At its peak in 1920 the reported AFL membership reached more than 4 million, almost double the prewar level.[92] In the Bay Area, where labor was much more thoroughly organized than in most American cities, the increase in union numbers was proportionately not so large. But the local labor movement experienced a notable expansion in size and strength.

Bay Area workers who had met defeat in 1916 strikes found the war boom bringing them concessions from employers. The Steamboat Owners' Association raised the monthly wages of river boat deckhands in May, 1917. Soon afterward the lumber longshoremen reported their base wage increased to 65 cents an hour. In August the Restaurant Men's Association announced higher pay scales for most cooks, waiters, and miscellaneous culinary workers. Even the United Railroads increased its minimum hiring rate at the end of 1916 from $2.50 to $2.70 per ten-hour day.[93]

Unions encountered little serious difficulty in negotiating wage gains. By the end of 1917 most organized workers had won pay increases without striking. But the San Francisco Teamsters' Union, requesting its first wage increase since 1912 in December, 1916, was too hasty; the Draymen's Association would have been more yielding some months later. Mike Casey, who discouraged union belligerence, relied upon his reputation among employers for conservatism and integrity. Despite labor's antagonism toward the Law and Order Committee, Casey asked Frederick Koster to help the teamsters secure a higher scale. Koster, agreeing that a wage increase was justifiable, used his influence as Chamber of Commerce president to persuade the Draymen's Association to accede to the union's demands. The association signed a new agreement, effective in January, 1917, increasing the wage rates of several thousand teamsters by 50 cents a day.[94] Like several other unions, however, the Teamsters' Union made an error in judgment. With lack of foresight, it accepted a three-year contract in the midst of an accelerating rise in the price level.

Among the many unionized groups who won wage gains between the summer of 1916 and the close of 1917 were milk wagon drivers and other specialty teamsters, printing tradesmen, building tradesmen, laundry workers, streetcar men, bakers, butchers, coopers, and metal tradesmen. A few unions, including the organizations of seamen, longshoremen, and building trades laborers, won a second annual round of pay boosts in 1917. The demands for wage increases in 1916 and 1917 approximated 50 cents a day, or $3 a week, with few unions exceeding this level. Even fewer had sufficient bargaining strength to push wage rates up as rapidly as retail prices. At the close of 1916 the estimated cost of living in the San Francisco–Oakland area was only 8 per cent higher than before the outbreak of the European war in mid-1914. But during 1917 the cost of living soared a further 20 per cent.[95] This meant a deterioration in real wages for most union members. More overtime work and steadier employment enabled many workers to prevent a decline in real earnings, but all categories of labor became acutely aware of the pinch of inflation as the war progressed.

Although price rises wiped out the benefits of wage increases, a number of Bay Area unions seized the wartime opportunity to establish a shorter workday, especially those in the transportation and distribution industries. During 1917 and 1918 the eight-hour day was won by sailors, marine firemen, longshoremen, inside creamery workers, and bakery drivers.[96] Substantial reductions in working hours were achieved before the end of the war by general teamsters, building material teamsters, milkdrivers, culinary workers, butchers, and grocery clerks, most of whom won the eight-hour day immediately after the war.

New Organizing Drives

By early 1917 the wartime boom had quickened union organizing activity in the Bay Area. The San Francisco Tailors' Union sought to extend its membership among clothing and department store bushelmen, and reported that a number of the stores granted wage increases. Late in 1917 the Stationary Firemen's Union claimed that organization among PG&E employees was approaching the level that had been reached before the 1913 strike. Various locals of the International Brotherhood of Teamsters made notable organizing gains during 1916–1917. In 1916 the Bakery Drivers' Union, under the leadership of George Kidwell, launched an aggressive campaign which brought it the eight-hour day early in 1918. Kidwell, a mildly radical, adroit leader with leanings toward industrial unionism, also succeeded in organizing wrappers, slicers, and other less skilled bakery workers who had been ignored by the Bakers' Union. In 1917 he renewed the effort to unionize the drivers employed by Latin bakeries, but succeeded in only a handful of firms. In 1916 the Milkers' Union, one of the oldest of San Francisco's AFL federal unions, organized the inside workers in creameries and milk-processing plants. The Milk Dealers' Association granted the union the eight-hour day as of January 1, 1917. After winning this concession the Milkers' Union merged into the Milkdrivers' Union, which continued to organize and bargain for the in-plant workers. The Milkdrivers' Union in the East Bay likewise extended its jurisdiction to embrace inside workers and unionized them with little difficulty in 1916–1918. The San Francisco Teamsters' Union, in 1917, organized the majority of drivers employed by the city's wholesale meat firms. And on both sides of the Bay, the teamsters finally achieved recognition from the Bekins Van and Storage Company, the largest firm of its industry and one that had held out for years against unionization. After a brief strike in mid-1917, the company accepted the contract terms negotiated by the teamsters with the California Transfer and Storage Association.[97]

In the summer of 1917 the Alameda County Central Labor Council, feeling that the East Bay was ripe for an intensive organizing drive, asked the AFL to assign a full-time organizer to the greater Oakland area. The AFL refused, however, stating that no funds were available. Left to their own resources, the council and some individual East Bay unions succeeded in gaining a foothold among a few largely untouched groups of workers: slaughterhouse butchers; laborers in the shops and yards of the Southern Pacific Railroad; fruit and produce workers; and building service employees.[98] In the closing months of 1917 organizing activity in the East Bay increased. But neither in the East Bay nor in San Francisco was there any large-scale expansion of unionism among previously unorganized workers. The chief gains in union membership during 1917 were made in the industrial sector most stimulated by the drive for war production—the metal trades and, above all, the shipbuilding industry.

Wartime Labor Relations in the Metal Trades

When the United States entered the war in April, 1917, Bay Area metal tradesmen were working under long-term agreements due to expire in the fall of the year. These agreements had been reached only after prolonged friction over the eight-hour day, the equalization of the competitive position of Bay Area firms with those elsewhere, and the demand of employers for three- to five-year contracts assuring them wage and cost stability. The 1910 compromise settlement between the California Metal Trades Association and the Iron Trades Council expired late in 1913. Protracted negotiations before and after its expiration made little headway toward a new agreement. The stalemate led the foundry owners affiliated with the CMTA to believe that they could attain a more satisfactory, harmonious labor-management relationship by forming their own bargaining association. The foundries dealt primarily with only one union—the Molders' Union—rather than with a group of metal trades crafts. They had accepted the long-established Molders' Union more wholeheartedly than other employers had accepted their newer relationships with the aggressive Machinists' Union and other metal trades unions. Indeed, some foundry employers suspected that the CMTA was not negotiating in good faith in 1913, and was basically uninterested in maintaining a settled bargaining relationship with the metal tradesmen.[99]

The California Foundrymen's Association was thus created by secession from the CMTA in the spring of 1914; it included almost every foundry in San Francisco and in Alameda County. Several months later it signed a three-year agreement, running to September, 1917, with the molders, the patternmakers, and a rather weak union of unskilled foundry employees. The agreement retained the eight-hour day and left wages unchanged. The CMTA, representing both the shipyards and the "uptown" machine shops and metal products manufacturers, negotiated for still another year before signing, in 1915, a two-year contract with the Iron Trades Council. By that time the issue of the eight-hour day was no longer seriously controversial, for the stimulus of war production for the Allies was aiding skilled metal tradesmen to win the shorter workday in an expanding segment of Eastern industry. The new contract raised the machinists' daily wage to $4, giving them their long-sought parity with molders, boilermakers, and blacksmiths. Like previous contracts between the CMTA and the ITC, it was silent on the question of union security, although employers recognized that in practice union-shop conditions were generally maintained among their skilled workers. Most of the unskilled men and boys employed by CMTA firms were not, however, union members.[100]

Militant Unionism in the Shipyards

During the war years no other branch of the Bay Area metal trades industry approached shipbuilding as a center of booming employment expansion and recurrent labor conflict. On the Oakland as well as the San Francisco side of the Bay, the establishment and enlargement of shipyards drew thousands of workers into the industry. This prodigious growth was accompanied by a degree of labor unruliness which made shipbuilding the chief focus of attention for those concerned with wartime industrial relations on the Pacific Coast.

The shipbuilding boom began in the Bay Area late in 1915 and gained momentum throughout the following year. In mid-1916 Bethlehem Steel's Union Iron Works, the largest San Francisco shipyard, reported that its work force had grown to 4,000 men—twice the 1914 level—and that it held contracts for the construction of approximately thirty vessels. In 1917, when America went to war, shipbuilding activity spurted upward at a greatly increased rate. At their peak point of expansion in 1919 Bay Area yards employed an estimated 55,000 workers, almost ten times the number reported for the entire California shipbuilding industry before the war.[101]

With union leaders confident of their powerful bargaining position, and with the rank and file pressing for gains, there was militant labor action in the shipyards. In 1917, as compared with World War II, federal authorities moved less rapidly and effectively to prevent work stoppages affecting war production. Both workers and employers lacked, on the whole, the emotional involvement in the war effort which was so characteristic of the more crucial struggle a generation later. Public opinion was not so potent a deterrent to wartime strikes or lockouts. Labor relations in Pacific Coast shipbuilding were thus sufficiently disturbed in 1917–1918 to evoke recurrent governmental intervention and, from business spokesmen, frequent denunciations of the metal trades unions as greedy, irresponsible, and unpatriotic. During the war shipbuilding temporarily superseded the construction industry as the target of open-shop advocates attempting to demonstrate the intolerable power and arrogance of organized labor. The turbulence of the industry's labor force also brought to the fore the perennial conflict between conservative union leaders and the more radical industrial unionists.

A few minor shipbuilding strikes occurred in mid-1916, when unorganized laborers, helpers, and apprentices staged brief walkouts for higher pay at the Union Iron Works. The Boilermakers' Union organized several hundred apprentices and helpers into a separate auxiliary, announcing that it was ridding these less skilled workers of obvious IWW influence among them. The first upheaval of consequence in local shipbuilding came early in 1917, when the AFL granted a federal charter to the new Shipyard Laborers' Union. From the outset this union of unskilled workers was in disfavor with metal trades craftsmen. The Boilermakers' Union protested the granting of the charter on the ground that the laborers were under its jurisdiction. M. J. McGuire, head of the boilermakers, was charged with having openly threatened to disrupt the upstart organization rather than allow it independent status.[102] The new union also aroused opposition by its refusal to accept supervision and advice from leaders of the older unions of skilled craftsmen.

The Shipyard Laborers' Union demonstrated its militancy within two weeks after receiving its charter. Early in March, 1917, its several hundred members struck against the East Bay's two leading shipyards—Moore and Scott, and the Alameda plant of the Bethlehem Shipbuilding Corporation—for recognition and an increase to a minimum $3 daily wage from the low prevailing level of $2 to $2.25. Hundreds of unskilled workers as yet unorganized joined the strike. Although the union's claim that 3,000 men had walked out was probably an exaggeration, the strike closed both yards for a brief period and elicited the offer of a compromise wage increase. The union disturbed Bethlehem executives, moreover, by establishing the nucleus of another Shipyard Laborers' Union in the corporation's Union Iron Works in San Francisco. The East Bay strikers remained out for more than two weeks, initially spurning the insistence of employers, supported by conservative metal trades union leaders, that bargaining would not begin until the workers had returned to their jobs. On

March 20, however, the Shipyard Laborers' Union called off its strike when the employers promised to negotiate. The settlement reached shortly afterward gave the union a higher wage scale and at least tacit recognition from the two largest East Bay shipyards.[103]

The skilled metal trades unions, although displaying little sympathy for the shipyard laborers' strike, also adopted aggressive tactics in 1917 as the cost of living rose and the demand for skilled labor became increasingly acute. Under higher pay scales voluntarily established by employers early in the year the prevailing minimum daily wage for experienced craftsmen was $4.25 to $4.50, a temporarily satisfactory rate. But by September 15, when its long-term contracts with the California Metal Trades Association and the California Foundrymen's Association expired, the Iron Trades Council had demanded a one-third increase in wage rates. The council, claiming to embrace almost 25,000 workers, approximately 90 per cent of them in the shipyards, was primed for drastic action to enforce its demand.[104]

Although labor's initial position was modified as bargaining proceeded, the gap between employer offer and union demand was still wide on September 17, 1917, when the council called out approximately 30,000 men in a strike that shut down shipyards, foundries, machine shops, and other metal trades plants throughout the Bay Area. In terms of the number of workers involved, it was the largest individual strike that had ever been called on the West Coast. It was also one of the most important labor disputes in American war industry during 1917–1918, paralyzing war production in the Bay Area metal trades. After one week, however, anxious representatives of the federal government managed to mediate a settlement. They persuaded the Iron Trades Council, the CMTA, and the CFA to sign a temporary agreement ending the walkout and establishing immediate wage increases on a sliding-scale basis, ranging from 20 per cent for workers with rates less than $4.25 per day to 10 per cent for those with rates above $5. "It is understood," the signatories carefully proclaimed, "that the object in agreeing to this advance in wages at this time is purely patriotic on both sides. . . ." A final determination of wage rates, the settlement provided, would be made by the new national Shipbuilding Labor Adjustment Board, created in mid-1917 by agreement between the federal government's Emergency Fleet Corporation and leaders of the AFL.[105]

Although the Boilermakers' Union held out for almost a week against a clause in the interim contract which prohibited on-the-job secondary boycotts against materials or equipment supplied by "unfair" firms, all affiliates of the Iron Trades Council had sent their members back to work by October 1. But the West Coast shipbuilding industry continued to give deep concern to federal authorities in the fall of 1917, as metal trades unions maintained disruptive walkouts for some days in Pacific Northwest shipyards. All strikes had been called off, however, by early November, when the Shipbuilding Labor Adjustment Board announced its wage award. This award established a uniform, coast-wide wage schedule that was known through the war period as the "Macy scale," after the board's chairman, V. Everitt Macy. Because of the rise in the cost of living, the board fixed rates for most categories of shipyard labor at approximately 30 per cent above the 1916 level. The daily wage of craftsmen such as boilermakers, machinists, and molders was standardized at $5.25; the wage rate of unskilled laborers was raised to $3.25 per day. The board, hoping to attract labor to the shipyards and pacify unrest, gave the metal tradesmen substantially larger gains than were achieved by most unions during 1917. The Macy award, nevertheless, was immediately protested as inadequate by metal trades leaders in both the Bay Area and the Puget Sound district.[106]

Before 1917 closed, dissatisfaction over the award led to more trouble. A delegation from the Iron Trades Council, headed by R. W. Burton and M. J. McGuire, went to Washington, D.C., in November, to demand improvements in the Macy scale. With the persuasive assistance of leaders of several AFL international unions, and of John I. Nolan, San Francisco's labor congressman, the delegation achieved a quick success. The Macy Board, apprehensive of another strike on the Pacific Coast, announced a supplemental wage increase of 10 per cent, effective December 15, on all shipyard work under government contract. The new award boosted the journeymen's scale in the principal crafts to $5.80 per day, 45 per cent above the $4 level prevailing in 1916. Although the board's ruling applied only to shipbuilding, the Iron Trades Council immediately served notice that the higher rates would be enforced on all firms in the California Metal Trades Association. On December 26, 1917, after the CMTA had balked at this ultimatum, several thousand metal tradesmen struck Bay Area plants turning out gas engines, pumps, airplane motors, and other products. Within a week the CMTA surrendered, agreeing that the augmented Macy scale would be observed by all its affiliated firms.[107]

The metal trades unions thus made impressive gains in 1917. Their employers, thanks to the inflationary war boom, could concede these gains with little economic difficulty. But an open-shop advocate reported that the CMTA's members were "fighting mad and helpless—at present." [108] When the war ended, he predicted, they would take their revenge for labor's exactions.

Labor Conflict in 1917

American industry in 1917 was beset by continuing labor conflict.[109] The Bay Area also experienced more strike activity than in the immediate prewar years. But the number of labor disputes was not particularly large. Most of the man-days lost in the Bay Area were attributable to work stoppages in the metal trades. There was no widespread wave of strikes in local industry, as workers and employers usually made peaceful adjustments to the rapid upward movement in prices, wages, and employment.

Many of the Bay Area strikes in 1917 were spontaneous outbreaks by groups of workers who were either unorganized or only recently touched by unionism. The cause was most often the lag of wages behind the soaring cost of living. The strikes were typically short ones that won wage concessions but failed to establish well-rooted organizations among the workers involved.

An exception was a mid-1917 strike by a new local of butchers employed in several West Oakland slaughterhouses. Aided by a boycott imposed by Bay Area butchers' unions on the products of the struck plants, the strike lasted until the spring of 1918, when an apparently satisfactory settlement was negotiated. The new union remained intact.[110]

Briefer and less well-organized strikes were called in 1917 by other groups of workers, including a new union of men and women in San Francisco trunk and suitcase manufacturing shops; freight handlers at the San Francisco depot of the Southern Pacific

Railroad, and laborers in the railroad's shops and yards in Oakland; unorganized confectionery workers in the large Ghirardelli candy and chocolate factory; and unskilled laborers in such plants as the Pacific Coast Steel Company and the Pacific Oil and Lead Company.[111]

In 1917 labor unrest also appeared in the nonunion Bay Area industry of fruit and vegetable canning. In the spring a union calling itself the "Toilers of the World" and including some members of the IWW among its founders enlisted a large number of cannery workers in and around San Jose. It soon acquired an AFL federal charter. Late in July, with the canning season approaching its height, the new union led hundreds of men and women out on strike for a minimum daily wage of $2.50 and an eight-hour day. Claiming more than 1,000 members, the Toilers of the World surprised the cannery owners with the first large-scale uprising among their workers. Intensive picketing impeded canning operations, and employers denounced the strike as an IWW conspiracy. Charging that the IWW was determined to sabotage the "capitalist" war effort by disrupting vital food industries, they demanded the imposition of martial law and the wholesale arrests of strikers as "enemies of this country." [112]

A government official later described the cannery conflict as "perhaps the most acute situation" the Federal Food Administration encountered in its wartime efforts to prevent breakdowns in food production. On July 26 the strike spread to a large cannery in San Francisco, where an estimated 500 unorganized workers left their jobs. More than 100 of the San Francisco strikers traveled across the Bay to urge Oakland cannery employees to join in the strike. But police broke up their demonstration in the East Bay and herded them back to the ferryboat terminal to be "deported to San Francisco." A few days later Oakland police met and turned back another large band of strikers coming over to agitate before East Bay canneries. The San Jose conflict, meanwhile, had produced violence in which one striker was shot to death and several men injured. For two days the city was under military control, as troops were brought in to prevent disorders. The excitement was soon over, however, both in San Jose and the San Francisco–Oakland area. Harris Weinstock and Ralph P. Merritt, the federal food administrator for California, mediated a settlement which substantially raised the wage rates of cannery workers; the new scale gave adult males 30 cents an hour. At the end of July the union voted to call off the strike.[113] Emerging with success from this clash with employers, the Toilers of the World maintained itself through the war period; it was the only union of any importance to appear in California canning before the 1930's.

These 1917 strikes by embryonic unions and groups of nonunion workers were significant manifestations of the growing realization among Bay Area wage earners of their amplified power in the wartime boom. But the strikes did not constitute a large-scale upheaval of the unorganized. They usually did not involve substantial numbers of workers. Nor did local labor leaders try to convert these uprisings into disciplined trade-union action. They gave unorganized strikers assistance and advice, especially in the East Bay, but did not exploit the war-born opportunity to extend unionization among unorganized workers.

Renewed Onslaught on the United Railroads

Two 1917 strikes were revivals of previous conflicts. The Bay and River Steamboatmen's Union, defeated in 1916 with the aid of the Law and Order Committee, again challenged the open-shop Steamboat Owners' Association. And the wartime upsurge of unionism brought a new attack on the United Railroads, the most hated symbol of the open shop in San Francisco. It was labor's last futile effort before the 1930's to subdue this formidable opponent.

By the spring of 1917 the Bay and River Steamboatmen's Union had regained sufficient strength to join the Marine Engineers' Beneficial Association in threatening to strike against Bay Area ferryboats. The threats won wage and hour concessions for the members of both unions employed on ferries of the Southern Pacific Railroad and the Key System. Late in April member firms of the Steamboat Owners' Association announced a wage increase for crews on other classes of vessels. The ambitious Steamboatmen's Union, however, now demanded recognition and a union-shop agreement. When the demands were rejected, the union called several hundred men out on strike in May. But the steamboatmen's 1917 struggle proved no more successful than that of

1916. By late summer the strike of deckhands and firemen had faded away, leaving the union thoroughly disrupted. Within a few months the union was dissolved.[114]

The renewal of the struggle against the United Railroads came in August, 1917. Edward Vandeleur, president of the Municipal Carmen's Union, had resigned his position earlier in the year to help lead another organizing drive among the company's employees. By the end of July Vandeleur and his fellow organizers had secretly enrolled a sufficient membership to make them hopeful of touching off a contagious uprising. Accordingly they planned, with success, to launch the strike that Tom Mooney had so thoroughly failed to start a year earlier. On Saturday, August 11, without warning, a dozen or more crews abandoned their cars in downtown San Francisco and called upon the other streetcar men to join them. The strike spread rapidly as the enthusiastic carmen paraded along Market Street and before the carbarns. The Labor Council wholeheartedly supported this new revolt against the open shop. On Saturday, August 18, Secretary John O'Connell and other council leaders spoke to a mass meeting claimed to number at least 5,000 strikers and sympathizers. By that time more than 1,000 had reportedly left their jobs to enlist in the newly chartered carmen's union. According to an open-shop spokesman, the United Railroads was attempting to maintain service with approximately 700 carmen, still loyal "though their lives were in danger every hour." Reassuringly, however, "hundreds of strikebreakers were on the way." [115]

The use of strikebreakers, detectives, and armed guards by the United Railroads, and violence on the part of the strikers, gave San Francisco its most inflamed industrial conflict of 1917. Labor Council officers warned the carmen to avoid disorders that could antagonize the public. Community opinion and the press appeared strongly sympathetic to the carmen's demands for the $3.50 daily wage and the eight-hour day currently enjoyed by employees of the Municipal Railway. Even the conservative *Chronicle* criticized the United Railroads by pointing out that the "minimum rate of wages for the commonest form of labor" employed by the city was $3 for an eight-hour day. The United Railroads hired men at $2.80 for ten hours of work within a fifteen-hour period, and allowed them to reach the maximum wage of $3.70 only after nine years of service. Some carmen worked seven days a week without overtime pay.[116]

In an effort to halt streetcar service, the striking carmen assaulted strikebreakers, stoned streetcars, and attempted to sabotage United Railroads tracks and equipment. In the first month of the strike, according to employer spokesmen, more than 300 of the company's employees had been injured. Most of the injuries were minor, but one man had been killed and a number critically wounded. This violence led the Law and Order Committee to intervene publicly in the strike, one of the few times it so acted after 1916. Frederick Koster and his fellow leaders of the Chamber of Commerce were convinced that city officials had once again failed to protect strikebreakers from vengeful unionists. The police and police court judges, it was alleged, had combined to prevent nonunion men from defending themselves. More than 100 United Railroads carmen and detectives were arrested during the strike for carrying concealed weapons, and several were given unusually severe sentences by police court judges up for early reëlection.[117]

Mayor Rolph, while insisting that an augmented police force was keeping this "occasionally" violent contest the most peaceful streetcar strike in San Francisco history, was clearly antagonistic to the United Railroads and its open-shop supporters. He resented President Jesse Lilienthal's refusal to meet with representatives of the strikers, and publicly recommended municipal purchase of the company to ensure its employees better working conditions. The mayor also took issue with the Law and Order Committee. On the night of August 23 a nonunion carman was shot to death and several others were injured when strikers attacked a streetcar. Koster immediately sent Rolph a telegram charging him with responsibility for a breakdown of law and order.[118] Rolph answered the "hysterical telegram" with an open letter in which he accused the Law and Order Committee of fomenting "industrial unrest and class hatred," and explosively lectured Koster:

The world is changing all around you, and you and your kind don't know it any more than the Czar knew what was happening. . . . Doubtless you are disappointed because the police have not yet turned machine guns on crowds in our streets, and killed a few dozen strikers, including the customary number of innocent bystanders.[119]

The 1917 strike against the United Railroads failed completely despite the unusually favorable circumstances of a tight labor market, the neutrality of city officials, a sympathetic public, and the encouragement and financial support of local labor. Edward Vandeleur later blamed the defeat on the antagonism aroused in the community by the strikers' continued violence. But the strike collapsed primarily because the United Railroads was able to maintain service despite sabotage and attacks by strikers. Approximately one-third of its workers refused to join in the walk-out, and another 200 or more returned to their jobs during the strike. Despite an increasing shortage of labor by mid-1917, the company managed to recruit more than 1,000 additional men to work as streetcar operators.[120]

On November 22, 1917, after three months of struggle, the Carmen's Union voted to call off its strike. It requested that donations be continued for some time to support its "aged and disabled" members who might have difficulty in finding other jobs. A few weeks later the union turned in its charter. To maintain its strike against the United Railroads more than $40,000 had been contributed, chiefly by San Francisco Labor Council unions. The Law and Order Committee did not publicize the amount it had spent in support of the company, but Koster later said that the defeat of this strike alone would have justified the entire expense of the committee since its creation.[121]

The Mooney Case and the Fickert Recall Election

During the latter weeks of the strike against the United Railroads, interest was building up in San Francisco over the approaching special election to determine whether District Attorney Charles Fickert was to remain in office. Aroused by the exposure of Frank Oxman, Fickert's star witness in the Mooney case, thousands of voters had signed the petition for a recall election. As the campaign between the pro- and anti-Fickert forces progressed, it revealed a deep split in the labor movement over the Mooney issue and illuminated the latent antagonism of many unionists toward conservative "labor politicians."

During the campaign the Mooney case precipitated a factional fight in the Labor Council which brought this antagonism to the surface. The council's president was Arthur Brouillet, a young and ambitious lawyer who was an officer of the Retail Clerks' Union. Brouillet also held a salaried position in the state's Republican administration. Violently opposed to union support for Mooney and Billings, even after the Oxman revelation, Brouillet alleged that certain labor leaders sympathetic to the defense had "guilty knowledge" of the Preparedness Day bombing. Paul Scharrenberg, with whom Brouillet had clashed over the Mooney case, retaliated by describing him in the *Coast Seamen's Journal* as a "horrible example of a type of parasite" trading on "his prestige as a 'labor leader'" to win political preferment. Brouillet, the *Journal* warned, demonstrated the "imperative necessity for electing none other than bona fide working men to positions of trust in the labor movement." [122]

Charged with making baseless accusations against fellow unionists, Brouillet was ousted as president of the Labor Council in November, 1917.[123] "No matter what may be justly said or unjustly whispered about . . . certain 'labor leaders,'" Scharrenberg wrote, "the 'common herd' is still true to itself." [124] But James Mullen, in the *Labor Clarion*, attacked the removal of Brouillet as part of a conspiracy by "radicals" to gain control of the San Francisco labor movement. The Brouillet issue divided union leaders into opposing factions. Supporting the ouster were Andrew Furuseth, Hugo Ernst, Daniel Murphy, and George Kidwell, who led a mixed group including men upholding Socialist or industrial unionist principles, and others chiefly moved by sympathy for Mooney. Prominent among Brouillet's adherents were Mike Casey, John P. McLaughlin, Andrew Gallagher, and other relatively conservative, politically influential labor leaders who showed no visible concern over Mooney's impending execution.[125] Before the controversy died away it had brought into sharp focus the division within San Francisco's labor movement.

While Labor Council delegates wrangled over the ouster of Brouillet, District Attorney Fickert was campaigning against his own ouster from office on a platform of "Americanism versus Anarchy." The comparative tolerance which had long characterized San Franciscans' attitudes toward political radicals and other nonconformists had been dealt a severe blow by America's entry into the war. Accordingly, Fickert now assumed the mantle of righteous patriotism. By late 1917 vague apprehensions of "Reds" and "anarchists" were mounting amid hysterical and unreasoning fear, not only among business groups, but among California unionists who had once defended the IWW's right to freedom from suppression. In October the annual convention of the State Federation of Labor adopted a resolution calling for the expulsion of all IWW members from AFL unions. In preceding weeks there had been rumors of an IWW plot to burn the crops in Alameda County, a mob of several hundred servicemen had wrecked the IWW headquarters in Oakland, and federal agents had arrested IWW members in San Francisco and other American cities on blanket charges of obstructing the war effort.[126] Growing alarm over the IWW and other antiwar groups gave Fickert a favorable setting for his campaign against recall, and he exploited the public's phobia to the full.

The district attorney also gained from the split within the labor movement. The Union Labor Recall League, headed by such men as Paul Scharrenberg, Daniel Murphy, and Hugo Ernst, opposed Fickert. In response the Union Labor Fickert League was established by labor officials representing mainly the unions of building tradesmen and teamsters. Some prominent union leaders, such as P. H. McCarthy, joined the league and openly backed Fickert. Others, more circumspect, gave the league their tacit support. Just before the election the league, in a large advertisement in the *Labor Clarion*, pointed out that Fickert, at the request of "your representatives in Union Labor," had filled certain political patronage jobs with union members. And it loosed a sweeping tirade against all "Reds, pacifists, seditionists," and "avowed anarchists." [127]

Energetically supported by the Chamber of Commerce and its Law and Order Committee, and benefiting from antiradical hysteria and from a disunited labor leadership, Fickert was retained in office by a large majority at the election on December 18, 1917. Frederick Koster claimed for the Law and Order Committee a major share of the credit for this victory over "anarchy." Scharrenberg, whose *Coast Seamen's Journal* was the only one of San Francisco's three labor papers to back the recall attempt,

350 | *Wartime Ferment*

reported that "the overwhelming majority of local labor leaders either openly supported Fickert or remained silent altogether." Fremont Older later commented in the *Bulletin* that at least three-fourths of the city's prominent union officials had considered Fickert's reëlection to be to their own personal political advantage.[128]

In December, 1917, the month of Fickert's election victory, President Woodrow Wilson's Federal Mediation Commission was in San Francisco investigating the Mooney-Billings case as part of its survey of wartime labor disturbances in the West.[129] Felix Frankfurter, a young lawyer who later became a justice of the United States Supreme Court, was secretary of the commission and author of its report on the case. The report, which brought Frankfurter denunciation as a "Bolshevik" by the judge who had presided over Billings' trial, was released in January, 1918. It accepted fully the class-war explanation of the case and stated its conclusions forcefully:

> Mooney is the center of the case. The other defendants have significance only because of their relation to him. . . . The utilities against which Mooney directed his agitation . . . undoubtedly sought "to get" Mooney. Their activities against him were directed by Swanson, private detective. . . . When Oxman was discredited, the verdict against Mooney was discredited. . . . The "Mooney Case" resolved itself into a new aspect of the old industrial feud . . . just as Mooney symbolized labor for all the bitter opponents of labor, so he came to symbolize labor irrespective of his personal merits, in the minds of workers.[130]

The commission's report added fuel to the growing agitation in the United States and abroad against Mooney's execution. Upon receiving the report President Wilson wrote Governor William Stephens to remind him that "the case has assumed international importance" and to ask for a retrial in view of the new evidence that had emerged since Mooney's conviction. But the California Supreme Court, in March, 1918, confirmed the death sentence, ruling that the new evidence afforded no basis, under state law, for setting aside a conviction.[131] In the following months protest mass meetings were held in San Francisco and other cities, and President Wilson sent repeated requests for executive clemency to the unsympathetic Governor Stephens.

Wartime Labor Relations in 1918

During 1918 the forces set in motion by the wartime boom gained impetus. The cost of living rose at an accelerated pace, climbing by approximately 30 per cent.[132] Wages of union and nonunion workers increased more rapidly than in 1917. And the unionization of unorganized workers, after proceeding at a moderate tempo through most of 1917, picked up speed.

Wage adjustments in 1918 were reached with less friction than in the early war months, as employers realized that the prolonged inflation made repeated pay increases justifiable and indeed inevitable. Throughout the nation, and in the Bay Area, the incidence of industrial conflict receded from its high level of 1917. Both labor and management were learning to accommodate themselves to the new environment of steadily rising prices and wages. Both sides also felt the inhibiting influence of governmental insistence that labor strife must not hamper the war effort. The tripartite National War Labor Board, created in the spring of 1918, received from the AFL and from employers pledges to accept the board's program for maintaining labor peace: a ban on strikes and lockouts for the duration of the war; referral of wage and other unresolved issues to the board or to special federal labor boards established in certain vital industries; explicit recognition of the right of workers to organize, bargain collectively, and be protected from discharge or discrimination on the basis of union membership; the waiving by labor of attempts to force strict union-shop conditions upon employers who had not previously accepted them.[133] The NWLB was called upon during the war to settle relatively few Bay Area labor disputes, but knowledge of its availability as a court of appeal lessened the impulse of unions to resort to the strike weapon against employers.

The war brought to collective bargaining in the Bay Area a greater participation by outside mediators or arbitrators. In 1917, with the creation of the United States Conciliation Service as an agency of the Department of Labor, governmental provision of mediation facilities expanded rapidly. Federal commissioners of conciliation, other governmental representatives, and private individuals who possessed the confidence of both labor and management were called upon repeatedly by Bay Area employers and unions for assistance in settling incipient wartime disputes. The war and its attendant inflation also stimulated the utilization of economic data by the parties engaged in collective bargaining. Arguments for wage adjustments based upon changes in the cost of living, upon wage movements in related occupations and industries, and upon the equity of maintaining prewar interoccupational and interregional wage differentials were prepared with greater precision and advanced with far more frequency. Although still limited, the employment as consultants of professional statisticians and economists expanded, as labor and management retained their services in negotiation and arbitration proceedings. The increased wartime use of arbitration to resolve economic issues in contract bargaining furthered this trend, since arbitrators relied heavily upon price, wage, and family budget data in reaching their decisions.

Rising Wages in 1918

In the final year of the war wages continued on the upward course that began in 1916. The large increases granted to shipbuilding workers by the 1917 Macy awards set the pace for wage rates elsewhere in the Bay Area economy. They forced matching increases from other metal trades firms and, in the view of resentful employers, stimulated unrest and unrealistic wage demands among the workers of firms not blessed with cost-plus government war contracts. The pattern set in shipbuilding was followed particularly in the utility industry, where the Pacific District Council of Electrical Workers persuaded PG&E and the Great Western Power Company, in mid-1918, to sign renewed contracts raising daily wages of electrical linemen to the $5.80 level established for most skilled craftsmen under the Macy award.[134]

Most employers acceded to union arguments that fairness called for increases in wages to accompany the rising cost of living. Voluntary acceptance of the same principle by nonunion firms, combined with the tightness of the labor market, kept wage scales of unorganized workers also climbing through 1918. The United Railroads, as an example, raised its minimum hiring rate to 37 cents an hour by mid-1918, almost one-third above the 28-cent rate prevailing before the August, 1917, strike. Some employers received union commendation for a generous approach to the wage issue. Early in 1918 the Coopers' Union praised Frederick Koster's California Barrel Company and several other firms for voluntarily raising pay scales 10 per cent beyond the level asked by the union. Employers of laundry workers, teamsters, and other workers whose unions had signed long-term wage contracts early in the war boom did not attempt to hold them to these agreements.[135]

Negotiations gave rise, however, to a number of strike threats. The San Francisco Teamsters' Union announced a strike for May 1, 1918, after the Draymen's Association, although publicly acknowledging that teamster wages were lagging far behind the cost of living, had pleaded the inability of its members to pay substantial increases. A compromise settlement was soon reached, however, raising wages by 50 cents a day and cutting the workday to 9.5 hours. The San Francisco Milkdrivers' Union came closer to carrying out a threatened strike in January, 1918, before Mike Casey negotiated a compromise embodying sizable wage increases for both drivers and inside workers. This union, although it had signed a three-year contract early in 1917, presented demands twice more during 1918, with exceptional success. It won a nine-hour day and successive wage increases * to $135 per month for drivers—almost 40 per cent above the scale at the end of 1917.[136]

Strikes over wage and hour issues were also threatened in 1918 by electrical linemen, teamsters, milkdrivers, and culinary workers in the East Bay, and press feeders, sausage makers, taxicab drivers, and garment cutters in San Francisco. Several of these disputes resulted in brief walkouts of small numbers of

* The final increase was the outcome of an informal arbitration hearing before Ralph P. Merritt, federal food administrator for California. Merritt had requested all unions in food manufacturing and distribution to refer disputes to his office before taking strike action. He thus played important mediation and arbitration roles during 1917–1918 in wage controversies involving such groups as milkdrivers, teamsters, butchers, and cannery workers. At the end of the war, in late 1918, Merritt publicly thanked Bay Area unions for carrying out their pledges to refer threatened conflicts to him, and stated with pride that no seriously disruptive wartime strike had occurred in California's food industries after the August, 1917, cannery walkout led by the Toilers of the World. (*Tri-City Labor Review*, Aug. 16, 1918; *Labor Clarion*, Sept. 20, 27, Dec. 13, 1918.)

workers.[137] Outside the metal trades and shipbuilding industry, however, there were only a few, small-scale labor conflicts involving well-established Bay Area unions in 1918. Clashes between employers and new unions were more common, but no prolonged strikes developed.

Union Organizing in 1918

By early 1918 the tendency toward unionization among unorganized workers had become more pronounced in the Bay Area, compared with the slow growth of interest in 1916 and 1917. The upswing in organizing activity received some of its impetus from the unprecedented official recognition which President Wilson's wartime administration had extended to the labor movement and to the principle of collective bargaining. Nationally prominent union leaders were honored by appointment to federal boards and commissions created to further the war effort. A corps of government representatives were constantly alert to head off industrial conflict by bringing employers, both the willing and the reluctant, into negotiations with unions. The National War Labor Board called upon employers to respect their workers' right to organize freely. Organized labor thus achieved more prestige and apparent security than ever before in the United States.

Awareness of labor's enhanced status influenced workers in the Bay Area as elsewhere. Prospective, but timid, union recruits could be lured with assurances—by no means always fulfilled in practice—that federal authorities would prevent employers from firing them for union affiliations. But although governmental policies encouraged the growth of unionism, the Bay Area's pronounced expansion in organizing activity during 1918 was due primarily to the cumulative effect of months of rising prices, growing labor shortage, and contagious examples of success set by unions throughout the local economy. Few of the new organizations established found it necessary to rely directly and heavily upon government intervention for maintenance of their existence during the war.

One group of workers in whose attempted unionization federal authorities did play a prominent role was that of the telephone operators. When America entered the war, the Pacific Telephone and Telegraph Company was operating under a system-wide contract signed by the Pacific District Council of Electrical Workers as bargaining agent for about 3,000 electrical linemen, cable splicers, and other skilled craftsmen. In the fall of 1917, as this agreement approached expiration, the council asked PT&T for a wage increase and a union-shop contract for its male membership, and for recognition and higher wages for new locals of telephone operators now being formed by the IBEW among approximately 9,000 girls. A threat of a coast-wide strike developed when PT&T opposed these demands. In particular the company objected to recognizing the unions of telephone girls, for it regarded them as ephemeral wartime organizations incapable of achieving either stability or maturity. Strikes of operators, supported by sympathy walkouts of linemen, broke out in the Pacific Northwest late in October, 1917, and a coast-wide strike was only narrowly averted by efforts of the Federal Mediation Commission. After publicly warning that it might recommend government seizure of PT&T, the commission entered into negotiations in San Francisco between representatives of the company and the IBEW Pacific District Council. The bargaining sessions ended late in November with an agreement, signed by the two parties and the commission, providing compromise wage increases for both the male craftsmen and the operators, and embodying the company's promise to recognize operators' unions. The union shop, however, was not established for any category of PT&T workers.[138]

The organization of telephone girls in the Bay Area lagged well behind that in the Pacific Northwest. Local IBEW union leaders enthusiastically cited the assurances received from Felix Frankfurter, of the Mediation Commission, that the operators now had "union recognition under the protection of the United States government" and that the government's representatives were busily "educating some of the subordinate officials" of PT&T to honor the recently signed agreement. Nevertheless, the organizing proceeded slowly, amidst constant complaints to federal authorities of discrimination and intimidation by PT&T, and denials by the company of these charges. Not until the early fall of 1918 could two new IBEW operators' locals in San Francisco and the East Bay claim to be building substantial memberships.[139] These organizations were still of questionable strength and solidity, but they represented the first resurgence of unionism among Bay Area telephone girls since the disastrous strike of 1907.

A more firmly rooted young union appeared late in 1917 in San Francisco's warehousing industry. Drawing chiefly upon employees of water-front firms, the Warehouse and Cereal Workers' Union, with a new AFL federal charter, had several hundred members by the winter of 1917–18. By the spring of 1918 it had joined the Waterfront Workers' Federation and had pushed wages for some of its members up to $3.50 per nine-hour day, a moderate level for unskilled workers. Then, in May, 1918, it demonstrated surprising power by bringing out approximately 1,000 men in a strike that tied up the movement of goods from San Francisco docks by shutting down the public warehouses owned by member firms of the Warehousemen's Association. The strike came after lengthy negotiations with the association over the union's demand for the eight-hour day and a $4 daily wage. Within twenty-four hours the walkout was ended, however, through the mediation of Federal Food Administrator Ralph P. Merritt. The warehouse workers won a favorable compromise settlement giving them a minimum wage of $4.50 for a nine-hour day. Their organization continued to grow throughout the year and by early 1919, with a membership of 1,500, claimed to be one of the largest unions in San Francisco.[140]

Other organizing gains were made during 1918 by a variety of both old and new unions. A union of ships' clerks took out a federal charter in the spring and joined the Waterfront Workers' Federation. It quickly organized most of the cargo checkers and the weighers on the docks, and followed the lead of the longshoremen in negotiating the eight-hour day from the Waterfront Employers' Union in 1918. The culinary workers, by 1918, were recovering from their 1916 defeat, with union memberships and wage rates rising among most categories of restaurant employees. A vigorous drive by the Waiters' Union brought in several hundred new and reinstated members, chiefly from leading restaurants and hotels in which it had long proved difficult to maintain effective organization. For the first time in its history, this union gained tacit recognition from the prominent Saint Francis, Palace, and Fairmont hotels, as it negotiated an increase from $2 to $2.50 in the hotel waiters' minimum daily wage. The ILGWU Cloakmakers' Union, disrupted by its 1913 strike and reviving slowly before the war, once again established influence throughout its jurisdiction and won bargaining agreements from the ladies' cloak industry's employer association. The Chauffeurs' Union, after a 1918 organizing drive, reported that only one taxicab firm was still holding out against unionization. A sufficient number of new members joined the formerly obscure Elevator Operators' Union to enable it, in mid-1918, to negotiate an increased wage scale from the Building Managers' and Owners' Association. And a new local of the Commercial Telegraphers' Union, formed in the spring, fought an uphill battle in San Francisco throughout the year as part of the union's nationwide drive to revive organization among the employees of Western Union and Postal Telegraph.[141]

New unions also appeared, or established unions expanded, among such groups of San Francisco workers as soft drink bottlers and drivers, tailors, watchmen, tannery and leather goods workers, women grocery clerks, janitors, and jewelry workers.[142] Although most of these efforts brought only piecemeal membership gains to the local labor movement, they contributed toward making 1918 the year of the most contagious spread of unionization seen in the city since the first years of the century.

New Unions among the Unskilled in the East Bay

By the early months of 1918, the East Bay was experiencing a pronounced upsurge in organizing activity, especially among unskilled workers. The Alameda County Central Labor Council gave the movement strong encouragement and a measure of unified direction. In the spring the council voted to hire a full-time, salaried organizer for six months. Concentrating his efforts chiefly among workers not belonging to recognized crafts, the council's organizer had, by October, helped to form new unions with a total of almost 1,500 members. Both these and older Alameda County unions recruited energetically during the year. The large combined organization of culinary workers grew substantially in strength and reported, late in 1918, that it had won the eight-hour day from almost all unionized restaurants. Organizing attempts were made, though often with disappointing results, among laundry workers and drivers, inside creamery workers, taxicab drivers, garment workers, and yard and shop laborers of the Key System transit company.[143] In addition, with the aid of the council's organizer, a significant effort was made to extend unionism into the ranks of unskilled industrial workers.

In mid-1918 the council announced the formation of the Factory, Mill and Warehouse Employees' Union, and its organizers predicted that it might soon become the largest labor body in Alameda County. Possessing an AFL federal charter, the new organization was a conglomerate industrial union open to most of the noncraft workers in manufacturing and distributive industries. Leaders of the council wanted first to bring these unskilled workers into one big union, and later have them distributed under the jurisdictions of existing crafts. Taking in men and women from groups not always welcome to established AFL unions—Portuguese immigrants, Mexicans, Negroes—the Factory, Mill and Warehouse Employees' Union by late 1918 had gained a foothold in a number of manufacturing industries. Its membership embraced workers in plants producing paint, paper, sulphur, fertilizer, textiles, and canned fruits and vegetables.[144]

The new union met with some hostility from craft organizations, whose leaders claimed that it infringed upon their jurisdictions. And it met hostility from employers. The large Paraffin Paint Company was an exception; though hitherto unorganized, it adopted a conciliatory policy toward both this union and a new local of the International Brotherhood of Papermakers in mid-1918. The company granted wage increases, removed a foreman against whom employees had protested by staging a brief walkout, and won praise from union leaders for its "unusual and gratifying fairness" in its relations with them. But the factory union was in constant friction with the establishments where the large majority of its claimed membership of more than 1,000 was concentrated—the strongly open-shop California Cotton Mills, and a canning plant of the California Packing Corporation. A few leaders of the union were discharged by these firms. Several active unionists at the California Cotton Mills were arrested on suspicion of draft evasion and then questioned about reports that they were subversive members of the IWW. Oakland police and agents of the federal Department of Justice appeared at meetings of the union, ostensibly to watch for any signs of IWW activity. On one occasion they abruptly closed down a large mass meeting held for the cotton mill workers. Officials of the Alameda County Central Labor Council charged that employers instigated these incidents in order to intimidate union organizers and prospective union members.[145]

Though it provided a rallying point for the East Bay's unskilled workers, the Factory, Mill and Warehouse Employees' Union made only nominal economic gains in 1918. It directed brief, spontaneous strikes of cannery workers over alleged failures of the California Packing Corporation to observe the minimum scales prescribed by Federal Food Administrator Merritt. It was unable, however, to bargain effectively for higher wages. Pressure from the union induced John R. Millar, manager of the California Cotton Mills, to meet with William Spooner of the Central Labor Council, and, reluctantly, to submit the mill workers' wage demands to determination by the War Labor Board.[146] But the union failed to establish a bargaining relationship with any firm. Its haphazard organizing efforts penetrated into only a few of the East Bay's manufacturing plants. Yet it represented, for the area's long-neglected industrial workers, the high-water mark of their participation in the local labor movement.

An Industrial Union for the Oil Workers

During 1918 the oil refineries in Contra Costa County were subjected to strong organizing efforts by branches of a new international union of oil field and refinery workers. Formed on an industrial rather than a craft union basis, it sprang up in California and soon began to spread toward the East. It received an AFL charter in mid-1918. Its first California refinery local was established in May, 1918, at the Shell plant in Contra Costa County. Other locals soon appeared at the Union and Standard refineries. By late 1918 these three Contra Costa County organizations claimed a combined membership of approximately 1,200 workers. The union at Standard, largest of the refineries, was destined to have only a brief existence; the company refused to negotiate and allegedly demoralized the union by discharging its leaders. But the locals at Shell and Union were brought amicably under the "Memorandum of Terms" drawn up in 1918 between the international and all major oil companies in California except

Standard.[147] Technically, each party signed the memorandum only with the Federal Mediation Commission, which had fostered negotiations in order to maintain oil production. The memorandum thus provided employers with a face-saving substitute for an acknowledged collective bargaining agreement. But by participating through their international in this quasi contract, the two Contra Costa County refinery locals received virtual union recognition.

Shipbuilding and the Metal Trades

In 1918, as in 1917, the most conspicuous center of union growth and activity in the Bay Area was shipbuilding and the metal trades. The huge expansion in employment in war industries, and the attendant expansion in union membership, greatly enhanced the position of the metal trades organizations in the local labor movement. For example, by mid-1918 the three largest unions in the East Bay were those of boilermakers, shipyard laborers, and machinists, with memberships ranging from 1,500 to almost 5,000.[148] Such union growth was not guaranteed, as it was in World War II, by union-shop contracts compelling thousands of new war workers to become members. But the unions gained recruits readily, especially in the skilled trades, where a nonunion craftsman found it difficult to resist pressure from shop stewards and other coworkers.

Aside from the shipyards, the most vigorous union organizing activity in 1918 was pursued in metal trades plants of the East Bay. Local unions of structural iron workers and of relatively unskilled foundry employees gained strength at such large establishments as Caterpillar Tractor, Dow Pump, and the Judson Manufacturing Company. Through brief strikes and threats of strikes, they pushed wage rates at several recalcitrant firms up to the level fixed for shipyards by the Macy award. A new local of the Brotherhood of Railway Carmen claimed that it had won several hundred members by mid-1918 in the long-unorganized Richmond shops of the Pullman Company. An international organizer for the boilermakers established unions among craftsmen in the Santa Fe and Southern Pacific railroad repair shops, and at the antiunion Western Pipe and Steel Company in Richmond. In July, after a brief strike, boilermakers and machinists employed by Western Pipe and Steel won the Macy wage schedule.[149]

By late 1917 the East Bay's aggressive young Shipyard Laborers' Union had launched an organizing campaign among the unskilled workers of the metal trades, announcing that it proposed to embrace all those "who cannot be taken care of by any other union." Its leaders rejected the race barriers characteristic of AFL organizations. The union enrolled a large number of Negroes, elected a Negro among its officers, and marched in the 1918 Oakland Labor Day Parade with a banner proclaiming its freedom from racial discrimination.[150] Outside the shipyards it unionized scattered groups of laborers in such plants as Judson Manufacturing and Standard Gas Engine, but fell far short of organizing the broad jurisdiction it had ambitiously outlined.

In the San Francisco metal trades, union organizing efforts and union-employer friction were less evident than across the Bay. The San Francisco industry was governed by the master contract between the California Metal Trades Association and the Iron Trades Council, which coöperated with apparent amity during 1918. A high level of organization was maintained with little difficulty among skilled craftsmen. Unionism among the less skilled was also strengthened, but vigorous leadership was not provided for this task. The Shipyard Laborers' Union in San Francisco received little encouragement and did not attain the size, nor display the initiative, of its militant counterpart in the East Bay. An unusual product of the wartime expansion of unionism in the metal trades was the Draftsmen's Union, formed in mid-1918 under an AFL federal charter. Soon claiming more than 200 members in shipbuilding firms, this white-collar organization affiliated with the Iron Trades Council and ambitiously demanded that employers have a union label stamped on all drawings. The union was apparently tolerated by metal trades firms, but attained no significant bargaining power.[151]

As the Bay Area's outstanding war industry and locus of expanded union power, shipbuilding continued in 1918 to draw the hostile scrutiny of those who resented organized labor's wartime influence. Unionized shipyard workers were portrayed as commonly soldiering on the job, despite occasional patriotic exhortations by their leaders. Unions were accused of imposing costly restrictions on productivity through enforcement of their working rules and jealous guarding of jurisdictional borders. Radical leaders in the metal trades were alleged to be exploiting the war boom as an opportunity to conduct their own warfare against employers.[152] These charges were encouraged, in part, by frequent displays of labor unruliness in the shipyards. Although the Pacific Coast shipbuilding industry experienced no serious strikes between the fall of 1917 and Armistice Day, 1918, union-management tension remained high. Labor relations were relatively calm in the San Francisco yards, under the influence of Iron Trades Council officers whose conservatism was in notable contrast to the aggressive militance of metal trades leaders in the Seattle area. But during 1918 shipbuilding in the East Bay was repeatedly overshadowed by threats of work stoppages.

The East Bay Boilermakers

Labor-management difficulties in the East Bay shipyards chiefly revolved around Boilermakers' Local 233, which in 1918 became the largest union in Alameda County. It also soon became the Bay Area's focal point of rebellion against conservative labor leadership. Chartered during the war as an offshoot of the San Francisco boilermakers' local, whose jurisdiction had previously covered both sides of the Bay, this union was led by men inclined toward left-wing political views and reliance upon militant tactics. In the view of one indignant employer, they formed a "scarlet clique" headed by a "deep red radical." They rejected the conciliatory policies of conservative San Francisco metal trades union officers and openly defied their attempts to maintain control over wartime union conduct in the East Bay industry. In 1918, in fact, the boilermakers seemed to resent the officers of the Iron Trades Council as much as they resented the executives of the Bethlehem Shipbuilding Corporation. Bethlehem's Alameda shipyard was repeatedly denounced as hostile to unionism and as the chief offender in paying new workers below the Macy wage scale while charging their labor at the full scale under cost-plus government contracts.[153]

In July this issue came to a head when the Boilermakers' Union struck against Bethlehem and the two other major East Bay shipyards, demanding that the firms sign formal stipulations that they would observe the Macy scale and allow union business agents free access to the yards at all times. This strike—the only shipyard work stoppage of significance during 1918—closed down shipbuilding operations employing an estimated 15,000 men. It ended, however, within two days, as the Iron Trades Council immediately condemned the unauthorized walkout, international officers of the boilermakers ordered a return to work, and federal mediators intervened with assurances of a fair hearing for wage claims. The union's aggressive leaders bowed under the combined weight of these pressures. The strike led to an investigation by Mortimer Fleishhacker, prominent San Francisco businessman serving as local examiner for the Emergency Fleet Corporation, who ruled that a number of members of the Boilermakers' Union were entitled to back pay in accordance with the Macy scale.[154]

Leaders of the East Bay boilermakers continued, through the closing months of the war, to be a source of disturbance to employers, government authorities, and the Iron Trades Council. In August threats of a renewed strike over wage grievances again placed Fleishhacker and other federal representatives in the role of pacifiers. In September the Boilermakers' Union concocted a scheme to force Bethlehem's Alameda shipyard to retain the shorter forty-four-hour workweek to which it had temporarily shifted during the summer months. Despite protests from the Iron Trades Council that the union was dishonoring the wartime shipbuilding agreement, the boilermakers instituted a series of "strikes" commencing at the noon hour on successive Saturdays.[155] The controversy over this campaign was approaching the boiling point when the war ended on November 11, 1918.

Internal Dissension

The defiant behavior of the East Bay Boilermakers' Union in 1918 was a manifestation of the rebelliousness that the turbulence of the war and postwar periods evoked within labor ranks. World War I radically altered the environment of the labor movement and placed uncomfortable pressure upon many entrenched union leaders. Unions were enlarged by an influx of workers with little comprehension of union tradition or discipline. These new members were restless because of rising prices and the excitement of the war, confident of their strength, and ready to respond to aggressive leadership. Older members, too, were quick to resent the real or imagined failure of union officials to adjust to rapidly changing conditions. The atmosphere was ripe for challenges to established labor leadership; and the metal trades, as the principal area of union growth, offered a promising field for insurgent unionists ambitious to throw off control by veteran officials. By the fall of 1918 a number of East Bay metal trades unions, led by the boilermakers and the shipyard laborers, were agitating for independence from the Iron Trades Council, whose headquarters were in San Francisco. Proclaiming that "Oakland is no longer a second-class town . . . ," they demanded formation of a separate East Bay council, free from domination by San Francisco unions and able to pursue its own militant and "progressive" policies. The secessionist movement was accompanied by denunciations of Iron Trades Council officers as apathetic toward the needs of the rank and file, overcompromising toward employers, and hostile to the cause of Mooney and Billings. And, inevitably, they were charged with being "political grafters . . . professional politicians . . . who manage year in and year out to avoid working with their hands at their trades." [156]

In 1918 this antagonism flared up in an editorial battle between the *Labor Clarion*, organ of the San Francisco Labor Council, and the *Tri-City Labor Review*, a privately owned paper designated as the official journal of the Alameda County Central Labor Council. The *Review* championed industrial unionism, Mooney and Billings, greater rank-and-file control of the labor movement, and release of local unions from the tight checkreins held by their internationals. The Oakland paper hammered away steadily at San Francisco union officialdom, with special emphasis upon such "labor politicians" as P. H. McCarthy, Mike Casey, and John P. McLaughlin, and proudly claimed that organized labor in Oakland was relatively free of politically ambitious leaders. James Mullen, in the *Labor Clarion*, attacked the "red terror organ" across the Bay and issued a stream of warnings against "unscrupulous agitators," IWW's, "Bolsheviks," and other assorted "Reds" who were fomenting a revolution against responsible, experienced labor leadership. The East Bay Boilermakers' Union in particular, he avowed, was "honeycombed with Bolsheviks." [157] Although these vituperative attacks and counterattacks exaggerated the extent of factional strife, the feeling between conservative and less conservative elements within the Bay Area labor movement had become very bitter by Armistice Day.

The Mooney Case at the Close of the War

The fate of Tom Mooney was one of the factors aggravating factionalism in the Bay Area labor movement. Mooney's adherents continued to protest that "Fickert politicians" and other influential San Francisco labor leaders were traitorously failing to assist the effort to save Mooney from execution. At the close of the war agitation over the case continued with undiminished intensity. A banner in the victory parade of Oakland shipyard workers on November 11, 1918, proclaimed that "we are celebrating, but we have not forgotten our fellow worker, Tom Mooney." [158] With the execution scheduled for mid-December, tension was running high.

Several months before Armistice Day the Mooney issue had again become relevant to a political contest. In June District Attorney Charles Fickert announced his candidacy for governor. As in his 1917 recall election, Fickert planned to run on a chauvinistic platform capitalizing on the growing wartime hysteria against IWW's and all other radicals. It was rumored that Fickert, expecting Governor William Stephens to grant Mooney executive clemency, would charge the incumbent with yielding to the forces of "anarchy." The governor, on the other hand, would alienate thousands of voters if Mooney were executed during his campaign for reëlection. Stephens side-stepped the Mooney issue in approved political fashion. Late in July he announced postponement of the execution to December 13 in order to give himself time to consider the case fully.[159] The new date conveniently fell after the November election.

In August Stephens defeated Fickert and other challengers in the Republican primary, and in November won a new term as governor. But he remained under severe pressure to reach a decision in regard to Mooney's execution. Mooney's more impassioned supporters were agitating for a nationwide general strike, to begin early in December, 1918, and continue until his release from prison. Although the concept of a general strike was anathema to traditional AFL leaders, it was confidently predicted that more than half a million rank-and-file unionists would join in the walk-out. In the Bay Area surprisingly strong sentiment developed for this proposal to paralyze all economic activity. On November 18 the Alameda County Central Labor Council called on all affiliated unions to poll their members on the question of taking part in the strike. Within a week, a number of unions ranging from the unruly one of shipyard laborers to the normally staid organizations of milkdrivers, bakery drivers, and musicians had voted to participate. The council promptly appointed a committee to direct the strike, which was scheduled to commence on December 9. In San Francisco enthusiasm was less widespread, but by late November a major effort was under way to induce unionists to disregard their conservative leaders and join in the uprising. Agitation was especially vigorous within the Machinists' Union and the culinary and clothing trades unions, whose leaders were particularly sympathetic toward socialism and industrial unionism.[160]

Amid the furor over the approaching execution, Fremont Older delivered another telling blow to Mooney's prosecutors. Earlier in 1918 Older had left the *Bulletin* to become editor of the *Call*, because, he said, the *Bulletin*'s owners had attempted to muzzle him after being threatened by the Law and Order Committee with an advertising boycott unless the paper ceased agitating the Mooney issue.[161] In the *Call*, on November 22, 1918, Older began publication of a confidential report just made to Secretary of Labor William B. Wilson by J. B. Densmore, a federal investigator assigned to conduct a secret probe into the Mooney case. Densmore's report consisted mainly of a verbatim transcript of certain conversations recorded in the fall of 1918 on a dictaphone surreptitiously planted in the district attorney's office. Although the transcript did not prove that Fickert had actually attempted to frame prosecution evidence, it did reveal the callous cynicism with which he and his subordinates played their roles in the trials of the bomb case defendants. In one outstanding passage, Assistant District Attorney Edward Cunha told Fickert: "Chief, if you can get a witness who will put Mrs. Mooney at Steuart and Market Streets, I don't give a damn if you put her there in a balloon." [162] The record showed that Fickert had frequently consulted with Frank C. Drew, attorney for the Chamber of Commerce, and

F. W. Henshaw, former justice of the California State Supreme Court—the two men whom Densmore claimed were "the real brains of the anti-labor forces arrayed against Mooney." [163] Moreover, the recorded conversations provided a devastating self-exposure of Fickert's official conduct and personal morality. Even when expurgated of unprintable material, the published transcript revealed Fickert in all the crudity and petty corruption of his day-to-day dealings with political cronies, bail bond brokers, and "fixers" of minor criminal cases. Densmore's report administered the *coup de grâce* to Fickert's dwindling prospects of a successful political career, and embarrassed his erstwhile supporters both inside and outside the labor movement. Paul Scharrenberg commented in the *Coast Seamen's Journal* some days after the exposé: "It is gratifying to note . . . that to this date no labor 'leader' has publicly come to Mr. Fickert's rescue. . . ." [164]

On November 28, six days after Older's publication of the Densmore report and fifteen days before the scheduled execution date, Governor Stephens commuted Mooney's sentence to life imprisonment.[165] The governor may have been influenced in part by the exposure of Fickert, or by a nagging uneasiness over the possibility that Mooney might be innocent. Stephens cited, however, only the repeated appeals of President Wilson as the basis for his decision to grant executive clemency. Had Woodrow Wilson not been so alarmed over the effects that the creation of an American labor martyr might have upon workers throughout Europe, it is highly improbable that Mooney would have been alive by the close of 1918.

The commutation of sentence relieved immediate tension, but it did not still the clamor of protest over the case. Until well into 1919, in fact, agitation remained near its peak level of late 1918. Mooney reacted to his reprieve with characteristic belligerence and rhetoric: "I prefer a glorious death at the hands of my traducers . . . to a living grave." [166] George Kidwell, Daniel C. Murphy, and other unionists denounced Governor Stephens' action as a flagrant evasion of the fundamental question of Mooney's guilt or innocence. Early in December they failed by only one vote to have the Labor Council pass a resolution directing that all unions be queried upon their willingness to turn out in a general strike to force full pardons for Mooney and Billings.

Alarmed by this flare-up of semirevolutionary spirit, Mike Casey and John P. McLaughlin called a meeting of the Teamsters' Union, which voted not to take part in a general strike.[167] The agitation died down, however, when Mooney publicly requested that the nationwide strike scheduled for December 9 be called off. But the issue of justice for Tom Mooney and Warren Billings did not die down. The Mooney-Billings case had repercussions, for years to come, on the California labor and political scene.

The Question of the Future

The 1900–1918 era in Bay Area industrial relations history had begun amid the excitement of organized labor's upheaval at the turn of the century; it ended with another period of unusual turbulence, the wartime boom of 1916–1918. Both the opening and the closing years of this era were thus characterized by invigorating success for labor, as union growth proceeded rapidly in the context of a general movement toward higher wages and shorter hours. But in each of these periods of dramatic expansion in union membership and in collective bargaining, the question inevitably arose: Would organized labor be able to consolidate the extensive gains it had so quickly won, and retain them when the favorable conditions gave way to less auspicious circumstances? This question had been answered in the affirmative for the vigorous Bay Area unionism that had sprung up in 1899–1903. The postwar years would provide the answer for the newly expanded union movement of 1916–1918.

Chapter IX | *A*

Retrospective

View

WORLD WAR I marked the end of an age in America's history; it marked also, for the Bay Area labor movement, the climax of the era of strength which had begun with the turn-of-the-century boom in economic activity. At the close of the war local union membership was at a new peak, and union power had never seemed so impressive. Labor spokesmen claimed almost 100,000 union members in San Francisco and Alameda County at the end of 1918, with about three-fourths of them in San Francisco. Though probably exaggerated, this estimate can serve as an index of the wartime expansion in organized labor's ranks. It showed an increase of more than 25 per cent and 75 per cent, respectively, in the claimed union membership in San Francisco and in Alameda County since 1915.[1] Since America's entry into the war, the labor movement had flourished in a favorable environment. Unions enjoyed the unaccustomed experience of winning repeated gains in wages and hours at relatively short intervals and against little employer resistance. In more than two years few Bay Area unions had suffered defeat in industrial disputes. And union policy had become increasingly aggressive in pressing demands in the continuing wartime inflation and labor shortage. Now the war was over, and Bay Area industrial relations were entering into a new phase in which many unions were destined to undergo severe ordeals. The coming decade, for the local labor movement, would be markedly different from the war and pre-war years of ascendant, vigorous unionism.

Labor in San Francisco—A Retrospective View

In the period of almost twenty years from the turn of the century to the close of 1918, the union movement centered in San Francisco had more power and influence than labor in any other major American metropolitan area. The Bay Area labor movement, it is clear, was predominantly the movement in San Francisco. Despite the relatively more rapid growth of population and industry in the East Bay between 1900 and 1918, San Francisco overshadowed Oakland and its neighboring cities as a center of economic activity. Business leadership was concentrated in San Francisco, northern California's seat of financial and commercial power and the headquarters city for many firms operating establishments in the East Bay and elsewhere. And, in the labor sphere, San Francisco was the center of major policy decisions, negotiations, and events with repercussions that spread well beyond the boundaries of the city. It was the site of the most significant collective bargaining relationships and the main arena of critical industrial conflicts. It provided the Bay Area's—and California's—outstanding labor leadership. It was a labor stronghold whose existence gave needed encouragement to the less vigorous unionism in peripheral areas. The labor movement in the East Bay would have thrived less well had San Francisco been dominated by open-shop employer forces.

At the end of the war San Francisco retained its long-held reputation as the country's foremost exhibit of a labor barony. Since the first years of the century it had been nationally hailed —and decried—as a "good union town," a "closed-shop city," a community in which organized labor wielded economic and political power over the public and over employers. Though this view was highly exaggerated, the strength of the local labor movement gave the city a unique quality. In an era when organized labor still had only limited significance in American society, San Francisco residents were aware of unions as an important element in community life. A few labor leaders would have been included on any list of San Francisco's best-known and most politically active citizens. News of central labor body meetings, of affairs of individual unions, of factional rivalries, and of union-employer negotiations was given wide publicity by the daily press. Labor never failed to maintain substantial influence within the city administration; its representatives were always to be found among those holding strategic elective and appointive offices. And labor's economic power was widely acknowledged and respected. Major industrial conflicts, directly affecting large segments of the public, did not develop frequently, but San Francisco was always conscious of the capabilities strong unions possessed for waging stubborn and disruptive battles with employers.

The strength of organized labor and the course of industrial relations in San Francisco in the period 1900–1918 resulted from a number of factors: traditions and influences carried over from earlier years; the composition of the local labor force; the structure of the San Francisco economy and the physical isolation of the city; the character of leadership of the labor movement and of the business community; the trend of economic conditions; the political potency of the working-class vote; and certain key events of the period. Though some of these factors were of special importance, none of them was an overriding, predominant force in determining the nature of local labor relations. Each blends into an explanation of the course of developments on the labor scene.

The Turn of the Century—Decisive Developments

At the opening of the 1900–1918 era the strength of the local union movement was reviving; its revival was part of organized labor's general upsurge throughout the country at the turn of the century. This upsurge, however, carried labor to special heights in San Francisco, from which it was not dislodged for the remainder of the period. The city provided a particularly favorable setting for the flourishing new unionism of the early 1900's. Traditionally a high-wage area, its labor force had never become habituated to docile acceptance of a meager standard of living or to unquestioning submission to arbitrary employers. Its workers did not have to compete with an unremitting influx of immigrants from southern and eastern Europe. "Cheap labor" was Chinese, not white, labor. Since the 1850's the San Francisco worker had enjoyed a more favored economic and social position than his counterpart in the East, and he was more accustomed to confident assertion of his demands. The union movement had appeared early in San Francisco, and by 1900 had already experienced several periods of exceptional vigor. Though the movement was relatively small and weak at the outset of the boom of the late 1890's, it was nevertheless well rooted. Unionism possessed a tradition and a solid base from which to spread, and confronted a local labor force with a high degree of receptivity to proposals for strong, organized action by workers. The ground was thus well prepared for the dramatic union growth touched off by returning prosperity toward the end of the century.

Favorable as conditions were for the resurgence of unionism, they could not in themselves assure that organized labor in San Francisco would achieve success. The movement was subjected to critical tests early in the period of revival, and its emergence with unimpaired strength from these tests was a major determinant of its subsequent development. The key episodes were the millmen's lockout and the teamsters' and water-front strike. In 1900 the Building Trades Council, already under P. H. McCarthy's leadership but still in the process of consolidating its power, faced a resolute challenge from the Planing Mill Owners' Association. Had the association been able to rally employers throughout the industry behind a stand for the open shop, and had council leaders been less resourceful in conducting this lengthy contest, the outcome might well have been a sharp setback for labor. Building trades employers had a clear and timely opportunity to form an industry-wide united front and so halt the continuing advance of unionism. But their failure to respond revealed their apathy and lack of organization, and gave evidence both to unionists and to disappointed open-shop advocates that they would not be likely to rally against the Building Trades Council later on, when the council had entrenched itself as the center of power in the industry.

The 1901 teamsters' and water-front conflict presented a much more serious challenge to San Francisco labor. The leaders of the Employers' Association correctly sensed the urgent need for an open-shop counteroffensive to shackle expanding unionism while it was still vulnerable. Their assault focused on the young organization of teamsters, the point of greatest strategic significance to the labor movement. Victory for the employers would have destroyed unionism among one of the largest bodies of San Francisco workers, who possessed a unique potential for disrupting the economic life of the city. It would have seriously impeded organizing efforts among specialty teamsters and workers in service and other industries who needed the support of the Teamsters' Union. Furthermore, an open-shop victory might have inspired the business communuity to support a coördinated attack against union influence in all local industry.

Leaders of the Labor Council and the City Front Federation immediately realized the crucial nature of the battle. Elimination of the Teamsters' Union would smooth the road for a campaign to drive unionism from the water-front and maritime transport industry. Local labor's hope to extend unionism beyond the ranks of highly skilled craftsmen would be dealt a heavy blow by destruction of the Teamsters' Union, the largest and strongest of the new unions of comparatively unskilled workers. Thus the conflict in the teaming industry became a mortal struggle between the Employers' Association and San Francisco labor, a dramatic battle to decide whether unionism or the open shop would prevail.

The 1901 strike, in character and purpose if not in scope, was virtually a general strike. In its essential aspects it was fully comparable to the San Francisco water-front and general strike of 1934. Like the latter, it ended in an apparent standoff which was, in actuality, a momentous victory for labor. But it was a victory gained by the narrowest of margins. Union leaders had forged a solid alliance of teamsters, longshoremen, and seamen, a rare achievement on the San Francisco water front. Nevertheless, as the strike continued, the scales appeared to be shifting toward the Employers' Association. The open-shop forces would very likely have won had Governor Henry Gage been willing to send in state militia to protect the movement of goods by strikebreakers. It was labor's good fortune that Governor Gage chose instead to exert pressure on the employers to call off their no-quarter battle against unionism. In the face of Gage's unsympathetic attitude, the stubborn resistance of the strikers, and the resentment of many businessmen at this costly industrial war, the leaders of the Employers' Association lost the determination and the disciplined control over their followers needed to achieve a decisive triumph for the open shop.

The 1901 struggle stands out as the most significant episode in San Francisco labor relations in the period 1900–1918. It is doubtful that the local union movement could have recovered from a crushing defeat, for in San Francisco, as in the nation, the turn-of-the-century upsurge in union strength had lost most of its momentum by late 1903. An open-shop victory by the Employers' Association in the fall of 1901 would have been a critical setback for labor at a time when it was of the utmost importance to take full advantage of a period so propitious for union expansion. As it was, the 1901 strike ended favorably for labor, and San Francisco unionism continued to push forward vigorously. By 1904, when the Citizens' Alliance next confronted labor with an open-shop challenge, it was well entrenched in the position it held with little change until the boom period of World War I.

Reverberations of the 1901 teamsters' and water-front strike were felt long afterward. The Union Labor Party, which captured the city administration in 1901 and held it for the next six years, was essentially a by-product of this battle. Controlled though it was by opportunists who had capitalized on the emotions stirred up among workers by the events of 1901, the ULP was nevertheless of significant value to labor. The presence of Eugene Schmitz in the mayor's office was an impressive and visible symbol of labor's political strength. San Francisco wage earners were attracted to a labor movement powerful enough to beat off a massive employer attack and then sweep its candidates into control of key municipal offices. Advocates of the open shop were disheartened at the prospect of undertaking new campaigns in the face of a hostile city administration. Unions gained additional confidence and freedom of action from the knowledge that the police force would not be utilized as a weapon against them in industrial conflicts, and employers feared that police "neutrality" would remove effective curbs upon strike violence.

Aside from the political power that the 1901 struggle had helped labor to win, the experience of the struggle itself deterred employers from rekindling such a conflict. The weeks of economic disruption and physical violence had demonstrated how unpleasant the alternative to labor peace could become. The prevailing conservatism of San Francisco labor leadership was reinforced by a strong desire to confine strikes more closely and prevent another general engagement. Likewise, recollections of the battle of 1901 dampened employer sentiment in later years for renewed efforts to launch a broad attack against unionism. Leaders of the Draymen's Association, in particular, were determined not to undergo again the costs of a head-on clash with the Teamsters' Union. After 1901 collective bargaining was thoroughly accepted in the local drayage industry, and this vital area of union strength was not touched by later open-shop movements in San Francisco.

Unionism and the Structure of San Francisco Industry

The aftermath of the 1901 conflict found collective bargaining relationships beginning, or settling down, in many industries. The economic structure of San Francisco was favorable to the widespread acceptance of collective bargaining in the early 1900's. Most of its industries sold their products in local or regional markets. The city was not dominated by major manufacturing interests which marketed goods competitively on a nationwide scale. It was primarily a financial, shipping, and distribution center. It processed and exported the products of its rich agricultural hinterland, and imported goods to be redistributed throughout northern California. It was also, in the first decade of the century, an especially busy site of construction activity called forth by the city's rapid rate of growth. Such an economic structure fitted well the structure of AFL unionism. Union strength was not concentrated in mass-production or large-scale manufacturing industries, but was found chiefly in industries characterized by small firms, competing in geographically limited markets, with labor costs constituting a high percentage of total costs. In large part San Francisco achieved early prominence as a stronghold of organized labor because so much of its economic activity was accounted for by industries adaptable to the unionism of the time.

In several industries of outstanding importance in San Francisco —printing, building construction, shipping—relatively strong unions had developed before 1900. These unions were well entrenched by the end of the period of expansion in 1903. The teaming industry, of special significance owing to the city's isolated peninsular location and comparative lack of railroad facilities, was unionized in 1900–1901. Unionism spread likewise through the specialty teaming trades employed in the distribution of milk, bakery, and other products. With the exception of shipping, these industries were confined to local or regional markets. Because of their high proportion of labor costs, employers realized that unionization could help to stabilize costs and curb cutthroat competition.

In the early 1900's the San Francisco labor movement successfully embraced other local product market industries, including laundry service, baking, the restaurant trade, meat retailing, carriage and hack rentals, and theatrical entertainment. In these industries, too, many employers accepted, and even welcomed, the union as an aid in preventing unprofitable competition. The fact, moreover, that these industries were composed of small firms, with scanty individual resources for combating union action, furthered the expansion of unionism among them.

The growth of labor organizations was more limited, however, in the public utility industries. Here unions confronted large, well-financed firms with substantial resistance power. These firms were not subject to competitive forces pushing them toward either acceptance or rejection of unionization, although they were under pressure to keep labor costs down, owing to the lack of flexibility in the rates they were allowed to charge. Company policy appears to have been the essential determinant of the relationships of the public service corporations with labor organizations. Unions gained and held a relatively secure position during 1900–1918 in the power and light industry; the locally owned Pacific Gas and Electric Company was willing, within limits, to accept collective bargaining. The nationwide open-shop policy of the American Telephone and Telegraph Company, however, was reflected by its subsidiary, Pacific Telephone and Telegraph. Though electrical workers' unions at times induced PT&T to negotiate with them, it was not until the war period that collective bargaining, on a major scale, was forced upon the West Coast telephone industry. Another local subsidiary controlled by Eastern corporate interests, the United Railroads, first resisted, then accepted, and at last threw off permanently its bargaining relationship with the streetcar men. The history of its dealings with its workers in the 1900–1918 period gave evidence that the United Railroads possessed the power to implement its decisions in regard to labor matters. Thus, although the absence of competition gave unions an advantage in attempting to win recognition from public service corporations, the formidable strength of the companies kept their industry, on the whole, from becoming one of the areas of major union influence in San Francisco.

In San Francisco industries that faced competition from other centers of trade and manufacturing, organized labor had appreciable, though mixed, success. Employers in such industries, who had strong incentives to keep labor costs at a competitive level, could easily look upon an aggressive union as a threat to their continued existence. For the most part, however, the need to survive did not impel them to strong resistance to unionization. San Francisco, after all, had been a high-wage community from the beginning, and few of its manufacturing industries attempted to sell their products competitively in the national market. Eastern producers enjoyed the advantages not only of lower wages, but also of easier access to raw materials, closer location to large bodies of customers, and cheaper freight rates. Bay Area manufacturing was adapted in large degree to products that could be sold with modest success in a Western regional market, even if produced by comparatively high-wage labor. The mountain barrier and the distance from Eastern industrial centers gave local manufacturers a measure of protection in distributing their goods to this market. Thus in a number of industries employers could accommodate themselves to unionization without seriously compromising their competitive positions. The thoroughly unionized brewing industry, for example, marketed its beer only in the West. Manufacturers of work clothing, deriving advantage from the union label and enjoying a comfortable relationship with an unaggressive union, retained their share of the Western market. Even in the metal trades, where employers were continually protesting that unionism menaced them with destruction, most firms conformed to a pattern of products and services not gravely threatened by Eastern competition. They engaged primarily in ship repairing, shipbuilding, and the manufacture of mining and agricultural machinery, marine equipment, engines, tin cans, stoves, and the job-lot orders of small foundries and patternmaking shops. In these branches of the industry Bay Area firms found a continuing, if limited, regional market for their goods.

To summarize, the over-all character of the local economy was an important factor in the comparative lack of violent antiunion sentiment. Relatively few firms were in the unenviable position of the California Cotton Mills in East Oakland, for example, which bid for its labor supply in a high-wage area but competed in the extremely low-wage textile industry. Certain industries, of course, were under severe competitive pressure. Illustrative of these were the shoe and ladies' garment manufacturing industries, struggling to hold small portions of their markets against the domination of major production centers in the East. Unionism failed to sink strong and healthy roots in these hard-pressed industries, although the failure was probably due as much to poor leadership and internal dissension as it was to employer opposition to unions as a source of increased labor costs.

Difficulty in Arousing Antiunion Fervor

In an economic environment allowing considerable latitude for employer adjustments to the impact of unionism, it was difficult after 1901 to build open-shop spirit up to the level demanded for a serious challenge to the vigorous San Francisco labor movement. There was, certainly, a significant undercurrent of antiunion feeling in the business community, and prominent business leaders strove at various times throughout the period to transform that feeling into overt action against labor. As they were preoccupied, not very realistically, with making San Francisco a major manufacturing center, they accused labor of frightening new industry away from the city. But resentment toward unionism was not strong enough to enable open-shop forces to carry out their programs of "freeing" San Francisco from labor domination.

A number of factors weighted the scales against the development of antiunion militance in the business community. Aside from the character of the local economy and the painful experience of the 1901 strike, a traditional San Francisco atmosphere of tolerance and liberality affected the policies of employers. The existence of such an organization as the Commonwealth Club gave testimony to this liberal spirit. Under the influence of Harris Weinstock and other civic leaders, this institution enabled union officials to mingle and to be accepted on equal terms with prominent business and professional men. The environment of this cosmopolitan seaport city was not conducive to the flourishing of moralistic or repressive attitudes, or to the tendency to perceive issues in simple terms of black and white. From the early years to the present, in fact, the course of local labor relations indicates that San Francisco employers were not disposed to take rigid or dogmatic positions toward trade unionism. Though most of them might well have preferred not to negotiate with unions, they adjusted fairly rapidly, and without severe emotional stress, to collective bargaining. Their sophistication concerning labor matters enabled them to accept philosophically a policy of expedience in dealing with strong labor organizations.

Little success was ever achieved in arousing the enthusiasm of San Francisco employers for the type of antiunionism exemplified by the *Los Angeles Times* and the Los Angeles Merchants' and Manufacturers' Association. To shame San Franciscans into a campaign against union labor, open-shop advocates repeatedly cited the faster rate of expansion of Los Angeles. But, although San Francisco employers may have envied the growth of the southern city, they did not have great respect for Los Angeles and were hardly inclined to take lessons from that city in regard to labor policy or anything else. Over the years, relations between unions and employers in San Francisco showed little evidence of having been significantly influenced by the existence, 400 miles to the south, of the nation's outstanding center of the open shop.

The San Francisco business community, moreover, was comparatively insulated from the influence of antiunion organizations in the East. Local metal trades firms were not affiliated with the National Metal Trades Association, one of the stanchest opponents of organized labor after 1900. San Francisco industry was also largely outside the orbit of the National Association of Manufacturers. The NAM did have as members a number of the city's prominent employers, several of whom were in the forefront of local open-shop movements. But San Francisco was viewed by the NAM leadership as esentially missionary territory, too many of whose inhabitants obstinately refused to receive the true gospel of the open shop.* The only encouraging reports to reach the

* For years the attitudes and policies of the city's employers were of recurrent concern to the NAM. This continued even into the 1930's and the 1940's, when leading San Francisco employers flaunted NAM doctrines by accepting the constitutionality of the Wagner Act and, later, advocating industry-wide collective bargaining.

NAM from San Francisco in the 1900–1918 period came during 1916–1917, when Frederick J. Koster was leading the Law and Order Committee in a drive against union power. The NAM rejoiced at the news of this redemption of a long-lost prodigal, but the claims of large-scale victory for the open shop proved to be premature.

The geographical isolation of the San Francisco Bay Area also contributed to the difficulty of undertaking effective battles for the open shop. Despite the development of the transcontinental railway network in the late nineteenth century, a large supply of nonunion labor was not readily available. Struck firms often had to go as far as Chicago, St. Louis, New Orleans, or points even further east to recruit substantial numbers of strikebreakers. Costs of recruitment, transportation, housing, and protection of workers after arrival could easily mount to a prohibitive level for all but a few large, well-financed companies. In this period employers lacked a central body, with ample resources at its command, which could recruit strikebreakers as needed for any industrial conflict.

The distance from other major population centers also permitted San Francisco to develop a unique labor relations atmosphere. As the leading city of the Pacific Coast and of the entire region west of St. Louis, San Francisco was beyond the influence of larger metropolitan areas. The local labor movement grew up in comparative isolation, and throughout the 1900–1918 period remained largely free from close direction or supervision by national union officers whose headquarters were in the East. It possessed proud native traditions and an *esprit de corps* that was almost certainly heightened by the lack of proximity to areas under the domination of the open shop. Whatever demoralizing blows were administered to labor in distant parts of the country, the union movement in San Francisco was accustomed to success, with its confidence as yet unshaken. Local employers, likewise, were not in close contact with developments in other cities where business interests were achieving greater success in restraining unionism. Indeed, employers could question whether the experiences of firms in combating organized labor in less strongly unionized communities were really relevant to the San Francisco situation. To a notable degree the relationships between local unions and employers were thus free to unfold in their own way, in relative detachment from the norms prevailing elsewhere. San Francisco, one of the most distinctive and unconventional of American cities, was distinctive also in the area of industrial relations.

Leadership among Employers and Unions

In addition to the environmental factors that handicapped efforts to arouse San Francisco employers to action, organizational and leadership deficiencies prevented full use of potential resources for the support of open-shop movements. Not until late in the 1900–1918 period did there emerge the type of leadership requisite for creating an effective antiunion front.

The Employers' Association of 1901 was an *ad hoc* organization, hastily put together in belated response to the threat of rising unionism. It was not well staffed, nor widely representative of employers. During its brief existence it was unable to win the general loyalties of San Francisco businessmen. By contrast, ample time existed for building up the Citizens' Alliance and preparing its antiunion campaigns. But the alliance was not wise in choosing its executive leadership. Instead of entrusting its affairs to a local businessman with broad personal contacts and the respect of the community, it imported Herbert George, a professional promoter. George's heavy-handed tactics, blustering public utterances, and unimpressive accomplishments lost for the alliance much of the influence it might otherwise have had among San Francisco employers. The alliance achieved no better results under George's successors.

Meanwhile, until 1916, none of the well-established businessmen's organizations took up the task of mobilizing employers. For years the Merchants' Association and the Chamber of Commerce officially held aloof from labor matters. In 1916, when it at last decided to challenge organized labor, the Chamber of Commerce demonstrated that it could be a formidable antagonist, able to tap extensive financial resources and to provide leaders of wide prestige. Though the antiunion campaign of the chamber's Law and Order Committee was largely frustrated by the economic boom of the war period, it was an ominous development for the local union movement. It foreshadowed the role played by the chamber in the early postwar years, when organized San Francisco employers finally struck telling blows at labor power.

On the union as well as the employer side, the caliber of leadership constituted an important influence upon the course of labor relations in the 1900–1918 period. The leadership factor was especially critical for the success of the union movement. In the hands of inept, reckless, or overaggressive leaders, labor would have failed to gain and hold the position made possible by the favorable San Francisco environment. On the whole, however, the labor movement remained under the control of men who fitted into the mold of the conservative AFL business unionist. They were content to make progress slowly through bargaining and compromise, and did not overplay labor's hand in pressing demands upon employers. They could, on occasion, effectively utilize the techniques of mass meetings, demonstrations, and parades in order to fire the enthusiasm of the rank and file, but normally they eschewed the outward trappings of militance. Their penchant was for quiet, personal negotiations to iron out new contract terms and other disputed issues. And they were adept, at critical moments, at working with city officials and key business and civic leaders to avert serious industrial conflicts or keep them under control.

The Building Trades Council and the Labor Council gave the labor movement a type of leadership relatively palatable to the business community. P. H. McCarthy maintained a tight control over the building trades unions, restraining the more aggressive ones from making frequent or costly demands upon employers. Despite the widely publicized portrait of him as a despotic "labor czar," exacting whatever terms he desired from helpless employers, McCarthy was careful to follow a policy with which the building trades firms could live in reasonable comfort. He sought to maintain the economic health of the industry and to suppress strikes and jurisdictional squabbles, and was conciliatory—even compromising—on the few occasions when he was confronted by an aroused group of employers.

Leaders of the Labor Council also exerted a moderating influence upon overmilitant unions, and were ready to intervene as mediators in situations which threatened open conflict. Probably to a greater extent than central labor bodies in other cities, the council was an active force in setting the tone of local labor relations. Such officers as Andrew J. Gallagher and John O'Connell, and such unofficial powers within the council as Mike Casey, were widely acquainted with and respected by San Francisco businessmen. Their support of the Republican Party gave leading labor officials a reputation for soundness and enlarged their circle of friends among employers. They were strongly dedicated to the goal of labor peace, quick to urge compromise settlements upon parties in dispute, and bitterly opposed to class warfare.*

The conservatism of San Francisco union officialdom may not always have served the local labor movement well. In certain important strikes the outcome might have been better for labor if all unionists had been urged to support the strike, and if the teamsters or other strategic groups had been called upon to assist the striking organization. The lack of reformist or idealistic goals on the part of most prominent labor officials may have encouraged their pursuit of personal political ambitions to the neglect of their obligations as union leaders; and it certainly led others to a narrow concentration upon the interests of their own organizations, with limited concern about the fortunes of the local labor movement as a whole. Weaknesses of leadership and shortsighted failures to link unions tightly together for mutual defense were revealed in the postwar years of crisis and repeated defeat for labor.

But, on net balance, the San Francisco labor movement probably had more effective direction in the 1900–1918 period than it would have had under the radical and dissident unionists who criticized the "labor politicians" and "reactionaries." The fiasco of Tom Mooney's 1916 strike against the United Railroads was an

---

* Mike Casey had a particularly strong personal influence in the sphere of labor relations. As the head of the city's most powerful individual union, a prominent Republican, and a resourceful mediator with a firm belief in the wastefulness of strikes, Casey contributed significantly to smoothing relations between San Francisco unions and employers. By restraining teamster organizations from sympathy strikes after 1901, he was a key figure in blocking the spread of labor conflicts. The high regard in which he was held by leaders of the Draymen's Association, moreover, helped to keep this strategic body of employers from being drawn again into a general battle for the open shop. And the defection of the Draymen's Association was a serious impediment to any employer movement aimed at overthrowing the power of union labor.

example of the results achieved by rash, inadequately prepared action. Few of the Socialists, doctrinaire industrial unionists, and other opponents of conservative labor leadership were, of course, as immature as Mooney. Nevertheless, they would have been much more likely than conventional business unionists to dissipate labor's strength in ill-advised strikes, arouse employers to anti-union militance, and antagonize the general public. Although the men influential in the San Francisco labor movement may have fallen short of an idealist's conception of a dedicated, selfless union leader, they were skillful, judicious, and honest representatives of the city's wage earners. The Union Labor Party provided a few spectacular examples of criminal financial dealings on the part of labor leaders in political office. But, in the sphere of collective bargaining, San Francisco employers dealt with a union movement largely free of racketeering and corruption, and led by responsible officials whom businessmen could understand and respect. Under these circumstances employers had no powerful stimulus to react violently against organized labor.

A Favorable Economic Environment

On the whole, economic conditions during the years after 1901 were also conducive to peaceful retention of the position gained by labor in its turn-of-the-century revival. The local economy's rapid growth in the early years of the 1900–1910 decade permitted unionism to entrench itself firmly, in a time of continuing heavy demand for labor. After the boom tapered off, by 1904, organized labor in San Francisco possessed comparative stability which, except for the unsettled period of 1906–1907, lasted until 1916. During these twelve years the local labor movement did not expand greatly in size or influence. The economy was growing more slowly, with the only interlude of feverish activity occurring during the rebuilding of San Francisco after the 1906 earthquake. Sustained boom conditions, stimulating a new surge of union growth, did not reëmerge until well into the period of World War I, but there was no severe downturn in the economy. Business activity and employment fell off markedly in the comparatively brief depressions of 1907–1908 and 1913–1914, but unions weathered both of these economic squalls without severe damage. From 1897 through the close of World War I the local labor movement experienced its longest period of freedom from serious depression since the decade of the 1860's. It thus did not come under heavy economic pressure to give up the ground it had won; indeed, the economic climate facilitated the stabilization of collective bargaining relationships.

In years of stable prices and of moderate looseness in the labor market, local unions were content to maintain the *status quo.* There is little indication that union leaders strove constantly to exploit to the utmost organized labor's vaunted position of strength in San Francisco. The Building Trades Council, as noted previously, imposed a policy of moderation upon its affiliates. Mike Casey's powerful Teamsters' Union furnished a conspicuous example of restraint in seeking gains for its membership. Despite employer resentment, labor organizations in shipping and the metal trades presented but few demands, spaced at wide intervals, during the years between 1901 and the business boom of World War I. After the turbulent period of 1906–1907 many unions waited almost a decade before they once again pressed for significant improvements in wages or hours, amid the acute inflation of 1916–1917. On the whole, through most of the first two decades of the twentieth century, San Francisco unions moved at a leisurely pace toward the goal of a better standard of life for their members.

Political and Other Influences

Other features of the San Francisco environment also helped explain the strength of the labor movement and the course of union-employer relations over the years 1900–1918. Unionism received valuable support from some of the San Francisco daily newspapers. William R. Hearst's *Examiner,* in the early years of the period, championed the workingman; Edward W. Scripps's *Daily News* was consistently and strongly sympathetic to labor. Throughout the period the labor movement possessed one or more journalistic allies to give wide and favorable publicity to union activities.

At all times after 1901 organized labor in San Francisco enjoyed a potent, if varying, degree of political influence. The election of 1911 marked the end of the Union Labor Party's direct control of the city administration, but the succeeding regime of Mayor James Rolph was friendly to labor. Union officials or their close associates continued to receive appointments to key municipal boards and commissions and to win election to the Board of Supervisors. District Attorney Charles Fickert, despite his co-operation with the Law and Order Committee in exploiting the Preparedness Day bombing, did not otherwise lend his office to antiunion activity. Open-shop forces did not attain the political dominance that would have enabled them to use the police as a weapon against unions. San Francisco police court and Superior Court judges, conscious of the labor vote, tended to be cautious in their handling of cases arising from industrial disputes. Severe penalties were seldom imposed on unionists guilty of strike violence, and employers found the courts far less prone than those of many other cities to grant injunctions against picketing, boycotting, and other union activities. In short, no important sector of local governmental authority represented a hostile counterforce to the labor movement.

Finally, a number of more or less accidental episodes and factors of personality left their marks upon the labor relations scene. The fact that Henry T. Gage, rather than an opponent of unionism, was the governor of California in 1901 was fortunate for the young union movement. The presence of Harris Weinstock, a highly respected and unusually objective mediator, contributed greatly to the maintenance of labor peace in the metal trades industry in 1910 and the years immediately following. The San Francisco earthquake in 1906 abruptly ended the significant activities of the Citizens' Alliance. It also permanently disrupted unionism among some groups of manufacturing workers and set the stage for several of the more important industrial conflicts of the 1900–1918 period. The decision by Congress to award San Francisco the Panama-Pacific Exposition of 1915 helped bring about a moratorium on open-shop campaigns during the years of preparation for this world fair; both business leaders and union officials, imbued with civic spirit, held overt labor conflict to a minimum. In 1916 the Preparedness Day bombing occurred at a most propitious moment for the new open-shop movement that had just emerged under the aegis of the Chamber of Commerce. The bombing gave the chamber a made-to-order propaganda weapon for its drive to reduce union power, and it set under way the Mooney-Billings *cause célèbre* which exerted influence upon the labor movement for more than twenty years to come. Thus arbitrary and chance events, determined neither by environmental conditions nor by the logic of past developments, played a significant role in affecting the course of local industrial relations.

Organized Labor in the East Bay

The union movement in the East Bay had considerably less stature than its counterpart across the Bay. San Francisco's location at the tip of a peninsula, separated from the East Bay by an unbridged expanse of water, impeded the flow of union spirit from the one area to the other. Little real progress was made toward bringing about close, continuous liaison and coöperation between labor organizations on the two sides of the Bay. East Bay unionism was definitely encouraged by the presence of a powerful body of unions in San Francisco, but it did not derive direct financial or other support, on a major scale, from that city. The labor movement in the East Bay was largely left to develop on its own, in a setting appreciably less favorable than that provided by San Francisco.

In the northern section of the East Bay, in Contra Costa County, such communities as Richmond, Martinez, and Crockett were small and not far removed from the status of company towns. The scattered groups of unionized workers in these towns did not attain enough numerical strength, nor become linked together sufficiently through central labor bodies, to constitute a local union movement of substantial influence.

In Alameda County, the three principal East Bay cities of Oakland, Berkeley, and Alameda constituted one continuous metropolitan area. Industry expanded considerably over the 1900–1918 period, giving the area less of a quiet, residential flavor than it had earlier possessed. But the Alameda County communities were not so transformed as to create for unionism a social and political environment comparable to that in San Francisco. It remained more difficult to organize workers effectively for either union or political action. Their homes, and the establishments in which they were employed, were more widely dispersed over a larger geographical area. There was lacking the compactness of San Francisco, with its high concentration of apartment dwellers which made for easier, closer contact among large groups of workers. The East Bay cities did not develop districts like San Francisco's heavily populated working-class neighborhood south of Market Street. Workers were less easily mobilized for meetings or demonstrations, and the contagion of union spirit did not so readily spread among them. Fewer East Bay workers, comparatively, could feel a sense of being caught up in a powerful movement embracing most of their friends and neighbors, and leading them to join unions as a matter of course.

Moreover, organized labor in the East Bay lacked the prestige derived by the San Francisco movement from the success of the Union Labor Party. The labor vote in San Francisco was more effective because many of the city's business executives and white-collar employees were commuters, whereas labor's political potential across the Bay was reduced because a large proportion of these commuters resided in the East Bay area. Oakland offered a more promising field for union political activity than did the more residential Alameda County cities; but here also labor never attained the political influence that might have contributed significantly to the strength of the union movement.

It is probable that unionism would have become a more important force in the East Bay had the area been better developed at the beginning of the century. San Francisco was already a major city by the late 1890's, with thousands of workers at hand to respond to organizational drives when business prosperity returned. In the East Bay, however, population and industry were much smaller. Oakland, Berkeley, and Alameda together had less than one-third the population of San Francisco. They were even less important in terms of economic activity. Thus, when the nation-wide surge of union organization tapered off in 1903 or 1904, it left in the East Bay a labor movement of rather modest dimensions. During the next dozen years, up to the boom period of World War I, the East Bay enjoyed a higher rate of economic growth than San Francisco. But organized labor in the East Bay did not keep pace with this expansion. The years 1904–1915 were, on the whole, a time of limited progress for unionism, both nationally and in the Bay Area. Although the East Bay economy was expanding, the favorable conditions prevailing at the turn of the century did not recur.

During these years a vigorous campaign by San Francisco labor might have stimulated the spread of unionism in the East Bay.

Outside assistance was certainly needed, since the East Bay labor movement demonstrated little capacity for mustering resources of its own for organizing drives. Although there were limits to the aid that San Francisco unionists could provide, the impressive sum raised for the 1910–1911 campaign in Los Angeles indicated their ability to support union movements elsewhere. Had San Francisco labor spent a comparable sum on organizing activity in the East Bay, the results might have been considerably more satisfactory than they were in Los Angeles.

But the structure of AFL unionism was not conducive to campaigns to unionize workers generally throughout an area. No city or regional central body was made responsible for the dissemination of unionism among organizable groups within the local labor force. Recruiting activity was primarily a function of national unions, operating within their own occupational boundaries. San Francisco labor leaders accordingly felt no mandate to organize the unorganized on a region-wide scale. Furthermore, the new jobs being provided by the growing East Bay economy were, to a greater extent than in San Francisco, relatively unskilled production jobs in manufacturing industries. A larger proportion of wage earners were thus factory employees outside the claimed jurisdictions of the national unions. Organization of these workers into federal locals was, for the most part, left to the AFL itself, and the federation never displayed the willingness or the capacity to undertake the job in the East Bay.

The advent of the war boom in 1916–1917 enlivened the East Bay labor scene. With the shipbuilding industry expanding and aggressive new unions developing, the local labor movement increased greatly in size. The spirit of organization was caught by many groups of workers beyond the normal scope of craft unionism. Organized labor in the East Bay, during the war years, thus narrowed the commanding lead held by the San Francisco movement. San Francisco remained the more important area in labor relations, but the coming of the war resulted in numerically large union movements on not only one but both sides of the Bay.

The Balance of Power in 1900–1918

Although organized labor was unusually strong in San Francisco and had significant pockets of strength in the East Bay, the period 1900–1918 was not characterized by union dominance over local employers. It has always pleased business spokesmen to cast employers in the appealing role of underdogs, helpless to protect themselves or the public from the exactions of "big labor." In San Francisco, particularly, many firms, and sometimes entire industries, were portrayed as subject to the near-dictatorial authority of unions. Nevertheless, in the years after 1900 there was a large reservoir of employer strength. Outside the San Francisco building trades, very few unions were confident of their ability to impose terms unilaterally upon employers. Even in the building trades, P. H. McCarthy frowned upon aggressive demands that might have provoked employers into revolt.

The fact that most Bay Area labor leaders moved slowly and cautiously toward their objectives indicated their respect for their opponents' powers of resistance and retaliation. Unions did not often enter lightly into open tests of strength, or resort immediately to strikes when firms balked at their demands. Moreover, the results of strikes did not support the view that local unions possessed overwhelming might. Notwithstanding the vigor of Bay Area unionism, most major conflicts ended either in decisive employer victories or in compromise settlements. Large firms proved particularly formidable. The Southern Pacific Railroad, PG&E, Sunset Lumber, C and H Sugar, and Western Union administered unequivocal defeats to Bay Area unions venturing to challenge them by strikes. And the United Railroads, both in 1907 and 1917, gave impressive demonstrations of an employer's power to crush hard-fought strikes that had gained widespread labor support.

This period in Bay Area labor history reveals the importance, to both unions and employers, of the establishment and maintenance of united fronts. The balance of power was determined in large part by the strength of the alliances on opposite sides of the bargaining table or picket line. The combination of widespread union organization and small-scale industry led to a notable development of employers' associations, particularly in San Francisco. The small- to moderate-sized business firms of the city were well aware of their need to close ranks in dealing with strong unions. Probably in no other major American community in this period was bargaining so extensively "collective" on the employer side. The building industry, of course, was a conspicuous example of an imbalance of strength resulting from employer failure to organize effectively. More representative of stable collective bargaining in San Francisco were the relationships between unions and the California Metal Trades Association, the Milk Dealers' Association, the Waterfront Employers' Union, and the Draymen's Association.

The importance of solidarity was emphatically demonstrated in a number of key labor disputes. Both sides were given repeated opportunities to witness the demoralizing effects of disunity. In such strikes as those of the millmen in 1900, the culinary workers in 1903, the printing tradesmen in 1905, and the structural iron workers in 1916, the failure of employers to maintain a solid front resulted in favorable outcomes for the striking unions. In the crucial struggle of 1901, only the alliance forged by the members of the City Front Federation enabled San Francisco labor to halt the open-shop drive of the Employers' Association. Other strikes of the period—those, for example, of the stablemen in 1904, the telephone workers in 1907, the pressmen in 1913, and the short-lived Light and Power Council in 1913—revealed the damage that could be done to a union cause by intralabor factional quarrels and the absence of support from fellow unions of workers employed in the same industry. The outcome of an industrial conflict thus did not always depend on economic conditions, the attitudes of governmental authorities, or the size, financial strength, and fighting spirit of the opponents. Certain major strikes in the Bay Area might have ended differently had employer or union forces created more effective alliances and maintained a more disciplined unity.

In retrospect it seems apparent that neither organized labor nor the employer community fully exploited its potentialities for achieving increased power during the 1900–1918 period. After having gained an influential position in San Francisco by 1903, the union movement failed to make further substantial progress until midway through World War I. Yet possibilities for expansion did exist. Speculative though these questions are, one may ask: What results would have been attained had the San Francisco labor movement launched and sustained a long-term program of organizing workers throughout local industry? Would the warehousing and wholesale distribution industry have been converted into a stronghold of unionism, if the powerful and strategically placed teamsters' organizations had adopted a broader concept of their jurisdictions? Could not a more energetic effort have been made to nurture unionism among manufacturing production workers? Was there not substantial neglect of opportunities for the judicious use of sympathy action by unions, particularly the Teamsters' Union, in support of strikes and organizing drives?

A continuing, large-scale campaign to expand the boundaries of unionism would, of course, have placed heavy demands upon both the leadership and the rank and file of the San Francisco labor movement. It would have required of them a sense of class solidarity among all wage earners, a willingness to make financial sacrifices, and an intensity of fervor well above the level characteristic of American labor circles. It would have necessitated more sympathy strikes, secondary boycotts, and refusals to cross picket lines, with the risks incurred by such actions. And, as previously indicated, it would have forced San Francisco labor leaders to assume the unusual responsibility of making a coördinated effort to organize all workers possible in the area.

Perhaps such a high degree of initiative and crusading spirit could hardly have been expected of the labor officials of any American city in this period, in the prevailing context of craft unionism and its traditional approach to organizational problems. Certainly the labor leadership of San Francisco was of high caliber, judged by the standards of the time. Yet it could have been more dynamic. It did not respond with great imagination and energy to the opportunity to make labor's strong position in San Francisco the base from which to maintain a drive for continued expansion of unionism in the Bay Area.

Even more clearly than labor, employers failed to utilize completely their potential resources for gaining power in the industrial relations arena. In San Francisco union strength stimulated firms to form industry employer associations through which they could bargain on equal terms with their respective unions. But, as already noted, the business community did not organize itself effectively into a counterforce to the local labor movement. It did not establish during the 1900–1918 period an over-all employers' association devoted exclusively to labor matters and comparable to the Los Angeles Merchants' and Manufacturers' Association, which conducted a continuous battle against unionism. The lack of such a permanent employers' central body was an important reason for the seeming impotence of San Francisco businessmen. Inadequate organization and insufficient motivation among employers, rather than a basic deficiency in economic strength, impeded the development of more formidable open-shop drives. Vigorous as organized labor was in San Francisco, it is nevertheless probable that unified and determined campaigns by employers would have put unionism on the defensive and curtailed its sphere of influence. The status of the union movement was not an entirely accurate indication of the underlying relative power positions of labor and the business community. Despite its apparent security, San Francisco labor was vulnerable to well-organized employer attacks, as later events made only too clear.

In 1916, with the stirring of new unrest on the labor scene, there were signs that employers were at last being mobilized competently behind a major drive to establish the open shop in San Francisco. The Chamber of Commerce, through its Law and Order Committee, had indicated its readiness to lead a battle to settle the question of unionism's position in local industry. But America's entry into the war postponed the possibility of carrying out the campaign launched by the chamber. At the close of 1918 the issue of the balance of power between organized labor and the forces of the open shop remained to be fought out in the postwar period.

Notes

Unless otherwise indicated, newspapers cited in the notes were published in San Francisco.

Notes to Chapter I | The Background Years

(Pages 1–38)

[1] *Ninth Biennial Report, 1899–1900,* California Bureau of Labor Statistics (Sacramento: 1900), pp. 60, 61.

[2] Edward P. Eaves, "A History of the Cooks' and Waiters' Unions of San Francisco" (unpublished M.A. thesis, University of California, Berkeley, 1930), p. 1; Beatrice V. Taylor, "Labor Relations on the Street Railways of San Francisco" (unpublished M.A. thesis, University of California, Berkeley, 1928), p. 1; Ira B. Cross, *A History of the Labor Movement in California* (Berkeley: University of California Press, 1935), p. 339; *Tenth Biennial Report, 1901–1902,* California Bureau of Labor Statistics (Sacramento: 1902), p. 44.

[3] Cross, *op. cit.,* p. 296.

[4] Lucile Eaves, *A History of California Labor Legislation* (Berkeley: The University Press, 1910), p. 6.

[5] Cross, *op. cit.,* p. 14.

[6] *Ibid.,* p. 297.

[7] Frederick L. Ryan, *Industrial Relations in the San Francisco Building Trades* (Norman: University of Oklahoma Press, 1936), p. 10.

[8] "San Francisco," *Encyclopaedia Britannica* (11th ed.; 1911), XXIV, 147.

[9] Cross, *op. cit.,* pp. 24–27.

[10] *Ibid.,* p. 303.

[11] *Ibid.,* pp. 30, 33.

[12] *Ibid.,* pp. 32–33.

[13] *Ibid.,* p. 304.

[14] *Ibid.,* p. 36; Lucile Eaves, *op. cit.,* pp. 13–14.

[15] Cross, *op. cit.,* p. 58.

[16] *Ibid.,* pp. 41–44, 49; Lucile Eaves, *op. cit.,* pp. 198–201.

[17] Cross, *op. cit.,* p. 48.

[18] *Op. cit.,* p. 14.

[19] Cross, *op. cit.*, pp. 57, 308.

[20] Lucile Eaves, *op. cit.*, pp. 16–19.

[21] Cross, *op. cit.*, p. 50.

[22] *Ibid.*, p. 73; Lucile Eaves, *op. cit.*, pp. 117–122, 142–145.

[23] Cross, *op. cit.*, pp. 74–75, 315.

[24] *Ibid.*, pp. 80, 317.

[25] *Ibid.*, p. 54.

[26] *Ibid.*, pp. 62–63.

[27] *Ibid.*, p. 308; Lucile Eaves, *op. cit.*, pp. 208–209.

[28] Cross, *op. cit.*, p. 51; Ryan, *op. cit.*, pp. 14–16.

[29] John R. Commons and Associates, *History of Labor in the United States* (New York: Macmillan, 1921–1935), II, 266.

[30] *Ibid.*, II, 253; Cross, *op. cit.*, pp. 89–90.

[31] Cross, *op. cit.*, pp. 91–92.

[32] Commons and Associates, *op. cit.*, II, 254–257, 268.

[33] Cross, *op. cit.*, p. 107.

[34] Lucile Eaves, *op. cit.*, p. 31.

[35] *Ibid.*, p. 36; Cross, *op. cit.*, pp. 113–123.

[36] Cross, *op. cit.*, pp. 131–132.

[37] *Ibid.*, p. 127.

[38] Commons and Associates, *op. cit.* II, 268.

[39] Cross, *op. cit.*, pp. 131–132.

[40] *Ibid.*, pp. 325, 327; Ryan, *op. cit.*, p. 17.

[41] Ryan, *op. cit.*, p. 18; *Third Biennial Report, 1887–1888*, California Bureau of Labor Statistics (Sacramento: 1888), p. 171; Cross, *op. cit.*, p. 146.

[42] *Third Biennial Report, 1887–1888*, California Bureau of Labor Statistics, p. 172; Ryan, *op. cit.*, p. 24.

[43] Cross, *op. cit.*, pp. 147–149.

[44] *Third Biennial Report, 1887–1888*, California Bureau of Labor Statistics, p. 173; Cross, *op. cit.*, pp. 167, 330; Paul S. Taylor, *The Sailors' Union of the Pacific* (New York: Ronald Press, 1923), pp. 46–49.

[45] Cross, *op. cit.*, pp. 177–181.

[46] *Ibid.*, pp. 180, 184.

[47] *Ibid.*, p. 182.

[48] *Ibid.*

[49] Paul S. Taylor, *op. cit.*, p. 52.

[50] Cross, *op. cit.*, p. 185.

[51] *Ibid.*, p. 192; Frank Roney, *Frank Roney, Irish Rebel and California Labor Leader*, ed. Ira B. Cross (Berkeley: University of California Press, 1931), p. 465.

[52] *Third Biennial Report, 1887–1888*, California Bureau of Labor Statistics, p. 168.

[53] *Ibid.*, p. 114.

[54] Hermann Schluter, *The Brewing Industry and the Brewery Workers' Movement in America* (Cincinnati: International Union of United Brewery Workmen of America, 1910), p. 3; Lucile Eaves, *op. cit.*, pp. 50–57.

[55] *Third Biennial Report, 1887–1888*, California Bureau of Labor Statistics, pp. 115–116, 128.

[56] *Ibid.*, pp. 114, 154.

[57] Cross, *op. cit.*, p. 201.

[58] *Ibid.*, pp. 199–200; Lucile Eaves, *op. cit.*, p. 52.

[59] Clara E. Mortenson, "Organized Labor in San Francisco from 1892 to 1902" (unpublished M.S. thesis, University of California, Berkeley, 1916), p. 25; Cross, *op. cit.*, p. 209.

[60] Ryan, *op. cit.*, p. 82; Cross, *op. cit.*, p. 201.

[61] Cross, *op. cit.*, pp. 207–209.

[62] Robert C. Francis, "A History of Labor on the San Francisco Waterfront" (unpublished Ph.D. dissertation, University of California, Berkeley, 1934), pp. 71, 73–74; Paul S. Taylor, *op. cit.*, p. 64.

[63] Cross, *op. cit.*, p. 210.

[64] *Ibid.*, p. 213; Lucile Eaves, *op. cit.*, p. 55.

[65] Cross, *op. cit.*, pp. 210–211.

[66] Robert V. Ohlson, "The History of the San Francisco Labor Council, 1892–1939" (unpublished M.A. thesis, University of California, Berkeley, 1940), p. 6; Mortenson, *op. cit.*, p. 42; Lucile Eaves, *op. cit.*, p. 59.

[67] Cross, *op. cit.*, p. 86; "San Francisco," *Encyclopaedia Britannica*, XXIV, 146.

[68] Cross, *op. cit.*, pp. 212, 213.

[69] Mortenson, *op. cit.*, p. 23.

[70] *Coast Seamen's Journal*, Aug. 7, 1901.

[71] Cross, *op. cit.*, p. 219.

[72] Almont Lindsey, *The Pullman Strike* (Chicago: University of Chicago Press, 1942), pp. 161–169.

[73] *Seventh Biennial Report, 1895–1896*, California Bureau of Labor Statistics (Sacramento: 1896), pp. 145–148, 153; Ryan, *op. cit.*, p. 25.

[74] Ryan, *op. cit.*, pp. 26, 27.

[75] *Seventh Biennial Report, 1895–1896*, California Bureau of Labor Statistics, p. 159.

[76] Cross, *op. cit.*, p. 224.

[77] *Seventh Biennial Report, 1895–1896*, California Bureau of Labor Statistics, p. 156.

[78] *Ibid.*, p. 157; Ryan, *op. cit.*, p. 103.

[79] Cross, *op. cit.*, pp. 226–227.

[80] Mortenson, *op. cit.*, p. 59.

[81] Ed Rosenberg, "The San Francisco Strikes of 1901," *American Federationist*, 9 (Jan., 1902), 14.

[82] Cross, *op. cit.*, p. 227.

[83] Ryan, *op. cit.*, p. 33.

[84] *Ninth Biennial Report, 1899–1900*, California Bureau of Labor Statistics, p. 113; Lucile Eaves, *op. cit.*, p. 60.

[85] Ryan, *op. cit.*, p. 104; Cross, *op. cit.*, pp. 228–231.

Notes to Chapter II | The Resurgent Labor
Movement, 1900–1901

(Pages 39–95)

[1] Leo Wolman, *The Growth of American Trade Unions, 1880–1923* (New York: National Bureau of Economic Research, 1924), p. 10.

[2] *The Population of California*, Commonwealth Club of California (San Francisco: 1946), p. 5.

[3] Grace H. Stimson, *Rise of the Labor Movement in Los Angeles* (Berkeley and Los Angeles: University of California Press, 1955), p. 272.

[4] *Ninth Biennial Report, 1899–1900*, California Bureau of Labor Statistics (Sacramento: 1900), p. 97.

[5] *Ibid.*, p. 107; Robert V. Ohlson, "The History of the San Francisco Labor Council, 1892–1939" (unpublished M.A. thesis, University of California, Berkeley, 1940), p. 3.

[6] *Proceedings of the Fourteenth Annual Meeting of the United Typothetae of America*, 1900, p. 22; *Coast Seamen's Journal*, Aug. 22, 1900.

[7] Ira B. Cross, *A History of the Labor Movement in California* (Berkeley: University of California Press, 1935), p. 143; *Ninth Biennial Report, 1899–1900*, California Bureau of Labor Statistics, p. 110.

[8] *Coast Seamen's Journal*, July 25, 1900; Cross, *op. cit.*, p. 338.

[9] *Coast Seamen's Journal*, Oct. 24, 1900; *Labor Clarion*, Sept. 4, 1908.

[10] Robert C. Francis, "A History of Labor on the San Francisco Waterfront" (unpublished Ph.D. dissertation, University of California, Berkeley, 1934), p. 84.

[11] *Coast Seamen's Journal*, Dec. 19, 1900. See also Charles F. Marsh, *Trade Unionism in the Electric Light and Power Industry* (Urbana: University of Illinois, 1930), p. 111.

[12] Francis, *op. cit.*, p. 84; *Coast Seamen's Journal*, June 27, July 25, 1900.

[13] Cross, *op. cit.*, p. 338.

[14] Clara E. Mortenson, "Organized Labor in San Francisco from 1892 to 1902" (unpublished M.S. thesis, University of California, Berkeley, 1916), p. 87; *Labor Clarion*, Sept. 4, 1908.

[15] Lucile Eaves, *A History of California Labor Legislation* (Berkeley: The University Press, 1910), p. 413; Mortenson, *op. cit.*, pp. 88–89; *Coast Seamen's Journal*, Oct. 17, 1900.

[16] Frederick L. Ryan, *Industrial Relations in the San Francisco Building Trades* (Norman: University of Oklahoma Press, 1936), p. 35.

[17] *Ibid.*, p. 34.

[18] *Ibid.*, pp. 55–57.

[19] Cross, *op. cit.*, p. 231; *Coast Seamen's Journal*, July 11, 18, 1900.

[20] Mortenson, *op. cit.*, p. 35; Ryan, *op. cit.*, p. 105.

[21] Ryan, *op. cit.*, pp. 105, 109, 131.

[22] *Ibid.*, pp. 106, 107; Cross, *op. cit.*, p. 233; *Organized Labor*, Oct. 20, 1900.

[23] *Organized Labor*, Sept. 28, 1900; Feb. 23, 1901; Mortenson, *op. cit.*, p. 78; Ryan, *op. cit.*, pp. 108, 109.

[24] Ryan, *op. cit.*, pp. 109, 131.

[25] Mortenson, *op. cit.*, pp. 78–79; Cross, *op. cit.*, p. 222.

[26] Ryan, *op. cit.*, p. 45.

[27] *Ibid.*, pp. 42–43.

[28] Interview with Archie J. Mooney; *Labor Clarion*, March 21, 1902.

[29] *Organized Labor*, Jan. 12, 1901.

[30] Bernard C. Cronin, *Father Yorke and the Labor Movement in San Francisco, 1900–1910* (Washington: Catholic University of America Press, 1943), p. 39.

[31] *Ibid.*, p. 40; Robert M. Robinson, "A History of the Teamsters in the San Francisco Bay Area, 1850–1950" (unpublished Ph.D. dissertation, University of California, Berkeley, 1951), p. 28.

[32] *Examiner*, Sept. 1, 1901; Robinson, *op. cit.*, pp. 23, 28.

[33] *Examiner*, July 28, 1901; Robinson, *op. cit.*, p. 29.

[34] Cronin, *op. cit.*, p. 42; Robinson, *op. cit.*, p. 32.

[35] Paul S. Taylor, *The Sailors' Union of the Pacific* (New York: Ronald Press, 1923), pp. 93–94.

[36] George C. Jensen, "The City Front Federation of San Francisco" (unpublished M.S. thesis, University of California, Berkeley, 1912), p. 39.

[37] *Ibid.*, p. 37; *Coast Seamen's Journal*, April 10, 1901; Robinson, *op. cit.*, p. 45.

[38] Thomas W. Page, "The San Francisco Labor Movement in 1901," *Political Science Quarterly*, 17 (Dec., 1902), 666.

[39] *Coast Seamen's Journal*, Jan. 23, 1901.

[40] *Ibid.*, April 24, 1901.

[41] *Organized Labor*, June 22, 1901.

[42] *Coast Seamen's Journal*, Jan. 30, March 20, 1901; Ed Rosenberg, "The San Francisco Strikes of 1901," *American Federationist*, 9 (Jan., 1902), 16; Robinson, *op. cit.*, p. 36.

[43] *Coast Seamen's Journal*, March 6, Aug. 7, 1901. The quotation comes from the latter issue.

[44] Ohlson, *op. cit.*, p. 50; Eaves, *op. cit.*, p. 65.

[45] Page, *op. cit.,* p. 669; *Examiner,* May 11, 1901.

[46] *Examiner,* May 5, 1901; *Argonaut,* May 13, 1901; Cronin, *op. cit.,* pp. 10, 49.

[47] *Coast Seamen's Journal,* May 15, 1901; Page, *op. cit.,* p. 670; Rosenberg, *op. cit.,* p. 15.

[48] *Coast Seamen's Journal,* May 15, 1901; Rosenberg, *op. cit.,* p. 16.

[49] *Argonaut,* May 13, 1901; *Coast Seamen's Journal,* Aug. 7, 1901.

[50] *Labor Clarion,* Sept. 4, 1908; Cross, *op. cit.,* p. 339.

[51] John R. Commons and Associates, *History of Labor in the United States* (New York: Macmillan, 1921–1935), IV, 115–116; Rosenberg, *op. cit.,* p. 15.

[52] *Coast Seamen's Journal,* May 22, 1901.

[53] Rosenberg, *op. cit.,* p. 16.

[54] *Ibid.;* Page, *op. cit.,* p. 674; *Coast Seamen's Journal,* Aug. 7, 1901.

[55] Rosenberg, *op. cit.,* p. 15; Cross, *op. cit.,* p. 239; *Labor Clarion,* March 28, 1902.

[56] Cronin, *op. cit.,* p. 43; Robinson, *op. cit.,* p. 47.

[57] Robinson, *op. cit.,* p. 41.

[58] *Ibid.,* pp. 44, 47.

[59] *Ibid.,* p. 47; Cronin, *op. cit.,* p. 43; *Examiner,* Aug. 1, 1901.

[60] Cronin, *op. cit.,* pp. 43, 44; *Bulletin,* July 21, 1901.

[61] Cronin, *op. cit.,* pp. 45, 46; Robinson, *op. cit.,* pp. 54–55.

[62] Cronin, *op. cit.,* p. 50; *Coast Seamen's Journal,* July 31, 1901.

[63] *Coast Seamen's Journal,* Aug. 7, 1901.

[64] Page, *op. cit.,* p. 678.

[65] Cronin, *op. cit.,* pp. 46, 47; *Coast Seamen's Journal,* July 31, 1901.

[66] *Chronicle,* July 30, 1901.

[67] *Coast Seamen's Journal,* July 31, 1901.

[68] *Ibid.*

[69] Francis, *op. cit.,* p. 15; Robinson, *op. cit.,* p. 79; Rosenberg, *op. cit.,* p. 16.

[70] Page, *op. cit.,* p. 679; Robinson, *op. cit.,* p. 77.

[71] Page, *op. cit.,* p. 679; Robinson, *op. cit.,* p. 77; Francis, *op. cit.,* p. 103; Jensen, *op. cit.,* pp. 45–46.

[72] *Coast Seamen's Journal,* Aug. 28, 1901.

[73] *Organized Labor,* Aug. 17, 1901.

[74] Page, *op. cit.,* p. 683; *Argonaut,* Aug. 12, 1901; *Coast Seamen's Journal,* Aug. 14, 1901; Cronin, *op. cit.,* p. 55.

[75] *Coast Seamen's Journal,* Sept. 4, 1901; Robinson, *op. cit.,* p. 80; *Organized Labor,* April 23, 1910.

[76] Rosenberg, *op. cit.,* p. 18; *Argonaut,* Aug. 26, Sept. 30, 1901; interview with Andrew J. Gallagher.

[77] *Argonaut,* Aug. 5, Sept. 23, 1901; *Coast Seamen's Journal,* Aug. 28, 1901.

[78] *Examiner,* Aug. 6, 1901.

[79] Page, *op. cit.,* p. 682.

[80] Jensen, *op. cit.*, p. 40.

[81] *Coast Seamen's Journal*, Aug. 21, 1901.

[82] *Merchants' Association Review*, Oct., 1901, pp. 5–6.

[83] *Argonaut*, Sept. 9, 1901; Cronin, *op. cit.*, pp. 65–67.

[84] Ohlson, *op. cit.*, p. 50; Francis, *op. cit.*, p. 110; Jensen, *op. cit.*, p. 47.

[85] *Coast Seamen's Journal*, Aug. 21, 28, 1901; Page, *op. cit.*, p. 678; Rosenberg, *op. cit.*, p. 18.

[86] *Argonaut*, Sept. 9, 1901; Robinson, *op. cit.*, p. 68.

[87] *Coast Seamen's Journal*, Oct. 2, 1901.

[88] *Argonaut*, Sept. 30, 1901.

[89] *Coast Seamen's Journal*, Sept. 25, 1901; Rosenberg, *op. cit.*, p. 18.

[90] Cronin, *op. cit.*, p. 163.

[91] *Chronicle*, Sept. 23, 28, 1901; *Call*, Sept. 24, 1901; Robinson, *op. cit.*, p. 71; Page, *op. cit.*, p. 686; *Coast Seamen's Journal*, Oct. 2, 1901.

[92] Jensen, *op. cit.*, p. 47; Page, *op. cit.*, p. 687; Cronin, *op. cit.*, p. 82.

[93] *Examiner*, Oct. 3, 1901.

[94] *Argonaut*, Oct. 7, 1901.

[95] Cronin, *op. cit.*, p. 82; *Examiner*, Sept. 22, 1901.

[96] *Coast Seamen's Journal*, Oct. 9, 1901.

[97] *Ibid.*, Oct. 9, 16, 1901; Walter Macarthur, "A Climax in Civics" (unpublished manuscript, University of California Library, *ca.* 1906), p. 13; *Labor Clarion*, Sept. 4, 1908; Rosenberg, *op. cit.*, p. 18.

[98] Cronin, *op. cit.*, p. 86; *Coast Seamen's Journal*, Oct. 16, 1901.

[99] Eaves, *op. cit.*, p. 60.

[100] Francis, *op. cit.*, p. 115; Robinson, *op. cit.*, p. 87; Cronin, *op. cit.*, p. 86. Time has a way of catching up with authors. In 1959, after this book had been written but before it went to press, the San Francisco teamsters called their first strike since 1901 against the Draymen's Association.

[101] *Examiner*, July 23, 1901.

[102] *Coast Seamen's Journal*, May 2, 22, 29, June 5, 1901; April 9, 1902; *Argonaut*, Sept. 9, 1901; Taylor, *op. cit.*, p. 98.

[103] *Labor Clarion*, May 16, 23, 1902; Francis, *op. cit.*, p. 87.

[104] *Coast Seamen's Journal*, Jan. 8, 1902; *Labor Clarion*, March 7, 1902.

[105] *American Federationist*, Jan., 1902, p. 23; *Labor Clarion*, March 7, April 4, 1902.

[106] *Labor Clarion*, April 11, May 30, June 20, 1902; Feb. 6, 1903.

[107] *Examiner*, Sept. 1, 1901.

[108] *Ibid.*, Sept. 6, 1901; Edward J. Rowell, "The Union Labor Party of San Francisco, 1901–1911" (unpublished Ph.D. dissertation, University of California, Berkeley, 1938), pp. 24, 34.

[109] Rowell, *op. cit.*, p. 23.

[110] *Ibid.*, p. 50; Cross, *op. cit.*, p. 245; *Bulletin*, Oct. 2, 1901.

[111] *Coast Seamen's Journal*, Oct. 16, 1901.

[112] *Ibid.*, April 9, 1902.

Notes to Chapter III | Collective Bargaining
Relationships, 1902–1903
(Pages 96–138)

[1] Edward J. Rowell, "The Union Labor Party of San Francisco, 1901–1911" (unpublished Ph.D. dissertation, University of California, Berkeley, 1938), p. 121; Harry A. Millis and Royal E. Montgomery, *Organized Labor* (New York: McGraw-Hill, 1945), p. 83.

[2] Robert V. Ohlson, "The History of the San Francisco Labor Council, 1892–1939" (unpublished M.A. thesis, University of California, Berkeley, 1940), p. 71; *Labor Clarion*, Aug. 22, 1902; March 13, 1903.

[3] *Examiner*, Sept. 3, 1902; *American Federationist*, Oct., 1902, pp. 115–116.

[4] *Labor Clarion*, Sept. 5, 1902.

[5] *Ibid.*, Aug. 15, 1902; Sept. 4, 1908.

[6] Interviews with San Francisco union officials.

[7] Frederick L. Ryan, *Industrial Relations in the San Francisco Building Trades* (Norman: University of Oklahoma Press, 1936), pp. 87, 113; *Labor Clarion*, Nov. 6, 1903; *Star*, Dec. 12, 1903.

[8] *Labor Clarion*, March 28, 1902; Robert M. Robinson, "A History of the Teamsters in the San Francisco Bay Area, 1850–1950" (unpublished Ph.D. dissertation, University of California, Berkeley, 1951), pp. 106, 108, 112.

[9] *Examiner*, Dec. 6, 1902; Ray Stannard Baker, "A Corner in Labor," *McClure's Magazine*, 22 (Feb., 1904), 369; Robinson, *op. cit.*, p. 116.

[10] *Labor Clarion*, Dec. 12, 1902.

[11] Ryan, *op. cit.*, p. 113; *Labor Clarion*, Nov. 6, 1903; *Star*, Dec. 12, 1903.

[12] *Labor Clarion*, Nov. 21, 1902; March 27, April 10, 1903; *Star*, Jan. 3, 1903.

[13] *Labor Clarion*, April 24, 1903.

[14] *Ibid.*, Oct. 23, 1903.

[15] *Ibid.*, Aug. 22, 1902.

[16] *Ibid.*, Aug. 29, 1902.

17 *Ibid.*, May 15, July 10, 1903.

18 Robert C. Francis, "A History of Labor on the San Francisco Waterfront" (unpublished Ph.D. dissertation, University of California, Berkeley, 1934), p. 127.

19 Ryan, *op. cit.*, p. 48; Herbert V. Ready, *The Labor Problem* (San Francisco: [c. 1904]), p. 11; *Coast Seamen's Journal*, June 17, Aug. 5, 1903.

20 Francis, *op. cit.*, p. 127; *Star*, Jan. 25, 1902.

21 *Labor Clarion*, March 13, 20, 27, April 3, 10, 17, 1903; Lillian R. Matthews, *Women in Trade Unions in San Francisco* (Berkeley: University of California Press, 1913), pp. 40, 42.

22 *Labor Clarion*, March 28, 1902; Feb. 27, 1903.

23 *Ibid.*, May 2, 1902; March 27, April 10, 1903.

24 *Ibid.*, Dec. 19, 1902; June 19, 1903; Edward P. Eaves, "A History of the Cooks' and Waiters' Unions of San Francisco" (unpublished M.A. thesis, University of California, Berkeley, 1930), pp. 37, 39, 43.

25 *Labor Clarion*, May 30, July 11, Dec. 19, 1902; May 8, 1903; Paul Chatom, "Industrial Relations in the Brewery, Metal, and Teaming Trades of San Francisco" (unpublished M.S. thesis, University of California, Berkeley, 1915), pp. 1, 7.

26 *Labor Clarion*, June 27, 1902; March 13, 27, Oct. 9, Nov. 27, Dec. 11, 1903.

27 *Eleventh Biennial Report, 1903–1904*, California Bureau of Labor Statistics (Sacramento: 1904), p. 46.

28 *Labor Clarion*, April 4, 1902; April 3, June 19, Sept. 18, 1903.

29 *Ibid.*, Sept. 26, 1902.

30 *Ibid.*, Sept. 4, 1902; Nov. 14, 1908.

31 *Ibid.*, April 18, 1902; *Argonaut*, April 21, 1902; Matthews, *op. cit.*, pp. 59, 60.

32 *Labor Clarion*, March 6, April 24, Oct. 9, 1903.

33 *Ibid.*, Feb. 13, March 20, April 24, May 15, 1903; Matthews, *op. cit.*, p. 84.

34 *Twelfth Biennial Report, 1905–1906*, California Bureau of Labor Statistics (Sacramento: 1906), p. 186; *Labor Clarion*, Nov. 14, 28, Dec. 19, 1902; April 10, 1903; *American Industries*, Dec. 15, 1902.

35 *Twelfth Biennial Report, 1905–1906*, California Bureau of Labor Statistics, pp. 190, 191; *Labor Clarion*, Aug. 29, Dec. 12, 1902; Sept. 25, 1903; Sept. 4, 1908.

36 *Twelfth Biennial Report, 1905–1906*, California Bureau of Labor Statistics, p. 190; *Labor Clarion*, Aug. 8, 15, Sept. 26, Oct. 31, 1902; July 24, 1903; *Star*, Jan. 3, 1903.

37 Lucile Eaves, *A History of California Labor Legislation* (Berkeley: The University Press, 1910), p. 421; *Twelfth Biennial Report, 1905–1906*, California Bureau of Labor Statistics, p. 191; *Labor Clarion*, Nov. 21, 1902; Jan. 23, 1903; Jan. 17, 1904; *Star*, Dec. 20, 1902.

38 *Coast Seamen's Journal*, May 7, 1902.

39 Bernard C. Cronin, *Father Yorke and the Labor Movement in San*

Francisco, 1900–1910 (Washington: Catholic University of America Press, 1943), p. 137; *Examiner,* March 5, 1902.

[40] *Labor Clarion,* April 18, 1902; *Chronicle,* April 18, 1902; *Coast Seamen's Journal,* May 7, 1902; Cronin, *op. cit.,* p. 138.

[41] *Coast Seamen's Journal,* May 7, 1902.

[42] *Examiner,* April 20, 1902; *Coast Seamen's Journal,* April 30, 1902.

[43] Cronin, *op. cit.,* p. 138; interview with John Forbes; *Chronicle,* April 23, 1902; *Coast Seamen's Journal,* April 30, 1902.

[44] *Constitution and By-Laws of the Building Trades Council of San Francisco,* 1901.

[45] Ryan, *op. cit.,* pp. 116, 117; *Twelfth Biennial Report, 1905–1906,* California Bureau of Labor Statistics, p. 192.

[46] Ryan, *op. cit.,* pp. 112, 114.

[47] *Daily News,* Dec. 30, 1913; Baker, *op. cit.,* p. 374; William Haber, *Industrial Relations in the Building Industry* (Cambridge: Harvard University Press, 1930), p. 171.

[48] Haber, *op. cit.,* pp. 404–405; Ryan, *op. cit.,* pp. 58, 110.

[49] *Labor Clarion,* June 5, 1903.

[50] Ryan, *op. cit.,* p. 118.

[51] *Ibid.,* pp. 46–47; *Labor Clarion,* March 21, 1902; interviews with San Francisco building trades union officials.

[52] Rowell, *op. cit.,* p. 145; *American Industries,* May 1, 1903; Baker, *op. cit.,* pp. 366, 370.

[53] *Labor Clarion,* March 4, 1904.

[54] *Ibid.,* March 13, May 22, 1903.

[55] *Star,* Nov. 7, 1903.

[56] Cronin, *op. cit.,* p. 114; Rowell, *op. cit.,* p. 180.

[57] *Star,* Nov. 19, 1904.

[58] Rowell, *op. cit.,* pp. 59–60, 65; Cronin, *op. cit.,* p. 104.

[59] *Thirteenth Biennial Report, 1907–1908,* California Bureau of Labor Statistics (Sacramento: 1908), pp. 167–170, supplemented by my own estimates and extrapolations.

[60] *Star,* March 14, 1903.

[61] Interview with Andrew J. Gallagher.

[62] *Twelfth Biennial Report, 1905–1906,* California Bureau of Labor Statistics, pp. 186–207.

[63] *Ibid.,* p. 195; *American Federationist,* Jan., 1903, p. 78.

[64] *Labor Clarion,* April 4, Sept. 19, Oct. 24, 31, 1902; March 6, April 24, Dec. 11, 1903; *American Federationist,* March, 1903, p. 38; *Twelfth Biennial Report, 1905–1906,* California Bureau of Labor Statistics, p. 195.

[65] Frank T. Stockton, *The Closed Shop in American Trade Unions* (Baltimore: Johns Hopkins Press, 1911), p. 46; Albion G. Taylor, *Labor Policies of the National Association of Manufacturers* (Urbana: University of Illinois, 1928), p. 39; Clarence E. Bonnett, *Employers' Associations in the United States* (New York: Macmillan, 1922), p. 25.

[66] Stockton, *op. cit.,* pp. 46, 48.

[67] Cronin, *op. cit.*, p. 139; *Labor Clarion,* March 20, April 3, 1903; *Coast Seamen's Journal,* March 25, 1903; *Examiner,* March 31, 1903.

[68] *Labor Clarion,* Nov. 13, 1903.

[69] *Ibid.*, June 12, 26, 1903; *Twelfth Biennial Report, 1905–1906,* California Bureau of Labor Statistics, p. 212.

[70] *Labor Clarion,* June 19, 26, Aug. 21, 1903; Jan. 4, March 25, 1904; *Twelfth Biennial Report, 1905–1906,* California Bureau of Labor Statistics, p. 199.

[71] *Labor Clarion,* Oct. 31, Nov. 14, 1902; June 19, 26, July 17, 24, 31, Aug. 14, 21, 28, 1903.

[72] *Ibid.*, Aug. 7, 14, 21, Sept. 18, Nov. 6, 1903; *Coast Seamen's Journal,* Oct. 7, 1903.

[73] *Labor Clarion,* Nov. 27, 1903.

[74] *Ibid.*, Aug. 7, Oct. 16, Nov. 27, Dec. 4, 1903; *Twelfth Biennial Report, 1905–1906,* California Bureau of Labor Statistics, p. 134.

[75] *Labor Clarion,* Dec. 11, 1903; Edward P. Eaves, *op. cit.*, p. 46.

[76] *Argonaut,* Dec. 14, 1903.

[77] *Ibid.*

[78] Edward P. Eaves, *op. cit.*, p. 47; *Labor Clarion,* Dec. 25, 1903.

[79] *Labor Clarion,* Feb. 5, 12, 19, March 11, May 13, Aug. 26, Sept. 16, 1904.

[1] *Argonaut,* Jan. 18, March 7, 18, 1904; *Labor Clarion,* Jan. 1, Feb. 5, March 18, 1904.

[2] *Labor Clarion,* Feb. 5, 1904.

[3] Interview with Frederick J. Koster.

[4] Grace H. Stimson, *Rise of the Labor Movement in Los Angeles* (Berkeley and Los Angeles: University of California Press, 1955), p. 258; *American Industries,* Feb.–Aug. *passim,* Dec. 15, 1904; *Evening Post,* June 28, Aug. 6, 1904; *Labor Clarion,* Oct. 28, 1904.

[5] *Evening Post,* Nov. 11, 1904.

[6] Interview with Frederick J. Koster; *Labor Clarion,* May 27, June 3, Oct. 28, 1904; *Evening Post,* Jan. 4, 1905; *American Industries,* Jan. 26, 1905.

[7] As published in *Labor Clarion,* Jan. 1, 1904.

[8] *Coast Seamen's Journal,* April 6, 1904.

[9] *Labor Clarion,* April 22, 1904.

[10] *Ibid.,* Jan. 22, Oct. 21, 1904; Robert M. Robinson, "A History of the Teamsters in the San Francisco Bay Area, 1850–1950" (unpublished Ph.D. dissertation, University of California, Berkeley, 1951), p. 118.

[11] *Twelfth Biennial Report, 1905–1906,* California Bureau of Labor Statistics (Sacramento: 1906), p. 200; Robinson, *op. cit.,* pp. 120, 122; *Labor Clarion,* April 29, May 13, 1904; *Examiner,* May 8, 1904.

[12] *Examiner,* July 1, 1904; *Evening Post,* Aug. 6, 13, Sept. 13, 1904; *Pierce v. Stablemen's Union* (1909), 156 Cal. 70.

[13] Printed circular distributed by the employment agency of Murray & Ready, dated July 30, 1904, in the collection of Archie Green, San Francisco.

[14] *American Industries,* Dec. 15, 1904.

[15] Robinson, *op. cit.,* p. 125; *Labor Clarion,* June 17, 1904; *Evening Post,*

Aug. 29, 1904; *Examiner*, Aug. 31, 1904; *Coast Seamen's Journal*, Sept. 7, 1904.

[16] Robinson, *op. cit.*, pp. 127–128; *Labor Clarion*, Oct. 21, 1904.

[17] Lucile Eaves, *A History of California Labor Legislation* (Berkeley: The University Press, 1910), pp. 422–425.

[18] *Pierce v. Stablemen's Union* (1904), Case No. 91122, Superior Court, City and County of San Francisco; *Evening Post*, Aug. 6, 1904; *American Industries*, Sept. 15, 1904.

[19] Eaves, *op. cit.*, pp. 426–431; G. A. Strong, "A Study of the Development of the California Law on Picketing" (unpublished M.A. thesis, University of California, Berkeley, 1952), pp. 23–26; *Goldberg Bowen Co. v. Stablemen's Union* (1906), 149 Cal. 429.

[20] *Evening Post*, Aug. 29, 1904.

[21] *Labor Clarion*, April 15, May 13, June 3, 1904; Nov. 10, 1905; *Examiner*, July 1, 1904; *Evening Post*, July 7, 11, 15, Sept. 30, 1904; *Twelfth Biennial Report, 1905–1906*, California Bureau of Labor Statistics, p. 202.

[22] *Evening Post*, Sept. 1, Oct. 4, 14, 22, Dec. 13, 22, 31, 1904; *Labor Clarion*, Oct. 21, Dec. 2, 9, 1904; Sept. 22, 1905; *Oakland Tribune*, June 1, 1905; *Twelfth Biennial Report, 1905–1906*, California Bureau of Labor Statistics, pp. 204, 206.

[23] *Labor Clarion*, March 4, 11, June 10, 1904; *East Bay Labor Journal*, Sept. 6, 1940, Labor Day Supplement; John L. Davie, *My Own Story* (Oakland: Post-Enquirer Publishing Co., 1931), p. 146.

[24] *Evening Post*, Oct. 3, 1904.

[25] *Labor Clarion*, Jan. 29, Oct. 7, 1904; Oct. 13, 1905; Jan. 26, 1906; *Evening Post*, Oct. 7, 1904.

[26] *National Civic Federation Review*, April, 1905, p. 23; *Labor Clarion*, June 9, 1905; Jan. 26, 1906.

[27] Cf. *Twelfth Biennial Report, 1905–1906*, California Bureau of Labor Statistics.

[28] *Labor Clarion*, June 10, 1904; *Coast Seamen's Journal*, Nov. 23, 1904.

[29] *Labor Clarion*, 1904–1905 *passim; Coast Seamen's Journal*, May 31, 1905; Robinson, *op. cit.*, pp. 111–112.

[30] *Star*, April 9, 1904; *Coast Seamen's Journal*, April 20, 1904; *Labor Clarion*, April 29, 1904; Beatrice V. Taylor, "Labor Relations on the Street Railways of San Francisco" (unpublished M.A. thesis, University of California, Berkeley, 1928), p. 41.

[31] *Chronicle*, April 25, 1904.

[32] Taylor, *op. cit.*, p. 41; Bernard C. Cronin, *Father Yorke and the Labor Movement in San Francisco, 1900–1910* (Washington: Catholic University of America Press, 1943), p. 140; *Labor Clarion*, May 6, 1904.

[33] *Argonaut*, Aug. 8, 1904.

[34] *Labor Clarion*, May 13, 20, 1904; Aug. 18, Sept. 8, 1905; *Evening Post*, July 5, 1904; *Star*, July 23, 1904; *Twelfth Biennial Report, 1905–1906*, California Bureau of Labor Statistics, p. 200.

[35] *Labor Clarion,* April 8, May 20, June 3, Sept. 16, 1904; Jan. 20, 1905; *Star,* June 4, 1904; *Twelfth Biennial Report, 1905–1906,* California Bureau of Labor Statistics, p. 212; interview with Warren Billings.

[36] Herbert V. Ready, *The Labor Problem* (San Francisco: [c. 1904]), p. 5.

[37] *Labor Clarion,* March 18, April 8, 15, 29, May 6, Aug. 19, Sept. 4, 23, 1904; March 17, 1905; Sept. 2, 1927; Charles F. Marsh, *Trade Unionism in the Electric Light and Power Industry* (Urbana: University of Illinois, 1930), p. 49.

[38] *Evening Post,* Oct. 3, 1904.

[39] *Ibid.,* Nov. 11, 1904.

[40] *American Industries,* Dec. 15, 1904.

[41] *Argonaut,* Oct. 31, Nov. 28, 1904; *Los Angeles Times,* Nov. 9, 1904; *Coast Seamen's Journal,* Nov. 16, 1904.

[42] *Evening Post,* Aug. 29, 1904; *American Industries,* Dec. 15, 1904; *Fresno Republican,* April 12, 1905; *Argonaut,* Sept. 18, 1905; Cronin, *op. cit.,* p. 134.

[43] *Evening Post,* Jan. 4, 1905; *Coast Seamen's Journal,* Jan. 11, 1905.

[44] *Evening Post,* Nov. 28, 1905.

[45] Edward P. Eaves, "A History of the Cooks' and Waiters' Unions of San Francisco" (unpublished M.A. thesis, University of California, Berkeley, 1930), p. 49; *Labor Clarion,* March 17, 24, 1905.

[46] *National Civic Federation Review,* April, 1905, p. 21.

[47] *Ibid.*

[48] Edward P. Eaves, *op. cit.,* p. 51; *Labor Clarion,* July 7, Aug. 11, 1905.

[49] Edward P. Eaves, *op. cit.,* pp. 51–52; *Labor Clarion,* Sept. 29, 1905; April 13, 1906.

[50] Frederick L. Ryan, *Industrial Relations in the San Francisco Building Trades* (Norman: University of Oklahoma Press, 1936), p. 118; *Evening Post,* July 6, 1904; *American Industries,* March 1, 1905; Oct. 15, 1906; *Organized Labor,* Sept. 2, 23, 1905; Jan. 13, 1906.

[51] *Argonaut,* May 4, 1904; *American Industries,* May 15, 1905; *Organized Labor,* Jan. 13, 20, 1906; *Twelfth Biennial Report, 1905–1906,* California Bureau of Labor Statistics, pp. 200–201, 212.

[52] *Star,* June 3, 17, 1905; *Daily News,* June 5, 1905; *Organized Labor,* June 10, 1905.

[53] David F. Selvin, "History of the San Francisco Typographical Union" (unpublished M.A. thesis, University of California, Berkeley, 1935), p. 53; *Examiner,* June 29, 30, 1905; *Evening Post,* July 9, 1905.

[54] *Bulletin,* July 4, 1905; *Labor Clarion,* July 7, 1905.

[55] Selvin, *op. cit.,* pp. 53, 54; *Examiner,* July 16, Sept. 18, 1905; *Labor Clarion,* July 21, 28, Aug. 4, Nov. 17, 1905; *Bulletin,* Sept. 18, 1905.

[56] "The World of Labor," *International Socialist Review* (Feb., 1907), 501.

[57] Edward J. Rowell, "The Union Labor Party of San Francisco, 1901–1911" (unpublished Ph.D. dissertation, University of California, Berkeley, 1938), p. 97.

[58] *Labor Clarion,* Nov. 10, 1905.

[59] Walton Bean, *Boss Ruef's San Francisco* (Berkeley and Los Angeles: University of California Press, 1952), p. 60; *Labor Clarion,* Sept. 8, 1905; *Argonaut,* Nov. 13, 1905.

[60] *Star,* May 20, 1905.

[61] *Argonaut,* May 22, 1905.

[62] Bean, *op. cit.,* p. 58; Rowell, *op. cit.,* p. 99; *Chronicle,* Nov. 2, 4, 1905.

[63] Bean, *op. cit.,* p. 64.

[64] *Coast Seamen's Journal,* Dec. 20, 1905.

[65] *Chronicle,* July 21, 1907.

[66] *Labor Clarion,* Jan. 26, 1906.

[67] *Argonaut,* March 24, 1906.

[68] Edward P. Eaves, *op. cit.,* pp. 52–53; *Labor Clarion,* Jan. 26, March 16, April 13, 1906.

[69] Robinson, *op. cit.,* pp. 128–130; *Examiner,* March 15, 20, 21, 23, 26, 1906; *Call,* April 4, 1906.

[70] *Examiner,* March 20, April 11, 1906; *Call,* April 7, 1906.

Notes to Chapter V | Labor Relations after
the San Francisco
Earthquake, 1906–1907
(Pages 167–199)

[1] "San Francisco," *Encyclopaedia Britannica* (11th ed.; 1911), XXIV, 148.

[2] *Coast Seamen's Journal*, April 25, 1906; *Labor Clarion*, May 4, 1906.

[3] *Twelfth Biennial Report, 1905–1906*, California Bureau of Labor Statistics (Sacramento: 1906), p. 221; *Coast Seamen's Journal*, May 23, 1906.

[4] *Labor Clarion*, May 11, 18, June 1, 1906.

[5] *Argonaut*, July 14, 1906.

[6] Hyman Weintraub, "Andrew Furuseth—Abraham Lincoln of the Sea" (unpublished manuscript, *ca.* 1955–1957); *Coast Seamen's Journal*, June 6, 1906.

[7] Paul S. Taylor, *The Sailors' Union of the Pacific* (New York: Ronald Press, 1923), p. 104; *Coast Seamen's Journal*, May 16, June 6, 1906.

[8] Weintraub, *op. cit.;* Taylor, *op. cit.*, p. 104; *Coast Seamen's Journal*, June 6, July 11, 1906. The quotation is from the latter issue of the paper.

[9] Robert C. Francis, "A History of Labor on the San Francisco Waterfront" (unpublished Ph.D. dissertation, University of California, Berkeley, 1934), p. 139; *Coast Seamen's Journal*, June 13, 1906.

[10] Francis, *op. cit.*, p. 139; George C. Jensen, "The City Front Federation of San Francisco" (unpublished M.S. thesis, University of California, Berkeley, 1912), p. 50; *Coast Seamen's Journal*, June 20, 1906; Jan. 16, 1907.

[11] *Coast Seamen's Journal*, June 20, 1906.

[12] Taylor, *op. cit.*, pp. 105–106; Edward J. Rowell, "The Union Labor Party of San Francisco, 1901–1911" (unpublished Ph.D. dissertation, University of California, Berkeley, 1938), p. 133; *Labor Clarion*, June 22, 29, 1906; *Coast Seamen's Journal*, Aug. 22, 29, 1906.

[13] *Coast Seamen's Journal*, July 18, 1906.

[14] *Ibid.*, Jan. 16, 1907; Taylor, *op. cit.*, pp. 100, 106; Weintraub, *op. cit.*

[15] Francis, *op. cit.*, p. 133; Weintraub, *op. cit.*

[16] *Coast Seamen's Journal*, Jan. 16, 1907.

[17] *Ibid.*, Aug. 22, 1906; Weintraub, *op. cit.*

[18] *Thirteenth Biennial Report, 1907–1908,* California Bureau of Labor Statistics (Sacramento: 1908), p. 170; *Examiner,* March 17, 27, 29, April 3, 4, 1906; *Labor Clarion,* April 6, 1906.

[19] Beatrice V. Taylor, "Labor Relations on the Street Railways of San Francisco" (unpublished M.A. thesis, University of California, Berkeley, 1928), p. 43; Bernard C. Cronin, *Father Yorke and the Labor Movement in San Francisco, 1900–1910* (Washington: Catholic University of America Press, 1943), p. 143; *Labor Clarion,* July 20, Aug. 10, 24, 1906; *Argonaut,* Sept. 8, 1906.

[20] Beatrice V. Taylor, *op. cit.,* p. 45; Cronin, *op. cit.,* p. 143; *Labor Clarion,* Sept. 14, 1906; *Argonaut,* Sept. 15, 1906.

[21] Beatrice V. Taylor, *op. cit.,* pp. 49–51; *Labor Clarion,* March 1, 1907; *Argonaut,* March 9, April 27, 1907.

[22] Frederick L. Ryan, *Industrial Relations in the San Francisco Building Trades* (Norman: University of Oklahoma Press, 1936), p. 121; *Twelfth Biennial Report, 1905–1906,* California Bureau of Labor Statistics, p. 220; *Argonaut,* July 14, 1906.

[23] *Labor Clarion,* July 17, Aug. 3, 24, 31, Sept. 7, 21, Oct. 12, Nov. 16, 1906; May 1, 1907; *Argonaut,* Dec. 15, 1906; Edward P. Eaves, "A History of the Cooks' and Waiters' Unions of San Francisco" (unpublished M.A. thesis, University of California, Berkeley, 1930), p. 57; Robert M. Robinson, "A History of the Teamsters in the San Francisco Bay Area, 1850–1950" (unpublished Ph.D. dissertation, University of California, Berkeley, 1951), p. 130.

[24] *Thirteenth Biennial Report, 1907–1908,* California Bureau of Labor Statistics, pp. 169–171; Ryan, *op. cit.,* p. 121; *Labor Clarion,* Aug.–Oct. *passim,* 1906; Feb. 15, 1907.

[25] *Thirteenth Biennial Report, 1907–1908,* California Bureau of Labor Statistics, p. 170; *Labor Clarion,* Feb. 16, 1906.

[26] *Thirteenth Biennial Report, 1907–1908,* California Bureau of Labor Statistics, p. 170; *Labor Clarion,* Feb. 16, 1906.

[27] Lillian R. Matthews, *Women in Trade Unions in San Francisco* (Berkeley: University of California Press, 1913), pp. 58, 85; *Labor Clarion,* Dec. 14, 1906; June 28, Aug. 23, 1907.

[28] Paul Chatom, "Industrial Relations in the Brewery, Metal, and Teaming Trades of San Francisco" (unpublished M.S. thesis, University of California, Berkeley, 1915), pp. 103, 105; *Thirteenth Biennial Report, 1907–1908,* California Bureau of Labor Statistics, p. 170.

[29] *American Industries,* Oct. 15, 1906.

[30] *Coast Seamen's Journal,* Sept. 19, 1906.

[31] *Ibid.,* Sept. 26, 1906.

[32] *Labor Clarion,* Oct. 19, 1906.

[33] Austin Lewis, "The Day After," *International Socialist Review* (Dec., 1911), 358.

[34] Walton Bean, *Boss Ruef's San Francisco* (Berkeley and Los Angeles: University of California Press, 1952), pp. 52, 76, 170.

[35] *Ibid.*, p. 78.

[36] *Bulletin,* May 16, 1907.

[37] Bean, *op. cit.*, pp. 157, 193, 196, 211; Rowell, *op. cit.*, p. 163.

[38] Bean, *op. cit.*, pp. 88–90.

[39] *Ibid.*, pp. 103, 104.

[40] *Ibid.*, pp. 113–117, 136; Rowell, *op. cit.*, p. 167; *Labor Clarion,* June 1, 1906.

[41] Bean, *op. cit.*, pp. 197, 211–218, 232.

[42] *Twelfth Biennial Report, 1905–1906,* California Bureau of Labor Statistics, p. 220; Ryan, *op. cit.*, p. 122; *Coast Seamen's Journal,* Jan. 16, 1907; interview with Edwin McKenzie.

[43] Matthews, *op. cit.*, p. 16; *Labor Clarion,* April 5, May 3, 1907.

[44] Chatom, *op. cit.*, p. 31; *Labor Clarion,* April 26, May 3, 1907; Sept. 4, 1908; March 1, 1912; *Coast Seamen's Journal,* May 8, 15, 1907; *Argonaut,* June 1, 1907; *Iron Trades Review,* Dec. 16, 1909.

[45] *Labor Clarion,* April 5, 12, May 3, 1907; *Examiner,* May 3, 1907.

[46] Beatrice V. Taylor, *op. cit.*, pp. 58–59; *Labor Clarion,* April 26, May 3, 1907; *Chronicle,* May 6, 1907; Fremont Older, *My Own Story* (San Francisco: Call Publishing Co., 1919), p. 89; Cronin, *op. cit.*, p. 152.

[47] *Chronicle,* May 7, 1907; *Labor Clarion,* May 10, 1907.

[48] Cronin, *op. cit.*, p. 152; Bean, *op. cit.*, pp. 218, 241.

[49] Beatrice V. Taylor, *op. cit.*, p. 65; *Examiner,* May 5, 1907; interview with John Forbes.

[50] *Chronicle,* May 7, 8, 1907.

[51] *Labor Clarion,* May 10, 1907; *Coast Seamen's Journal,* May 15, 1907.

[52] *Coast Seamen's Journal,* July 3, 1907.

[53] *Ibid.*, May 15, July 3, 1907.

[54] *Ibid.*, May 15, 1907.

[55] *Argonaut,* June 29, July 13, 20, 1907.

[56] *Proceedings of the Twelfth Annual Convention* (1907), National Association of Manufacturers, p. 41; *American Industries,* June 1, 1907; *Square Deal,* June, 1907; *Open Shop,* July, 1907; Clarence E. Bonnett, *Employers' Associations in the United States* (New York: Macmillan, 1922), p. 369.

[57] *Argonaut,* June 1, 22, 1907.

[58] *Coast Seamen's Journal,* May 15, 1907; *Labor Clarion,* Sept. 4, 1908; *Iron Trades Review,* Dec. 16, 1909; copy of 1907 agreement in files of Molders' Union Local 164, San Francisco.

[59] *Labor Clarion,* June 7, 1907; *Coast Seamen's Journal,* June 12, 1907; interview with Al Wynn.

[60] Matthews, *op. cit.*, p. 16; Robinson, *op. cit.*, p. 138.

[61] *Argonaut,* June 8, 1907; *Labor Clarion,* Nov. 1, 1907; March 6, 1908.

[62] *Labor Clarion,* May 10, June 14, 1907; *Argonaut,* June 8, 1907; Bean, *op. cit.*, p. 233.

[63] *Labor Clarion,* July 19, Aug. 9, 1907; *Examiner,* July 24, 1907.

[64] Beatrice V. Taylor, *op. cit.*, p. 60; *Examiner,* Aug. 3, 1907; *Labor Clarion,* Oct. 11, 25, Dec. 13, 1907.

[65] Vidkun Ulriksson, *The Telegraphers, Their Craft and Their Unions* (Washington: Public Affairs Press, 1953), p. 75; "The World of Labor," *International Socialist Review* (Aug., 1907), 117–118; *Examiner,* July 18, 20, 1907; *Final Report and Testimony of United States Commission on Industrial Relations* (Washington: 1916), X, 9389.

[66] *Examiner,* July 20, Aug. 9, 10, 1907; *Labor Clarion,* Aug. 23, 1907.

[67] Beatrice V. Taylor, *op. cit.,* p. 61; interview with Judge Marcus C. Sloss; *Chronicle,* May 18, 1907; *Examiner,* July 21, Sept. 3, 6, 1907; Gertrude Atherton, "San Francisco and Her Foes," *Harper's Weekly,* 51 (Nov. 2, 1907), 1590–1591; Bean, *op. cit.,* p. 243.

[68] *Examiner,* Aug. 25, 1907.

[69] *Labor Clarion,* June 14, 1907; Beatrice V. Taylor, *op. cit.,* p. 69.

[70] Bean, *op. cit.,* pp. 220, 226, 262, 266.

[71] *Ibid.,* pp. 236, 266.

[72] *Ibid.,* p. 266; Rowell, *op. cit.,* p. 147.

[73] Robinson, *op. cit.,* p. 103; Bean, *op. cit.,* p. 264; *Examiner,* Aug. 21, 23, 1907.

[74] *Argonaut,* July 6, 1907; *Chronicle,* Aug. 7, 10, 1907; Beatrice V. Taylor, *op. cit.,* p. 67; Cronin, *op. cit.,* p. 156.

[75] Beatrice V. Taylor, *op. cit.,* pp. 67, 68; *Examiner,* Sept. 3, 6, 1907; *Labor Clarion,* Sept. 13, 1907.

[76] *Chronicle,* Sept. 15, Oct. 10, 1907; *Argonaut,* Sept. 21, 1907; *Examiner,* Oct. 10, 1907; *Labor Clarion,* Oct. 25, 1907.

[77] *Chronicle,* Jan. 7, 1908; *Leader,* Jan. 11, 1908; *The World* (Oakland Socialist weekly), Aug. 7, 1909; Robinson, *op. cit.,* p. 189.

[78] *Chronicle,* May 7, 1907.

[79] Cronin, *op. cit.,* p. 174.

[80] *Ibid.,* pp. 191–200; Rowell, *op. cit.,* pp. 147, 197, 200.

Notes to Chapter VI | Depression and Revival
1908–1910
(Pages 200–235)

[1] *Coast Seamen's Journal,* June 12, 1907.

[2] Alvin H. Hansen, *Business Cycles and National Income* (New York: Norton, 1951), p. 11.

[3] *Argonaut,* Nov. 9, 1907; July 3, 1909; *Labor Clarion,* Nov. 15, Dec. 6, 1907; Jan. 17, March 13, 1908; Feb. 26, March 5, 1909; *The World,* Jan., 1908; *Organized Labor,* Jan. 16, 23, March 13, May 8, 1909.

[4] *Argonaut,* Oct. 17, 1908.

[5] Citizens' Alliance Annual Report for 1908, as reprinted in *Labor Clarion,* Feb. 26, 1909; *Daily Journal of Commerce,* Jan. 13, 1909.

[6] *Labor Clarion,* Sept. 4, 25, Oct. 2, 16, 1908; *Thirteenth Biennial Report, 1907–1908,* California Bureau of Labor Statistics (Sacramento: 1908), p. 171.

[7] David F. Selvin, "History of the San Francisco Typographical Union" (unpublished M.A. thesis, University of California, Berkeley, 1935), p. 69; *Labor Clarion,* May 1, 22, 1908; April 29, 1910.

[8] *Labor Clarion,* July 31, Aug. 7, 1908; Feb. 5, May 17, 1909; Howard Thor, "A History of the Marine Engineers' Beneficial Association" (unpublished M.A. thesis, University of California, Berkeley, 1954), p. 67; Charles J. Stowell, *Studies in Trade Unionism in the Custom Tailoring Trade* (Bloomington, Ill.: Journeymen Tailors' Union of America, 1913), p. 115.

[9] *Labor Clarion,* Feb. 14, April 3, June 12, Aug. 28, Sept. 25, Dec. 4, 18, 1908; July 23, 1909; Beatrice V. Taylor, "Labor Relations on the Street Railways of San Francisco" (unpublished M.A. thesis, University of California, Berkeley, 1928), p. 72; Emerson P. Schmidt, *Industrial Relations in Urban Transportation* (Minneapolis: University of Minnesota Press, 1937), p. 182.

[10] *Labor Clarion,* May 1, June 19, Aug. 14, 1908; March 5, April 9, May 7, June 11, 19, Sept. 10, Nov. 13, Dec. 10, 1909; *Organized Labor,* June 19, 1909.

[11] *Labor Clarion,* Sept. 4, 1908; June 11, 19, July 9, 23, 1909; *Examiner,* June 2, 1909; *Organized Labor,* June 19, 1909.

[12] *The World,* April 9, 1910; *Organized Labor,* April 16, 1910; *Daily News,* Nov. 9, 26, 1910; *Labor Clarion,* Dec. 2, 1910.

[13] *Coast Seamen's Journal,* July 24, 1907; *Labor Clarion,* July 3, 1908; *Organized Labor,* Jan. 30, Feb. 6, 1909; Jan. 28, 1911.

[14] *Organized Labor,* Jan. 22, Feb. 5, 1910.

[15] *Ibid.,* Jan. 28, 1911; interview with James Rickets.

[16] *Organized Labor,* Jan. 23, 1909.

[17] *Argonaut,* July 25, 1908; *Organized Labor,* Jan. 23, 30, March 30, 1909.

[18] *Organized Labor,* Feb. 5, 1910.

[19] *Ibid.,* Jan. 22, Feb. 5, 1910.

[20] *Ibid.,* April 24, 1909; Jan 28, 1911; interview with Andrew J. Gallagher. For account of early career of Anton Johannsen, cf. Hutchins Hapgood, *The Spirit of Labor* (New York: Duffield, 1907).

[21] *Organized Labor,* Jan. 21, 28, 1911.

[22] *Ibid.,* Jan. 23, 1909; Jan. 28, 1911; Jan. 25, 1913; *Daily Journal of Commerce,* April 21, 1910; *Fourteenth Biennial Report, 1909–1910,* California Bureau of Labor Statistics (Sacramento: 1910), pp. 302–317.

[23] *Labor Clarion,* Oct. 11, 1907; *Chronicle,* Jan. 20, 1915; interview with Andrew J. Gallagher.

[24] Interview with Andrew J. Gallagher.

[25] Taylor, *op. cit.,* p. 72; *Labor Clarion,* May 29, July 10, Sept. 25, 1908; March 12, April 23, 1909.

[26] *Labor Clarion,* May 22, Nov. 6, 27, 1908; Feb. 7, Nov. 4, Dec. 23, 1910; *Organized Labor,* Dec. 18, 1909; interview with Andrew J. Gallagher; Robert M. Robinson, "A History of the Teamsters in the San Francisco Bay Area, 1850–1950" (unpublished Ph.D. dissertation, University of California, Berkeley, 1951), p. 146; Synopsis of Minutes, Alameda County Central Labor Council, Oct. 18, 1909; Feb. 14, 1910 (as published in *Labor Clarion*).

[27] *Labor Clarion,* June 12, Dec. 18, 1908; Feb. 15, 1909; Feb. 25, Aug. 19, 1910; *Daily News,* Dec. 16, 30, 1910; *Fourteenth Biennial Report, 1909–1910,* California Bureau of Labor Statistics, p. 302; *Fifteenth Biennial Report, 1911–1912,* California Bureau of Labor Statistics (Sacramento: 1912), p. 591.

[28] *Labor Clarion,* Feb. 12, March 12, 1909; *Organized Labor,* June 26, 1909; *Daily News,* Dec. 30, 1910; Charles H. Green, *The Headwear Workers* (New York: United Hatters, Cap, and Millinery Workers International Union, 1944), pp. 121–122; Lillian R. Matthews, *Women in Trade Unions in San Francisco* (Berkeley: University of California Press, 1913), p. 60.

[29] *Labor Clarion,* March 5, April 9, 26, 1909; March 25, April 15, 22, 1910; Synopsis of Minutes, Alameda County Central Labor Council, Oct. 18, 1909 (as published in *Labor Clarion*); Robinson, *op. cit.,* p. 161; Paul Chatom, "Industrial Relations in the Brewery, Metal, and Teaming Trades

of San Francisco" (unpublished M.S. thesis, University of California, Berkeley, 1915), p. 95.

[30] *Labor Clarion,* March 25, 1910.

[31] *Ibid.,* Feb. 25, 1910; *Daily News,* Nov. 30, 1910.

[32] Ira B. Cross, *A History of the Labor Movement in California* (Berkeley: University of California Press, 1935), p. 338; *Labor Clarion,* April 24, 1908.

[33] Matthews, *op. cit.,* pp. 34–35; Cross, *op. cit.,* p. 265; *Daily News,* Dec. 19, 1910.

[34] *Labor Clarion,* June 19, July 10, 31, 1908.

[35] *CMTA Newsletter,* as published in *Labor Clarion,* Oct. 9, 1908.

[36] *Labor Clarion,* May 14, 1909; *Iron Trades Review,* Dec. 16, 1909.

[37] *Daily Journal of Commerce,* Nov. 3, 1908.

[38] *Ibid.,* Dec. 28, 1909.

[39] *Labor Clarion,* Jan. 15, Feb. 12, April 16, June 25, 1909; April 15, June 3, July 1, 1910; *Daily Journal of Commerce,* Dec. 28, 1909; *Daily News,* Dec. 10, 1910.

[40] Chatom, *op. cit.,* p. 53.

[41] *Bulletin,* July 7, 1909.

[42] *American Industries,* July, 1909; *Proceedings of the Fifteenth Annual Convention* (1910), National Association of Manufacturers, p. 289.

[43] *Labor Clarion,* Aug. 21, 1908; Feb. 26, April 6, 1909; *American Industries,* Sept., Oct., 1910; *Daily News,* Nov. 16, 1910.

[44] *Chronicle,* Nov., 1909, *passim; Proceedings of the Fourteenth Annual Convention* (1909), National Association of Manufacturers, pp. 201–202.

[45] *Chronicle,* Nov. 7, 1909.

[46] *Labor Clarion,* Dec. 10, 1909.

[47] Walton Bean, *Boss Ruef's San Francisco* (Berkeley and Los Angeles: University of California Press, 1952), p. 252.

[48] *Ibid.,* pp. 254–255, 268, 274, 285, 288.

[49] *Ibid.,* pp. 293, 298.

[50] Edward J. Rowell, "The Union Labor Party of San Francisco, 1901–1911" (unpublished Ph.D. dissertation, University of California, Berkeley, 1938), p. 216.

[51] *Ibid.,* p. 206; *The World,* Aug. 7, Dec. 11, 1909.

[52] *Organized Labor,* June 19, 26, July 3, 1909; *Labor Clarion,* Sept. 10, 1909.

[53] *Organized Labor,* Nov. 6, 1909; Franklin Hichborn, *"The System,"* as *Uncovered by the San Francisco Graft Prosecution* (San Francisco: James H. Barry Co., 1915), p. 417; Rowell, *op. cit.,* pp. 214–216.

[54] *Daily Journal of Commerce,* Nov. 4, 1909; Jan. 8, 1910; Rowell, *op. cit.,* pp. 206, 214, 226.

[55] *Organized Labor,* June 5, 1909; Bean, *op. cit.,* pp. 297, 300–303, 305, 310.

[56] Frederick L. Ryan, *Industrial Relations in the San Francisco Building Trades* (Norman: University of Oklahoma Press, 1936), p. 49; *Organized Labor,* Jan. 22, 1910.

[57] Ryan, *op. cit.*, p. 122; Rowell, *op. cit.*, p. 230.

[58] *Labor Clarion*, May 20, July 15, 1910; *Daily News*, Nov. 18, 1910.

[59] *Daily News*, Sept. 13, 15, 19, Oct. 8, 19, 1910; *Organized Labor*, Oct. 22, 1910; *Final Report and Testimony of United States Commission on Industrial Relations* (Washington: 1916), VI, 5371.

[60] Synopsis of Minutes, Alameda County Central Labor Council, March 7, 1910 (as published in *Labor Clarion*); *Labor Clarion*, April 8, Dec. 9, 1910; *Argonaut*, Nov. 19, 1910; *Daily News*, Nov. 29, 30, Dec. 2, 8, 1910; Chatom, *op. cit.*, pp. 96, 99–100; Cross, *op. cit.*, pp. 324, 325.

[61] Ryan, *op. cit.*, pp. 122, 123; Rowell, *op. cit.*, p. 228; *Daily Journal of Commerce*, July 28, 1910.

[62] *Argonaut*, Aug. 6, 1910.

[63] Rowell, *op. cit.*, p. 229; Ryan, *op. cit.*, p. 123; *Daily Journal of Commerce*, Aug. 4, 1910; *Organized Labor*, Aug. 13, 1910; *Argonaut*, Aug. 13, 1910; *Shop Review*, Oct., 1910.

[64] *Labor Clarion*, Jan. 21, 1910; *Shop Review*, March, 1910; *American Industries*, April–June, 1910.

[65] *Transactions of the Commonwealth Club of California*, I (Nov., 1903), 44–45.

[66] *Ibid.*, V (April, 1910), 75.

[67] *Ibid.*, p. 163.

[68] *Ibid.*, p. 19.

[69] *Ibid.*, p. 121; *Labor Clarion*, March 25, 1910.

[70] Andrew J. Gallagher, "Something Doing in Los Angeles," *International Socialist Review* (Sept., 1910), 167; Grace H. Stimson, *Rise of the Labor Movement in Los Angeles* (Berkeley and Los Angeles: University of California Press, 1955), pp. 334, 340.

[71] *Organized Labor*, June 18, 1910; Stimson, *op. cit.*, pp. 340–341.

[72] *Labor Clarion*, May 27, 1910.

[73] *Ibid.*, June 17, 1910; *Organized Labor*, June 18, 1910; interview with Andrew J. Gallagher; *Final Report and Testimony of United States Commission on Industrial Relations*, V, 4336–4342, 4520–4523.

[74] Stimson, *op. cit.*, pp. 344, 345; interview with Andrew J. Gallagher.

[75] *Oakland Enquirer*, Aug. 22, 1910; interview with Andrew J. Gallagher.

[76] Stimson, *op. cit.*, p. 368.

[77] *Labor Clarion*, Aug. 12, Sept. 30, 1910; *Daily News*, Sept. 22, 27, 1910.

[78] *Daily News*, Oct. 12, Nov. 11, 1910; *Labor Clarion*, Nov. 18, 1910; interview with Andrew J. Gallagher.

[79] *Daily News*, Dec. 20, 1910; *Chronicle*, Jan. 11, 1911.

[80] *Final Report and Testimony of United States Commission on Industrial Relations*, V, 4520–4524; Stimson, *op. cit.*, pp. 359, 365.

[81] *Organized Labor*, July 16, 1910.

[82] Cf. William J. Burns, *The Masked War* (New York: George H. Doran Co., 1913); Richard C. Searing, "The McNamara Case: Its Causes and Results" (unpublished M.A. thesis, University of California, Berkeley, 1952); Stimson, *op. cit.*, pp. 378–397.

[83] Burns, *op. cit.*, p. 136; Stimson, *op. cit.*, p. 388; *Daily News,* March 10, 1913; Hapgood, *op. cit.*, pp. 375–380.

[84] Stimson, *op. cit.*, p. 401.

[85] Clarence Darrow, *The Story of My Life* (New York: Scribner, 1932), pp. 179–181.

[86] John A. Fitch, "The Dynamite Case," *Survey,* XXIX (Feb. 1, 1913), 607–608.

[87] *Ibid.; Daily News,* March 10, 1913; *Labor Clarion,* July 10, 1914; *Final Report and Testimony of United States Commission on Industrial Relations,* XI, 10672.

[88] Interview with Edwin V. McKenzie; *Labor Clarion,* Oct. 29, 1915.

[89] *Labor Clarion,* Sept. 15, 1911.

[90] *Daily News,* Sept. 20, Nov. 6, 1911; July 17, 1912; *Labor Clarion,* Nov. 10, 1911; Chatom, *op. cit.*, pp. 35–36.

[91] Stimson, *op. cit.*, pp. 421, 422–423.

[92] *California Labor's Greatest Victory; Final Report of the General Campaign Strike Committee for the Unionizing of Los Angeles* (San Francisco: 1912).

Notes to Chapter VII | Years of Stability
1911–1915

(Pages 236–298)

[1] *Argonaut*, Feb. 4, 1911; *Daily News*, April 6, 1912.

[2] *Daily News*, Nov. 18, 1910; *Shop Review*, Dec., 1910; *Labor Clarion*, April 7, 1911.

[3] *Proceedings of the Eighteenth Annual Convention* (1913), National Association of Manufacturers, pp. 45–49; Frederick L. Ryan, *Industrial Relations in the San Francisco Building Trades* (Norman: University of Oklahoma Press, 1936), p. 213.

[4] *Proceedings of the Eighteenth Annual Convention* (1913), National Association of Manufacturers, pp. 45–49; *Organized Labor*, June 28, 1913; Jan. 17, 1914.

[5] *Proceedings of the Eighteenth Annual Convention* (1913), National Association of Manufacturers, pp. 39–40; *Final Report and Testimony of United States Commission on Industrial Relations* (Washington: 1916), VI, 5247–5249.

[6] *Argonaut*, Jan. 28, 1911; *Shop Review*, Feb., 1911.

[7] *Argonaut*, Jan. 28, 1911.

[8] *Daily News*, April 14, 1911.

[9] *Ibid.*, Jan. 21, 1911.

[10] *Final Report and Testimony of United States Commission on Industrial Relations*, VI, 4326–4328; *Daily News*, April 12, 13, May 24, July 28, 1911; *Daily Journal of Commerce*, Aug. 10, 1911; *American Industries*, Dec., 1915.

[11] *Final Report and Testimony of United States Commission on Industrial Relations*, VI, 5431.

[12] George E. Mowry, *The California Progressives* (Berkeley and Los Angeles: University of California Press, 1951), p. 92.

[13] *Ibid.*, pp. 92–93, 143.

[14] Earl C. Crockett, "The History of California Labor Legislation, 1910–1930" (unpublished Ph.D. dissertation, University of California, Berkeley, 1931), pp. 285–290.

[15] *Ibid.; Labor Clarion,* March 3, 17, 1911.

[16] George W. Bemis, "Sectionalism and Representation in the California State Legislature, 1911–1931" (unpublished Ph.D. dissertation, University of California, Berkeley, 1935), p. 92; Mowry, *op. cit.,* pp. 143, 146; *Labor Clarion,* Feb. 17, April 7, 1911.

[17] Crockett, *op. cit.,* pp. 280, 291; Mowry, *op. cit.,* p. 222; *Labor Clarion,* Jan. 3, 24, May 16, 1913; Nov. 6, 1914; Jan. 22, May 14, 1915; *The World,* Nov. 13, 20, 1914; *Daily News,* Oct. 21, 1915.

[18] *Organized Labor,* Aug. 26, 1911; *Labor Clarion,* Sept. 8, 1911; *Daily News,* Sept. 20, 25, 1911; Edward J. Rowell, "The Union Labor Party of San Francisco, 1901–1911" (unpublished Ph.D. dissertation, University of California, Berkeley, 1938), p. 237.

[19] Rowell, *op. cit.,* pp. 233, 238, 241. The quotation appears on page 238.

[20] *Ibid.,* pp. 241–242; *Organized Labor,* Nov. 11, 1911; *Daily News,* Nov. 18, 1911; *Daily Journal of Commerce,* Jan. 6, 1914; *Argonaut,* Jan. 2, 1915.

[21] Crockett, *op. cit.,* p. 300; *Labor Clarion,* Sept. 1, 1911; Nov. 8, 1912.

[22] *Daily News,* July 22, 1911; *Labor Clarion,* March 22, 1912.

[23] *Labor Clarion,* Feb. 16, 23, March 1, 8, 1912; *Daily News,* April 6, 1912; postcard in collection of Archie Green, San Francisco.

[24] Eleanor A. Todd, "History of the Milk Wagon Drivers' Union of San Francisco County, 1900–1933" (unpublished M.A. thesis, University of California, Berkeley, 1936), pp. 47, 50; Charles C. Brisco, "Industrial Relations in the East Bay Fluid Milk Distribution Industry" (unpublished M.B.A. thesis, University of California, Berkeley, 1953), p. 39; Robert M. Robinson, "A History of the Teamsters in the San Francisco Bay Area, 1850–1950" (unpublished Ph.D. dissertation, University of California, Berkeley, 1951), p. 150; *Labor Clarion,* Oct. 5, 1906; *Daily News,* April 19, 1911.

[25] Robinson, *op. cit.,* p. 487; Todd, *op. cit.,* p. 52; Brisco, *op. cit.,* p. 39; *Daily News,* Jan. 31, Feb. 2, 3, April 19, 1911; *The World,* Feb. 4, 11, 1911; *Labor Clarion,* June 27, 1913.

[26] *Final Report and Testimony of United States Commission on Industrial Relations,* VI, 5247–5250, 5396–5399.

[27] *The World,* March 25, 1911.

[28] *Final Report and Testimony of United States Commission on Industrial Relations,* VI, 5247–5250, 5398; *Chronicle,* Aug. 8, 1911; *The World,* Aug. 12, 1911; *Daily News,* Sept. 23, 1911; *Organized Labor,* Jan. 27, 1912.

[29] *Final Report and Testimony of United States Commission on Industrial Relations,* VI, 5248–5249; *Organized Labor,* March 18, 1911; Feb. 8, 1913; Feb. 7, 1914; March 27, 1915; *The World,* Oct. 14, 21, 1911.

[30] *Organized Labor,* March 27, 1915.

[31] *Daily News,* Oct. 21, 1910; May 19, 1911; *The World,* May 13, 1911; *Seventeenth Biennial Report, 1915–1916,* California Bureau of Labor Statistics (Sacramento: 1916), p. 260.

[32] *Daily News,* May 19, 25, 1911; April 4, 1913.

[33] *The World,* May 13, 1911; *Daily News,* May 19, 25, July 4, 1911.

[34] Minutes of the Executive Council of the California State Federation of Labor, March 24, 1907 (as published in *Labor Clarion,* April 5, 1907).

[35] *Labor Clarion,* Jan. 17, 1908.

[36] *Ibid.*

[37] *Contra Costa Gazette,* June 17, July 1, 15, 22, 1911; *Labor Clarion,* Aug. 4, 1911; *Daily News,* Aug. 7, 1911; *Chronicle,* Aug. 7, 8, 1911.

[38] *Final Report and Testimony of United States Commission on Industrial Relations,* XI, 9775, 9863; *The World,* June 24, 1911.

[39] *Labor Clarion,* Aug. 4, 1911.

[40] *Shop Review,* Aug., 1909; *Final Report and Testimony of United States Commission on Industrial Relations,* XI, 9863.

[41] *Daily News,* Sept. 30, 1911; *Final Report and Testimony of United States Commission on Industrial Relations,* XI, 10054–10058.

[42] *The World,* Oct. 7, 14, 21, Nov. 11, 1911; Feb. 10, 1912; *Daily News,* Oct. 23, 1911; *Labor Clarion,* Feb. 8, 1912; *Final Report and Testimony of United States Commission on Industrial Relations,* XI, 9901.

[43] *Machinists' Monthly Journal,* Nov., 1915.

[44] Ira B. Cross, *Collective Bargaining and Trade Agreements in the Brewery, Metal, Teaming, and Building Trades of San Francisco, California* (Berkeley: University of California Press, 1918), pp. 240–241; *Daily News,* Sept. 30, 1915.

[45] Paul Chatom, "Industrial Relations in the Brewery, Metal, and Teaming Trades of San Francisco" (unpublished M.S. thesis, University of California, Berkeley, 1915), p. 90.

[46] *Daily News,* June 15, 1911.

[47] Chatom, *op. cit.,* p. 90; Robinson, *op. cit.,* p. 194; *Daily Journal of Commerce,* July 3, 1911.

[48] *Daily News,* April 25, June 1, 1911; May 13, Oct. 10, 1912; Feb. 26, 1913; *Labor Clarion,* April 28, Aug. 25, Nov. 24, 1911; Sept. 27, Nov. 18, 1912; April 18, Sept. 5, Nov. 17, 1913; May 8, Dec. 4, 11, 1914; *Organized Labor,* July 15, 1911; Lillian R. Matthews, *Women in Trade Unions in San Francisco* (Berkeley: University of California Press, 1913), p. 73. Cf. *Sixteenth Biennial Report, 1913–1914,* California Bureau of Labor Statistics (Sacramento: 1914); *Seventeenth Biennial Report, 1915–1916,* California Bureau of Labor Statistics.

[49] *Labor Clarion,* March 8, July 5, 19, Oct. 11, 18, 1912.

[50] *Daily News,* Feb. 17, 1913; Feb. 24, 26, March 18, 1914; *Labor Clarion,* Nov. 21, Dec. 5, 1913; May 29, July 24, 1914; Feb. 26, May 14, Aug. 6, 1915.

[51] Matthews, *op. cit.,* p. 65; *Daily News,* Oct. 3, 1911; May 1, July 17, 24, Nov. 14, 1912.

[52] *Argonaut,* Nov. 30, 1912.

[53] *Star,* Dec. 5, 1912.

[54] *Daily News,* Nov. 22, Dec. 7, 9, 1912; Jan. 20, 23, 1913; *Labor Clarion,* Feb. 6, July 7, 1914; March 26, April 30, 1915.

[55] *Labor Clarion,* April 21, May 12, June 23, Nov. 3, 1911; July 26, 1912; March 14, 1913.

[56] *Daily News,* Aug. 21, Sept. 5, 23, Oct. 8, 16, Nov. 6, 1913; *Labor Clarion,* Sept. 12, 26, 1913.

[57] *Daily News,* Oct. 31, 1913.

[58] *Labor Clarion,* March 20, 1914.

[59] Francis C. Head, "Trade Unionism in the Clothing Industries of San Francisco" (unpublished M.A. thesis, University of California, Berkeley, 1935), p. 69; *Daily News,* Oct. 12, 1915.

[60] *Daily News,* March 7, 1912; *Labor Clarion,* Jan. 3, 1913; Beatrice V. Taylor, "Labor Relations on the Street Railways of San Francisco" (unpublished M.A. thesis, University of California, Berkeley, 1928), p. 74.

[61] *Daily Journal of Commerce,* May 23, 1914; *Argonaut,* May 30, 1914.

[62] *Daily News,* Oct. 20, 1913.

[63] *Argonaut,* Dec. 20, 1913; *Organized Labor,* Jan. 31, 1914; *Chronicle,* April 5, 1915; *Daily News,* May 1, 12, 1915.

[64] *Motorman and Conductor,* Dec., 1915, p. 35; *Daily Journal of Commerce,* Dec. 5, 1915.

[65] *Labor Clarion,* Dec. 9, 1910; April 21, 1911; Nov. 12, 1915.

[66] *Oakland Enquirer,* Sept. 3, 1910; *Daily News,* June 29, 1912; Oct. 9, 1913.

[67] *Labor Clarion,* Dec. 27, 1912; *Daily News,* Jan. 10, Feb. 13, March 13, April 24, July 17, 1913; June 11, July 30, 1914; *Seventeenth Biennial Report, 1915–1916,* California Bureau of Labor Statistics, p. 155.

[68] *Daily News,* Dec. 6, 1910; May 29, Dec. 13, 1913; *Organized Labor,* Jan. 28, 1911; Jan. 27, 1912; Feb. 7, 1914; *The World,* Aug. 17, 1912.

[69] *The World,* April 8, July 29, Aug. 12, 1911; *Daily News,* Aug. 2, 1912; *Organized Labor,* Feb. 8, 1913; Edgar J. Hinkel, ed., *Oakland, 1852–1938* (Oakland Public Library, 1939), pp. 762, 763.

[70] *Seventeenth Biennial Report, 1915–1916,* California Bureau of Labor Statistics, p. 165.

[71] *Shop Review,* Oct., 1912; *Final Report and Testimony of United States Commission on Industrial Relations,* VI, 5247, 5381–5383.

[72] *Final Report and Testimony of United States Commission on Industrial Relations,* VI, 5383.

[73] *Labor Clarion,* Oct. 31, 1913; April 9, 1915; *Daily News,* April 14, 1915.

[74] *Daily News,* Jan. 6, Feb. 13, April 5, 1911; April 1, 4, May 28, 1913; *Organized Labor,* Jan. 21, 1911; Feb. 7, 1914; March 27, 1915; *Contra Costa Gazette,* April 29, 1911; *Labor Clarion,* April 11, July 18, Aug. 22, 1913; April 9, 1915; *Final Report and Testimony of United States Commission on Industrial Relations,* VI, 5385.

[75] *The World,* Nov. 5, 1910; March 9, 16, July 13, Aug. 10, 1912; *Labor Clarion,* Jan. 19, May 31, 1912; *Organized Labor,* Feb. 8, 1913.

[76] *Labor Clarion,* March 22, April 19, May 3, 31, 1912.

[77] Hyman Weintraub, "The I.W.W. in California, 1905–1931" (unpub-

lished M.A. thesis, University of California, Los Angeles, 1947), pp. 21, 33, 34; *The World,* July 1, 29, Oct. 7, 1911; Jan. 13, 27, 1912; Austin Lewis, "The Drift in California," *International Socialist Review* (Nov., 1911), 273.

[78] F. Monaco, "San Francisco Shoe Workers' Strike," *International Socialist Review* (May, 1913), 818–819; *Daily News,* Feb. 8, 12, 1913; interview with Warren Billings.

[79] Interview with Warren Billings.

[80] *Daily News,* Feb. 8, 12, 1913; letter from Tom Mooney published in *International Socialist Review* (May, 1910), 1052–1053.

[81] *Tom Mooney Betrayed by Labor Leaders* (San Francisco: Tom Mooney Molders' Defense Committee, 1931), p. 24.

[82] Cf. *Revolt,* May, 1911–May, 1912, *passim.*

[83] William Z. Foster, "The Molders' Convention," *International Socialist Review* (Dec., 1912), 486–487.

[84] *Labor Clarion,* March 7, April 25, May 16, 1913; *Daily News,* March 11, Sept. 1, 1913; interview with Warren Billings.

[85] Matthew Josephson, *Union House, Union Bar* (New York: Random House, 1956), pp. 79–80, 112; *Labor Clarion,* April 12, Oct. 11, Nov. 22, 1912; Sept. 13, 1913.

[86] *Daily News,* May 15, 17, 27, June 17, 1912; *Labor Clarion,* June 21, 1912.

[87] *Daily News,* Oct. 11, 1912.

[88] Robert C. Francis, "A History of Labor on the San Francisco Waterfront" (unpublished Ph.D. dissertation, University of California, Berkeley, 1934), pp. 146, 147, 148; *Labor Clarion,* Jan. 26, May 24, 1912; *Daily News,* March 14, Dec. 8, 1914.

[89] Cf. Hyman Weintraub, "Andrew Furuseth—Abraham Lincoln of the Sea" (unpublished manuscript, *ca.* 1955–1957).

[90] Francis, *op. cit.,* pp. 146–147; *Organized Labor,* Feb. 10, 1912; *Labor Clarion,* July 16, 1915; *Daily News,* Dec. 19, 1915.

[91] *Daily News,* July 6, 1914.

[92] *Labor Clarion,* March 19, 1915; *Daily News,* March 22, 1915.

[93] *Daily News,* Dec. 7, 1911; *Labor Clarion,* Dec. 6, 1912; Dec. 24, 1915; *Machinists' Monthly Journal,* Nov., 1914.

[94] *Organized Labor,* Sept. 21, 1912; Phillips Russell, "The Class Struggle on the Pacific Coast," *International Socialist Review* (Sept., 1912), 236–238.

[95] *Daily News,* Jan. 21, 1914.

[96] Ryan, *op. cit.,* p. 94; *Organized Labor,* Feb. 7, 1914; March 6, 1915; *The World,* Sept. 18, 1915.

[97] *Labor Clarion,* Sept. 3, Oct. 1, Dec. 24, 1909; Nov. 3, 1911; March 8, 1912; March 3, 1913; *Final Report and Testimony of United States Commission on Industrial Relations,* V, 4972–4976.

[98] *Final Report and Testimony of United States Commission on Industrial Relations,* V, 4913–4917, 4972–4976.

[99] *Labor Clarion,* Oct. 3, 1913.

[100] Stuart M. Jamieson, "Labor Unionism in American Agriculture" (un-

published Ph.D. dissertation, University of California, Berkeley, 1943), p. 151.

[101] *Seventeenth Biennial Report, 1915–1916,* California Bureau of Labor Statistics, p. 189; *Daily News,* July 9, 10, 1914.

[102] *Labor Clarion,* Nov. 14, 1913.

[103] *Daily News,* May 13, 1912.

[104] *Labor Clarion,* May 31, Aug. 9, 1912; *Daily News,* June 1, Aug. 29, 1912.

[105] *Labor Clarion,* March 28, April 11, May 22, June 6, Dec. 5, 1913.

[106] *Final Report and Testimony of United States Commission on Industrial Relations,* VI, 5283–5288; *Daily News,* June 25, 1913.

[107] Interview with Luis Ireland; *Labor Clarion,* July 18, Sept. 5, 1913; June 26, July 3, Nov. 13, 1914; *Daily News,* Dec. 5, 1914; *Organized Felony* (San Francisco: Franklin Printing Trades Association, 1914), pp. 4–5; *Final Report and Testimony of United States Commission on Industrial Relations,* V, 4235.

[108] *Final Report and Testimony of United States Commission on Industrial Relations,* VI, 5283–5286; "Renewing the Open Shop Fight," *Sunset,* 33 (Oct., 1914), 652.

[109] Interview with Luis Ireland; *Daily News,* Nov. 8, Dec. 11, 1914; July 4, 1915; *Labor Clarion,* June 11, Aug. 6, 1915.

[110] Charles F. Marsh, *Trade Unionism in the Electric Light and Power Industry* (Urbana: University of Illinois, 1930), p. 58.

[111] *Ibid.,* p. 55; *Daily News,* Aug. 27, Oct. 20, 1912.

[112] *Daily News,* April 8, May 7, 1913; *Labor Clarion,* April 11, 1913; *Daily Journal of Commerce,* May 2, 7, 1913; *Final Report and Testimony of United States Commission on Industrial Relations,* VI, 5423.

[113] *Daily Journal of Commerce,* May 17, 1913; *Daily News,* May 30, 1913; Marsh, *op. cit.,* p. 59.

[114] *Daily Journal of Commerce,* May 24, June 7, 1913; *Daily News,* June 7, 1913.

[115] *Daily News,* June 17, 1913.

[116] *Labor Clarion,* July 18, 1913.

[117] *Daily News,* July 17, 25, Aug. 15, 1913; Marsh, *op. cit.,* p. 61.

[118] *Labor Clarion,* Dec. 12, 1913.

[119] Marsh, *op. cit.,* p. 61; *Final Report and Testimony of United States Commission on Industrial Relations,* VI, 5423; *Daily Journal of Commerce,* May 15, June 12, 30, 1913; *Daily News,* May 27, June 13, 17, 1913; *The World,* June 21, 1913.

[120] *Daily News,* Nov. 27, Dec. 6, 15, 18, 1913; Jan. 13, 1914.

[121] Interview with Warren Billings; Marcet Haldeman-Julius, *The Amazing Frameup of Mooney and Billings* (Girard, Kansas; Haldeman-Julius Publications, [c. 1931]), p. 6.

[122] *Daily News,* March 20, June 20, July 1, 1914; *Labor Clarion,* March 27, May 22, 1914; interview with Andrew J. Gallagher.

[123] Interview with Andrew J. Gallagher. Cf. *Tom Mooney Betrayed by Labor Leaders.*

[124] *Labor Clarion,* July–Dec., 1913, *passim; Daily Journal of Commerce,* Jan. 2, 1914; E. Guy Talbott, "The Armies of the Unemployed in California," *Survey,* 32 (Aug. 22, 1914), 523–524.

[125] *Daily News,* Feb. 11, March 3, 7, 9, 18, July 17, 1914; Talbott, *op. cit.,* p. 524.

[126] *Final Report and Testimony of United States Commission on Industrial Relations,* VI, 5316–5319.

[127] *Ibid.,* pp. 5310–5313, 5322–5324.

[128] *Ibid.,* pp. 5190–5192, 5376–5380.

[129] *Ibid.,* pp. 5376–5378, 5478–5481; Ryan, *op. cit.,* p. 127; *Daily News,* April 16, 22, 1914.

[130] *Daily News,* May 12, 1914; *Daily Journal of Commerce,* May 12, 1914; *Organized Labor,* May 16, 1914; Ryan, *op. cit.,* p. 127.

[131] *Final Report and Testimony of United States Commission on Industrial Relations,* VI, 5171–5174, 5310–5315, 5339–5343.

[132] *Ibid.,* p. 5171; Ryan, *op. cit.,* pp. 129, 140. Cf. Harold Seidman, *Labor Czars* (New York: Liveright, 1938).

[133] Ryan, *op. cit.,* pp. 138–139; *Daily News,* April 16, 1915.

[134] *Daily News,* Aug. 24, 1912.

[135] Cross, *op. cit.,* p. 244; *The World,* Nov. 21, 1914.

[136] *Final Report and Testimony of United States Commission on Industrial Relations,* VI, 5280.

[137] *Ibid.,* V, 4190, 4326; VI, 5444; *Law and Order and the San Francisco Chamber of Commerce* (San Francisco: Chamber of Commerce, 1918).

[138] *Final Report and Testimony of United States Commission on Industrial Relations,* V, 4773–4776, 4790–4793, 4809–4814, 4827–4835.

[139] *Ibid.,* V, 4812; XI, 10667–10672; *Daily News,* Oct. 17, 1914; *Labor Clarion,* April 9, July 30, 1915; Ernest J. Hopkins, *What Happened in the Mooney Case* (New York: Brewer, Warren, and Putnam, 1932), p. 87.

[140] *Daily News,* July 20, Sept. 4, 1914; *Labor Clarion,* Dec. 4, 1914; May 4, 1915; *Final Report and Testimony of United States Commission on Industrial Relations,* V, 4790–4799.

[141] *Daily News,* Sept. 7, 1914.

[142] *Transactions of the Commonwealth Club of California,* IX (Oct., 1914), 559.

[143] *Daily News,* Dec. 22, 1914; *Argonaut,* Jan. 2, 1915; *Coast Seamen's Journal,* Oct. 13, 1915.

[144] *Daily Journal of Commerce,* April 25, 1915.

[145] *Ibid.,* Oct. 29, 1915.

[146] *Ibid.,* July 14, Oct. 16, 1915; *Argonaut,* Dec. 11, 1915.

[147] *Daily Journal of Commerce,* Sept. 7, 1915; *Daily News,* Oct. 29, 1915.

[148] *Daily News,* Oct. 29, Nov. 8, 1915.

[149] *Ibid.,* Sept. 4, Nov. 10, 1915; *Labor Clarion,* Nov. 12, 1915; *Argonaut,* Oct. 2, 1915; *Law and Order and the San Francisco Chamber of Commerce,* p. 5.

[150] *Labor Clarion,* Nov. 12, 19, 1915.

Notes to Chapter VIII | Wartime Ferment

1916–1918

(Pages 299–368)

[1] Florence Peterson, *Strikes in the United States, 1880–1936* (Washington: Government Printing Office, 1938), p. 30.

[2] Paul S. Taylor, *The Sailors' Union of the Pacific* (New York: Ronald Press, 1923), p. 110; Howard Thor, "A History of the Marine Engineers' Beneficial Association" (unpublished M.A. thesis, University of California, Berkeley, 1954), p. 87; *Coast Seamen's Journal*, April 19, May 3, 1916.

[3] *Labor Clarion*, March 17, May 19, Aug. 25, 1916; *Daily Journal of Commerce*, May 17, 1916.

[4] Frederick L. Ryan, *Industrial Relations in the San Francisco Building Trades* (Norman: University of Oklahoma Press, 1936), p. 128; *Labor Clarion*, April 28, May 12, 19, 1916.

[5] *Labor Clarion*, May 5, 26, June 9, 1916; *Argonaut*, May 6, 1916; Ernest J. Hopkins, *What Happened in the Mooney Case* (New York: Brewer, Warren, and Putnam, 1932), p. 88; *The World*, Dec. 22, 1916.

[6] *Daily Journal of Commerce*, May 31, June 1, 1916; Robert M. Robinson, "A History of the Teamsters in the San Francisco Bay Area, 1850–1950" (unpublished Ph.D. dissertation, University of California, Berkeley, 1951), p. 201.

[7] *Law and Order in San Francisco: A Beginning* (San Francisco: Chamber of Commerce, 1916), pp. 1, 2.

[8] Taylor, *op. cit.*, p. 108; Robinson, *op. cit.*, pp. 201, 203; *Coast Seamen's Journal*, June 7, 1916; *Daily Journal of Commerce*, July 7, 1916.

[9] *Daily Journal of Commerce*, June 8, 9, 1917; Robert C. Francis, "A History of Labor on the San Francisco Waterfront" (unpublished Ph.D. dissertation, University of California, Berkeley, 1934), p. 152.

[10] *Bulletin*, June 7, 19, 21, 1916; *Daily Journal of Commerce*, June 17, 20, 1916; *Law and Order in San Francisco*, p. 12; Francis, *op. cit.*, p. 153.

[11] *Law and Order in San Francisco*, p. 4.

[12] *Ibid.,* pp. 5, 13; Robinson, *op. cit.,* p. 202; *Bulletin,* June 26, 1916; *Coast Seamen's Journal,* June 28, 1916; *Daily Journal of Commerce,* July 6, 1916; *Argonaut,* July 8, 1916.

[13] *Law and Order in San Francisco,* pp. 13–15.

[14] *Ibid.,* p. 17; *Bulletin,* July 11, 1916; *American Industries,* June, 1923, p. 27.

[15] *Daily Journal of Commerce,* July 13, 17, 1916; *Bulletin,* July 18, 1916; *Coast Seamen's Journal,* July 19, 1916; Francis, *op. cit.,* p. 154; Robinson, *op. cit.,* p. 201.

[16] Francis, *op. cit.,* p. 155.

[17] *Labor Clarion,* Feb. 25, 1916; Emerson P. Schmidt, *Industrial Relations in Urban Transportation* (Minneapolis: University of Minnesota Press, 1937), p. 154; *The World,* Jan. 19, 1917.

[18] Hopkins, *op. cit.,* p. 93.

[19] *Ibid.,* p. 94.

[20] Marcet Haldeman-Julius, *The Amazing Frameup of Mooney and Billings* (Girard, Kansas: Haldeman-Julius Publications, [c. 1931]), p. 74; *Labor Clarion,* July 21, 1916.

[21] *Chronicle,* July 14, 15, 1916; Haldeman-Julius, *op. cit.,* p. 75.

[22] *Labor Clarion,* July 21, 1916.

[23] Hopkins, *op. cit.,* pp. 91, 98, 101.

[24] Ryan, *op. cit.,* p. 129; *Labor Clarion,* Aug. 4, 1916.

[25] *The World,* 1916, *passim; Coast Seamen's Journal,* June 28, 1916.

[26] *Tri-City Labor Review* (Oakland), June 16, 1916; *Labor Clarion,* July 14, 1916; *Coast Seamen's Journal,* July 26, 1916; Richard H. Frost, "The Mooney Case in California Politics" (unpublished M.A. thesis, University of California, Berkeley, 1954), pp. 4, 23.

[27] *Bulletin,* July 22, 1916.

[28] Frost, *op. cit.,* p. 4; Hopkins, *op. cit.,* p. 24.

[29] Hopkins, *op cit.,* pp. 44, 115, 125, 178.

[30] *Ibid.,* p. 35.

[31] *Ibid.,* p. 113.

[32] Interview with Frederick J. Koster; *Chronicle,* July 27, 1916.

[33] *Argonaut,* Aug. 19, Sept. 30, 1916; *Chronicle,* Dec. 21, 1916; *American Industries,* Feb., 1917; *Law and Order and the San Francisco Chamber of Commerce* (San Francisco: Chamber of Commerce, 1918), p. 6; interview with Frederick J. Koster; framed testimonial on wall of Mr. Koster's office.

[34] *American Industries,* Feb., 1917.

[35] *Law and Order and the San Francisco Chamber of Commerce,* p. 11.

[36] *American Industries,* Aug., 1920; interview with Frederick J. Koster.

[37] *Labor Clarion,* Aug. 18, 1916; *American Industries,* Aug., 1920.

[38] Edward P. Eaves, "A History of the Cooks' and Waiters' Unions of San Francisco" (unpublished M.A. thesis, University of California, Berkeley, 1930), pp. 61–62.

[39] *Ibid.,* pp. 65–66.

[40] *Ibid.*, p. 77; *Daily Journal of Commerce*, Aug. 2, 3, 8, 1916; *Tri-City Labor Review*, Aug. 4, 1916; Matthew Josephson, *Union House, Union Bar* (New York: Random House, 1956), p. 122.

[41] Louise M. Ploeger, "Trade Unionism among the Women of San Francisco, 1920" (unpublished M.A. thesis, University of California, Berkeley, 1920), pp. 111, 112; Josephson, *op. cit.*, p. 24; Eaves, *op. cit.*, p. 84; *Labor Clarion*, Sept. 22, 1916.

[42] Josephson, *op. cit.*, p. 122; *Daily Journal of Commerce*, Aug. 9, Sept. 30, 1916; *The World*, Aug. 18, 1916.

[43] *Labor Clarion*, Aug. 11, 18, 1916; *Daily Journal of Commerce*, Aug. 15, 1916; Eaves, *op. cit.*, p. 73.

[44] Eaves, *op. cit.*, pp. 69, 77; *Law and Order in San Francisco*, p. 29; Josephson, *op cit.*, p. 122; *Daily Journal of Commerce*, Aug. 4, 1916; *Labor Clarion*, Sept. 15, 1916.

[45] *Daily Journal of Commerce*, Aug. 10, 1916; *Bulletin*, Aug. 18, 19, 1916; Josephson, *op. cit.*, p. 126; F. M. Davenport, "Did Hughes Snub Johnson?" *American Political Science Review*, 43 (April, 1949), 321–332.

[46] *Coast Seamen's Journal*, Aug. 23, Oct. 4, 1916; *Labor Clarion*, Aug. 25, 1916.

[47] *Daily Journal of Commerce*, Nov. 9, 1916.

[48] *Law and Order in San Francisco*, p. 35; *Chronicle*, Aug. 6, 1916; *Call*, Aug. 6, 1916; *Labor Clarion*, Oct. 27, 1916.

[49] Eaves, *op. cit.*, p. 85; *Labor Clarion*, Dec. 1, 1916.

[50] *Law and Order in San Francisco*, p. 29; Eaves, *op. cit.*, p. 80.

[51] *Labor Clarion*, June 8, 1917.

[52] *Law and Order in San Francisco*, p. 37; *Tri-City Labor Review*, June 30, July 14, 15, Aug. 18, 1916; Feb. 2, May 11, 1917; *Oakland Tribune*, July 16, 1916; *American Industries*, Dec., 1916.

[53] *Third Quarterly Meeting, November, 1916*, California Development Board (San Francisco: 1916), p. 31; *Argument on the Anti-Injunction Bill* (San Francisco: Chamber of Commerce, 1917); *Coast Seamen's Journal*, June 6, 1917.

[54] *Daily Journal of Commerce*, July 17, 25, 1916; *Argonaut*, July 29, 1916; Francis, *op. cit.*, p. 152.

[55] *Law and Order in San Francisco*, p. 33; *Daily Journal of Commerce*, Aug. 12, 24, 31, 1916.

[56] *Coast Seamen's Journal*, Nov. 29, 1916; Francis, *op. cit.*, p. 154.

[57] Ryan, *op. cit.*, p. 128; *Chronicle*, July 1, 1920.

[58] *Labor Clarion*, Aug. 4, 1916.

[59] *Chronicle*, July 1, 1920; *Labor Clarion*, Sept. 22, 1916; April 10, 1925. The quotation comes from the *Chronicle*.

[60] *Argonaut*, Oct. 14, 1916.

[61] *Labor Clarion*, Sept. 8, 1916.

[62] *Coast Seamen's Journal*, Dec. 23, 1916.

[63] *Ibid.*, Jan. 24, 1917.

[64] Ryan, *op. cit.*, p. 128.

[65] Hopkins, *op. cit.*, p. 178; *Bulletin*, July 27–31, 1916; *Daily News,* July 28, Aug. 4, 1916.

[66] Hopkins, *op. cit.*, p. 178; Robert R. Brooks, *As Steel Goes* (New Haven: Yale University Press, 1940), p. 28.

[67] *The Blast*, Feb. 23, 1916. See also *In the Matter of the Application of Thomas J. Mooney for a Pardon,* brief submitted by the district attorney of San Francisco, 1918.

[68] *Law and Order in San Francisco; Law and Order and the San Francisco Chamber of Commerce;* interview with Frederick J. Koster; speech by Koster, printed in *American Industries,* Feb., 1917.

[69] Interview with Andrew J. Gallagher; *Labor Clarion,* Sept. 8, 1916; *The World,* Sept. 22, 1916; *Tri-City Labor Review,* March 23, 1917.

[70] *Tri-City Labor Review,* Sept. 15, 1916; Sept.–Dec., 1916, *passim;* June 29, 1917.

[71] *The Mooney-Billings Report,* U.S. National Commission on Law Observance and Enforcement (New York: Gotham House, 1932), p. 26.

[72] Hopkins, *op. cit.*, pp. 131–133.

[73] *Ibid.,* pp. 132–161; *Labor Clarion,* Aug. 30, 1918.

[74] Lillian Symes, "Our American Dreyfus Case," *Harper's Magazine,* 161 (May, 1931), 645.

[75] Hopkins, *op. cit.*, p. 88; *The World,* Sept. 22, 1916; *Call,* Sept. 23, 1916; Henry T. Hunt, "Mooney and Billings." *New Republic,* 58 (April 10, 1929), 219–223.

[76] *Bulletin,* Sept. 25, 1916; *Labor Clarion,* Sept. 29, Oct. 13, 20, 27, Nov. 3, Dec. 22, 1916; *Coast Seamen's Journal,* Oct. 11, 1916.

[77] Hopkins, *op. cit.*, p. 193.

[78] *Ibid.,* pp. 218–220, 235–238.

[79] *Ibid.,* p. 246; *Bulletin,* April 20, 1917; *Labor Clarion,* May 3, 1917; Symes, *op. cit.*, p. 646; John A. Fitch, "The San Francisco Bomb Cases," *Survey,* 38 (July 7, 1917), 305–307.

[80] Harry F. Grady, "A Rejoinder," *Survey,* 37 (March 24, 1917), 717–718; *Connection of Certain Department of Labor Employees with the Case of Thomas J. Mooney,* U.S. Secretary of Labor, 66th Cong., 1st sess., H. Doc. 157 (1919), p. 90 (hereafter cited as *Densmore Report*).

[81] *Densmore Report,* p. 5; Fitch, *op. cit.*, p. 306; *Call,* April 21, 24, 1917.

[82] *Densmore Report,* p. 5.

[83] *Call,* April 28, 1917.

[84] *Argonaut,* May 5, 1917.

[85] *Coast Seamen's Journal,* May 2, 1917; *Labor Clarion,* May 4, 1917.

[86] *Labor Clarion,* July 13, 1917.

[87] *Coast Seamen's Journal,* July 25, 1917.

[88] *Tri-City Labor Review,* July 27, Nov. 30, 1917; Hopkins, *op. cit.*, p. 239.

[89] *Report on the Mooney Dynamite Cases in San Francisco,* Federal Me-

diation Commission, Public Information Committee Official Bulletin (Washington: 1918), p. 2; "Strange News from Russia," *New Republic*, 11 (May 5, 1917), 8–10; Frost, *op. cit.*, pp. 60, 84.

[90] *American Industries*, June, 1917.

[91] *Law and Order and the San Francisco Chamber of Commerce*, p. 12.

[92] Leo Wolman, *Ebb and Flow in Trade Unionism* (New York: National Bureau of Economic Research, 1936), p. 26.

[93] Francis, *op. cit.*, pp. 154–157; *Labor Clarion*, Dec. 29, 1916; Sept. 7, 1917.

[94] Interview with Frederick J. Koster; *Law and Order and the San Francisco Chamber of Commerce*, p. 8; Robinson, *op. cit.*, p. 194.

[95] *Labor Clarion*, 1916–1917 *passim;* June 8, Sept. 7, 1917; *Coast Seamen's Journal*, 1916–1917 *passim; Tri-City Labor Review*, 1916–1917 *passim; The Cost of Living in the United States, 1914–1926*, National Industrial Conference Board (New York: 1926), p. 174.

[96] *Eighteenth Biennial Report, 1917–1918*, California Bureau of Labor Statistics (Sacramento: 1918); *Nineteenth Biennial Report, 1919–1920*, California Bureau of Labor Statistics (Sacramento: 1920); Robinson, *op. cit.*, p. 148; Francis, *op. cit.*, p. 132; Eleanor A. Todd, "History of the Milk Wagon Drivers' Union of San Francisco County, 1900–1933" (unpublished M.A. thesis, University of California, Berkeley, 1936), p. 105.

[97] Francis C. Head, "Trade Unionism in the Clothing Industries of San Francisco" (unpublished M.A. thesis, University of California, Berkeley, 1935), p. 38; *Labor Clarion*, Feb. 11, March 10, Aug. 4, 1916; Nov. 23, 1917; *Tri-City Labor Review*, June 7, July 12, 1918; interview with Wendell Phillips; Robinson, *op. cit.*, pp. 148, 195, 196; Todd, *op. cit.*, p. 108; Charles C. Brisco, "Industrial Relations in the East Bay Fluid Milk Distribution Industry" (unpublished M.B.A. thesis, University of California, Berkeley, 1953), p. 58; interview with G. A. Silverthorn.

[98] *Tri-City Labor Review*, July 6, Oct. 19, Nov. 2, 17, 1916; June 15, July 6, 1917.

[99] Paul Chatom, "Industrial Relations in the Brewery, Metal, and Teaming Trades of San Francisco" (unpublished M.S. thesis, University of California, Berkeley, 1915), pp. 36–39; Ira B. Cross, *Collective Bargaining and Trade Agreements in the Brewery, Metal, Teaming, and Building Trades of San Francisco, California* (Berkeley: University of California Press, 1918), pp. 280, 285.

[100] Chatom, *op. cit.*, p. 37; *Machinists' Monthly Journal*, Nov., 1915; *Final Report and Testimony of United States Commission on Industrial Relations* (Washington: 1916), VI, 5233–5235.

[101] *Chronicle*, May 28, 1916; *California Shipbuilder*, Aug., 1919.

[102] *Labor Clarion*, May 19, 26, 1916; *Tri-City Labor Review*, Feb. 16, 23, 1917.

[103] *Chronicle*, March 4, 10, 12, 16, 1917; *The World*, March 23, 1917; *Tri-City Labor Review*, April 6, 1917.

[104] *Labor Clarion*, Jan. 19, March 16, Sept. 14, 21, 1917.

[105] *Chronicle,* Sept. 18, 1917; *Labor Clarion,* Sept. 28, 1917; Alexander M. Bing, *Wartime Strikes and Their Adjustment* (New York: Dutton, 1921), p. 20. The quotation comes from *Labor Clarion.*

[106] "To Hell with the Country," *Sunset,* 39 (Nov., 1917), 7; *Tri-City Labor Review,* Oct. 5, 1917; Bing, *op. cit.,* p. 23; Paul H. Douglas, "Labor Administration in the Shipbuilding Industry during Wartime," *Journal of Political Economy,* XXVII (1919), 362; *History of Union Shipbuilding on the Pacific Coast,* Pacific Coast District Metal Trades Council (Tacoma: Central Labor Council, 1943), p. 4.

[107] Bing, *op. cit.,* p. 24; *Labor Clarion,* Nov. 9, Dec. 21, 1917; *Chronicle,* Dec. 26, 31, 1917.

[108] Walter V. Woehlke, "Bolshevikis of the West," *Sunset,* 40 (Jan., 1918), 72.

[109] Peterson, *op. cit.,* p. 20.

[110] *Tri-City Labor Review,* July 6, Aug. 24, Nov. 16, 1917; March 22, 1918.

[111] *Chronicle,* April 30, 1917; *Coast Seamen's Journal,* July 11, 1917; *Labor Clarion,* Sept. 14, 1917.

[112] Hyman Weintraub, "The I.W.W. in California, 1905–1931" (unpublished M.A. thesis, University of California, Los Angeles, 1947), p. 91; *Chronicle,* July 26, 28, 1917.

[113] Bing, *op. cit.,* p. 104; *Chronicle,* July 27, 31, 1917; *Tri-City Labor Review,* Aug. 3, 1917.

[114] *Chronicle,* April 6, 10, 14, 28, 1917; *Coast Seamen's Journal,* May 2, 23, July 4, 1917; *Labor Clarion,* June 7, 1918; Francis, *op. cit.,* p. 157.

[115] Beatrice V. Taylor, "Labor Relations on the Street Railways of San Francisco" (unpublished M.A. thesis, University of California, Berkeley, 1928), pp. 77, 79; *Chronicle,* Aug. 12, 14, 24, 1917; Walter V. Woehlke, "The Striker and Low Justice," *Sunset,* 39 (Nov., 1917), 12.

[116] *Chronicle,* Aug. 16, 1917; *Labor Clarion,* Aug. 17, 1917; Woehlke, "The Striker and Low Justice," p. 73.

[117] Woehlke, "The Striker and Low Justice," p. 73; *Los Angeles Times,* Sept. 11, 1917; Schmidt, *op. cit.,* p. 183.

[118] Herman G. Goldbeck, "The Political Career of James Rolph, Jr." (unpublished M.A. thesis, University of California, Berkeley, 1936), p. 53; *Argonaut,* Sept. 29, 1917; Woehlke, "The Striker and Low Justice," p. 82.

[119] *Labor Clarion,* Aug. 31, 1917.

[120] Beatrice V. Taylor, *op. cit.,* p. 82; *Law and Order and the San Francisco Chamber of Commerce,* p. 6; *Examiner,* Sept. 4, 1917.

[121] *Labor Clarion,* Nov. 23, 1917; Schmidt, *op. cit.,* p. 182; *Law and Order and the San Francisco Chamber of Commerce,* p. 13.

[122] *Coast Seamen's Journal,* Oct. 24, 1917; *Tri-City Labor Review,* Oct. 26, 1917.

[123] *Labor Clarion,* Nov. 9, 1917.

[124] *Coast Seamen's Journal,* Nov. 7, 1917.

[125] *Labor Clarion,* Nov.–Dec. *passim,* Dec. 7, 1917; *Tri-City Labor Review,* Nov.–Dec. *passim,* 1917.

[126] *Examiner,* July 13, Aug. 11, 1917; *Labor Clarion,* Dec. 7, 1917; Woodrow C. Whitten, "Criminal Syndicalism and the Law in California, 1919–1927" (unpublished Ph.D. dissertation, University of California, Berkeley, 1946), p. 62.

[127] Frost, *op. cit.,* p. 69; *Tri-City Labor Review,* Dec. 7, 14, 1917; *Labor Clarion,* Dec. 14, 1917.

[128] *Tri-City Labor Review,* Dec. 21, 1917; *Coast Seamen's Journal,* Jan. 6, 1918; *Bulletin,* June 6, 1918; *Law and Order and the San Francisco Chamber of Commerce,* p. 12.

[129] Frost, *op. cit.,* p. 67.

[130] *Report on the Mooney Dynamite Cases in San Francisco,* p. 4.

[131] Hopkins, *op. cit.,* p. 240; Frost, *op. cit.,* p. 85.

[132] *Nineteenth Biennial Report, 1919–1920,* California Bureau of Labor Statistics, p. 394; *The Cost of Living in the United States, 1914–1926,* p. 174.

[133] Peterson, *op. cit.,* p. 20; Bing, *op. cit.,* pp. 119–123.

[134] *Chronicle,* June 12, 1918; *Coast Seamen's Journal,* June 26, 1918.

[135] Beatrice V. Taylor, *op. cit.,* p. 88; *Labor Clarion,* Jan. 18, 1918; Robinson, *op. cit.,* p. 194; Todd, *op. cit.,* p. 118.

[136] *Chronicle,* March 24, April 5, 1918; *Labor Clarion,* May 3, 1918; Todd, *op. cit.,* pp. 118, 128, 138.

[137] *Labor Clarion,* Jan. 18, Sept. 27, Oct. 4, 1918; *Tri-City Labor Review,* May 10, Oct. 11, 1918.

[138] *Argonaut,* Jan. 11, 1916; *Tri-City Labor Review,* Nov. 17, 1916; *Chronicle,* Oct. 20, 21, Nov. 3, 4, 10, 23, 1917; interview with E. P. Marsh.

[139] *Tri-City Labor Review,* Jan. 4, Sept. 13, 1918; *Labor Clarion,* Sept. 20, Oct. 11, 1918.

[140] Francis, *op. cit.,* p. 160; *Labor Clarion,* March 22, 1918; *Chronicle,* May 24, 1917; Robinson, *op. cit.,* p. 495.

[141] Francis, *op. cit.,* p. 159; Ploeger, *op. cit.,* pp. 104, 115; Josephson, *op. cit.,* p. 115; *Labor Clarion,* Nov. 16, 1917; Feb. 8, March 15, July 19, Aug. 23, Oct. 4, Nov. 8, 22, Dec. 20, 27, 1918; *Chronicle,* June 4, 13, July 1, 1918; April 13, 1919.

[142] Reinaldo Pagano, "History of the Building Service Employees' International Union in San Francisco, 1902–1939" (unpublished M.A. thesis, University of California, Berkeley, 1948), pp. 23–37; *Labor Clarion,* Jan. 25, March 15, May 17, Aug. 23, 1918.

[143] *Tri-City Labor Review,* April 12, May 3, July 5, 12, Aug. 30, Sept. 13, Oct. 11, 18, 25, 1918; interview with G. A. Silverthorn.

[144] *Tri-City Labor Review,* July 12, 19, Aug. 23, Oct. 11, 1918.

[145] *Ibid.,* June 28, Aug. 9, Sept. 20, Oct. 4, 11, Nov. 11, 18, 29, 1918; *Oakland Tribune,* Sept. 29, 1918; *Oakland Post-Enquirer,* Nov. 20, 1918.

[146] *Tri-City Labor Review,* July 26, Aug. 9, 16, 23, 1918.

[147] Harvey O'Connor, *History of Oil Workers' International Union (CIO)* (Denver: Oil Workers' International Union, 1950), pp. 262, 327; Louis J. Zitnik, "The Trend of Collective Bargaining in Petroleum Production, Refining, and Pipe Line Transportation Departments in California" (unpublished

M.A. thesis, University of California, Berkeley, 1947), p. 26; interview with E. P. Marsh.

[148] *Tri-City Labor Review*, May 24, Aug. 30, Dec. 13, 1918; *Chronicle*, Nov. 25, 1918.

[149] *Tri-City Labor Review*, Jan. 11, 18, March 28, May 31, June 14, July 26, Aug. 2, Sept. 6, Oct. 11, 18, Dec. 27, 1918; *Labor Clarion*, Aug. 2, 9, 1918; *Coast Seamen's Journal*, Oct. 9, 1918.

[150] *Tri-City Labor Review*, Sept. 6, Oct. 18, 1918.

[151] Walter V. Woehlke, "America's First Defeat," *Sunset*, 40 (April, 1918), 14; "Strikes for Pay Not Earned by the Men," *Sunset*, 41 (Sept., 1918), 7; *Labor Clarion*, April 12, June 7, 28, Nov. 8, Dec. 27, 1918; *Chronicle*, July 15, 1918.

[152] Cf. series of articles by Walter V. Woehlke: "The Shipyard Hold-up," *Sunset*, 40 (March, 1918), 11 ff.; "America's First Defeat," pp. 14 ff.; "Wages and Output," *Sunset*, 40 (May, 1918), 11 ff.

[153] *Ibid.*; "Strikes for Pay Not Earned by the Men," p. 7; interview with Archie J. Mooney; *Tri-City Labor Review*, June 21, 1918.

[154] *Chronicle*, July 15, 17, 1918; *Labor Clarion*, July 19, 1918; *Tri-City Labor Review*, July 19, Aug. 9, Sept. 13, 1918.

[155] *Tri-City Labor Review*, Aug. 2, 16, 1918; *Labor Clarion*, Aug. 16, 1918; *Chronicle*, Sept. 8, Oct. 2, 6, Nov. 25, 1918.

[156] *Tri-City Labor Review*, Sept. 20, Oct. 11, 1918.

[157] *Ibid.*, Nov. 2, 1917; May 31, Sept. 27, Oct. 4, Dec. 6, 13, 20, 1918; *Labor Clarion*, Jan. 4, 18, July 19, Aug. 16, Sept. 13, 1918.

[158] *Tri-City Labor Review*, Nov. 15, Dec. 6, 1918.

[159] Frost, *op. cit.*, pp. 88, 90, 96.

[160] *Ibid.*, p. 102; *Tri-City Labor Review*, Nov. 22, 29, 1918; *Labor Clarion*, Nov. 29, 1918.

[161] Fremont Older, *My Own Story* (San Francisco: Call Publishing Co., 1919), p. 182.

[162] *Densmore Report*, p. 26.

[163] *Ibid.*, p. 10.

[164] *Coast Seamen's Journal*, Dec. 4, 1918.

[165] *Chronicle*, Nov. 29, 1918.

[166] *Tri-City Labor Review*, Dec. 6, 1918.

[167] *Coast Seamen's Journal*, Dec. 4, 1918; *Labor Clarion*, Dec. 6, 13, 1918.

Notes to Chapter IX | A Retrospective View

(Pages 369–393)

[1] Cf. membership estimates as reported in *Tri-City Labor Review*, May 24, Oct. 4, 1918; Feb. 21, 1919; *Chronicle*, June 15, July 6, Aug. 30, 1919; *Labor Clarion*, July 11, Aug. 3, 1919.

Bibliography

Bibliography

Books, Theses, and Documents

Bean, Walton. *Boss Ruef's San Francisco.* Berkeley and Los Angeles: University of California Press, 1952.

Bemis, George W. "Sectionalism and Representation in the California State Legislature, 1911–1931." Unpublished Ph.D. dissertation, University of California, Berkeley, 1935.

Bing, Alexander M. *Wartime Strikes and Their Adjustment.* New York: E. P. Dutton & Co., 1921.

Bonnett, Clarence E. *Employers' Associations in the United States.* New York: The Macmillan Co., 1922.

Brisco, Charles C. "Industrial Relations in the East Bay Fluid Milk Distribution Industry." Unpublished M.B.A. thesis, University of California, Berkeley, 1953.

Burns, William J. *The Masked War.* New York: George H. Doran Co., 1913.

California. Bureau of Labor Statistics. *Third Biennial Report, 1887–1888.* Sacramento: 1888.

——. *Seventh Biennial Report, 1895–1896.* Sacramento: 1896.

——. *Ninth Biennial Report, 1899–1900.* Sacramento: 1900.

——. *Tenth Biennial Report, 1901–1902.* Sacramento: 1902.

——. *Eleventh Biennial Report, 1903–1904.* Sacramento: 1904.

——. *Twelfth Biennial Report, 1905–1906.* Sacramento: 1906.

——. *Thirteenth Biennial Report, 1907–1908.* Sacramento: 1908.

——. *Fourteenth Biennial Report, 1909–1910.* Sacramento: 1910.

——. *Fifteenth Biennial Report, 1911–1912.* Sacramento: 1912.

——. *Sixteenth Biennial Report, 1913–1914.* Sacramento: 1914.

——. *Seventeenth Biennial Report, 1915–1916.* Sacramento: 1916.

——. *Eighteenth Biennial Report, 1917–1918.* Sacramento: 1918.

——. *Nineteenth Biennial Report, 1919–1920.* Sacramento: 1920.

Chatom, Paul. "Industrial Relations in the Brewery, Metal, and Teaming

Trades of San Francisco." Unpublished M.S. thesis, University of California, Berkeley, 1915.

Commons, John R., and Associates. *History of Labor in the United States.* New York: The Macmillan Co., 1921–1935. 4 vols.

Commonwealth Club of California. *The Population of California.* San Francisco: 1946.

Crockett, Earl C. "The History of California Labor Legislation, 1910–1930." Unpublished Ph.D. dissertation, University of California, Berkeley, 1931.

Cronin, Bernard C. *Father Yorke and the Labor Movement in San Francisco, 1900–1910.* Washington: Catholic University of America Press, 1943.

Cross, Ira B. *Collective Bargaining and Trade Agreements in the Brewery, Metal, Teaming, and Building Trades of San Francisco, California.* Berkeley: University of California Press, 1918.

———. *A History of the Labor Movement in California.* Berkeley: University of California Press, 1935.

Darrow, Clarence. *The Story of My Life.* New York: Charles Scribner's Sons, 1932.

Davie, John L. *My Own Story.* Oakland: Post-Enquirer Publishing Co., 1931.

Eaves, Edward P. "A History of the Cooks' and Waiters' Unions of San Francisco." Unpublished M.A. thesis, University of California, Berkeley, 1930.

Eaves, Lucile. *A History of California Labor Legislation.* Berkeley: The University Press, 1910.

Federal Mediation Commission. *Report on the Mooney Dynamite Cases in San Francisco.* Public Information Committee Official Bulletin. Washington: 1918.

Francis, Robert C. "A History of Labor on the San Francisco Waterfront." Unpublished Ph.D. dissertation, University of California, Berkeley, 1934.

Frost, Richard H. "The Mooney Case in California Politics." Unpublished M.A. thesis, University of California, Berkeley, 1954.

Goldbeck, Herman G. "The Political Career of James Rolph, Jr." Unpublished M.A. thesis, University of California, Berkeley, 1936.

Green, Charles H. *The Headwear Workers.* New York: United Hatters, Cap, and Millinery Workers International Union, 1944.

Haber, William. *Industrial Relations in the Building Industry.* Cambridge: Harvard University Press, 1930.

Hansen, Alvin H. *Business Cycles and National Income.* New York: W. W. Norton, 1951.

Hapgood, Hutchins. *The Spirit of Labor.* New York: Duffield and Co., 1907.

Head, Frances C. "Trade Unionism in the Clothing Industries of San Francisco." Unpublished M.A. thesis, University of California, Berkeley, 1935.

Hichborn, Franklin. *"The System," as Uncovered by the San Francisco Graft Prosecution.* San Francisco: James H. Barry Co., 1915.

Hinkel, Edgar J., ed. *Oakland, 1852–1938.* Oakland Public Library, 1939. Mimeographed. 2 vols.

Hopkins, Ernest J. *What Happened in the Mooney Case.* New York: Brewer, Warren, and Putnam, 1932.

Jamieson, Stuart M. "Labor Unionism in American Agriculture." Unpublished Ph.D. dissertation, University of California, Berkeley, 1943.

Jensen, George C. "The City Front Federation of San Francisco." Unpublished M.S. thesis, University of California, Berkeley, 1912.

Josephson, Matthew. *Union House, Union Bar: the History of the Hotel and Restaurant Employees and Bartenders International Union, AFL–CIO.* New York: Random House, 1956.

Lindsey, Almont. *The Pullman Strike.* Chicago: University of Chicago Press, 1942.

Marsh, Charles F. *Trade Unionism in the Electric Light and Power Industry.* Urbana: University of Illinois, 1930.

Matthews, Lillian R. *Women in Trade Unions in San Francisco.* Berkeley: University of California Press, 1913.

Millis, Harry A., and Royal E. Montgomery. *Organized Labor.* New York: McGraw-Hill Book Co., 1945.

Mortenson, Clara E. "Organized Labor in San Francisco from 1892 to 1902." Unpublished M.S. thesis, University of California, Berkeley, 1916.

Mowry, George E. *The California Progressives.* Berkeley and Los Angeles: University of California Press, 1951.

National Industrial Conference Board. *The Cost of Living in the United States, 1914–1926.* New York: National Industrial Conference Board, 1926.

O'Connor, Harvey. *History of Oil Workers' International Union (CIO).* Denver: Oil Workers' International Union, 1950.

Ohlson, Robert V. "The History of the San Francisco Labor Council, 1892–1939." Unpublished M.A. thesis, University of California, Berkeley, 1940.

Older, Fremont. *My Own Story.* San Francisco: Call Publishing Co., 1919.

Pagano, Reinaldo. "History of the Building Service Employees' International Union in San Francisco, 1902–1939." Unpublished M.A. thesis, University of California, Berkeley, 1948.

Peterson, Florence. *Strikes in the United States, 1880–1936.* U.S. Bureau of Labor Statistics Bulletin no. 651. Washington: Government Printing Office, 1938.

Ploeger, Louise M. "Trade Unionism among the Women of San Francisco, 1920." Unpublished M.A. thesis, University of California, Berkeley, 1920.

Robinson, Robert M. "A History of the Teamsters in the San Francisco Bay Area, 1850–1950." Unpublished Ph.D. dissertation, University of California, Berkeley, 1951.

Roney, Frank. *Frank Roney, Irish Rebel and California Labor Leader.* Ed. Ira B. Cross. Berkeley: University of California Press, 1931.

Rowell, Edward J. "The Union Labor Party of San Francisco, 1901–1911." Unpublished Ph.D. dissertation, University of California, Berkeley, 1938.

Ryan, Frederick L. *Industrial Relations in the San Francisco Building Trades.* Norman: University of Oklahoma Press, 1936.

Schluter, Hermann. *The Brewing Industry and the Brewery Workers' Movement in America.* Cincinnati: International Union of United Brewery Workmen of America, 1910.

Schmidt, Emerson P. *Industrial Relations in Urban Transportation.* Minneapolis: University of Minnesota Press, 1937.

Searing, Richard C. "The McNamara Case: Its Causes and Results." Unpublished M.A. thesis, University of California, Berkeley, 1952.

Seidman, Harold. *Labor Czars.* New York: Liveright Publishing Corp., 1938.

Selvin, David F. "History of the San Francisco Typographical Union." Unpublished M.A. thesis, University of California, Berkeley, 1935.

Stimson, Grace H. *Rise of the Labor Movement in Los Angeles.* Berkeley and Los Angeles: University of California Press, 1955.

Stockton, Frank T. *The Closed Shop in American Trade Unions.* Johns Hopkins University Studies in Historical and Political Science, Series 29, no. 3. Baltimore: Johns Hopkins Press, 1911.

Stowell, Charles J. *Studies in Trade Unionism in the Custom Tailoring Trade.* Bloomington, Ill.: Journeymen Tailors' Union of America, 1913.

Strong, G. A. "A Study of the Development of the California Law on Picketing." Unpublished M.A. thesis, University of California, Berkeley, 1952.

Taylor, Albion G. *Labor Policies of the National Association of Manufacturers.* Urbana: University of Illinois, 1928.

Taylor, Beatrice V. "Labor Relations on the Street Railways of San Francisco." Unpublished M.A. thesis, University of California, Berkeley, 1928.

Taylor, Paul S. *The Sailors' Union of the Pacific.* New York: Ronald Press Co., 1923.

Thor, Howard. "A History of the Marine Engineers' Beneficial Association." Unpublished M.A. thesis, University of California, Berkeley, 1954.

Todd, Eleanor A. "History of the Milk Wagon Drivers' Union of San Francisco County, 1900–1933." Unpublished M.A. thesis, University of California, Berkeley, 1936.

Ulriksson, Vidkun. *The Telegraphers, Their Craft and Their Unions.* Washington: Public Affairs Press, 1953.

U.S. National Commission on Law Observance and Enforcement. *The Mooney-Billings Report.* New York: Gotham House, 1932.

U.S. Secretary of Labor. *Connection of Certain Department of Labor Employees with the Case of Thomas J. Mooney.* U.S. 66th Cong., 1st sess., H. Doc. 157. Washington: 1919.

U.S. Senate. *Final Report and Testimony Submitted to Congress by the Commission on Industrial Relations.* Washington: 1916.

Weintraub, Hyman. "The I.W.W. in California, 1905–1931." Unpublished M.A. thesis, University of California, Los Angeles, 1947.

Whitten, Woodrow C. "Criminal Syndicalism and the Law in California, 1919–1927." Unpublished Ph.D. dissertation, University of California, Berkeley, 1946.

Wolman, Leo. *Ebb and Flow in Trade Unionism.* New York: National Bureau of Economic Research, 1936.

————. *The Growth of American Trade Unions, 1880–1923.* New York: National Bureau of Economic Research, 1924.

Zitnik, Louis J. "The Trend of Collective Bargaining in Petroleum Production,

Refining, and Pipe Line Transportation Departments in California." Unpublished M.A. thesis, University of California, Berkeley, 1947.

Newspapers and Periodicals

American Federationist. Monthly journal of the American Federation of Labor.
American Industries. Journal of the National Association of Manufacturers.
Argonaut. San Francisco weekly.
California Shipbuilder. Publication of the California Metal Trades Association.
Coast Seamen's Journal. Journal of the Sailors' Union of the Pacific.
Contra Costa Gazette. Martinez, California, weekly.
Labor Clarion. Official journal of the San Francisco Labor Council.
The Leader. Periodical published by Father Peter Yorke, San Francisco.
Machinists' Monthly Journal. Official journal of the International Association of Machinists.
Motorman and Conductor. Official journal of the Amalgamated Association of Street Railway Employees.
Oakland Enquirer.
Oakland Post-Enquirer.
Oakland Tribune.
Open Shop. Publication of the National Metal Trades Association.
Organized Labor. Official journal of the San Francisco Building Trades Council.
Revolt—The Voice of the Militant Worker. Published by Thomas J. Mooney, 1911–1912, San Francisco.
San Francisco Bulletin.
San Francisco Call.
San Francisco Chronicle.
San Francisco Daily Journal of Commerce.
San Francisco Daily News.
San Francisco Evening Post.
San Francisco Examiner.
Shop Review. Publication of the National Founders' Association.
Square Deal. Publication of the Citizens' Industrial Association of America.
Star. San Francisco weekly.
Tri-City Labor Review. Official journal of the Alameda County Central Labor Council.
The World. Weekly publication of the Oakland Socialist Party.

Articles, Manuscripts, Pamphlets, and Proceedings

Atherton, Gertrude. "San Francisco and Her Foes," *Harper's Weekly*, 51 (Nov. 2, 1907), 1590–1593.
Baker, Ray Stannard. "A Corner in Labor," *McClure's Magazine*, 22 (Feb., 1904), 366–378.

Commonwealth Club of California. *Transactions of the Commonwealth Club of California.* San Francisco.

Davenport, F. M. "Did Hughes Snub Johnson?" *American Political Science Review,* 43 (April, 1949), 321–332.

Douglas, Paul H. "Labor Administration in the Shipbuilding Industry during Wartime," *Journal of Political Economy,* XXVII (1919), 362–396.

Fitch, John A. "The Dynamite Case," *Survey,* XXIX (Feb. 1, 1913), 607–609.

———. "The San Francisco Bomb Cases," *Survey,* 38 (July 7, 1917), 305–312.

Foster, William Z. "The Molders' Convention," *International Socialist Review* (Dec., 1912), 486–487.

Franklin Printing Trades Association. *Organized Felony: The Picket and the Wrecking Crew, Weapons of San Francisco's Labor Monopoly.* San Francisco: Franklin Printing Trades Association, 1914.

Gallagher, Andrew J. "Something Doing in Los Angeles," *International Socialist Review* (Sept., 1910), 166–167.

General Campaign Strike Committee for the Unionizing of Los Angeles. *California Labor's Greatest Victory; Final Report . . . Embracing Receipts and Expenditures June 1, 1910–April 1, 1912.* San Francisco: 1912.

Grady, Harry F. "A Rejoinder," *Survey,* 37 (March 24, 1917), 717–718.

Haldeman-Julius, Marcet. *The Amazing Frameup of Mooney and Billings.* Girard, Kansas: Haldeman-Julius Publications, [c. 1931].

Hunt, Henry T. "Mooney and Billings," *New Republic,* 58 (April 10, 1929), 219–223.

In the Matter of the Application of Thomas J. Mooney for a Pardon. Brief submitted by the district attorney of San Francisco. San Francisco, 1918.

Lewis, Austin. "The Day After," *International Socialist Review* (Dec., 1911), 357–359.

———. "The Drift in California," *International Socialist Review* (Nov., 1911), 272–274.

Macarthur, Walter. "A Climax in Civics." Typewritten manuscript in University of California Library, *ca.* 1906.

Monaco, F. "San Francisco Shoe Workers' Strike," *International Socialist Review* (May, 1913), 818–819.

National Association of Manufacturers. *Proceedings of the . . . Annual Convention.* Philadelphia.

Pacific Coast District Metal Trades Council. *History of Union Shipbuilding on the Pacific Coast.* Tacoma: Central Labor Council, 1943.

Page, Thomas W. "The San Francisco Labor Movement in 1901," *Political Science Quarterly,* 17 (Dec., 1902), 664–688.

Ready, Herbert V. *The Labor Problem.* San Francisco: [c. 1904].

"Renewing the Open Shop Fight," *Sunset,* 33 (Oct., 1914), 652–653.

Rosenberg, Ed. "The San Francisco Strikes of 1901," *American Federationist,* 9 (Jan., 1902), 15–18.

Russell, Phillips. "The Class Struggle on the Pacific Coast," *International Socialist Review* (Sept., 1912), 236–238.

"San Francisco," *Encyclopaedia Britannica* (11th ed.; 1911), XXIV, 143–149.

San Francisco Chamber of Commerce. *Argument on the Anti-Injunction Bill.* San Francisco: 1917.

———. *Law and Order and the San Francisco Chamber of Commerce.* San Francisco: 1918.

———. *Law and Order in San Francisco: A Beginning.* San Francisco: 1916.

"Strange News from Russia," *New Republic*, XI (May 5, 1917), 8–10.

"Strikes for Pay Not Earned by the Men," *Sunset*, 41 (Sept., 1918), 7.

Symes, Lillian. "Our American Dreyfus Case," *Harper's Magazine*, 161 (May, 1931), 641–652.

Talbott, E. Guy. "The Armies of the Unemployed in California," *Survey*, 32 (Aug. 22, 1914), 523–524.

"To Hell with the Country," *Sunset*, 39 (Nov., 1917), 7.

Tom Mooney Betrayed by Labor Leaders. San Francisco: Tom Mooney Molders' Defense Committee, 1931.

Weintraub, Hyman. "Andrew Furuseth—Abraham Lincoln of the Sea." Unpublished manuscript, *ca.* 1955–1957.

Woehlke, Walter V. "America's First Defeat," *Sunset*, 40 (April, 1918), 14–16, 72–74.

———. "Bolshevikis of the West," *Sunset*, 40 (Jan., 1918), 14–16, 70–72.

———. "The Shipyard Hold-up," *Sunset*, 40 (March, 1918), 11–13, 71–72.

———. "The Striker and Low Justice," *Sunset*, 39 (Nov., 1917), 11–13, 73, 82.

———. "Wages and Output," *Sunset*, 40 (May, 1918), 11–13, 56.

"The World of Labor," *International Socialist Review* (Aug., 1907), 117–118.

Interviews

Warren K. Billings.

John Forbes, past president, San Francisco Industrial Association.

Andrew J. Gallagher, past secretary, San Francisco Labor Council.

Luis Ireland, labor negotiator for San Francisco printing trades employers.

Frederick J. Koster, past president, San Francisco Chamber of Commerce.

Edwin V. McKenzie, of defense counsel for Tom Mooney and Matt Schmidt.

E. P. Marsh, federal mediator in Pacific Coast labor disputes, World War I.

Archie J. Mooney, former officer of San Francisco Carpenters' Union.

James Rickets, former business agent, San Francisco Building Trades Council.

Paul Scharrenberg, past secretary, California State Federation of Labor.

G. A. Silverthorn, past secretary, Alameda County Central Labor Council.

Marcus C. Sloss, former Superior Court judge, San Francisco, and justice of California Supreme Court.

Al Wynn, secretary, Molders' Union Local 164, San Francisco.

Index

Index

Alameda, 387; population of, 237, 388; wartime shipyard strikes in, 339–340, 362–363

Alameda County, 40, 45; antipicketing ordinance in, 319

Alameda County Building Trades Council. *See* Building Trades Council, Alameda County

Alameda County Central Labor Council, 45, 128, 211, 227, 262, 266, 325, 359, 364, 366; organizing efforts of, 336, 357–358; charter revoked by AFL, 380

Alexander, W. E., 142, 156

Alexander, Wallace M., 291

American Can Company, 82, 133, 153, 179

American Federation of Labor, 19, 21, 27, 33, 39, 41, 44, 57, 62, 63, 79, 93, 119, 277; membership of, 96, 131, 333–334; convention of 1904 (in San Francisco), 155; Executive Council of, 232, 280, 282–285; convention of 1913, 283; convention of 1915 (in San Francisco), 296

American-Hawaiian Steamship Company, 172

American Railway Union, 33

American Steel and Wire Company, 132–133

American Stevedore Company, 320

Anti-injunction bills, 145–146, 242–243, 319

Anti-Jap Laundry League, 191, 213–214

Antipicketing ordinances: in Los Angeles, 228; in Bay Area, 265, 317–319

Antiradical hysteria in World War I, 348–350, 364–365

Arbitration, 24, 112, 315; in building trades, 55, 288; in shoe manufacturing, 117, 153; on street railways, 132, 175, 186; in printing trades, 204; Weinstock plan, 225–226, 243; in metal trades, 229–230, 234; in World War I, 351, 353

Argonaut, 69, 85, 136, 189, 195, 202, 223, 257, 330

Asiatic Exclusion League, 213

Atlas Engine Company, 264, 291

Automobile mechanics, San Francisco, 256; 1916 strike of, 301, 309, 327

Bag factory workers, San Francisco, 133

Bakers' Association, Master, 154

Bakersfield, 141

Bakery drivers: San Francisco, 68, 113, 182, 271, 335–336; East Bay, 211, 366

Bakery workers: San Francisco, 19, 23, 24, 42, 44, 46, 68–69, 106–107, 113–114, 146, 148, 154, 335, 376; East Bay, 261; 1912 strike of, 271

Bakery Workers' International Union, 107

Bank of California, 305

Barbers, San Francisco, 44

Bartenders, San Francisco, 213

Bay and River Steamboatmen's Union, 334; 1916 strike of, 302–307; 1917 strike of, 344–345

Beer bottlers, San Francisco, 113, 222; 1901 strike of, 75, 90–92

Date Due